The New Management

The New Management

THIRD EDITION

Robert M. Fulmer

Emory University

MACMILLAN PUBLISHING CO., INC.
NEW YORK

Collier Macmillan Publishers
London

Macmillan Publishing Co., Inc.
866 Third Avenue, New York, New York 10022

Collier Macmillan Canada, Inc.

Library of Congress Cataloging in Publication Data

Fulmer, Robert M.
   The new management.

   Bibliography: p.
   Includes indexes.
   1. Management.   I. Title.
HD31.F85   1982   658   81-3763
ISBN 0-02-339740-3   AACR2

Printing: 1 2 3 4 5 6 7 8   Year: 3 4 5 6 7 8 9

Preface

In the first edition of *The New Management*, I identified my major objective as the treatment of "the basics of management in a concise, interesting, and understandable manner." It has been most gratifying to learn from colleagues throughout the country that this objective was successfully attained. The market acceptance of the *The New Management* confirmed the judgment that professors share an interest in learning vehicles that are stimulating, creative, practical, and comprehensive. Thus, the major emphasis of this book remains the same in revision.

The book title evoked considerable comment. Frequent questions were, "Is there anything really new in management?" or "What was wrong with the old management?" As I suggested in 1974, the new management was new in somewhat the same sense that the "new math" and "new grammar" were when they first appeared: the presentation is innovative; the basic data are not.

There are several features that I believe justify the title and, more important, differentiate this book from many other texts intended for courses in the principles of management:

1. It is the first book consciously to bridge the gap between the study of the humanities and the study of business. It is my hope that the student will be thus comfortably drawn from the familiar subject matter studied in earlier college courses to the unfamiliar field of management and made to see the interrelationship between business and the social sciences. The study of management becomes a clear continuation of the earlier education but gives that education a professional slant.

2. It discusses management theory with an emphasis on the future, because most students will be applying the concepts taught here over a period of many years.

3. It is written expressly for the student. Without in the least meaning to patronize the student, I have sought a format that should make learning management principles interesting and even entertaining. The language is straightforward, deliberately intended to gain and hold interest. The style is unusual for a textbook, but its aim is to motivate students to learn more about management, both during this early exposure and later in their education. I hope, of course, that both instructors and students will find the book a pleasure to read.
4. This text will also identify several areas where management concepts are applicable to a personal setting. The reader is challenged to apply the concepts presented in this book to the challenge of managing the most difficult subordinate—the one that confronts you in the mirror each morning.

Obviously, this edition is even newer than its predecessor. Each chapter has been updated to reflect the latest in research and practice. Considerable new material in the area of contingency management and systems theory has been added. Because of a need by many schools for material relating to production and operations management, Part IV is completely revised. While this edition continues it emphasis on the future, the general view of the future has changed dramatically during the past four years.

The New Management has five major parts. I believe they are logically arranged for teaching a basic course. However, the chapters need not be covered in the strict order found here, and alternative organizations are suggested in the instructor's manual that accompanies the book. Perhaps a few words about the contents will be useful.

Part I, "The Past Is Prologue," builds, in general, on the student's previous studies in the humanities but does not presuppose more than casual knowledge of any specific discipline. The historical events and persons described in Chapter 1 are probably familiar ones seen here in a new context, the social and intellectual history of management. After showing that management and managers are not new to the student or to the world, Part I explores the development of industrial and postindustrial society in the United States. After establishing the relationship between history and the evolution of management philosophy and practice, the part concludes with a survey of the major approaches to management theory.

Part II contains the heart of the administrative discipline. It deals with the functions of planning, decision making, organizing, controlling, and staffing. The process of integrating these various functions into a productive, efficient management style is also developed. The role of authority in making this goal possible concludes the section.

In Part III there is a basic overview of behavioral science that emphasizes the importance of men and women in management. The first two chapters are intended to encourage self-development, self-awareness, and the understanding of others, along with a knowledge of basic group dynamics. Key components of organizational behavior such as communications, leadership, and employee and organizational development are explored in the subsequent chapters, along with the manager's role as an agent of change.

Part IV was entirely new in the second edition, and has been completely revised for the third. It recognizes the importance of a manager's role in overseeing the operations of an organization and the production function. Several analytical and quantitative tools for effective decision making are introduced and illustrated. Finally, this section identifies the components of several managerial systems that are essential for organizational success.

In Part V, I have asked the future executive to take a serious look at the world outside the present organizational setting and to examine the major ethical and social ramifications of management decisions. This is followed by a discussion, based on various forecasting studies, of the sort of world the student will probably encounter when he or she fully assumes managerial responsibilities. The probable changes in administrative techniques that may be needed to be an effective manager in the society of the next decade are also introduced.

R.M.F.

Acknowledgments

In any treatment of a basic subject, even one entitled *The New Management*, there is little that the author can claim to be uniquely his own. Typically, ideas have been molded, influenced, and shaped by the academic and business associations enjoyed by the author. In a special way, I wish to acknowledge the contributions my former professors have made to the thinking that is conveyed in this book.

As an undergraduate, I was especially influenced by M. J. Martin and Axel Swang. At the University of Florida, Bill Wilmot and Bill Fox were particularly helpful in shaping my interest in the management discipline. At UCLA, Melville Dalton, Wayne McNaughton, Bill Ryan, Cyril O'Donnell, and George Steiner were articulate, helpful, and stimulating management mentors. Harold Koontz, my major professor, was clearly the most influential individual in shaping my management thinking, as well as my professional goals. This book owes a great deal to the systematic, operational approach to management that he has labored so diligently to popularize.

Specific improvements in the writing have come about as a result of generous help afforded by early readers of the manuscript. Readers such as Keith Davis of Arizona State University, Leon Megginson of The University of South Alabama, Barry Richman of UCLA, Ted Herbert of The University of North Carolina at Chapel Hill, Joseph Pecenka of Northern Illinois University, Russel Sigler of Miami-Dade Junior College, and Robert Bukofzer of Central State University, Oklahoma, all made invaluable suggestions that helped improve and sharpen the focus of the first edition.

Reviewers for the second edition included:
William R. Allen, University of Rhode Island
Stephen Butcher, Emporia State University
Ray Curtis, Lorain County Community College

Jere L. Crago, Delgado College
John Harpell, West Virginia University
Walter E. Jones, St. Petersburg Junior College
Jack Magee, Washington State University
W. A. Meinhart, Oklahoma State University
Mildred Pryor, Stephen F. Austin State University
Linda Zaich, Long Beach City College

Former students such as Steve Franklin, Ray Bressler, George Jacobs, Ted Shead, and Jim Higgins were helpful at various stages of research and editing for the original manuscript. Donna Wood (University of Pittsburgh) and Charlie Walton provided extensive editorial input and assistance with the first two editions. Jack Goodwin of Emory University provided invaluable assistance with the revisions of Part IV. His assistance greatly contributed to the improvement of this edition. Pat Roney and Pat Farmakis deserve special commendation for their secretarial assistance and support. Joan Edmonson provided valuable aid in proofreading. Dean George M. Parks of Emory University helped provide an environment that was productive during the challenging task of text revision.

Contents

part III
The Human Dimension in Management

part IV
The Management of Operations

part V
The World Outside

part I

The Past Is Prologue

1

The Intellectual Heritage of Management

CAREER OPPORTUNITY—If you are a bright, hard-working individual with management capabilities and skill in motivation by flogging, then set your sights on an unlimited advancement career with Apex Pyramids, the nation's fastest-growing fabricator of monumental sepulchers. Because of recent innovations by our Engineering Department, building blocks are now precut to size prior to transport to the client's building site. If you have experience in getting people to go your way, there could be a place for you in our blockbusting or drag-team operations. As an Apex Slide Ruler, you will work with over fifteen hundred reluctant (but nonunion) workers. We are interested in results and do not question your methods if you can guarantee that your men will meet or exceed daily block-moving quotas. Our motto is : Spare the rod and spoil the mile.

Our benefits are second to none and include free burial insurance, two meals per day, a leisurely sixteen-hour day at the whip handle, and generous profit-sharing plan (except on government jobs).

You owe it to yourself to check out this wonderful opportunity. With pyramids being completed now at the rate of one every twenty years, make sure you get in on the ground floor.

> Do not be distracted by the claims of our competitor, Sphinx Inc. Check with our man from Apex and get the lowdown on career opportunities in a fast-growing industry. Remember, when it comes to sepulchers, Sphinx stinks, but Apex gets to the point!

It is not very difficult for us to imagine familiar modern management techniques in the days of the pharaohs. True, we can get a laugh or two thinking of profit sharing and other twentieth-century terms appearing in the ancient land of the Nile, but the generic relationships of people managing people must have borne a great many similarities. In fact, many ancient documents have been translated to reveal that, through the ages, wherever people have worked together to accomplish their goals, many of the same phenomena have prevailed.

Most scholars suggest that management, in its most basic format, has existed since one person persuaded another—whether with club or carrot—to do something. I would argue that management concepts were first developed by astute individuals who sought greater efficiency by using concepts that would later help organizations achieve larger objectives. Frequently, management is defined as the challenge of creating an environment where people can work together to achieve a mutual objective. While this is true for managers in business, government, and other organizations, I hope that each management student will recognize the opportunities for applying management concepts to personal challenges. For our purposes, management can be defined as the concepts, techniques, and processes that enable goals to be achieved efficiently and effectively.

Each generation has struggles with its own problems of supply and demand, profit and loss, labor and management, and death and taxes. However, in all fairness to our own hard-pressed generation, it should be pointed out that we do have one affliction that the ancients did not have. We have more history to learn!

Although it is fairly obvious that human relations have followed many of the same patterns through the ages, ideas about management and productivity have not always been as we see them today. Throughout most of the history of civilization, people have shown a startling lack of the practical business sense or management acumen that we take so much for granted. It seems so natural to us that activities should have a purpose . . . a goal . . . a reason for being. We would feel disorganized and slipshod going through life with no idea of ultimate destination. But, regardless of how naturally we accept the necessity of productivity, it has not always been the case. In fact, it has almost never been the case.

The Dawning of the Age of Practicality

Historians point out that there have been only two great eras of practicality in the history of mankind. One occurred between 6000 B.C. and 3000 B.C., and the second, in which we currently find ourselves, began in the eighteenth century or thereabouts.[1]

During the first great age of practicality, people particularly in the Near East, learned quite a bit about how to conquer the environment. They learned to harness oxen, sail boats, build arches, and plow furrows. They also discovered metallurgy and learned how to irrigate their fields artificially. They discovered the secrets of fermentation and other useful things. Toynbee has suggested that the inventions of this period were far more important than those of any other period.[2] This is easy enough to agree with when you try to picture Henry Ford trying to get his company going without the wheel or Colt manufacturing a worthwhile .45 before gunpowder. And, for a real clincher, picture Gutenburg trying to print the first book on banana leaves!

We don't know much about the period that gave us these early inventions—some historians even call it a precivilization era. The little knowledge we do have indicates that 3000 B.C. marked a tapering off of an age of great progress. The time that followed this rapid progress began to be called civilization.

The Pleasures of Productivity

As we look briefly at the development of the intellectual heritage of management through the ages, we can see a consistent correlation of productive periods with times of capitalism and individual competition. Although the concepts of this book are for managers and prospective managers in both nonprofit and for-profit organizations, the author feels that our capitalistic system with its emphasis on private enterprise is the backbone of any sound managerial philosophy. This system recognizes and encourages achievement in every sector of employment. As we will notice in the following pages, material progress and improvement remained severely limited until private enterprise and capitalism became dominant systems.

The B.C. Years (Before Capitalism)

Back in the early days of civilization—even before the *Wall Street Journal* and the Rotary Club—only a few folks were utilizing admirable management practice. Solomon, the Biblical king of Israel, directed the

---

[1] Joseph McGuire, *Business and Society* (New York: McGraw-Hill Book Company, 1963), p. 13. This chapter has been influenced by McGuire's excellent treatment on pp. 12–27.
[2] Arnold J. Toynbee, *Survey of International Affairs* (Oxford: British Institute of National Affairs, 1931), pp. 478–488.

establishment of elaborate trade agreements and hammered out several political and economic treaties to enable the craftsmen of his time to hammer out a massive temple to Yahweh.[3] Solomon's kingdom was whirring along like a well-oiled time-and-motion study in the tenth century B.C.

Of course, management and efficiency are sure to have been significant ingredients in every situation—whether historic or prehistoric— in which one individual emerged as leader, the chieftain (the force to be reckoned with). Is it degrading to the profession of management to suggest that effective management practice is primarily common sense and was utilized by primitive people? It is no insult . . . because common sense is such an uncommon quality in most generations. In fact, some of the most disappointed students ever to emerge from learning institutions are those who think that, by taking a degree in management, they will receive inside knowledge of the secret words and formulas for manipulating people. The truth is that even the best management education curriculum can only hope to sharpen the skills and understanding that students already have.

Auditing the Sumerian Priests

Some of the oldest written documents that have ever been found are temple records of the Sumerian civilization of about 3000 B.C.[4] The Sumerian temple priests were rather lax in their separation of church and state and soon collected and controlled vast amounts of worldly goods. The religious tax system put the priests in charge of flocks, herds, revenues, and estates.

Somebody in Sumer got the wild idea that priests might be subject to human forgetfulness (especially if it tended to line their holy pockets), and an elaborate system of accounting was instituted. The priests were required to give account of their stewardship on a regular basis to the chief priest—note the managerial control via organizational reporting.

Because these Sumerians recognized the need for managerial control, virtually the earliest written documents in the world are the five-thousand-year-old accounts of their inventories. In fact, it is highly probable that the managerial needs of this early civilization prompted the invention of the Sumerian script. The initiating force was economic; and although developed by the priests, the script's first use was for managerial control purposes and not for doctrinal purposes.

[3] Kings 6:7 suggests that the construction of this temple, a wonder of the ancient world, was so carefully planned that, "there was neither hammer or ax nor any tool of iron heard in the house while it was in the building."—Obviously a masterpiece of prefabrication and of managerial planning.

[4] V. Gordon Childe, *Man Makes Himself* (New York: The New American Library, Inc., 1951), p. 143.

The Original Pyramid Climbers

Approximately four thousand years B.C., the Egyptians were building a civilizational edge on the rest of the world. Very few of us can comprehend the extent to which this culture zoomed ahead of its times. If it were possible to make a reliable comparison, we would probably find that no nation in our time is as far ahead of its contemporaries as the land of the Pharaohs was between 4000 B.C. and 525 B.C.

The most obvious demonstration of Egyptian prowess is the construction projects that remain even today. Without the service of cranes, bulldozers, or coffee breaks, the Egyptians constructed mammoth structures of admirable precision. The great pyramid of Cheops, for example, covers thirteen acres and contains 2,300,000 stone blocks.[5] The blocks weigh about two and a half tons each and were cut to size in quarries many miles away—the foundation stones of prefab housing! The stones were transported and set in place by slave labor and precision planning. The help-wanted ad that appears at the beginning of this chapter is a joke, but it also makes one quite serious point. The men who built the enduring structures of ancient Egypt not only knew how to plan a project, but they demonstrated great skill in the mobilization and use of human resources. Managing 100,000 workers in a twenty-year project should certainly merit a solid gold sundial upon retirement.

In their business and governmental affairs, the Egyptians kept documents to show exactly how much was received and from whom, when it came in, and exactly how it was used. The military, social, religious, and governmental aspects of Egyptian life were highly organized. There were many inefficiencies, but the final task was accomplished. Three commodities, which virtually rule modern efforts, seem to have been only minor considerations along the Nile: time, money, and the satisfaction of the worker.

Meanwhile, Over in Babylonia

In their own way, the Babylonians were making tremendous strides. Around 2000 B.C., a king named Hammurabi united the cities along the Tigris and Euphrates rivers into a single powerful nation. Hammurabi authored a set of laws, which coincidentally came to be called the Code of Hammurabi. The code covered regulations about personal property, real estate, trade and business, the family, and labor. In fact, virtually all the laws coming to us from the Babylonian civilization are of a business nature dealing with such items as sales, loans, contracts, partnerships, agreements, and promissory notes.

---

[5] Adolf Erman, *Life in Ancient Egypt*, trans. from the German by Helen M. Tirard (London: Macmillan & Company, Ltd., 1894), p. 472.

The Code of Hammurabi described in detail the legal procedure to be followed in questions of minimum wages, control, responsibility, and retribution.[6] Following the passing of Hammurabi and his strength of leadership and organization, the country stumbled along for about fifteen hundred years before another able manager came to the helm of the Babylonian ship of state.

Nebuchadnezzar reunited the Babylonians and led them to great heights in both military and domestic endeavors. From the textile mills of this period come examples of color-coding methods of production control and incentive wage payments. Colored tags were used to indicate the various types of yarn entering the mills. The wages paid the women engaged in the spinning and weaving operations were determined on the basis of production.

The Hebrews

The Hebrews demonstrated frequent wisdom in the management of people and activities. The Old Testament recounts the life of Joseph, who rose from slavery to a position of power and influence in Egypt. His able administration of the granaries is said to have seen Egypt through seven years of famine that nearly wiped out the surrounding nations.

Moses, the most famous of the Jewish leaders, was educated in Egypt. He organized and led the exodus of over a million Israelites from slavery in Egypt. The Law of Moses contains a highly structured set of rulings on every aspect of Jewish life. Both civil and religious laws are included.

The eighteenth chapter of Exodus describes the rationalizing of the principle of delegation. Moses was trying to judge all the cases brought to him. His father-in-law suggested the appointment of assistant judges to handle the simple decisions of the "lower courts." This account gives us one of the earliest and most commonly available records of a philosophy and plan for organizational delegation.

Jethro's advice to Moses also illustrates early use of the principle of management by exception. Moses' father-in-law suggested, "Every small matter they shall judge, but every great matter they shall bring to thee."

The examples of Joseph, Moses, and Solomon point up the exceptional managerial talent of the Hebrews. In spite of (and in some cases because of) persecutions and forced migration, the Jews have consistently demonstrated themselves to be an organizationally oriented people.

---

[6] Robert F. Harper, *The Code of Hammurabi, King of Babylon* (Chicago: University of Chicago Press, 1904).

The Classical Era

The classical era shifted the eye of history back to the Mediterranean for a thousand years or so. The Greeks dominated from 400 B.C. until about 100 B.C., at which time the Romans took over everything until their organizational chart came apart at the seams around A.D. 500. The Greeks and Romans had a rather similar view of the business community. The fraternity of traders, merchants, and moneylenders was considered a sort of necessary evil. It was okay to be on a first-name basis with your neighborhood trader . . . but you wouldn't want your sister to marry one.

In spite of its low popularity rating, the merchant population prospered in both Greece and Rome. The Mediterranean made possible the trading of exotic goods as well as necessities. Commercial institutions developed a relatively high degree of sophistication. Local markets expanded and the port cities became the centers of activity. Particularly in the military state of Rome did the merchant prove necessary. The term *military-industrial complex* may be fairly recent, but the arrangement is as old as war and business. It is difficult to picture the Roman sword maker praying for peace.

Banking became quite well established among individual customers and within temple walls. Competition, advertising, and public relations were very much in evidence, as demonstrated by the following bank advertisement, which appeared in the middle of the third century B.C.

> To citizens and foreigners this bank gives equal dealing; deposit and withdraw, when your account is correctly made up. Let another make excuse, but Caicus even at night pays foreign money to those who want it.[7]

The social philosophy of the Greeks and Romans kept the barriers up for the merchant classes. The teachings of some of the renowned thinkers of the time created an environment that was generally hostile to business activities. "How degrading to spend one's time and effort dealing with people and things instead of dwelling upon enlightened investigation of philosophy and law!"

Laws reflected these prevailing social attitudes. Merchants were not allowed to own property in Greek city-states. They could not hold public office, and in times of war they did their fighting in the ranks of the foot soldiers rather than among the more elite cavalry. Three of the well-known classical thinkers represent the unsteady social climb of the merchant class. They are Plato, Aristotle, and Xenophon.

Plato (427?– 347 B.C.) looked down on commercial activity as base

---

[7] George A. Bullock, "Bank Advertisements: Ancient and Modern," *Barrons*, July 30, 1928, p. 3.

and common. On the other hand, when he described his ideal state, he did recognize the necessity for the services and skills of men of commerce and craftsmanship. Plato recognized that even the citizens of the ideal state would eat food, live in houses, and freeze without clothing. He could see that no city is capable of supplying all man's wants, and therefore there must be a merchant class to bring these "necessities" from afar.

Aristotle (384–322 B.C.) studied under Plato and shared his dislike for commercial activities, particularly when someone came away with a profit. The writings of Aristotle eventually proved to have great influence on social and economic philosophies. His "scientific method of thinking" became part of the foundation for the development of modern decision-making technique. He discussed economic questions such as exchange, division of labor, money, interest, and usury. Some historians feel that Aristotle's writings have ultimately had more influence on later social and economic philosophies than those of any other man.[8]

Xenophon (434?–355 B.C.) viewed business activities from a different, more realistic, point of view. He looked at business as an opportunity for increasing state treasuries and urged that commerce be encouraged. Xenophon looked upon foreigners and merchants as assets to the city-state. He pointed to the number of goods and services brought in as well as the excess goods that were exported by the merchants. He suggested that foreigners be allowed to own land and build buildings, that they be exempt from conscription into the army, that they be honored with seats of distinction on public occasions, and that they be provided with public funds for ships and ventures.

Early Stages of Capitalism

The period of history from A.D. 500 until A.D. 1500 has been kicked about quite a bit by historians. Because there was comparatively little enlightenment and progress, some historians call the period the Dark Ages. More than one youngster in school has wondered how things must have looked during those "dark" days . . . Was each day overcast and gloomy?

The most commonly used term for this historic period is the *Middle Ages* or *medieval* times. Actually, such designations are always applied by subsequent ages. It is very doubtful that the average person in 750 thought about living in either middlish or uncommonly dark times. How might they have named this era? "Modern times," perhaps.

[8] Quoted by Keith Davis and Robert Blomstrom, *Business and Its Environment* (New York: McGraw-Hill Book Company, 1966), p. 26

Prebusiness Capitalism (500–1100)[9]

There had been a considerable development of private business capitalism in the days before the Middle Ages. However, the cooperative collective economy seemed to dominate life on the manors. Under the feudal system, three necessary elements of business activity were lacking: (1) There was little or no ability to change individual standing by individual effort. (2) The purpose of production was consumption primarily, with only limited consideration given to production for exchange. (3) The philosophy of the times did not highly value individual progress in material affairs.

It would be naive to say that no business happened during this period. Regular patterns of work were developed. Work was divided somewhat to fit the peculiar talents of workers. Feudal lords developed some administrative, supervisory, and accounting techniques. As long as there are humans, there will be business and management, but compared to other periods of management history this time was rather bland and unexciting.

The grass is always greener in another time's social system. From time to time, reformers and malcontents demand that we return to the collective, noncompetitive economics of the past. Such demands for the good old days seem unrealistic in view of the many times that such an existence has been tried and rejected by mankind.

Petty Capitalism (1100–1400)

Petty capitalism introduced business to society. During prebusiness capitalism, people manufactured things, but only for their own use. As petty capitalism dawned, craftsmen began to see the wisdom of producing goods for exchange as well as consumption. One step beyond the barter system was the more convenient system of exchange for some common medium. Such an accumulation of work and effort in the form of capital gave people the leisure to contemplate, plan, and specialize in those areas in which they could make their greatest contribution to society and to their bank accounts.

One of the important aspects of commerce that became acceptable with petty capitalism was the practice of investing or putting out capital. By this device, capital could be made to work for the individual who possessed it. It became wise and acceptable to build capital by (1) investing in a business partnership, (2) loaning goods or money, or (3) making a charge for selling goods on credit.

The individual petty capitalist became the building block from which our present business world has grown. The petty capitalist was motivated by a set of ideals and values different from those held in the previ-

---

[9] Although the author has modified the divisions of time, the classification of stages within the development of capitalism was originally suggested by Moore, ibid., pp. 7–16.

ous era. He believed that status could be obtained by economic attainment. He was an individualist and believed in the individual's right to economic independence. Because of an emphasis upon the individual, he avoided any control by others. Also, he would willingly assist others in gaining their independence by offering apprenticeships to promising youngsters. The foundation policy of the petty capitalist is summarized in the term *democratic economic equality*.

Thomas Aquinas may have contributed more than any other person to the opening of the doors to capitalism. The writings of Aquinas gave the air of acceptability to several aspects of enterprise that had previously been taboo. Two of the concepts that proved troublesome in this transition period were "just price" and "usury."[10]

Aquinas held that everything had one "just price." He felt that the value of a commodity was objective, inherent in the article, and completely outside the fluctuating of supply and demand and market values. The exchange price should cover the "just price" paid by the merchant plus whatever markup would help maintain his standard of living. If the price charged by the merchant allowed him to *improve* his standard of living, the merchant was operating outside canon law. In our day, it is almost impossible to conceive of a business run only to provide services. Even our so-called nonprofit organizations are seeking to guarantee growth of assets and capabilities. We are accustomed to businesses that claim to be interested in "satisfied customers" and "return business." However, we could hardly believe a businessperson who was not concerned ultimately with turning a profit.

Business progressed in spite of the doctrine of "just price." As the benefits of trade began to be appreciated by society, the enforcement of Aquinas' highly idealistic doctrines became more and more lenient. The doors were open and the natural growth and expansion of philosophy and practice were only beginning.

Protestant Capitalism and Mercantilism (1400–1776)

The period extending from the final days of the Middle Ages to the emergence of the American system of private enterprise is called the era of Protestant capitalism and mercantilism. The primary understanding of the mercantile capitalist was that if business was to grow the market had to be extended. This simply stated understanding paved the way for many developments. New and better goods brought in from a wider area could vastly extend the market. The merchant who delegated the tasks of manufacturing, shipping, and marketing would be able to produce a greater profit. Accordingly, the sedentary merchant adapted administrative techniques, policies, and practices that would fulfill the

---

[10] McGuire, op. cit., p. 19.

guiding principle of extending the market (and the number of marketeers).

Each expansion step in the mercantile capitalist's interests brought new evidence that unique and innovative business functions would be required. Sedentary merchants learned to let others do the work. They began to specialize in exporting or banking, cooperating with others who were specializing in importing and the transportation of goods. Mercantile capitalism lasted for about six centuries, longer than any other system. It was by no means a perfect system, but it worked well for its times. It contributed to much of the exploration and experimentation that eventually changed the world and outdated the mercantile capitalist. A system of business is good or bad, adequate or inadequate according to its context.

Many inventions had to come before the barriers were removed from capitalist explosion. James Watt had to fiddle with his teapot and discover a principle that led to the steam engine. Coal became recognized and available as an industrial power source. Innovative methods of mining, transportation, communication, and production had to become accepted before the stage was set for the Industrial Revolution.

With all factors working together—changing religious and social attitudes, rising nationalism, migration to the cities, and the coming of pivotal inventions—the world was ready to move into a period of prosperity, production, and problem-packed progress. One discovery, however, was to overshadow all others in its importance to the history of American management. It was called the "freedom to make a profit," and it was christened in 1776.

Industrial Capitalism in the New World (1776–1890)

The fledgling nation was ripe for the development of a new kind of businessperson. The industrial capitalist believed in specializing, streamlining, and delegating tasks. He used power machinery whenever applicable, drove employees hard, and remained strictly in control of operations.

The industrial capitalist's guiding principle was to reduce costs—sell more—and make more profit. The young American society provided the perfect climate for such goals. With the population (work force) continuing to swell, new frontiers (markets) opening up, and transportation and communication improving, the times were right for the person who comprehended the potential of being the local merchant to the whole nation.

The Wealth of Nations

One of the classic books on economic philosophy was written by Adam Smith, an eighteenth-century professor at Glasgow, Scotland. At the age of thirty, Smith accepted the post of traveling companion and tutor to the son of Charles Townshend, the Chancellor of the Exchequer for England at the time of the American Revolution. During his travels throughout Europe, Smith began the writing of his treatise. He called his book *An Inquiry into Nature and Causes of the Wealth of Nations*. The title is usually remembered as *The Wealth of Nations*.[11]

Though published in 1776, Smith's book was remarkably forward-looking. *The Wealth of Nations* described in its 900 pages the workings of an ideal free market economic society. It set forth a prescription for a vigorous and successful business system and earned its author the title of the "father of classical economics."

Smith believed that people were motivated by a relatively small number of basic forces, among which were the desires for independence and trade. If each person were free to pursue personal goals, the public interest would be facilitated more than if people actually set out to promote public goals. "It is not from the benevolence of the butcher, the brewer, or the baker, that we expect our dinner," observed Adam Smith, "but from their regard to their own interest."

It takes very little thought about the freedom of business to conclude that there must be some kind of controls lest the enthusiasm of businesspeople abuse the privilege of commerce. In Smith's plan, the necessary control will be supplied by the element of competition. He felt that rigorous and efficient competition would cause the system to produce an adequate supply of goods and services in the most efficient manner and at the lowest possible prices. The trouble with ideal systems of anything is that they exist only in somebody's mind and generally break down when applied to the complicated relationships of nonideal human beings.

In Smith's opinion, the forces of the marketplace would work out any economic problems—in the long run. During the 1930's many classical economists argued that, in the long run, the free forces of the marketplace would solve this "temporary" difficulty. Perhaps this was true, but much suffering was taking place in the short run. As the famous British economist John M. Keynes pointed out, "In the long run, we are all dead!"

Smith's emphasis on the principle of specialization showed him to be ahead of his time. He believed that increasing specialization was the key to productivity. Productivity would produce more income, higher

---

[11] Adam Smith, *The Wealth of Nations* (New York: Modern Library, Inc., 1937). Originally published in 1776.

wages, larger families, increased demand, further division of labor and . . . the cycle would never stop. Smith's contribution to the literature of economics is only exceeded by his optimism about the predictability of man.

Financial Capitalism (1890–1933)

At first, things went exceptionally well for the industrial capitalists because they were competing only with petty capitalists and mercantile capitalists who were using the old techniques. They were easy prey for the streamlining time-and-motion of the industrial capitalists. However, hard times came for the industrial capitalists when the competition became a more sophisticated test between two or more firms having the same technical expertise and equipment. The industrialists' strong point was production methodology. When that field became a standoff and the emphasis shifted to financial aspects as determiners of success or failure, many of the industrial capitalists went under. Their production was fine, but their forecasting let them down. Those who were skillful enough to manage production and finance equally well became the forerunners of the next emerging period: financial capitalism.

The financier was the skilled practitioner who would answer the cry for help from the industrial capitalists. Financiers didn't know much about production methods, but they were masters of financial juggling. Instead of specialization, they emphasized diversification of products and multiple economic functions. The profits, which the industrialist had always put back into new equipment, were set aside as cash reserves by the financial capitalist. Cutthroat competition was replaced by a new concept of cooperative competition. The system of financial capitalism had a flexibility that could have negotiated a workable relationship between the principal interest groups of the economy: the workers, the consumers, the producers, and the investors. Unfortunately, financial capitalism did not dominate the scene long enough to bring about the positive effects within its capability.

Many people learned to dislike the financier, and most would probably now blame financial capitalism for the crescendo of events that led to its own demise in the Depression of the 1930's.

When the financial capitalists had decided that they could all make more money together than in competition with each other, an interesting era in American business was dawning. For the next few decades there was a continuing battle of wits and legal technicalities. Businesses banded together to make their profits secure. The government legislated to protect the consumers and perpetuate competition.

Business Combines

Among the most widely used devices for business combinations were the trust and the holding company. A trust is the product of the transfer of the stock of previously competing companies to a group of trustees who issue trust certificates to the participating companies and then proceed to solidify their monopoly. Companies who are not part of the trust can easily be run out of business by united action of the trust members. After competition is eliminated, the trust is free to price its products and services at almost any level it pleases.

The great industrial trusts (railroads, salt, oil, sugar, etc.) came under attack from a variety of sources in the late 1800's. Political parties, state governments, and federal legislation crippled the trust movement. A death blow was intended by the passage of the Sherman Antitrust Act in 1890. This act explicitly prevented the ". . . contract, combination in the form of trust . . . in restraint of trade or commerce." Yet the Anti-Trust Division of the Justice Department still manages to stay busy.

The *holding company*, born of loopholes in antitrust legislation, has been the most effective means of combining the activities of a number of companies under single leadership. The holding company is a company that owns controlling interests in other companies. The holding company is highly representative of the financial capitalism period in that its prime purpose is financial management and manipulation—production questions are left to the companies being bought and sold. The holding company was in high gear at the turn of the century. It is still legal today, and its use has been steadily increasing. It is common today to hear a company describe itself as "a wholly owned subsidiary of." It is likely that the conglomeration of business will accelerate in the future. Already, the five hundred largest firms produce one half of all the goods and services that are available annually in the United States.

Social Darwinism

In the mid 1800's, Charles Darwin presented his famous theory of biological evolution in *The Origin of Species*.[12] Darwin suggested that all forms of organic life originated from a small number of primitive types and that all organisms we know today evolved from them through the natural laws of survival. His theory was soon tagged with the identifying phrase "survival of the fittest." If that phrase didn't ring a bell with competitive businessmen, the writings of Herbert Spencer did.[13]

Spencer applied Darwin's biological principles to social development. He said, in effect, that the weaker social institutions and busi-

[12] (London: J. Murray, 1859.) See Richard Hofstadter, *Social Darwinism in American Thought*, rev. ed. (Boston: Beacon Press, 1955), pp. 31–50.
[13] Herbert Spencer, *Principles of Sociology* (New York: Appleton & Company, Inc., 1898).

nesses might have to be sacrificed to develop the stronger movements. This rationalization for "survival of the fittest" business ethics was very popular with the surviving fit.

Men like Vanderbilt, Carnegie, Rockefeller, Gould, and Hill had built gigantic financial empires. It was inevitable that some of the "little people" had to be crowded out as these captains of industry pursued their goals. As Thorstein Veblen said, "The captain of industry was a man who started out to do something and ended up doing somebody."

The financiers were making new money and new enemies every day. In such a situation, Spencer's doctrine of Social Darwinism was extremely comforting. Not everyone, he argued, could expect to rise to the top of the business, social, or political heap—only those who were the "fittest" should expect to survive. Even more popular than the fitness factor of Spencer's theory was the idea that it was best for these things to occur without intervention—especially intervention from government. If the natural development of society were left alone, Spencer felt that the end result would be the ideal condition of all humanity. He thus gave "scientific proof" to what the financiers had believed all along.

Near the end of the 1890's, Spencer came to the United States and was wined and dined by the so-called robber barons of the era. In fact, John D. Rockefeller was so impressed with Spencer's Social Darwinism that he made his famous "American Beauty Rose" speech at one of these meetings. Rockefeller pointed out that in order to cultivate a prize-winning rose, it was necessary for many of the shoots and branches to be pruned away to allow the full strength and vitality to flow into a single branch that could then produce the very best of its species. It did not take a great deal of insight to see the point of Rockefeller's analogy: many small, struggling petroleum companies might need to fall by the wayside so that there could be one American beauty, known as Standard Oil.

National Capitalism (1933–1950)

With nations, corporations, and individuals, change often represents a rebound from whatever has gone before. When the industrial capitalists became too engrossed with their processes to give proper attention to finances, the financiers supplanted them. In the same way, the barons of financial capitalism brought about abuses and conditions that pushed the nation into a reaction phase.

At first, people were supportive of the captains of industry. Not only did these self-made millionaires fulfill the American dream, but their enterprises represented progress to the man in the street. It is said that when Mussolini first came to power in Italy, the people preferred to ignore the abusive actions he took to get results. "Who cares?" they are quoted as saying. "He at least makes the trains run on time."

This same series of events seems to follow in every area of life. A problem arises. Everyone flocks to the most obvious cure and wholeheartedly embraces it. Soon, they begin to realize that either (1) the cure was worse than the disease, or (2) the cure worked and then became diseased itself. The wise student of history will develop a mature caution from the bitter experiences of previous ages. We should be skeptical of any new thing that promises to solve all the present problems and usher in an age of flawless utopia. It *may* solve the current problems, but its side effects and abuses will be the seeds of its own eventual undoing.

Robert Moore[14] suggests that national capitalism took control of business not on behalf of commercial interests but on behalf of labor and the petty capitalists. Ownership of business remained in private hands, but the government, acting for concerned consumers, began to tighten controls and enact protective legislation. National capitalism—that is national control of the capitalistic system—came about to remedy the inequities created under industrial and financial capitalism.

The Role of Roosevelt

National capitalism rose to its peak during the New Deal years when Franklin D. Roosevelt first entered the White House. The Great Depression had left the people frustrated and begging for drastic political changes. They voted Roosevelt into office, and he gave them their money's worth in political changes. Congress established the Federal Emergency Relief Administration and appropriated $500 million for its operation. Roosevelt's administrators granted funds to state relief agencies for direct relief. Congress established the Civilian Conservation Corps, which employed as many as 500,000 young men in reforestation and flood control. Mortgage relief aided millions of persons. The Farm Credit Administration in two years refinanced one fifth of the nations' farm mortgages, and the Home Owner's Loan Corporation saved one sixth of the nation's home owners from losing their homes. The Federal Housing Administration came into being to insure new home mortgages. Fifteen billion dollars was loaned to small and large businesses by the government. Financial capitalism had gotten the country in debt, and everybody agreed that national capital could get the country out.

The unfortunate characteristic of government programs is that they always tend to increase. A tax-financed social institution almost never goes out of business—unless it is to split into two or more subagencies. Such agencies are self-perpetuating and can eventually become as big a

---

[14] Robert E. Moore, "The Evolution of Capitalism," in W. T. Greenwood (ed.), *Issues in Business and Society* (Boston: Houghton Mifflin & Company, 2nd edition, 1971), pp. 7–16.

problem as the one they were originally created to solve. We should recognize that national capitalism and social democracy are transitional systems along the way to much less desirable arrangements. At the end of the road there are two unwelcome alternatives, socialism and fascism. Socialism substitutes government ownership of business for private ownership. Fascism retains private ownership but establishes tight political control over business. Each of the two alternatives has the undesirable but inevitable consequence of sacrificing personal liberty for autocracy.

To many, it would seem that we have never left the national capitalism period. It is true that many governmental restraints still exist, and a growing amount of "national capital" is flowing in the marketplace. Still, the emergency control aspect of the post-Depression years has passed away. Each new election renews the charges that this candidate or that one wants everything run by big government or has sold out to big business.

The business-government relationship (i.e., the socialism-private enterprise balance) must be carefully cared for by all segments of the population. The public must realize the extreme importance of business in the growth and continuation of our way of life. On the other hand, business must learn that responsibility for public well-being is not just a gimmick the public relations department dreamed up. Business must *serve* the public as well as make a profit. Public trust is a commodity to be earned and treasured by business.

Managerial Capitalism (1950–   )

In our present age of capitalism, the decisions are made and the trends are set by the managerial breed. Unlike their predecessors, the captains of today's business do not own their own companies. More often, they are slaving away in the service of a vast number of stockholders, who range from prosperous individuals, pension plans, and holding companies all the way down to one-share dabblers in the market.

Managerial capitalists are like all the other historic leaders of business, and—at the same time—like none of them. They must know the whole business but have control over only one small part. They must be product oriented, process conscious, financially responsible, and public spirited. They must be all things to all people, yet still function as only one cog in the wheel. They must ambitiously pursue their own ends without endangering the goals of the company as a whole. It is easy to see how the managerial capitalist could gather fringe benefits from such an uncertain job: ulcers, alcoholism, and identity crises are common commodities in the executive suite of the managerial capitalism years.

Peter Drucker, one of the most respected spokesmen of American management thought, expresses the opinion that the "management boom" has ended. Drucker traces the wildfire spread of American management technique during the quarter-century following World War II. He recounts many examples of recovering and developing nations that asked the renowned American management consultants to come and say the magic words over their efforts between 1945 and 1970. Drucker suggests that the boom has ended, and now the time of management *work* has come.

It is true that the buyers of management advice and counsel are more sophisticated; yet, *good* management will always be in demand. What Drucker calls the "end of the management boom" might more accurately be termed "the emergence of the careful consumer of management advice . . . a healthy demand for *results* instead of fancy words and promises."

If the history of management tells us anything, it is that, no matter what happens, peace or war, prosperity or famine, this world will always be in need of *good* managers . . . the kind who can get society from "where it is" to "where it wants to be."

Summary

Throughout most of the history of civilization, people have shown a startling lack of the practical business sense that we take so much for granted. Historians point to only two great eras of practicality in the history of mankind—one from about 6000 to 3000 B.C. and the other from the eighteenth century to the present.

America has had many qualities that provided open doors to the emergence and perfection of an outstanding business system. In addition to vast physical resources, it has had a heritage of management and industrial experimentation from the Old World countries. Immigrants have supplied the manpower, and democracy has supplied the open doors to business. Emphasis on innovation and education has paved the way. The eras of American business may be grouped into four distinct time periods according to the type of people who were at the helm.

Industrial capitalism (1776–1890) was the era of the efficiency expert and the production manager. Many of the businessmen subscribed to Adam Smith's *Wealth of Nations* philosophy that healthy competition left alone would produce quantity goods and quality life for all. The industrial capitalists's weakness was a lack of attention to the financial aspects of business.

Financial capitalism (1890–1933) was dominated by the financier. Without being concerned with the production of goods, this titan focused on the manipulation of financial resources to produce the greatest advantages. The robber barons liked the Social Darwinism of Herbert Spencer, which taught that the "survival of the fittest" in social realms was not only permissible but the best possible way to attain well-being for all.

National capitalism (1933–1950) came into power when the people, represented by government, had to rise up and defend themselves against the abuses and excesses of the financial capitalists. The multitudinous programs of big government characterized the national capitalism period. This characteristic is still apparent in our society. Indeed, a continuing effort is required to maintain the delicate balance between business and government.

Managerial capitalism (1950–   ) characterizes the present era, in which people *manage* rather than *own* their companies. Rarely are decisions made on individual entrepreneurial risk. The large corporation blends the talents and abilities of great hosts of individuals. Occasionally, however, people get lost in the bigness of the operation. All reports to the contrary, management is alive and well. It may have lost some of its mystique, but *good* managerial technique is always in demand.

Review Questions

1. What ingredients are necessary for productive business activities?
2. Define *petty capitalism; Protestant capitalism.*
3. Using the chapter opening as a guide, write a want ad for other historical management opportunities.
4. How would you compare the efficiency of management in constructing a pyramid with that of contemporary government projects? Why is there a difference?
5. Identify and discuss early examples of long range planning.
6. Why are most of the early illustrations of management concepts found in religious, government, or military settings rather than in business?
7. According to George Contenau, Babylonian supervisors were punished if their workers failed to produce. Apply this concept of supervisory responsibility to the classroom.
8. Who is the father of classical economics? Are his concepts still accepted?
9. What are the four main periods in the emergence of the American business system?
10. Managerial capitalism started around 1950. In your opinion, how long is this era likely to continue? Why?
11. Give an example of Social Darwinism.

2

The Emergence of American Business and Management Thought

"Oh . . . is it time to go down to the operating room now? Okay, what do you want me to do? Just slide over onto that little cart? Okay . . . how's that? You know . . . you really ought to put a couple of larger wheels on the back of this cart— it would make your job easier.

Hey . . . and while you're working on it, I think you might find that there is a soft rubber substance put out by Acme that will cushion those shocks as you roll through the doors like that. In fact, you should check on the cost of installing automatic door-openers because that could reduce the number of employees needed to get these carts from one place to another. You know . . . I was just noticing the blank ceiling above as we roll down this hall. If you were to put your mind to it, you could paint some cheery pictures on the ceiling for the people who have to ride along here like this looking straight up. Humm? We're in the operating room already? My goodness . . . I had no idea it would take so many people to perform a simple operation . . . I bet we could. . . . What? Oh hello . . . you must be the anesthesiologist. You know, if you would hold that little mask in the other hand and stand on the left side of me, you'd find it a lot easier to. . . . ZZZzzzzzz."

The American manager is known around the world as the person who can always find the better way to accomplish whatever work is to be done. It is often pointed out that a skilled manager can manage a soap factory or a computer facility or a warehouse or a football team. The skill is *management*, and it supersedes the specific understanding of the specific field to be managed The unique American habit of finding the better way has been admired, emulated, and sought after by America's international friends . . . and enemies. In the process of copying, these internationals have also learned that management does have its limitations and abuses.

All of us are familiar with those times when "the tail has wagged the dog" or "the cure has been more awesome than the disease." The field of management has had to endure its share of hair splitters and stopwatch maniacs along the way to the development of management concepts. Yet without the dedication to detail and the worship of efficiency, American industry would not command its current leadership position. It took men and women who valued "the better way" to make American industry hum. It was the efficiency fanatic who streamlined American industrial production into world leadership. Frank Gilbreth is said to have always buttoned his vest from the bottom up instead of from the top down. His reason was efficiency—the bottom-to-top process took him only three seconds, while top-to-bottom took seven. Think what a mind like that could—and did—do with a more complicated process like building houses or bridges.

Links in the Management Chain

American production efficiency has a worldwide reputation. But scientific management of *production* is only one link of the three-link chain of management thought. It didn't take many experiments with the stopwatch to discover that the mover is just as crucial as the motion. Thus, the link of *human relations* was recognized for its importance in the management process. Writers began to stress the importance of the human element in getting any job done. The middle link of the management chain—the link that holds the whole thing together—is *administration*. As used here, "administration" refers only to the coordinative aspects of planning, organizing, and controlling required of every manager. It is necessary that both scientific management and human relations be tied together for the total efficiency approach.

Over the years these three links of the chain have leapfrogged in prominence. For a while the leading experts were those whose gospel was that scientific approaches produce efficiency. Then, for a while, the human relations specialists were the consultants in vogue. The administrative approach also enjoyed its heyday. From the fortunate vantage point of the present, we can see the obvious necessity for all three links of the management chain.

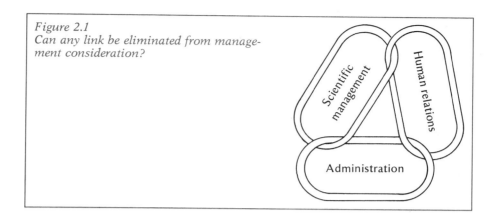

Figure 2.1
Can any link be eliminated from management consideration?

In this chapter, we will look briefly at the leaders in each of the three areas. We will look at some of their experiments, discoveries, and accomplishments. However, no vote will be taken at the end of the chapter to determine which is our favorite figure of management history. Rather, we will attempt to gain from each those concepts that should be included in a multifaceted management philosophy. No problems involving people ever had simple, one-word solutions. The manager's value to a company will always be in recognizing and treating total problems . . . not in citing simple formulas from some historical expert.

Scientific Management: "To build the mousetrap better"

Charles Babbage lived in the early 1800's and was one of the first to apply scientific inquiry to the study of production. His studies of production problems resulted in two major concepts, both of which seem common sense to us but were quite innovative in 1832. Babbage's first contribution to producers was to suggest that various parts of the total job should be assigned to workers on the basis of worker skills.

Division of labor was useful for four reasons, according to Babbage:[1] (1) Learning time is reduced because one worker must learn only one skill. (2) Less time is lost in changing from one skill to another during production. (3) Workers are likely to develop proficiency because they are repeating the same operation time after time. (4) Because the job is

[1] *On the Economy of Machinery and Manufacturers* (London: Charles Knight, 1832), pp.121–140.

broken down into its component parts, special tools and equipment are likely to be developed.

The second area in which Babbage pioneered was in providing guidelines by which managers could weigh the relative values of machine processes versus human operations. The newest machine on the market was an automated pin-maker. Babbage evaluated the machine's product and cost and gave the following questions:

1. What defects is the machine product liable to have?
2. What advantages does the machine product possess?
3. What is the prime cost of the machine?
4. What is the expense of keeping the machine in repair?
5. What is the expense of moving and attending to the machine?

Once again, the questions Babbage asked seem common sense to us. However, Babbage was one of the first to raise questions concerning quality and the cost of using machines, including human power and maintenance.

An interesting sidelight about Babbage is his experimentation with principles that are used in modern electronic computers.[2] Babbage first thought of computer principles in 1833, described them in great detail in 1840, spent most of his time attempting to make his "Difference Engine." He died disappointed in 1871. It was seventy years before anyone made a machine embodying all his ideas.

Charles Babbage had a mission: to make tedious computations and productions easier for workers. Today his pioneering theories are in daily use. However, his emphasis on production alone required that his theories be expanded and tempered to be useful in the "real world."

The Father of Scientific Management

Frederick W. Taylor is usually referred to as the "father of scientific management." His theories and experiments made revisions in two major areas—labor and management. Underlying the whole approach of scientific management is the belief that there is a one best way of doing any job. Both labor (the worker) and management (the supervisor) must be committed to this basic efficiency principle for the Taylor approach to be effective.

Taylor described two parts of a "mental revolution," which he said epitomized scientific management. The first part of the mental revolution, according to Taylor, is that both labor and management must stop quarreling about the division of the profits and get to the business of maximizing profits. The second phase of the mental revolution is to use the scientific approach to obtain information and determine procedure.

[2] Phillip and Emily Morrison (eds.), *Charles Babbage and Calculating Engines* (New York: Dover Publications, Inc., 1961), p. 9.

Taylor's unquestioning dedication to his statistical world represented his only major weakness. His results were often astonishing with regard to dollars and cents but discouraging to human workers. Taylor was by nature a stern and remote man. There was more in his writings than in his methods that reflects an insight into human nature. His associates, Carl Barth and H. L. Gantt, are given the credit for much of the humanizing and communicative development of the Taylor method.

There has been criticism of the Taylor doctrine of scientific management. Some critics have felt that application of the method sometimes requires more time and effort than the less efficient alternatives. In one instance Taylor experimented for twenty-six years to determine the best methods of machining metals. Under Taylor's concept of functional management, a single supervisor was replaced by eight different workers.[3]

1. The planner, who prepares written, detailed instructions.
2. The inspector, who sees that the workers understand the drawings and instructions.
3. The gang boss, who sets up the job and sees that the best methods are used.
4. The speed boss, who determines the proper tools, speeds, and so on.
5. The repair boss, who makes adjustments and cares for the machinery.
6. The time clerk, who handles pay, written reports, and returns.
7. The route clerk, who arranges the order of work and the movement of parts.
8. The disciplinarian, who is a troubleshooter and solves all the miscellaneous problems.

Taylor, like Babbage and the other leaders in production emphasis, tended to forget the human aspect of a job. At least one of his work revisions caused a strike. The nation owes a lot to Frederick Winslow Taylor, but none of us would be very happy working in a factory run by pure Taylorism. Nevertheless, the sheer dollars-and-cents proof of Taylor's work is impressive. Two examples of his work are described in the following sections.

Taylor and the Pig Iron Handlers

Perhaps the most widely publicized application of Taylor's scientific management philosophy was the handling of pig iron at the Bethlehem Steel Company in the late 1890's.[4] Because of prolonged low prices for pig iron, some eighty thousand tons of pig iron had been stored in small

---

[3] F. W. Taylor, *Shop Management* (New York: Harper and Row, Publishers, 1903), p. 96.
[4] Ibid., p. 47.

piles in an open field. With the outbreak of the Spanish-American War, the sudden demand for pig iron caused its price to rise and the iron in the field was sold. The immediate job was to load the piles of pig iron into railroad cars for shipment.

Pig iron had for many years been handled by workers (pig iron handlers) in gangs of about seventy-five people. Each pig iron handler picked up a pig of iron weighing ninety-two pounds, carried it up an inclined plank, and dropped it into the railroad car. A particular group of workmen was selected by Taylor and his associates in order to show the workers, the owners, and the managers, on a sufficiently large scale and in a very elementary kind of work, the advantages of his ideas over the existing day work and piecework plan.

Investigation revealed that the average pig iron handler was loading about 12½ long tons (2,240 pounds = a long ton) per day. The immediate problem? How to raise the output per worker to the higher level and still get the job done cheaply and efficiently.

Because the ultimate aim was "to develop each individual to the highest state of efficiency and prosperity," it seemed better to deal with the individual rather than with the group. The first step taken was the scientific selection of the worker to be used in the experiment. After a careful watching and studying of the gang for three or four days, four men were selected as possible candidates. The history of each candidate was obtained and inquiries were made as to his character, habits, and ambitions. One individual was then selected from among the four candidates. He was a Pennsylvania Dutchman named Schmidt.

Schmidt was noted for his frugality, energy, and physical characteristics. (Taylor later made the following statement, "Now one of the very first requirements for a man who is fit to handle pig iron as a regular occupation is that he shall be so stupid and so phlegmatic that he more nearly resembles in his mental make-up the ox than any other type." This outlook may help explain some of Taylor's later problems in interpersonal relations.) Being a proud man, or "high-priced" man, Schmidt was offered $1.85 per day rather than the usual wage of $1.15 per day to do exactly as he was instructed during the experiment: work when told to work, rest when told to rest. Schmidt was able to load 47½ tons per day.

A more detailed analysis of this rate reveals some interesting data.

Table 2.1 The Pig Iron- Handlers' Progress	Before	After
Long tons loaded per day	12½	47½
Wages	$1.15 per day	$1.85 per day
Labor costs	9⅕¢ per ton	3⁹/₁₀¢ per ton

The rate of $47\frac{1}{2}$ long tons per day equals 106,400 pounds or $53\frac{2}{5}$ short (regular) tons per day. There were 1,156 pigs loaded per day. The work days consisted of ten hours, of which Taylor determined that 42 per cent, or four hours and twelve minutes, was spent either returning to the pig iron pile from the railroad car or taking a rest (generally sitting down). The average distance of the pig iron piles from the railroad cars was 36 feet, so that a pig iron handler walked about 8 miles under load and 8 miles not under load each day. A pig of iron was loaded every thirty-one seconds on the average. Labor cost was reduced from $9\frac{1}{5}$¢ to $3\frac{9}{10}$¢ per long ton.

Other men subsequently were selected and trained to handle pig iron at this rate until all pig iron was handled in the Taylor method. Taylor noted that only about one man in eight of this gang of seventy-five pig iron handlers was physically capable of loading $47\frac{1}{2}$ tons per day.

> And indeed it should be understood that the removal of these men from pig iron handling, for which they were unfit, was really a kindness to themselves, because it was the first step toward finding them work for which they were peculiarly fitted, and at which, after receiving proper training, they could permanently and legitimately earn higher wages.

Taylor and the Optimum Shovel

A later experiment was conducted by Taylor at the Bethlehem Steel Company regarding the most efficient load for a worker to shovel. Investigation revealed that the existing practice was for each worker to provide his own shovel. The workers did not know in advance what type of material they were to shovel when they reported for work each day. Because of the widely varying density of the materials to be shoveled, each shovel load varied from four pounds for rice coal to thirty pounds for iron ore. Taylor concluded that with rice coal the worker was so underloaded and with iron ore so overloaded that it was impossible for the worker to do a proper day's work.

After experimenting, Taylor concluded that the best shovel load was about twenty-one pounds. Eight to ten different kinds of shovels were provided by the company and were issued in the morning to the workers according to the material to be shoveled that day. The number of shovel laborers in the yard was eventually reduced from about 500 to

Table 2.2 *Using the Right Tool Pays Off!*		Before	After
Number of workers		500	150
Worker output per day		16 tons	59 tons
Wages per man		$1.15 per day	$1.83 per day
Labor costs		$.072	$.033

150, resulting in an annual saving of $75,000 to $80,000, or a cost reduction from $.072 per long ton to $.033. For shoveling sixteen long tons each worker received $1.15 per day under the old plan. With the new plan each worker earned $1.88 per day for shoveling fifty-nine long tons.

Frederick W. Taylor was extremely evangelistic about the gospel of scientific management. In 1911 he published a book that was a sort of summary of his efforts. In the introduction to the book, he gave his reasons for his evangelistic zeal:

> To prove that the best management is a true science, resting upon clearly defined laws, rules, and principles, as a foundation. And further to show that the fundamental principles of scientific management are applicable to all kinds of human activities, from our simplest individual acts to the work of our great corporations, which call for the most elaborate cooperation.[5]

Gantt: the Human Side of Taylorism

Henry L. Gantt was a contemporary and co-worker of Frederick Taylor. Gantt tended to be more specialized, involving almost all his efforts in the steel and foundry industries. He also had a much greater concern for the human relations aspects of management than did the other efficiency experts of his time. In fact, Gantt and Taylor strongly disagreed when Gantt wanted to emphasize employee training. Taylor felt that the training would undermine the purity of the scientific approach to problem solving.

Gantt was one of the first to pioneer in the humanizing of the science of management. He belongs to the era of consultants who emphasized production, and he also represents the generation's awakening to the importance of the people. Gantt tried to fit the methods to the workers and take into consideration their state of mind. He insisted that the worker should be considered the variable and that all else should be adapted to him.

Gantt became the unrelenting foe of arbitrary, autocratic domination and of incompetent control and management. He tried to develop in his teaching and in practice truly democratic relations in business and industry. He believed that an action is right when it will advance the cause of humanity and wrong when it will not. He strongly supported Taylor's thesis that a knowledge of human activities is the best basis for action in industrial questions. It was on this premise that Gantt based the concepts he discussed in his book *Industrial Leadership*.[6]

Gantt held several patents, was the inventor of the Gantt chart, and rendered valuable consultant and managerial services during the World

---

[5] *The Principles of Scientific Management* (New York: Harper and Row, Publishers, 1911) p. 7.
[6] (New Haven, Conn.: Yale University Press, 1916).

War I production effort. He will, however, be remembered as the humanizing force in Taylor's scientific management approach.

Gilbreth: America's Best-known Efficiency Expert

Frank Gilbreth became America's best-known efficiency expert through the book *Cheaper by the Dozen*.[7] The book was written by two of the dozen Gilbreth children and successfully entertained the reading public with the quirks and eccentricities of a man for whom efficiency was a way of life. Gilbreth proposed marriage and a dozen children to Lillian Moller. By his calculations, a dozen children appeared to be the most efficient number.

Frank and Lillian Gilbreth were participants in good standing in the scientific management movement. Their slogan was "the one best way." They were intent on finding the one best way to do any job through the use of motion study, which reduced each job to its most basic movements. Their motion studies were used to set up more accurate job standards and eliminate wasted motion and effort.

Lillian Gilbreth pioneered in the field we now call personnel management. She was interested in the scientific selection, placement, and training of personnel. Few people realize the prowess of the female half of the Gilbreth team. In 1915 she was the first woman in the United States to receive a Ph.D. in psychology. An Oakland newspaper article revealed the prevailing attitudes of the day when it commented that "although a graduate of the University of California, the bride is nevertheless an extremely attractive young woman."

Frank Gilbreth was not only a consultant but quite a successful building contractor. He developed extensive field rules for his employees. These field rules eliminated wasted time and energy and speeded up the building pace. Interestingly enough, the employees did not seem to resent the rules because Gilbreth built into his system reward and respect for his employees.[8]

Gilbreth outlined 34 rules for workers and strictly enforced them as the key to higher pay and quicker promotions. He outlawed smoking on the job . . . except to finish the noon smoke. Extensive records were required, and most decisions went through the office. Preference was given to union laborers, but no employee could join the union without permission from Gilbreth. There was a system of whistle blasts to keep everyone starting and stopping in unison. Monthly reports were expected from everyone desiring promotion.

---

[7] Frank B. Gilbreth, Jr., and Ernestine Gilbreth Carey, *Cheaper by the Dozen* (New York: Thomas Y. Crowell Company, 1948).
[8] Based on W. R. Spriegel and C. E. Meyers (eds.), *The Writings of the Gilbreths* (Homewood, Ill.: Richard D. Irwin, Inc., 1953).

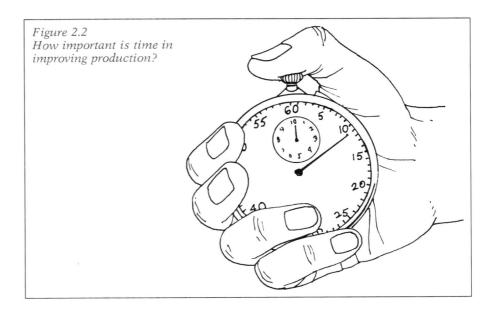

*Figure 2.2
How important is time in
improving production?*

Gilbreth also gave instructions regarding the behavior of all steady-pay workers, including what they were to do when it rained. Those who were employed in the Gilbreth organization were given white list cards that described their qualifications and character. These cards were treasured and were something of a status symbol.

The next section describes those management pioneers who emphasized the human relations link of the efficiency chain. In that section we will again mention the Gilbreths because their writings and practice brought both human relations and efficiency into play, and yet Frank Gilbreth's almost comical preoccupation with the split second makes him the perfect representative of the generation of experts who came charging into the shops and factories clicking stopwatches and quoting the Taylor doctrine of scientific management. Gilbreth's trial and error with his own shaving technique is an almost perfect capsule characterization of the time-and-motion man:

> For a while he tried shaving with two razors, but he finally gave it up.
> "I can save forty-four seconds," he grumbled, "but I wasted two minutes this morning putting this bandage on my throat."
> It wasn't the slashed throat that really bothered him. It was the two minutes.[9]

[9] Gilbreth and Carey, op. cit., p. 2.

Human Relations: "To build a better class of mousetrap builders"

Robert Owen was the successful manager of a textile mill in Scotland in the early 1800's. In 1813, he made an address to some of his colleagues that was far more renowned for its content than its title.[10] In "An Address: To the Superintendents of Manufacturers, and to those Individuals generally, who, by giving Employment to an aggregated Population, may easily adopt the means to form the Sentiments and Manners of such a Population," Owen said people were more important than machines!

Owen referred to his employees as "vital machines," and in describing how they should be regarded and treated he compared the importance of "vital machines" with that of the inanimate machines" of the factory. Owen referred to the practice of keeping machinery in good repair and pointed out that employees, too, have upkeep requirements. He claimed that as a result of his attention to personnel in his factory he was receiving more than 50 per cent return on any money so spent. Owen was an early spokesman of the coming emphasis upon human relations as a method of maximizing profits and motivating work. He stated that if the personal and social needs of workers were attended to, the economic repayment for such attention would take care of itself.

Munsterberg: Expert on Everything

Dr. Hugo Munsterberg was recruited from Germany for the Harvard Experimental Psychology Department in 1892. By 1908, he was receiving the highest salary at Harvard and becoming America's favorite authority on just about everything. He produced thirty books and monographs plus hundreds of speeches and articles for the popular press. He was quoted by *McClure's Magazine*, *The Ladies' Home Journal*, and evangelist Billy Sunday.

Munsterberg deserves credit for the creation of the new field of industrial psychology. As a private consultant, he developed aptitude and screening tests for several major corporations. He developed a test to indicate accident-prone motormen for the elevated railways. He investigated the decision-making aptitudes of naval and merchant marine officers. His trainees filled the first industrial psychologists' positions.

The German doctor became renowned in both the industrial and the scholastic fields. His political attachments with Germany and his lack of personal diplomacy led to public disfavor. As World War I was approaching, Dr. Munsterberg wrote to officials of his native Germany

[10] Robert Owen, "A New View of Society," reprinted in H. F. Merrill (ed.), *Classics in Management* (New York: American Management Association, Inc., 1960), pp. 21–25.

saying that he would use his personal influence to encourage President Wilson to stay out of the conflict.

The letter was intercepted by British intelligence, whereupon a wealthy Harvard alumnus from Great Britain offered the university a $10 million reward to fire Dr. Munsterberg.

True to the concepts of academic freedom, Harvard refused, but Dr. Munsterberg graciously offered to resign for half the sum even though he knew the university would not accept. Partly because of his notoriety, and despite his personal fame and involvement in business consulting, none of Dr. Munsterberg's disciples were able to carry on his work.

There was no more inspiring idea, he had said, than "this adjustment of work and psyche by which mental dissatisfaction in the work, mental depression, and discouragement may be replaced by overflowing joy and perfect inner harmony."[11] Although Dr. Munsterberg was unable to effect much joy and harmony in his personal relations, he did focus the attention of industry on the significance of scientific human relations programs.

Mayo: Father of Human Relations

Elton Mayo is frequently given the title "father of human relations." His now-famous Hawthorne experiments marked the point in management history when employees began to have rights. No doubt the transition would have taken place anyway, but Mayo's investigations and findings conveniently coincided with the changing attitude of managers.

Mayo, an industrial psychologist from Harvard University, agreed to participate in a study at the Hawthorne plant of Western Electric near Chicago.[12] The tasks were rather routine and were supposed to demonstrate worker productivity under varying environmental conditions—light, heat, room color, etc. Six of the women from the regular production line were moved to a special location where they could be carefully observed. Mayo's assistants began gradual changes of all the variables—less light, more rest time, different pay scales. Surprisingly, almost every change resulted in an increase in productivity. Even when the lights were down to the approximate level of moonlight, the girls increased production. Finally, to cap off the confusion, the experimenters returned to the original light, heat, and pay arrangements. Once again, the productivity increased!

[11] Editors of *Business Week, Milestones of Mangement* (New York: McGraw-Hill, Inc., 1965), Vol. 2, p. 21.

[12] Among the best sources for additional information on these experiments are Elton Mayo, *The Human Problems of an Industrial Civilization* (Boston: Division of Research, Harvard Business School, 1945); F. J. Roethlisberger and W. J. Dickson, *Management and the Worker* (Cambridge, Mass.: Harvard University Press, 1939); and F. J. Roethlisberger and W. J. Dickson, *Management and Morale* (Cambridge, Mass: Harvard University Press, 1942).

Mayo had uncovered what was later to be called the *Hawthorne effect:* special treatment—even abuse—can bring positive results because of the human factor. He had discovered that productivity is largely a function of the worker's attitudes. The attention paid to these workers gave them status and a feeling of importance. The worker's status in the mini- society of the job and the worker's self-enhancement opportunities are just as influential as the tools he or she uses.

Through the Hawthorne demonstration and others, Mayo was able to show that humane and respectful treatment of labor "pays" in the long run. In one textile mill, Mayo and his helpers tried many types of production incentives. Everything failed—even money—until the workers were involved in the decision making. Their personal involvement with the purpose of their labors caused production to increase, even though the machines could not run any faster.

The doctrine of fair treatment of personnel is so accepted in our day that it is hard to comprehend the thoughtless treatment prior to 1900. When workers were considered animals, and later raised to the status of machines, the bosses did only what they thought had to be done to avoid mutiny. When people became people, industry added something to its production tools that it had never recognized before—human pride.

The Hawthorne studies demonstrated that

1. Human social and psychological needs are every bit as effective as motivators as money.
2. The social interaction of the work group is as influential as the organization of the actual work.
3. The human factor cannot be ignored in any accurate management planning.

Lillian and *Frank Gilbreth* did the majority of their work before the tide of management thinking had turned to an emphasis on human relations. Even so, the writings of the couple place an extraordinarily perceptive emphasis upon the importance of the worker. "The emphasis in successful management," they wrote, "lies on the man, not on the work; therefore, that efficiency is best secured by placing the emphasis on the man, and modifying the equipment, materials, and methods to make the most of the man."[13]

Long before the Hawthorne experiments the Gilbreths were pointing out that for workers to be inspired to do their best work they must feel that they are recognized as individuals and not just part of a group of workers.

The Gilbreths designated two types of incentives—direct and indirect. Direct incentives include opportunities for ambition, pride, the

[13] Spriegel and Meyers, op cit.

love of play, competition, and desire for personal recognition to be achieved. The rewards under indirect incentives consist of promotion, pay, shorter hours, and other forms of external remuneration. It is a continuing struggle for managers to avoid slipping back into the simplistic but erroneous philosophy that more money buys more work.

Chester I. Barnard rose from being a Massachusetts farm hand at the age of twelve to a position of social and managerial respect as president of the New Jersey Bell Telephone Company. Often rated the greatest of modern theorists, Barnard was a scholar whose education extended far beyond his formal training. His boundless energy and Yankee zeal for good causes projected him into the management of countless public service organizations. His success in each endeavor could be traced to his emphasis upon the importance of the individual.

To Barnard an organization was "a system of consciously coordinated personal activities." He favored the term *organized activities* instead of *managed people,* and he stressed a "system of interactions," which depended on the maintenance of a balance between the contributions and satisfactions of its members. He made the handling of incentives one of the prime jobs of the executive.

In Chapter 2 of his classic, *The Functions of the Executive,*[14] Barnard points out that the first step in understanding individuals and individual behavior is cooperative systems.

Barnard articulated the human relations emphases that had been developing for centuries. Taylor's detailed investigation of scientific management had opened the doors on individual importance. As soon as the variables were quantified, it became apparent that there was an important efficiency factor outside the realm of physical facilities, tools, or rewards. The worker himself had to be considered in each decision. Human relations could never be ignored again.

Administration: "The best workers plus the best tools plus coordination equals the best mousetrap factory"

At the time Frederick Taylor was making his name with shovel sizes and pig iron in America, a French mining engineer, *Henri Fayol,* was making a great contribution to the science of management in Europe. At nineteen, Fayol had joined Commentry-Fourchambault, S.A., a large French mining conglomerate. By 1888, he had become its managing director and had built a great reputation as an engineer and scientist. When

[14] (Cambridge, Mass.: Harvard University Press, 1938.)

Apollo 17 Splashdown (NASA). The key to complex management tasks: scientific management, human relations, or administration?

Fayol became the managing director, the company was on the brink of bankruptcy. Within a few years, Fayol made it a successful company again by the application of good management, or "doctrine administrative," as he called it.

Fayol became well known in Europe during the years following World War I, even though his attainments seemed to be overshadowed by the European rush to embrace the teachings of Frederick Taylor. For years, Fayol's teachings were bypassed by Frenchmen who instead studied Taylorism.

Eventually, the genius of Fayol began to be seen. The professors started to quote him because his ideas had been worked out from a scientific analysis of his own practical and successful experience. In 1929, the first translation of Fayol's ideas appeared in America, but more than another twenty years passed before the wit and wisdom of Fayol's explanations came into common use.

At a time when the champions of scientific management were emphasizing the production problems of industry, Fayol was pointing to the importance of the executive's managerial role. He said that management played an important part in the administration of things—coordinating things large and small, industrial, commercial, political, religious, or any other.

Fayol: Teacher of Top Management

Fayol believed that better management depended on better training of managers. He founded a school that met once a week to study administrative problems of practicing managers. Until his death in 1925 at the age of 84, Fayol continued to be active in the application of his managing experiences to both public and private undertakings.

Fayol's general administrative principles were explained in a book published in 1916. *General and Industrial Management*[15] lists the following fourteen principles of management:

1. Division of work.
2. Authority.
3. Discipline.
4. Unity of command.
5. Unity of direction.
6. Subordination of individual interests to the general interest.
7. Remuneration.
8. Centralization.
9. Scalar chain (line of authority).
10. Order.
11. Equity.

[15] Trans. by Constance Storrs (London. Sir Isaac Pitman and Sons, 1949).

12. Stability of tenure of personnel.
13. Initiative.
14. Esprit de corps.

"Management," said Fayol, "is neither an exclusive privilege nor a particular responsibility of the head or senior members of the business; it is an activity spread like all other activities between the head and members of the body corporate.[16]

Mary Parker Follett was not discovered by the management disciples until she was in her mid-fifties and at the peak of her fame as a political philosopher and social critic. Her Radcliffe education and her life of culture and public service helped qualify her for fame as management's favorite friend and philosopher.

In 1920, Mary Follett published a book called *The New State*.[17] It made her an immediate power in the world of government and leadership. She had intelligently pointed out the flaws in many trusted social and political practices. Her searching examination of human relations was, perhaps, the first to promote "togetherness" and "group thinking"—in those terms. She precipitated a public outcry for a more scientific approach to management of government. She felt that if things were as they should be real harmony between capital and labor would depend upon an integration of motives and interests that would weld them into one group.

Business leaders flocked to Miss Follett. Her advice was treasured because she brought a nonbusinesss orientation to the problems of industries suffering from a slight overdose of Taylor's cold analysis. She renewed in business a valuing of things like professionalism, participation, creativity, and humanitarianism. She was at the right place at the right time to pull together the three links of the management chain— scientific management, human relations, and administration.

Colonel Lyndall Urwick had successful careers as a British military officer, as a civil servant, and as a management consultant. Urwick did much to discover and popularize the contributions made by Fayol. He has been a constant contributor to the discipline of management, typically viewing it from a professional, philosophical viewpoint.

R. C. Davis, in the early 1940's, attempted to read everything that the Library of Congress contained pertaining to the field of management. From that experience, Davis developed a comprehensive identification of management principles that for many years remained the standard in the field. He was the first American to develop a comprehensive theory of management functions and processes. For many years, Davis served as Dean of the College of Fellows within the Academy of Management, a tribute paid to him largely because his tenure at Ohio State

[16] Ibid., p.6.
[17] (London: Longsman, Green and Co., 1918.)

University served as inspiration to a large number of contemporary professors of management.

Harold Koontz co-authored the largest-selling management textbook in the world. *Principles of Management*,[18] now in its seventh edition, has been translated into 13 foreign languages. In addition to being the senior author of this text, Koontz is also widely known for his "management theory jungle"—a comprehensive classification of the means through which people study the subject of management. This concept will be further explored later in the third chapter.

Urwick, Davis, and Koontz are mentioned here because of their work in bringing the discipline together. Other scholars who have contributed important ideas and research will be introduced throughout the book.

Summary

Management thought can be described as an interlocking chain of three distinct philosophies. At one time or another, each link of the chain has received the overwhelming share of emphasis. Over the years, however, the evolution of management thought has established all three links as interdependent necessities.

The first link is *production.* Many hours of careful investigation and methods refinement made American production methods almost legendary. For years the time-and-motion specialists ruled the roost. Charles Babbage applied scientific inquiry to production problems as early as 1800. Frederick W. Taylor earned the name "father of scientific management" for his exhaustive studies and detailed findings on things like pig iron handling and optimum shovel sizes. Henry L. Gantt, a colleague of Taylor's, was also a production smoother but tended to take a more humanistic viewpoint. Frank and Lillian Gilbreth were leading industrial efficiency consultants of their time. Like Gantt, the Gilbreths seemed to give a little more consideration to the human factor in production, foreshadowing the shifting emphasis of management.

The human relations link of the management chain has received growing emphasis through the decades. Robert Owen recognized and made adjustments for his employees (whom he called "vital machines") early in the 1800's. Dr. Hugo Munsterberg, America's turn-of-the-century expert on everything, founded the new field of industrial psychology, which investigated worker aptitudes and needs. Elton Mayo earned the title "father of human relations" for his landmark experiments at the Hawthorne plant of Western Electric in 1927. His famous "Haw-

[18] (New York: McGraw-Hill Book Company, 1980.)

thorne effect" demonstrated the significance of the human component as a major variable of management planning. The Gilbreths deserve mention again among those who worked with the human side of industry. Mrs. Gilbreth probably had a great deal to do with this emphasis, being the first woman in the United States to receive a Ph.D. in psychology. Chester I. Barnard, the president of New Jersey Bell Telephone, was able to articulate in this century human relations emphases that had been developing for many centuries.

The *administration* link of the management chain has received much emphasis and, to some extent, ties the other two links together. Henri Fayol, a French mining engineer, published fourteen principles of management, eight of which are directed toward the administration of the organization. Mary Parker Follett was a famed political philosopher and social critic whose advice came to be treasured by management. She described people-centered, ideal organizational patterns for business people. Colonel Lyndall Urwick did much to discover and popularize the contributions made by Fayol. R. C. Davis, beloved management professor at Ohio State, developed a comprehensive identification of management principles. Harold Koontz, co-authored the largest-selling management textbook and is widely known for his definitive classification of the means through which people study the subject of management.

Production . . . human relations . . . and administration are the three links of management thought. A chain is only as strong as its weakest link.

Review Questions

1. What relationship exists between scientific management and electronic computers?
2. Explain Taylor's concept of "functional management."
3. Discuss Taylor's experiments in shoveling pig iron.
4. In what way did Henry L. Gantt's approach to management differ from Taylor's?
5. Describe the partnership that enabled Frank Gilbreth to achieve international stature as a management consultant.
6. According to Robert Owen, what are the most vital machines in any manufacturing operation?
7. What did the Hawthorne experiments prove about the impact of illumination on production?
8. Which of the pioneers of management thought can be referred to as "fathers" of specific fields?
9. Which women made the greatest contributions to the early development of management thought?

3

Paths Through the Management Maze

"Well, Sir . . . I can remember like it was only yesterday the way that boy could ask questions. One day, he was hanging around the garage as I was tinkering with the old jalopy, and he says, 'Grandpa, which part of a car is the most important part of all?'

"It was funny he should ask right then, cause I'd just been thinking about how I always just gave short answers to the boy . . . kinda neglecting his education an' all that . . . so I started in giving him the works. Well, I said, it won't move without the engine, but the engine can't do nothing without the gas tank, and it's gotta have wheels to do any moving around, and of course, there's gotta be a steering system or the driver can't. . . .

"Well . . . I looked around and that youngster had disappeared—didn't even wait for my answer. Later, I asked him why he'd ducked out on me.

"'Grandad,' he said very seriously, 'when you started saying everything was the most important, I figured you didn't know which one it really was'."

We like definite, absolute, exclusive answers to our questions. In a subject which involves complicated interworkings of many parts, there is sometimes a frustrating lack of clearcut superlatives and definite answers. That fact makes the truth no less true—it just means that we have to discipline ourselves to see the big picture, to fathom the intricacies instead of demanding meaningless simplicity.

The study of management is a dynamic study. It must be, because by its very nature it is a people-centered discipline. It employs people. It serves people. And with the peopleness of management comes the continuing effort to boil everything down into simplistic explanations. Yet no single word or formula or explanation is capable of including the whole topic. There is, for example, no simple summary of the skills that make a good manager.

In any field of study, there is a certain amount of historical and theoretical data to be mastered. It is useless to wish for the old days before the printing press catapulted every college professor into the authorship of a pet theory. The multiplicity of approaches is with us and, surprisingly, there is value in each approach. To alert students, each exposure to a new theoretical approach is stimulating. They need not agree with the new theory to skim off some value from it.

The Management Jungle

It is important that we adopt the proper objective for studying what Harold Koontz has called "the management theory jungle."[1] To seek a one-and-only doctrine of management is foolhardy. Each approach has something to offer the student who is intelligently building his or her own theory. To use names of professors or studies for scholastic name-dropping and seminar one-upmanship is useless. It does not prove that one is a manager—only that he can read.

The obvious practical purpose for sharpening your machette and entering the management theory jungle is to gain from the experience of others. A wise student learns from everyone he or she encounters . . . and students encounter everyone they can. But seeking for any single facet of the diamond that outshines all others is futile—any of the facets seems to sparkle most, depending upon the observer's viewpoint. The same is true of the varied nominations for "most important managerial trait." The opinion is largely a matter of the nominator's perspective.

Some of the best-known approaches to management are (1) the opera-

---

[1] Harold Koontz, "The Management Theory Jungle," *Journal of the Academy of Management*, Vol. 4, No. 3, pp. 174–188. See also Harold Koontz, "Making Sense of Management Theory," *Harvard Business Review*, July–August, 1962, pp. 24ff.

tional approach, (2) the empirical approach, (3) the human behavior approach, (4) the social system approach, (5) the decision theory approach, and (6) the mathematical approach. Each provides a different orientation . . . a different frame within which new knowledge may be organized. The theories have many similarities and many features in common. Their differences have occurred simply because some people can more easily understand things one way, whereas others get the message some other way. For this very reason (i.e., because different people think differently) it is important to become familiar with the many ways of analyzing the management task.

The ultimate intent of our study is action. We are learning so that we may do . . . or so that we may do better. Learning for the sake of having facts is wasteful. Because we are interested in the manager him-

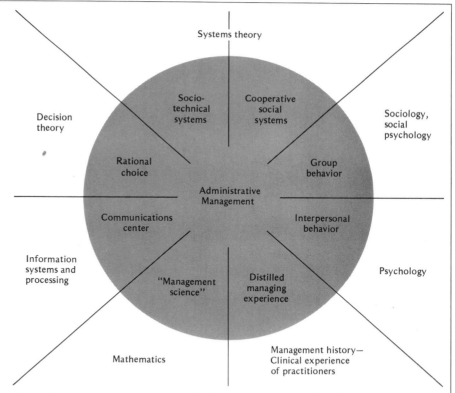

Figure 3.1
Management Theory and Science as a System Drawing on Other Areas of Organized Knowledge. [*Adapted from Harold Koontz, Cyril O'Donnell, and Heinz Weihrich, Management, 7th ed.* (*New York: McGraw-Hill Book Company, 1980*), *p. 75.*]

Systems theory

Socio-technical systems
Cooperative social systems

Decision theory

Sociology, social psychology

Rational choice

Group behavior

Administrative Management

Communications center

Interpersonal behavior

Information systems and processing

Psychology

"Management science"

Distilled managing experience

Mathematics

Management history— Clinical experience of practitioners

Operational-management theory and science are that part of the diagram enclosed in the circle. It shows how operational-management theory and science have a core of basic science and theory and draw from other fields knowledge pertinent to understanding management. It is thus, in part, an eclectic science and theory.

self, we will look at the theories of management in light of the complete manager. We will notice that each of the approaches to management is built around one of the qualities of the ideal manager, who must be a superhuman combination of many other occupations.

In this chapter, then, we will analyze "Super-Manager," that mild-mannered manipulator who is faster than a speeding rumor and able to leap tall pyramids at a single bound. What are the characteristics of Super-Manager, the mythical maximizer of profits and idealized idol of industry? What are the special skills and understanding used in the never-ending struggle for life, liberty, and the pursuit of a big Christmas bonus? And how do the varied talents of Super-Manager (Figure 3.2) fall into place within an organization?

Super-Manager is many people in one. His or her skills must all be present, but if any one skill takes over from the others, the manager is becoming lopsided and placing too much emphasis on a single facet. Let us look in this chapter at the many faces of Super-Manager.

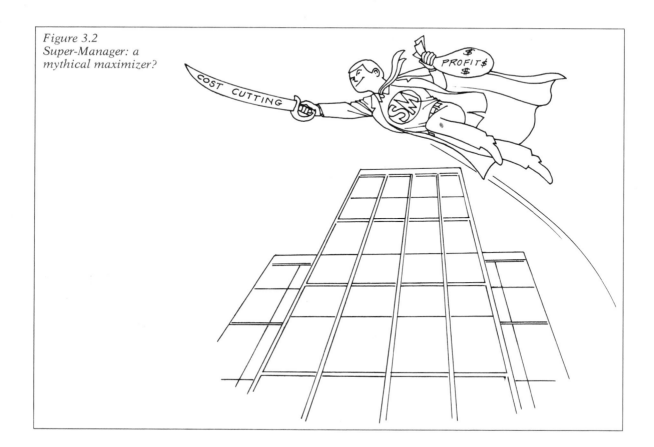

Figure 3.2
Super-Manager: a
mythical maximizer?

The Manager Is a Historian

Empirical theory is based on the premise that we must study the past or be doomed to repeat it. It is assumed that through the study of the successes and mistakes made by managers in the past, we can perfect the present and guard the future. Unfortunately, this past-is-prologue approach is a little too simple for complicated reality. Life situations may *resemble* each other, but each one is one of a kind. Management, unlike law, is not a discipline based on precedent. Symptoms may appear the same, but causes are sure to be as different as the people who make up the problem.

In fact, there is a danger involved in learning pat answers and canned solutions to management problems. Answers do not exist separately and independently of specific situations. A technique that was found to be right in the past may be the very worst thing that could be used in the present. When your employees walk out, would you (1) call in an expert labor consultant who knows nothing of your industry, (2) negotiate and attempt to settle the strike yourself, or (3) both? What advantages would each alternative offer?

All too often in government (but also in business) we watch as one regime or administration takes over and proceeds to automatically reverse the policies and procedures of its predecessor. The result is an unfortunate pendulum approach, which falls far short of meeting the needs. Some companies and countries swing forever from one extreme to another, passing only momentarily through the situation that should exist.

The ideal manager is able to draw generalizations from historical incidents in management and mismanagement. Nevertheless, such generalizations are only *guides* for present action—not *dictators* of guaranteed procedure.

One of the most common characteristics of those theorists who emphasize an empirical approach is the discussion and evaluation of simulated, hypothetical situations. Thus, the XYZ Real Estate Company or the Acme Production Corporation is described, discussed, and dissected on the assumption that the student is preparing for future similar corporate dilemmas. The famous case method used for instruction at many law schools and business schools does not always rest on simple cases. Lessons *can* be learned from the vicarious experience gained in making decisions about "paper" problems—and there is little danger that bad choices will cost more than a few quality points. Such experiences, of themselves, are neither good nor bad. If the student is using vicarious experience to sharpen personal perceptions and intuitions, the simulations can be valuable. On the other hand, the student who carefully files copies of the XYZ and Acme cases for easy retrieval in a future crisis is probably heading for trouble.

Another approach used by the empirical school of management theory is to study the methods of successful managers. Many service station managers were doubtless disappointed that Alfred P. Sloan's reorganization plan for General Motors was not a viable model for their operations. Yet, *My Years with General Motors*[2] became a best seller partially because of the managerial insight it provided.

While good managers would not think of an exclusively historic approach to decision making and problem solving, there is no doubt that they will be interested in the history of management. Furthermore, the wise manager makes mental notes of historic successes—but absorbs the principles, rather than memorizing the specifics. The Super-Manager draws historical generalizations—but acts independently. None of us would be nearsighted enough to suggest that *Moby Dick* is worthwhile reading only to one-legged whale hunters.

On the management theory diagram, the historian manager's attributes fall into the section called "distilled managing experience." The schematic emphasizes the place of the clinical experiences of aspiring managers, but clearly shows the fact that historical study and observation is only one piece of the pie.

The Manager Is a Psychologist

In addition to attention to the historical actions of people, the manager also gives heed to the characteristic nature of people. Natural intuition about people must be coupled with an updated understanding of scientific and psychological techniques. Both of these sides of people powers must be present. Managers can't be merely friendly and understanding. They can't be purely scientific. They must bring together existing and newly developed theories, methods, and techniques of the behavioral sciences with a common-sense understanding of people.

This approach to managing goes under many names. It has been called the "human relations," "leadership," and the "behavioral sciences" approach. The tactic is to concentrate on the *human* aspect of management. This school is always in danger of straying across the border into the forbidden territory of "manipulation." Most people like the sound of the term "managing," but the idea of deviously manipulating people is usually regarded very negatively. Falling into the error of manipulation is not automatically part of a psychological approach to management, but it is easy to fall into, once the primacy of systematic behavior modification is embraced.

In the same way that history must be studied in perspective, psycho-

[2] (New York: MacFadden-Bartell Books, 1965.)

logical events and evidence must also be weighed carefully. The laboratory performance of a bunch of rats may hold some *suggestions* about the performance of people in an office. But the manager must become the melting pot for all such input, tempering pure science with an understanding of the people involved. Workers are never *subjects* for experimentation, but people for understanding.

Human relations is a term that is somewhat involved in every aspect of life. Nevertheless, it is not a term that can be used interchangeably with *management*. There are some who like to equate managership with leadership. They wish to treat all led activities as managed situations. Obviously, many who are called leaders are not leading and many with the title of boss are more controlled than controlling. The complete manager understands and studies people. He or she is automatically interested in current theories and developments in psychology, group dynamics, and interpersonal relations. An effective manager is always somewhat of a psychologist—but a psychologist is not necessarily a manager.

A Good Manager Is a Social Scientist

Just as the manager's human relations characteristics provide an interest in psychological developments, a recognition of group power causes one to listen carefully to the social scientists. Psychology's emphasis is upon the individual and his or her motivations and reactions. Sociology and social psychology widen this approach to include collective psychology and the actions of people in groups. This is, without doubt, an important part of any manager's responsibility. The collective response is not necessarily a larger version of the individual response. Groups have unique personalities of their own—personalities distinctly different from those of their individual members.

The wise manager realizes intuitively that the worker's relationship to the small world of daily work can be a key factor in project attitudes and outcomes.

The social studies area of the manager's brain listens with interest to descriptions of incidents like the Hawthorne experiments mentioned earlier. The manager notes with interest and reflection what those experiments pointed up so clearly: group status is every bit as significant a production factor as machinery, lighting, heating, or even remuneration. The manager does not go around looking for an instance in which to apply the lessons learned at Western Electric. Rather, the Hawthorne experience can be stored in a personal bank of sociological experience. At the right time, actions rather than recitation will be called for.

One of the leading theorists in the social science approach to management was Chester I. Barnard.[3] From his prestigious position at the head of New Jersey Bell Telephone, Barnard wrote of his theory of cooperation grounded in the need of individuals to offset, through cooperation, the biological, physical, and social limitations affecting the person and the environment. Barnard defined an organization as any cooperative system in which people are able to communicate with each other and are willing to contribute action toward a conscious common purpose. Under this broad definition, even a rioting mob could be called an organization though we do not usually think of mob action as well organized and controlled.

Herbert A. Simon[4] and others of the social science school of management have emphasized the importance of the cooperative and purposeful group interrelationship or behavior. They have tended to want the group to be the primary orientation of the manager. Like the human relations discipline, this social science approach tends to equate leadership with managership. The two cannot be equated.

Basic sociology—the analysis of social behavior and the study of group behavior in social situations—does have value for the student of management. But it cannot include all of the aspects of management functions. The complete manager is a sociologist, but sociologists are not necessarily managers.

The Manager Is a Social Systems Specialist

At the top of Figure 3.1, a large chunk of the pie represents, "systems theory." It is perhaps appropriate that this section should be at the top of the chart, for the current emphasis in management could easily deceive beginning students into thinking that systems constitute the whole pie.

Every generation of management thought has seen scholars who insinuate that the human skills and aptitudes of the managerial task can be programmed and scheduled into automatic success. This is not true. A systematic approach can help . . . but systems can never replace feelings, innovation, or human response. It is true that there are unique relationships of groups and individuals in different types of work settings. Yet once again, it must be said that only a foolish student of management would expect to achieve automatic success by implementing some technical system that was a proven success in some other—even a

[3] *The Functions of the Executive* (Cambridge, Mass.: Harvard University Press, 1938).
[4] *Administrative Behavior* (New York: Macmillan Publishing Co., Inc., 1947).

similar—situation. In spite of their rave reviews, social systems are not the whole answer to the battery of question marks faced by the manager every day. The contributions of this theory are discussed more fully in Chapter 19.

The recent emphasis on business systems has tended to overshadow the fact that the best managers throughout history have been "systems people." Of course, PERT charts have only entered the scene within the last few years. But great managers have always had the ability to see systems whenever they looked at any task. This systems awareness does not suggest a cold, calculating, inhuman use of human components— though such abuses have occurred. Rather, the systematic manager perceives relationships and interdependencies of the various subtasks of the total operation.

Open and Closed Systems

A system can be defined as any collection of things that work together for a common purpose. A *closed system* is one which is stated or does not adapt to its environment. An *open system* exists when there are regular relationships and interactions between the system and its environment. When a *closed-loop feedback* is added to an open system, there is controlled monitoring of new information entering the system. Thus, a heating system with thermostatic control has "closed-loop" control. When a house is heated by a fireplace, the only way to provide feedback to the heating system is by external involvement. This is a closed system with an open feedback loop.

Systems management is more fully explored in Chapter 19. These basic concepts are introduced in order to explain the emphasis of some management scholars. Hopefully, this explanation will also point out the importance of managers understanding the relationship between various parts of their jobs. The concept of closed-loop feedback suggests the importance of managers serving as a center for communication flow. Communications input into the management system increases the ability of managers to respond to changing conditions in an efficient and productive manner.

The skillful and forward-looking manager rarely sees management systems as *closed*. Planning becomes more and more open as it becomes more realistic and better prepared for every eventuality. Among the tools which are absolutely necessary for efficient management must be listed the systems orientation . . . that set of mind or point of view which quickly senses and controls the variable interworkings of all the activities and people required for the victory.

The recent vogue has been the systems approach as the methodology for "getting it all together." This is both beneficial and detrimental. Systems *can* allow us to remain in touch with the total picture, the interacting nature of activities. And yet, the false security of having the whole world of possibilities reduced to a chart on the wall has paralyzed more than one operation. Possibly no organization utilizes systems more than the Federal bureaucracy, yet few businesses could survive with the resulting productivity. Systems can be useful, but they are not the all-inclusive method of unifying the other parts into a whole. The unifying factor is the intelligence and discretion of the manager—the skill of the manager is the common denominator in managerial success.

The Manager Is a Logician

Some theorists, particularly those who come from the discipline of economics, like to point to decision theory as the explanatory factor for all of management thought. Some limit themselves to specific kinds of decisions, like economic decisions. Others include anything about the organization that enters into the subject under analysis.

Once again, a group has taken one important factor and sought to make it the entire truth. These people believe that when all things are seen in the right light, every managerial activity is one of decision making. It is obviously true that nobody gets paid for propping her feet on an executive desk—managers make up in responsibility and ulcers what they appear to lack in physical exertion. Still, there are just too many other qualifications equally important ever to allow decision making to be considered the whole ball game.

Most of the enthusiasts for the decision theory school have a systems orientation. They like to think that every factor can be scientifically described, numbered, and manipulated. This is perhaps true with an internal combustion engine but not with individual or group responses. Some decision theory writers limit themselves purely to the economic decisions of the business. This cannot come close to providing an inclusive framework for management study. But even those who attempt to include all of the types of decisions involved will still find a great many managerial operations and involvements that will resist inclusion in their approach.

There are some decisions that cannot be quantified or stated in terms of relative economic value. Value considerations and aesthetic decisions are very real things that must be dealt with. Yet these and other important considerations are, in the final analysis, subjective decisions that reflect not pure data or alternative selection but the personal, entrepreneurial feeling in the bones of the experienced manager. Management history is replete with examples of individuals who succeeded by following intuitions that seemed contrary to all "logical" thought.

Murder by Death (Columbia Pictures Industries, Inc.). How is the logic of a manager like that of a detective?

The manager must be logical—especially in risk taking. But when you are head of a big company looking for a skillful executive, you want to hire a logical manager, not a managerial logician.

The Manager is Part Mathematician or Management Scientist

Mathematicians have always been a highly respected fraternity, but with the advent of the computer culture in which we live the mathematician was raised to the position of near-deity. One cartoon depicted two programmers puzzling over the printout sheet from a gigantic wall of a computer behind them. "It is demanding that we sacrifice a goat to it." one of the operators is saying. We are all amazed at the simplicity and one-twoism of the mathematical approach. The computer programmers, the systems analyst, and the perpetrators of PERT charts have built a growing fan club in management theory.

It is not the purpose of this chapter to tear down any of the wonderful accomplishments that the more systematic and mathematical management specialists have provided. Rather, this chapter's primary aim is to point out that mathematics, like all the other parts, should never be considered to be the whole. There can be no doubt about the usefulness —in fact, necessity—of a mathematical approach to inquiry. It forces the evaluator to define and describe; it provides functional symbols for parts and people; and it furnishes the set of mind that allows the simplification of complex phenomena.

Mathematicians have made a great contribution to logical thinking. They have demonstrated the values of goals and step-by-step procedure. Life, however, is not mathematical. When people are involved, one and one occasionally adds up to three. The unknown factors of human nature can throw a monkey wrench into the smooth machinery of the mathematical systems theorist.

The complete manager is part mathematician—and becoming increasingly dependent upon quantitative models and techniques. The manager can't do the job without the skills and precision of math, but realizes that mathematics is a tool rather than a school . . . a part rather than the whole.

The Communications-center Manager

"Communications" is a magic word. Everything we humans do together is dependent to some extent upon the skill with which we communicate about it. Because of this universal importance, and because of the blossoming centrality of the computer and other data-processing methodology, some people have sought to characterize good management as good communications performance.

According to this philosophy, the effective manager is only important in the abilities to receive, store, analyze, reshuffle, and redistribute information . . . more like the work in the mail room than in the executive suite. As in the other cases, this idea has some truth to it, but can hardly be inclusive of all the manager is and does.

The fatal flaw of the communications-center manager is the exclusion of the innovative and creative functions. There is minimal attention given to the information-generating office of the manager. And yet, it is the creative areas that separate the managers from the office workers. Managers bring together data all right, but there is a skill of perception and organization which far supersedes the mailroom worker's or the telephone switchboard operator's.

The Whole Manager

As will already be obvious, the stance of this text is to emphasize the manager. The various areas of study and occupational skill are important. Indeed, whole chapters will be dedicated to the study of various functions of management. Nevertheless, these will be treated as tools in the kit of the manager. If management skills and qualifications were as simple as some theorists would make it, the task of personnel departments would be much easier . . . they could hire managers from résumés and transcripts and never have to bother with interviews. But common sense tells us that the interview must be the most important part of the evaluative battery. It is not the *listing* of background that interests a wise employer, it is the *use* of that background. The manner in which the individual manager has woven together all of his disciplinary study and experiences is the crucial test.

The valuable graphic representation offered by Koontz allows us to realize that the whole manager lies in the totality of the circle. The operational manager in the center of the chart must look outward in all directions. In reality, the circle will never be so perfectly round, since various managers' aptitudes and interests will result in some inequities of skills and method. But that is reality—as long as we are discussing theory, we *can* conceive of Super-Manager, balancing with precision all the varied skills and tools of the managerial task.

This test will emphasize the manager as basic and the disciplines as ancillary. One of the most obvious characteristics of the creative manager is the ability to learn lessons from almost every experience of life. No matter where you are or what you are doing, you can always be observing principles of life. You can see management in everything. Rather than becoming a person who knows a field, you can be a person whose field embraces the basics of your environment. The world is made of people and things and the relationships between them—and so is management. The manager is historian, psychologist, social scientist, social systems specialist, logician, mathematician, communications center. There is not a field from which the manager cannot learn. But the manager is first of all an individual.

The overall job of any manager is to create within the enterprise an environment that will facilitate the accomplishment of its objective. To accomplish this job, many tools must be used. We will survey briefly the contents of the management tool box. Whole chapters will later be devoted to each of these tools. For now, we will observe them together. We will do this in an effort to avoid an error that is commonly made in the evaluation of management: the error of confusing the manager's tools with the work. We would never say that a carpenter's work is a hammer, but somehow we occasionally conclude that a manager's work is planning.

The manager is a craftsman. The tools are planning, organizing, staffing, controlling, and directing. These tools can be used on any job in management, whether it be government, education, sales, production, or research. The tools must be in good condition, but the finest tools in the world will not make a craftsman of a clod.

Planning

It is amusing to consider the insinuation made when companies establish planning departments. Planning for specific futuristic directions may be delegated to such a group, but the responsibility for planning can never be removed from any job. (Perhaps planning departments could more correctly be called environmental scanning and alternative generation departments.)

Each person plans work—*sets objectives and determines how to take action.* It sometimes appears that managers plan and workers do not. This appearance results from the fact that management's planning involves more variables and greater loss for mistakes. Management plans must be specific and clear enough to be communicated, whereas the line worker plots out an approach and readjusts for failure.

Planning is, of course, decision making because it involves selecting from among established alternatives. It is not necessarily good planning simply to say what action will be taken. Good planning says what *all* the possible actions might be, then places those courses in preferential order. A plan is incomplete if it lacks provisions for Plan B and maybe even Plans C and D.

Planning and the responsibility for planning cannot be completely separated from managerial performance. All managers have responsibility for planning whether they are at the top, middle, or bottom of the organizational structure. They have the *responsibility*, but to plan without the counsel and involvement of those who will execute the plan . . . is, in itself, poor planning.

Organizing

When planning has taken place, there exists an orderly explanation and description of the things that must be done to accomplish the overall objective. These may not be on paper, but unless the component parts have been identified and clarified, good planning has not yet taken place and the operation is not yet ready to be organized . . ."go back to the beginning and do not collect $200 for passing Go." Plan the work and then organize for the working of the plan.

Organization involves the arrangement of component jobs so they will get done in the most efficient way. Skills of organization include the grouping of the component jobs, the assignment of groups of activities to a manager, the delegation of authority to carry them out, and establishment of the relationship that shall exist between the working divisions.

Quite often the drawing of the organizational chart can reveal inconsistencies and inadequacies. On the other hand, many organizations possess an efficient and nicely drawn organizational chart but have no real organization. The chart hangs in dignity on the front office wall, while members of the staff run roughshod over the theoretical lines and staffs. This writer once requested an organizational chart of a consulting client. The request was denied on the excuse that "Things are changing so fast around here that any chart is obsolete before it can be printed." Reflection on that incident leads to the conclusion that if things were changing that fast, an organizational chart is even more necessary to provide some reference point for change and to reflect the basic organizational purposes.

Staffing is the securing and supporting of positions that become necessary as the work is organized. It involves the definition of personnel requirements; inventorying, appraising, and selecting candidates; and compensating, training, and keeping employees.

The organizational structure is not an end in itself but is one more tool of the manager craftsman. Efficient organization, like quality tools, will contribute to the success of the enterprise. The organizational chart must fit the task and should be an accurate statement of what actually happens.

Controlling

It is quite common for individuals to bear the title of *manager* even though they have no control over the task they have been given. In such cases, they are not managing but riding. And they are at the mercy of whatever factors or people are *really* controlling the activity.

Control is the challenge of making sure that events go as planned. Control is the attempt to eliminate all surprises. Carrying out the plans that have been made means controlling all the activities of employees that could cause a variation in results. Here the manager walks a tightrope

—in danger of letting employees get out of hand and equally in danger if they begin to feel too heavy a hand. The individual skill of the manager becomes most apparent at the point of control.

Direction, the human side of control, is another word that is loosely used in most descriptions of organizational function—how many times we have seen directors . . . who don't! On the other side of the ledger, there are many skilled and capable directors who move along letting the organization have *their* way—the director's way. One pitfall to avoid in effective direction is the assumption that "everyone knows what we know." Failure to make clear the goals, objectives, and methods is failure to direct. Organizations should be directed as a car is steered—with continuous, almost imperceptible, adjustments of course and speed . . . rather than with sudden, jerky changes and corrections. For the skillful, *direction* is sufficient to communicate clearly and monitor the job in process. For others, control becomes almost a reactionary thing, involving expensive correction, discipline, and retrenching.

Compelling events to go as planned means locating the persons responsible for deviations from the plans and taking the necessary steps to improve performance. Control is very important. A project that is out of control has little chance of ending according to plans. And it could very well do violence to other parts of the entire operation. Control is important, but it is only one tool of the management craftsman. Leadership and the human dimension is the focus of one major section of this book, and should be considered equally important in any thinking about control and direction. Analogies about driving cattle or sheep are useless, and we need to realize it and seek positive means for gaining control through sensitive, humanistic principles of direction.

Management — Coordination

Coordination is another term that might be tossed into the manager's tool box. At first glance, it would seem to be another thing that the manager does. And yet, on closer examination, coordination appears to be the essence of management. It is perhaps the closest thing to a synonym that we could find for *management.* Each of the basic functions of management (planning, organizing, and control) is an exercise in coordination. Each of the resource areas (history, psychology, social science, logic, and math) contributes to the manager's ability to coordinate skillfully. The interaction between these components and the complex relationship between management jobs in an organization were recognized in the concepts of system theory introduced earlier.

The challenge of coordination is that individuals often perceive the group's goals differently and also lean toward varying methods of reaching those goals. To impose sameness dictatorially is not to coordinate. A coordinator not only keeps everyone together but manages to draw out individual strengths in the process. The combined, coordinated result of a group's work should be a composite product, demonstrating the strengths of each member. "It becomes the central task of the manager to reconcile differences in approach, timing, effort, or interest and to harmonize cooperative and individual goals."[5]

One of the most unifying strategies of coordination is to make sure that each employee understands and appreciates the place of his job in the total picture. Understanding is easier than appreciating (especially when the job is turning wing nut 3A one-quarter turn to the right). Even so, the extent to which each employee feels he or she is contributing to the total effort is the extent to which coordination difficulties are likely to be avoided.

Mary Parker Follett had a great deal to say about the nature and importance of coordination.[6] She stated that it is achieved through interpersonal vertical and horizontal relationships of people in an enterprise. Ideas, ideals, prejudices, and purposes are passed from worker to worker more effectively than from memo to bulletin board. To unify the employees in working toward company goals, the wise coordinator will facilitate and participate in the communication among all levels of employees. Coordination is a communicated commodity, not an ordered one.

The timing for coordination is important . . . the earlier the better. The bulk of coordination is ideally accomplished as the plan is originally communicated to those involved. The later changes are made, the more complicated they are. The need for continuous, cooperative horizontal and vertical interchange of information can hardly be overemphasized. Good coordination attacks problems as they arise. Controlled coordination will anticipate them and prevent their occurrence.

Many methods are used to facilitate coordination. The most common is the supervisor, who can employ directional devices, teach principles of cooperation, illustrate desired methods, and monitor the effectiveness of the effort. In addition to personal contact, other methods may span the coordination gap. Written communications, procedures, bulletins, mechanical devices, group meetings, and liaison arrangements can keep everybody moving toward the same goal.

"The Moving Target"

It is easy for us, in discussing the things done by managers, to allow those things to appear isolated and static. This appearance is not

[5] Harold Koontz and Cyril O'Donnell, *Principles of Management* (4th ed.) (New York: McGraw-Hill Book Company, 1968), p. 50.
[6] Mary Parker Follett, *The New State* (London: Longmans, Green and Co., 1918).

fact . . . but has the limitation of still pictures trying to explain motion. In reaction to this problem, some writers have popularized the term "contingency management", making light of those "principles of management" writers who seek to reduce dynamic life decisions to test tubes.

The manager's task is to hit a moving target. Any observer knows that life is complicated, interwoven, and moves too fast for pat answers. The analytic approach is a good way to look at and understand the pieces one at a time, but there is no assumption that real events will occur in such a simplistic order.

While management pioneers like Frederick Taylor and Frank Gilbreth spent their lives looking for "one best way," the proponents of a "contingency" theory believe that there are no universal principles. As one writer expresses it:

> There is no one best way to plan; there is no one best way to lead; there is no one best way to organize a group; and there is no one best way to control the activities of an organization. The best concepts and techniques can be selected only after one is aware of the particular circumstances he is facing. . . .[7]

In many ways, the contingency approach to management is a manifestation of the same philosophy that developed situational ethics or the "new morality" during the 1960's. The ability to recognize the unique characteristics of any situation does not, however, negate the value of general principles. A reasonable utilization of the situational approach to morality, management, or life merely means that people should refrain from providing answers until they genuinely understand the question. Guidelines and principles are helpful in every walk of life. At the same time, management is too complex to be reduced to a set of simple rules or principles.

What the skilled manager is trying to achieve with all the available tools is coordination—so everybody can reach the group goal. "The better the tools" and "the better the manager"—the surer the victory.

This era has been dubbed "The Age of Management." Business, government education, and health care depend more and more on professional managers. Management courses are growing more rapidly in popularity than almost any other subject. Yet management's greatest challenge is only beginning to be subjected to analysis. This most important frontier is presented as an almost plaintive plea in the first eight letters of the word *management*. This message urges, "manage me!" Unfortunately, most treatments of management focus almost exclusively on the organizational setting where humans work together. Seldom has

---

[7] Howard M. Carlisle, *Situational Management: A Contingency Approach to Leadership;* (New York: AMACOM, 1973), p. 7.

attention been directed to the more universal and important challenge of applying sound management concepts to the various aspects of daily life. Everyone, from key corporate executives to undergraduate students or unemployed laborers, can achieve a greater degree of real success by gaining more control over his or her life.

Perhaps the most difficult challenge of management involves the application of management concepts to that most difficult subordinate — the one who faces you each morning in the mirror. As the sixteenth-century French novelist Rabelais suggested, "How shall I be able to rule over others if I have not full power and command of myself?"

Summary

There is a confusing multiplicity of theories about the management activities that are most inclusive of the management task. It is important that a proper understanding be adopted for reviewing the "management theory jungle." No single tool of the manager can be set apart as most important. Rather, the complete manager is able to use all of the appropriate tools toward the accomplishment of the goal.

The manager is many people. The manager is a historian, trying to benefit from the experience of others; a psychologist, giving heed to the characteristic nature of people; a social scientist, recognizing that group status is a highly significant management tool; an expert in group management through understanding social systems; a logician, utilizing the latest decision-making techniques; a mathematician, using a systematic approach to problem solution; and a complex communications center, receiving, adjusting, and redistributing data. While this text seeks to treat all these tools of the manager, it will present the manager as the crucial commodity.

The tools of the manager craftsman are planning, organizing, staffing, controlling, and directing. All managers have responsibility for planning, whether they are at the top, middle, or bottom of organizational structure. Organization involves the arrangement of component parts so that they will get done in the most efficient way. Staffing is the manning of positions that become apparent as the work is organized. Control is the practice of making sure that events go as planned. Direction is advance control.

Coordination is perhaps the closest thing to a true synonym for *management*. The challenge of coordination is to capitalize on individual differences while maintaining control. What the manager craftsman is trying to accomplish is coordination—so everyone works together in reaching the group goal.

Review Questions

1. You have read about several approaches to management. Name them. Why isn't one approach adequate?
2. What are the tools, or functions, of the manager?
3. How is coordination related to management? Why is it important?
4. Describe the "Super-Manager" profiled in the chapter.
5. Is the manager a manipulator? Does the term *manipulation* have a positive or negative connotation? Discuss.
6. Identify the major roles that a manager must play in exercising managerial responsibility.
7. Identify the school of management thought evidenced by the following statements.
   a. A happy sailor is a productive sailor.
   b. On this job, two is company but three is a crowd.
   c. This approach worked in 1908 and will work again now.
   d. Statistical analysis indicates that we should anticipate a problem in February.
8. On page 56, the text identifies five major tools or functions of management. Yet the following section focuses on planning, organization, and control. Why are the other functions overlooked?
9. If planning, organization, and other management functions are seen as tools, what word comes closest to being the tool box?

part II

The Job of Management

4

Effective Decision Making

"Well, we were driving back home from Florida when it happened. We were passing through Atlanta, and you may know the place where Interstate 75 and 85 separate. I-75 goes to the northeast toward Chattanooga, and I-85 goes to the northeast through the Carolinas. Since I wanted to go toward the northeast, I did what any normal, intelligent person would do, I veered to the right. Guess I didn't notice that the road kinda veered right for a little while, then swung to the left. Some blamed engineer laid it out just backwards!

First thing you know, my wife figured out that something was wrong. In her tender, loving way, she said, 'Stupid, you're on the wrong road again!'

"Well, I checked the road signs and there wasn't much I could say to argue with her. But then I checked the speedometer and we were going the speed limit. So I really shut her up. I said "That's all right, we're making such great time, let's stay on this road'."

Each of us is confronted from day to day with the need to do responsible decision making. This involves gathering accurate, dependable, and adequate data, and choosing between alternatives.

Almost every management action involves decision making. Some authorities like Claude George, Jr., go so far as to declare that decision making *is* management. In *Management in Industry*,[1] George says, "In the final analysis, managers are paid for doing only one thing: making decisions. In fact, the job of managing is the job of making decisions."

As we have noted in Chapter 3, one school of management philosophy says that the way to study management is to study decision making. Others, who shy away from making any one activity or characteristic the whole of the subject, still have to admit that the process is present in almost every management function. It is safe to say, therefore, that on the question of whether decision making is the whole of management . . . no final decision has been made.

In the next chapter we will consider planning as the process of making decisions before the fact. Planning itself is a process of advance or original decision making. Almost every chapter of this book (and almost every activity of the executive's day) involves decision making. It could be argued by the local cynic that most managers make no decisions but merely *implement* decisions made by someone else higher up. Of course it soon becomes obvious that decisions are necessary regarding (1) the methods by which the decisions will be implemented or (2) *whether* they will be implemented at all.

Sadly, many managers abdicate their responsibility and opportunity to make important decisions. Often they decide either not to decide or to give a "definite maybe" as an answer. In such a case they are judging themselves unworthy of their positions and proving that their job can be done by an unskilled person.

Rational Decision Making

Early theories about how individuals made decisions were based on the concept of an "economic man." Utilitarian philosophers such as Jeremy Bentham and John Stuart Mill assumed that the goal of all human behavior is to seek pleasure and avoid pain. The value (utility) of any object or action, according to their thinking, should be evaluated according to the difference between the pleasure it provides and the pain it costs. Bentham even went so far as to develop a hedonistic calculus that was a preliminary form of what might be called cost-benefit analysis.

The underlying assumption of the economic-man theory is that all in-

[1] 2nd ed. (Englewood Cliffs, N.J.: Prentice-Hall, Inc., 1964), p.19.

dividuals know the alternatives available in a given situation and all the consequences they will bring. It also assumes that people will behave rationally—that is, that they will make choices so as to maximize some desired value. Even today, most microeconomic theories are based on the assumption that there is an attempt to maximize profits.

Obviously, it is irrational to assume that people always behave in a rational manner. In 1947, Herbert A. Simon[2] wrote a book that was sharply critical of this economic theory. Simon argued that "administrative man" was a more valid model of reality because managers were never completely informed and were seldom able to maximize anything. Because of the physical limitations of the decision maker, Simon introduced the *principle of bounded rationality:*

> The capacity of the human mind in formulating and solving complex problems is very small compared to the size of the problem. It is very difficult to achieve objectively rational behavior in the real world . . . or even a reasonable approximation to such objective rationality.[2]

Because optimizing is viewed as too difficult for "administrative man," Simon suggested that "satisficing" was a more realistic and typical procedure.[3] The satisficer considers possible alternatives until finding one that meets a minimum standard of satisfaction. Instead of searching a haystack to find the sharpest needle in it, he or she will be content to find a needle sharp enough to sew with. In spite of the fact that many new quantitative tools (see Chapter 18) offer the manager an even better grasp of the decision-making situation, studies of actual decision-making behavior have supported this theory.[4]

Psychological Dimensions of Decision Making

It is easy enough to say that the executive must seek out the facts, weigh the variables, and then act decisively. We like to build pictures of the swashbuckling, self-assured manager dancing fearlessly onto a corporate limb, saying defiantly, "Just do as I say. I know I am right. Whatever happens, I'll take the responsibility."

It makes a nice dream. But the "real world" of business and management seems to be allowing less and less of this type of romantic foot-

---

[2] *Administrative Behavior* (New York: Macmillan Publishing Co., Inc., 1947).
[3] J. G. March and H. A. Simon, *Organizations* (New York: John Wiley & Sons, Inc., 1958), p. 141.
[4] See R. M. Evert and J. G. March, *Behavior Theory of the Firm* (New York: McGraw-Hill Book Company, 1963).

work. In fact, recent studies indicate that less gambling may be taking place in the board room than on the warehouse loading dock.

Chris Argyris tested the top management systems and decision-making activities of ten organizations. All the executives were interviewed and their behavior taped during critical decision-making meetings. When the results were analyzed, the conclusion seemed to be that

> executives represent a more potent source of dehumanization, conformity, and ineffective decision-making than does computer technology. More specifically: The biggest single barrier to effective decision-making and the biggest contributor to the dehuminization of the decision-making process, was the way the executives dealt with each other and the kind of group dynamics they created.[5]

Argyris felt that the managers he tested had plenty of individual decision-making and risk-taking ability. But in groups they tended to create interpersonal relationships and company politics that eliminated the opportunity to take risks. One of the problems certain to be confronted in multilithic organizations of the future is the amount of individual participation in the making of decisions. Certainly the company's well-being is to be protected. Yet we might wonder if the stifling of individual initiative is a positive or negative force for the company. On a broader scope, the science fiction writers have been, for years, predicting the demise of the individual and his or her capacity actually to make a difference.

Company pressures can operate in a number of ways to create indecision and fear of risk taking. Clearly, an important consideration for supervisors and those who must foster creativity and innovation is the structuring of an environment in which the qualities of good, innovative decision making are glorified rather than derided.

Deciding: Past, Present, and Future

Kepner and Tregoe[6] have developed a graphic representation of the fact that decisions have a somewhat cyclical nature. The chart, shown in Exhibit 4.1, demonstrates that managers should make sure they know at which point in its cycle the problem situation is being encountered. Any experienced manager can testify that decisions occur in spirals rather than lines.

The first stage in the cycle is preliminary decision making. This is analogous to the planning process and will receive more detailed discussion in the next chapter. Preventive problem solving is the process of anticipating the kinds of things that can go wrong. Finally, some prob-

[5] "How Tomorrow's Executives Will Make Decisions," *Think Magazine*, November–December 1967, p. 18.
[6] Kepner, Charles H., and Benjamin B. Tregoe, *The Rational Manager* (New York: McGraw-Hill Book Company, 1965).

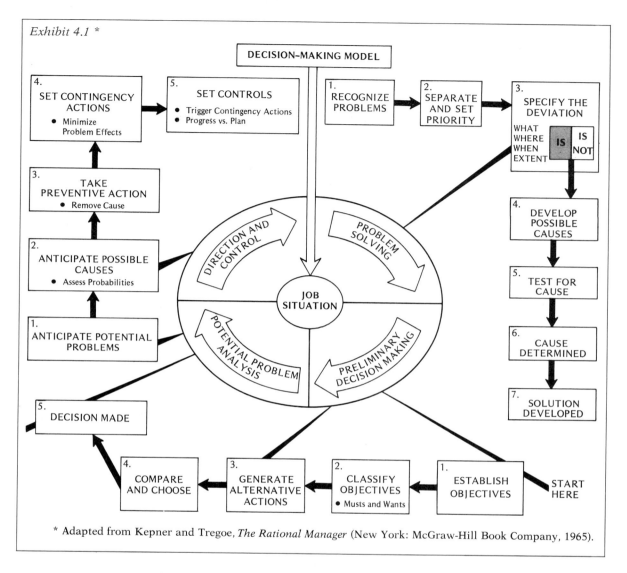

Exhibit 4.1 *

DECISION-MAKING MODEL

4. SET CONTINGENCY ACTIONS
- Minimize Problem Effects

5. SET CONTROLS
- Trigger Contingency Actions
- Progress vs. Plan

1. RECOGNIZE PROBLEMS

2. SEPARATE AND SET PRIORITY

3. SPECIFY THE DEVIATION

WHAT WHERE WHEN EXTENT | IS | IS NOT

3. TAKE PREVENTIVE ACTION
- Remove Cause

4. DEVELOP POSSIBLE CAUSES

2. ANTICIPATE POSSIBLE CAUSES
- Assess Probabilities

5. TEST FOR CAUSE

DIRECTION AND CONTROL

PROBLEM SOLVING

JOB SITUATION

1. ANTICIPATE POTENTIAL PROBLEMS

POTENTIAL PROBLEM ANALYSIS

PRELIMINARY DECISION MAKING

6. CAUSE DETERMINED

7. SOLUTION DEVELOPED

5. DECISION MADE

4. COMPARE AND CHOOSE

3. GENERATE ALTERNATIVE ACTIONS

2. CLASSIFY OBJECTIVES
- Musts and Wants

1. ESTABLISH OBJECTIVES

START HERE

* Adapted from Kepner and Tregoe, *The Rational Manager* (New York: McGraw-Hill Book Company, 1965).

lems will arise that the manager, even with astute forethought and analysis, will not have considered. The problem-solving process should be applied to correct these situations.

Preventive Problem Solving

The comic hero of America steps onto the pitcher's mound. Charlie Brown makes his windup and lets fly his best pitch. As the ball flies toward the slugger on the other team, Charlie philosophizes, "It's a mistake to try to avoid the unpleasant things in life."

Almost immediately, a line drive rifles back at him. Attempting to get out of the way, he loses his hat, glove, and one shoe. As he lies dazed next to the pitcher's mound, he adds, as an afterthought, "But I'm beginning to consider it."

We are all aware of the pressures of problem solving, firefighting, and crisis management that can keep managers at the end of their ropes. After hours of avoiding line drives, pacifying irate customers, or dealing with sticky production problems, managers may puzzle over the philosophy expressed by inventor Charles Kettering: "Problems are the price of progress. Don't bring me anything but trouble. Good news weakens me." A hard day of answerless dilemmas could make a manager throw in with Charlie Brown and decide to consider accepting the weakening influence of good news and, whenever possible, to avoid the unpleasant things in life.

For those managers who lack Kettering's perseverance, or who wish to avoid problems by anticipating them, a simple set of questions[7] about the decision can be of help:

1. What Is Right?

In order to anticipate or to recognize crisis situations, it is necessary for the manager to have an understanding of what is sought. In other words, it helps to know what is right before attempting to tell when something is going wrong.

Crises, like opportunities, often go unrecognized. As William Woodward commented, "The turning points of lives are not necessarily the great moments. The real crises are often concealed in situations so trivial in appearance that they may pass unnoticed." One of the biggest problems of managing is that it is so daily! To handle the demands of the job adequately, a manager must be constantly alert to any problem that can develop to crisis proportions.

Without adequate plans or standards for measurement, it is impossible to exercise control or to have a clear reading of what should take place. Too often managers are like the administrators described by Winston Churchill; "they are decided only to be undecided, resolved to be irresolute . . . and all-powerful for impotence."

2. What Can Go Wrong?
Shakespeare said it well:

> But since the affairs of men
> rest still uncertain,
> Let's reason with the worst
> that may befall.
>
> (*Julius Caesar*)

---

[7] This section is drawn from Robert M. Fulmer, "Crisis Management," *Association Management*, October 1971, pp. 71–74.

After Shakespeare came Edsel Murphy, who clarified and first stated the most universal and dependable principle of administration. Murphy's Law of Management, simply stated, says, "If anything can go wrong, it will."

Most executives have seen this law in operation, but only a few have taken time to anticipate and make allowances for it. To apply this concept successfully, the manager must follow the pessimistic practice of expecting the worst—and then making the most of it.

To demonstrate the all-pervasive nature of Murphy's Law, several engineering corollaries are cited. These have been taken from *The Contributions of Edsel Murphy to the Understanding of the Behavior of Inanimate Objects* by D. L. Klipstein.

1. All constants are variables.
2. In any given miscalculation, the fault will never be placed if more than one person is involved.
3. Any wire cut to length will be too short.
4. A dropped tool will land where it can do the most damage. (Also known as the Law of Selective Gravitation.)
5. If a project requires n components, there will be $n - 1$ units in stock.
6. An item selected at random from a group having 99% reliability will be a member of the 1% group.
7. Interchangeable parts won't.
8. Components that must not and cannot be assembled improperly will be.

Tom Baker of the American Soft Drink Association reports that the impact of the cyclamate ban would have been worse had his executive committee not adopted the practice of meeting regularly to discuss with each other "the worst things that could possibly happen to us."[8] Although they were not able to anticipate the exact nature of the problem that arose, they had recognized the constant threat that some ingredient would be declared dangerous or undesirable. According to Baker, "a problem recognized is already half-solved." This anticipation and preparation enabled the soft drink industry to take prompt and decisive action to minimize what could have been a catastrophic occurrence.

After a number of potential problems have been identified, it is desirable to group them. Some problems or crises must be avoided at all costs. Others are irritating enough so that considerable efforts should be directed to their elimination, and still others are so minor that only cur-

[8] An interview with Tom Baker, Executive Vice-President, American Soft Drink Association, June 3, 1971.

Exhibit 4.2
Potential Problem
Analysis*

What: The movement of furniture and office equipment.
Where: From fifth floor of building A to fourth floor of
new building B.
When: Sunday, starting 9 A.M. and finishing 4 P.M. for
inspection.
Extent: Twenty desks and tables, forty file cabinets, twenty
typewriters, twenty chairs. . .

Potential Problem: Possible Causes	Proba-bility (in %)	Preventive Actions	Residual Proba-bility (in %)	Contingent Actions
A. *Move will take too long:*				
1. Not packed and ready.	75	Instruct; set deadline; in-spect 3:00 P.M. Friday.	5	Have two-man packing crew on hand.
2. Not enough movers show up.	20	Check; get written com-mitment from movers.	10	Know of backup com-mercial mover.
3. Freight elevator not manned.	50	Check; arrange for operator.	5	Have backup operator on call.
4. Hand trucks not available.	20	Check and arrange.	0	Know where to borrow.
5. Lunch counters nearby closed, no food.	70	Check hours; locate nearest one that will be open.	10	Know cater-ing truck service to call.
6. Doors locked, no one has key.	50	Get passkey	0	
B. *Stuff will be mixed up, things all confused:*				
7. Stuff not properly labeled.	80	Instruct; in-spect mid-P.M. Friday.	10	Have assist-ant who can label stuff.
8. Movers don't know where to put stuff.	100	Lay out rooms with chalk; use signs and labels.	5	Have assist-ant who knows layout.
9. Someone else moving in, same time.	10	Check with building super-intendent.	5	Rearrange schedule; set up aisles to keep separate.

Exhibit 4.2
(Continued)

Potential Problem: Possible Causes	Proba-bility (in %)	Preventive Actions	Residual Proba-bility (in %)	Contingent Actions
C. *Stuff will be damaged:*				
10. Breakables not properly packed.	40	Instruct; provide packing materials; inspect.	10	Have two-man packing crew on hand.
11. Doors, corners, elevators not padded.	100	Check for critical spots; arrange for padding.	10	Have extra pads on hand.
D. *Stuff will be stolen, lost:*				
12. Unauthorized people come in, take things.	50	Place uniformed guards at doors; have mover post bond.	5	Spotcheck against list.
13. Desks, files not locked.	40	Instruct; check locks.	10	Have man lock same.

* Adapted from Kepner and Tregoe, *The Rational Manager* (New York: McGraw-Hill Book Company, 1965).

sory attention need be directed to them. The planning-decision sheet (Exhibit 4.1) provides more detail about this and related steps in potential problem analysis. This potential problem analysis approach is applied in Exhibit 4.2 to the type of preparation that might go into the planning of an office move.

✳ 3. What Could Cause This Problem to Occur?

It is not enough to know that something could go wrong. It is essential to recognize the causative factor. As J. Pierpont Morgan once pointed out, "There are two reasons for everything—the obvious reason and the real reason." Managers must have the persistence and intelligence to find the real reason. If a problem has already occurred, the job of determining causes is much easier. It essentially involves identifying changes that could have produced the precise effect associated with the problem. In the analyzing of potential crises, the causes have not happened and the job is more difficult. Here a manager must draw heavily on experience and judgment to list as many possible causes as can be seen for a given potential problem. Most will never create a problem, but his consideration may well be the proverbial "stitch in time." Treating symptoms instead of causes is somewhat analogous to treating a skin infection with cosmetics rather than penicillin.

✗ 4. What Preventive Action Can I Take?

As suggested previously, once the problem has been identified, the solution or prevention may be obvious. Crises find poor feeding grounds in a prepared organization. No wise wolf is going to leave a sheep to dine upon a porcupine. Similarly, trouble is less likely to visit a prepared organization. The analysis of the potential problem shows how simple steps can sometimes drastically reduce the probability of problem development. At a very simple level, the supervisor of a very carefully planned Sunday move would face a crisis situation if she arrived with the movers to find that the new office building was securely locked and that no building key was available. A very simple precautionary step (picking up the passkey on Friday) would eliminate this potential problem.

5. What Is My Contingency Plan?

After identifying potential problems, causes, and preventive action, it would appear that the manager has done all that can be expected. But the astute executive is acutely pessimistic. After doing everything possible to keep problems from occurring, it helps to go on to ask, "What am I going to do when something goes wrong anyway?" This truly calls for the kind of person who goes around building dungeons in the air. But, as illustrated in the plan for the Sunday move, this approach can be very helpful as a continuation of the process.

This process of decision making or crisis management can be a laborious one. Some managers excuse their lack of preparation by saying, "I simply don't have time to do all this." It is curious that although we may not have time to do something correctly, we always find time to do it over again when it goes wrong.

✗ 6. When Will My Alternative Plan Go into Action?

There must be a definite triggering mechanism built into a crisis plan. Otherwise managers may be like the cold-blooded frog who allowed himself to be cooked in a pan of water as the temperature was increased gradually. Sometimes individuals are credited with patience simply because they don't have the ability to make a decision. It is generally much easier to make a good decision about when you should move to Plan B before the pressure of a crisis situation strikes. For contingency actions, an executive should establish an early-warning system of mileposts that will alert him that *now* there is a problem. As soon as the designated bell rings or flag waves, the plan should shift itself to the predetermined contingency action.

Problem Solving

At first glance, it might appear that problem solving and decision making are only different terms for the same process. However, there is a very meaningful difference. Problem solving is the process that allows the manager eventually to make a decision. The best decision maker in the world is bound to fail if the wrong problem has been isolated to decide about. Problem analysis is the logical process by which the manager narrows down a broad body of information during progress toward a solution. Clearly, we ought to spend more time isolating the problem than worrying over the solution. And it is true that many times the process of getting the facts and eliminating every hazy area about the problem can actually remove the need for a decision. With proper fact-finding about the problem, the manager may eventually say, "If that is the way the problem really is, then, we have no alternative but to . . ."

The Problem-Solving Process

The problem-solving process begins with the identification of the problem, continues with the analysis by which the cause is isolated, and concludes with an act of choice. At each stage, specific information relevant to the problem drops out as the situation is refined. Next, the most important problem to be treated is established and things that might have caused it are listed. Finally, the list of causes is refined until the single most likely cause is remaining. Locating this cause makes it possible to take a specific, effective action on the problem.

A skilled mechanic gives a familiar demonstration of the problem-solving process. In answers to your frantic cry for help, a series of questions will help to isolate and refine the problem itself. It may seem to the stranded motorist that the problem is simple—the car won't go. Of course, that is not the problem at all—only an irritating symptom. It would be so easy to treat the symptom by pushing the car. But, in doing so, the motorist begins to realize that treating the symptom is ultimately rather unsatisfactory. What is really needed is a person who knows the process well—who knows how things are when they are as they should be. *A problem is the difference between what should be happening and what actually is happening.* The effective problem solver asks those questions that gradually eliminate the distracting symptoms and leave only the problem to be solved.

As with most processes, things are relatively simple until you involve the human element. Very often problem solvers will listen to a little evidence and jump to an immediate conclusion about the problem. Then, instead of welcoming further questions, they take a sort of pride of discovery and defend their statement of the problem against all comers. Suppose you rolled into a service station with a sick automobile and were greeted by a knowing mechanic who said, "I heard the car when you drove it in and it obviously needs a new battery." If your further listing of the car's symptoms all brought the same response, you might be wise to try another mechanic. This one seems less interested in *your* problem and more interested in the station's problem—moving more batteries this month.

As John Foster Dulles commented during his tenure as Secretary of State, ("The measure of success is not whether or not you have a tough problem, but whether it is the same problem you had last year.") Despite all the preventive action that can be taken, the best laid plans of mice and men will still "gang aft agley." The following list suggests a format that can be used for the analysis of unanticipated crisis situations that do occur. Essentially these steps involve using the same steps as the procedure for analysis of potential problems but with a present rather than a future orientation.

Through preparation, study, and analysis, the manager should strive to resemble the character described in Robert Nathan's *Road of Ages*, "Toward men and toward God, she maintained a respectful attitude, lightened by the belief that in a crisis she could deal adequately with either of them."

Steps in Problem Analysis

1. *State the problem.* The more specifically and clearly the problem is stated, the easier the rest of the problem-solving process will be.
2. *Define the present level.* State in specific and measurable terms the exact state of affairs at present.
3. *State your objective.* State in specific and measurable terms the exact difference between the present and the way things ought to be.
4. *List the possible causes.* Write down all the possible reasons why the present concern might have arisen. Consider all the possible causes, maybe even a few that seem impossible.
5. *Select the most likely cause.* This selection process itself may suggest other causes and send you back to Step 4.
6. *List alternative solutions.* Write down all the possible actions that would seem to meet the need you have isolated.
7. *Analyze your alternative actions.* Weigh each possible action with regard to effort, cost, and risk. Will the solution cost more than the problem?
8. *Make your decision.* Select the action alternative that has the highest total rating on your effort, cost, and risk evaluation.
9. *Make an action plan.* Carefully and with attention to minute de-

tails, plan the events that will have to occur to bring about the selected alternative. Give attention to the specific dates and objectives of each step toward accomplishing the solution.

10. *Accept the credit graciously.* When the problem-solving steps have been followed carefully and the plan has been executed completely, there are only two possible activities remaining. You may accept the praise of your colleagues graciously while humbly agreeing that you are, as they have suggested, wise, discerning, and perceptive. Or you may find that you have chosen the wrong alternative cause of the problem. In this case, recycle to Step 6 and begin again with the next most likely cause. But fear not! In the end, honor and glory await you.

Exhibit 4.3, "Problem Analysis Work Guide," has been designed to allow the manager to display graphically the various components of a problem. This chart and all other problem-solving systems demonstrate one basic concept: get the facts completely and accurately, and the problem will be relatively simple.

Japanese Decision Making

Japanese managers have long awed those American managers who have had the opportunity to deal with them. The awe occurs in two areas: the dragging pace with which the Japanese appear to make their decisions, and the lightning pace with which they can carry out their decisions once they are made. Peter Drucker's[9] analysis of the Japanese approach to decision making highlights the fact that in America we emphasize the answer, while in Japan the emphasis is on the question and all its implications.

The Japanese procedure is to be very deliberate in the initial stages of gathering information and polling the delegation. (The manager of a Japanese business may consult with people throughout the company over a long period of time to derive a true consensus about what ought to be done. American procedure may look the same—with token contacting of the rank and file—but the Japanese actually make the decision on the basis of majority opinion.)

American managers might be horrified at such a loss of control, but the success of the Japanese approach cannot be denied. Once the decision is made, there is almost no need to initiate a clever program to "sell" the top brass's decision to the troops . . . in Japan, the troops have already been through it all in the process of arriving at a decision.

[9] Peter F. Drucker, *Management: Tasks, Responsibilities, Practices* (New York: Harper & Row, Publishers, Inc., 1974), pp. 467–70.

Exhibit 4.3. Problem Analysis Work Guide

STATE THE PROBLEM

If you are faced with a particularly difficult problem in your work assignment, describe it here. If there are none, start with Step Two.

2. OBJECTIVE

State the goal that is jeopardized by this problem. (If you had no problem, describe a key end-result you very much hope to accomplish.)

3. LIST THE KNOWN FACTS

Note the pertinent facts about the problem. Write a brief history that would help account for your present dilemma.

4. FORCE FIELD ANALYSIS

Driving Forces   Restraining Forces

Lengthen Arrows
Where Force Should
Be Strengthened

Shorten Arrows
Where Force Can
Be Decreased

5. LIST ALTERNATE SOLUTION

Brainstorm with yourself all the possible things you might do to solve this problem.

6. VALUE ANALYSIS OF ALTERNATIVES

Failure Risk: Probability, Cause and Remedy	Check Favorability Factors					CHECK ALTERNATIVES MOST DESIRABLE
	Reduce Restraint Barriers	Contributes To Goal	Least Effort	Least Time	Least Risk	

DECISION

Think of several ways of checking the decision out. Bounce it off a friend. Try it out on a sample basis.

8. ACTION PLAN

Lay out steps for carrying out the decision.

Drucker also lauds the Japanese idea about which decisions need to be made at the top. He recounts experiences in which Americans wanted to establish cooperative business relations with a Japanese company. While the Americans waited impatiently for the discussion of terms, licenses, and other critical matters, the Japanese continued at length to discuss basic issues like whether or not the company ought to alter its product line at all. By the time the basic decisions were made (and the Americans had almost given up hope), the Japanese were ready to polish off the details in record time. The lesson for westerners lies in the Japanese emphasis on defining the question to such lengths that implementation is easy once the decision is made. Perhaps the Japanese system cannot be transferred completely to the United States, since there are so many dissimilar social patterns. Even so, American managers could benefit from a little more emphasis on participatory decision making.

Getting "At" Group Ideas

It is easy enough to say that managers ought to take advantage of the combined wisdom of their people in making decisions. But we all have a few choice words to say about the productivity of the last committee we were stuck in. It probably discussed the same questions over and over, changing the original idea several times, and finally surrendering to the initiative of the most aggressive member or to that of a "railroading" chairman—committees have a bad reputation, but proven potential.

In recent years, researchers have given a lot of attention to finding the best techniques for extracting the combined wisdom that must exist in the multiple experience banks of committees. The word "interacting" is now commonly used for what we usually do in a committee—a sort of sloppy, unstructured, loosely-led thrashing about in the topic until everybody grows sick of it and gives in to some sort of compromise.

Researchers have compared this interacting approach to two systems for structuring group contributions to the solution of any given problem. One of the approaches is called the Delphi method; the other is known as NGT, or nominal group technique.[10]

The Delphi method gets its name from the fact that the priestess at Delphi used to send runners to all parts of the country to bring back the best opinions of all the sages of the realm. The consensus of Delphian thought usually proved to be valid, giving rise to the saying "two delphs are better than one." Today, instead of runners, the modern Delphi sys-

[10] Andre L. Delberg, et al. *Group Techniques for Program Planning* (Glenview, Ill., Scott Foresman and Company, 1975), pp. 17–39.

tem uses questionnaires sent through the mail or via computer terminal. The difference is that, instead of a single questionnaire, several are sent in sequence. The result is that along with the second request for input, each participant receives a summary of the middle half of the opinions from questionnaire one. As the opinions and summaries go back and forth, experience has shown that the participants change and adjust their opinions toward a consensus which emerges with the passage of time. Delphian technique is applied to forecasting (as in Chapter 5) and is particularly valuable in finding close projections about topics where a sure answer cannot possibly be found—until it is too late.

Nominal group technique (NGT) is similar to the "brainstorming" technique that became popular a few years ago—and then was diluted in meaning until any discussion came loosely to be called brainstorming. The NGT procedure calls for a committee to sit silently around a table together and list on paper every possible solution or relevant factor regarding the stated problem. Once this is done, the group scribe consolidates the list into one list on the board or a chart. In this consolidation stage, there is no discussion of the suggested alternatives, except to clarify meanings. Once the list is whittled down to one unified list, the group begins discussing the alternatives, first placing them in some priority order, then elaborating on the ones that appear to be rising to the top of the list of alternatives.

Research studies[11] have produced conflicting results, with Delphi producing better in some instances and NGT doing better in others. Obviously, the reason is that some systems work better in getting some types of information out of some groups than others. No manager is naive enough to think that there is one and only one best trick to pull out of the committee hat. The information needed, the group involved, and the restrictions on time are sure to determine the best way. The important fact to remember is that, in our nation of tongue-in-cheek putdowns of the committee process, there is undeniable strength in the group approach. It is not just a matter of spreading the blame more widely—committees have more to offer. The problem for the manager is extracting it.

Though researchers disagree as to the best procedure for getting at the group's wisdom, they do agree that compared to individuals, committees are slower than most, less accurate than the best, and more accurate than most. It has been found, for example, that five-person groups take longer than the average individual working alone (50 per cent longer), but over three fourths of the groups produce better performance (an average of 30 per cent better). Most groups, however, are worse than the best individual in the group.[12]

[11] Ibid.
[12] Ross A. Webber, *Management* (Rev. ed. Homewood, Ill., Richard D. Irwin, 1979), p. 207.

Personal Goals and Decision Making

A program of goal setting and systematic decision making can be a vital asset not only to business organizations but also to individuals. Goals that you personally have set give your life a sense of assurance and can create and maintain a high motivation to achieve. Only the individual who has a sense of direction is in a position to judge whether or not real progress is being made. Almost all of the self-help success books place emphasis upon definite goals. The very essence of success in any endeavor is knowing exactly what you want.

One of the most widely read of the success manuals, Napoleon Hill's *Think and Grow Rich*, makes reference to a method by which desire for financial attainment can be realized. He says,

> First, fix in your mind the exact amount of money you desire. It's not sufficient to merely say, "I want plenty." Be definite as to amount. Second, determine exactly what you intend to give for what you desire. Third, establish a definite date when you intend to possess or achieve your goal. Fourth, create a definite plan for carrying out the desire and begin at *once*, whether you are ready or not, to put this plan into action. Fifth, write out a clear, concise statement of the amount of money you intend to acquire or the goal you intend to achieve. Name the time limit for its acquisition.[13]

Finally, Hill suggests that you read your written statement aloud twice daily, once just before retiring at night and once after arising in the morning. While reading, make every effort to see and feel yourself as having already attained the goal.

As one of the characters in *South Pacific* suggests, "If you don't have a dream, how you gonna make a dream come true?" Thomas Edison dreamed of a lamp that could be operated by electricity. He began where he was to put his plan into action. Despite more than *ten thousand failures*, he stood by his dream until he had made it a physical reality. The Wright brothers dreamed of a machine that would fly through the air. Today, of course, the evidence is everywhere that their dream was not as unreasonable as their friends said. Marconi once dreamed of a system for harnessing the intangible forces of the electromagnetic spectrum. Today we know that his dream was practical because every radio and television set gives evidence of it. However, few people realize that Marconi's "friends" had him taken into custody and examined in a psychopathic hospital when he announced that he had discovered a principle by which he could send messages through the air without the aid of wires or other direct physical means of communication.[14] Most dreamers today fare better than some of these earlier individuals.

[13] Greenwich, Conn.: Fawcett Publications, 1960), p.36.
[14] Napoleon Hill, op cit., p.36.

Guidelines for Decision Making

1. Marshal the Facts

Much of the difficulty of decision making could be removed if managers would develop mental on-off switches about facts. If all the necessary facts are present, make the decision; if not, make no decision until some facts *are* available. Although getting more facts can become an escape hatch for someone who just don't want to make a decision, it is usually a valuable use of the decision maker's time.

2. Consult Your Feelings

Sigmund Freud once gave the following advice regarding decision making:

> When making a decision of minor importance I have always found it advantageous to consider all the pros and cons. In vital matters, however, such as the choice of a mate or a profession, the decision should come from the unconscious, from somewhere within ourselves. In the important decisions of our inner life, we should be governed, I think, by the deep inner needs of our nature.[15]

John Mihalasky[16] has conducted some interesting research into his experimental notion that decision makers in business may have some special, measurable, dependable, predictive ability that can guide them in their use of information or serve when there is little or no information available.

Mihalasky divided 25 chief executives into two classes—those who had doubled profits in the past five years and those who had not. Of the managers whose companies had doubled profits, 11 scored above the chance level on a computer guessing game. One scored at the chance level. Of the 13 who had not doubled profits, 8 scored below chance and 5 scored above chance. The results indicate that there may be greater skills or abilities to successful decision making than the construction of decision trees. The power of intuition or the intuitive interpretation of data must not be ignored in the decision-making process. The study does not, however, indicate which comes first. Do people who have high intuitive skills or ESP naturally become high-level executives? Or do individuals who practice good techniques of managerial decision making develop a greater capacity to guess right? In either case, you—with your existing talent and skills—can improve only through practicing the fundamentals of logical decision making. Who knows what other fringe benefits will come from this exercise?

[15] Quoted in Robert L. Heilbroner, "How to Make an Intelligent Decision," *Think Magazine*, December 1960, p. 2.

[16] "What Do Some Executives Have More Of?" *Think Magazine*, November–December 1969, p. 25.

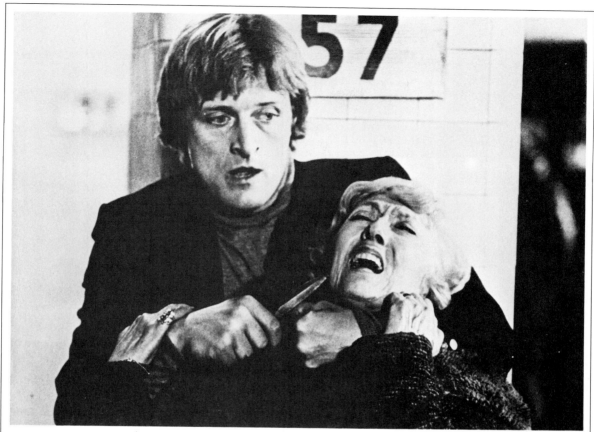

Nighthawks (Universal Pictures, 1981). [Copyright © by Universal Pictures, a Division of Universal Studios, Inc. Courtesy of MCA Publishing, a Division of MCA INC.] Is logic or persuasion more important in managerial decision making?

3. Use Wise Timing

A sense of timing requires that we know when *not* to make a decision. Research shows that when we are blue, low, our actions tend to be aggressive and destructive; when we are in good spirits, all fired up, our behavior swings toward tolerance and balance. As Chester I. Barnard, first president of the New Jersey Bell Telephone Company, has put it, "The fine art of executive decision making consists in not deciding questions that are not now pertinent, in not deciding prematurely, in not making decisions that others should make."[17]

4. Don't Infer Too Much

There is, as stated earlier, much value in intuitive feelings about a decision that is to be made. Nevertheless, it is imperative that we be *aware*

[17] *Functions of the Executive* (Cambridge, Mass.: Harvard University Press, 1938).

Exhibit 4.4

Bubbles LaVroom has been killed. Police have rounded up six suspects, all of whom are known criminals. All of them are known to have been near the scene of the murder at the approximate time that it occurred. All had substantial motives for wanting Bubbles killed. However, Dirty Dan has been completely cleared of guilt.

1. Dirty Dan is known to have been near the scene of the killing of Bubbles LaVroom.	T	F	?
2. All six of the rounded-up gangsters were known to have been near the scene of the murder.	T	F	?
3. Only Dirty Dan has been cleared of guilt.	T	F	?
4. All six of the suspects were near the scene of Bubbles' murder at the approximate time that it took place.	T	F	?
5. The police do not know who killed Bubbles.	T	F	?
6. Bubble's murderer did not confess of his own free will.	T	F	?
7. Dirty Dan did not kill Bubbles.	T	F	?
8. It is known that the six suspects were in the vicinity of the cold-blooded assassination.	T	F	?
9. Bubbles LaVroom is dead.	T	F	?

(Answers at end of chapter.)

and place appropriate weightings on feelings, especially if they should contradict the indication of all the data. Many times, upon receiving data, we fill in the gaps or jump to conclusions about what lies between the lines. And many times, the assumptions we make become the very weakness in our case that returns to haunt us after a faulty decision has been made. Do you remember the riddle from childhood that made use of the human tendency to infer too much: "What two coins add up to fifteen cents—and one of them cannot be a nickel?" Exhibit 4.4 suggests the ease with which we infer from limited data. Because of these comments you will probably be very suspicious and score better than most students. Without explaining the purpose, give the quiz to one of your friends.

5. Get on the Right Wavelength

The skills of communication play a vital role in decision making. Ideas must be clearly communicated among the person who finds the problem, the people who gather the answer-holding data, the decision maker, and the people who will carry out the solution plan. The best, most accurate decision in the world is useless if a communication breakdown has caused it to be made on incorrect data or if the solution plan is never implemented. Exhibit 4.5, an exercise in problem solving, illustrates the importance of being on the right wavelength. Once the common dimensions of the three problems are seen, the solution is simple.

6. Keep the Decision Flexible

Franklin D. Roosevelt was a great believer in flexible decisions. Frances Perkins, his Secretary of Labor, said of him, "He rarely got himself sewed tight to a program from which there was no turning back."[18]

"We have to do the best we know at the moment," he told one of his aides. "If it doesn't turn out all right, we can modify it as we go along."

Part of the worrisomeness of decision making comes from a natural tendency to overstress the *finality* of the choices we make. When in doubt, say no. It's a lot easier to change a *no* to a *yes* than vice versa.

7. Follow Through

"Thinking," wrote the Swiss psychiatrist Otto Fenichel,[19] "is usually preparation for action. People who are afraid of actions increase the preparation." Many times we have known people who preferred to go on forever "getting ready" rather than to act.

There is a delicate balance that must be maintained between making sufficient inquiries and laying proper groundwork! Nevertheless, when you feel yourself calling for information to reinforce information you already have, you might suspect that you are avoiding an obvious decision or looking for justification of a not-so-obvious alternative.

8. Have Courage

"One person with courage makes a majority," said Andrew Jackson. This statement is doubly applicable to the decision-making process. After all the steps have been taken and all the facts have been secured, there remains the question Will I do what is best—even though it is not the alternative chosen or favored by the majority?

This is a question that each person must answer on a daily basis. It takes courage to stand alone or to be the first to take what may become a popular stand. Regardless of the alternative chosen, the other alternatives will linger to haunt and tease: "What if you had decided to . . . ?"

When a decision has to be made, it is good to talk to others. Ultimately, however, the final *yea* or *nay* will have to be decided right there inside your own head . . . but you wouldn't want it any other way.

Summary

Many individuals feel that decision making is the essence of management. Many authorities have gone so far as to say that decision making *is* management. Although some people try to avoid decisions, it is easy

---

[18] Quoted in Heilbroner, op. cit.
[19] Ibid.

*Exhibit 4.5
Problem Solving
Perspective*

Nuclear Physics:
Yesterday you computed erg velocity. You therbled five nucleonics, as shown below. Compute the sum of these in fissioncybers.

	Fissioncybers
1 mass-velocity erg unit @ 14 blig points	.69
1 multiple coordinate @ .031254 inertial value	.12
3 millitherbs @ force-velocity E = mc² plus/minus	1.78
1 full-entity hydronucleus @ 3.2 square of unit	.32
2 electronuclear hygrocarbols @ force .89 pH2 std.	.97
Total fissioncybers	

Now increase these f/c's by 3% to find ultimate erg velocity.
Now go right on to the next problem.

Industrial Engineering:
Yesterday you made a time-and-motion study. You timed five elements, as shown below. Find the total time for these elements in decimal minutes.

	Decimal Minutes
Pick up assembly and place in position	.32
Run cutting tool 3.750″ to a starting position	.12
Make three cuts, .025″ each, 2.500″ apart	1.78
Reposition assembly and set gauge at "0" point	.97
Inspect assembly and put aside in #89 bin	.69
Total decimal minutes	

Now increase this time by 3% to find the standard allowance.
Proceed at once to the next exercise.

Consumer Economics:
Yesterday you went shopping. You bought five items, as shown below. Find the total cost of these items.

	Money Spent
1 box of carpet tacks @ 12¢ per box	$ .12
1 tube of toothpaste @ 32¢ per tube	.32
3 cans of scouring powder @ 23¢ per can	.69
1 car-polishing kit @ 97¢ per kit	.97
2 cans of floor wax @ 89¢ per can	1.78
Total money	$

Now add a 3% sales tax to find out what you spent altogether.

to see that decisions *will* be made—to put off deciding is to manage by default.

The psychological dimensions of decision making are attracting more and more attention as the bigness of business continues to reduce the opportunity for individuality in decision making. The research of Chris Argyris has indicated that executives are making fewer and fewer decisions and instead are rubber-stamping proposals from the system below them.

In the pressure of making crisis decisions, the wise manager will take the time to answer the following key questions: (1) What is right? (2) What can go wrong? (3) What could cause this problem to occur? (4) What preventive action can I take? (5) What is my contingency plan? And, (6) when will my alternative plan go into action?

Problem solving is the process that allows the manager to get the facts systematically for making a decision. The fact-finding process of asking an ever-narrowing series of questions is basic to problem solving.

The suggested steps of problem analysis are to (1) state the problem, (2) define the present level, (3) state your objective, (4) list the possible causes, (5) select the most likely cause, (6) list alternative solutions, (7) analyze your alternative actions, (8) make your decision, (9) make an action plan, and (10) accept the credit graciously or recycle.

The Japanese approach to decision making emphasizes the strengths of evaluation that lie within the group that is to be affected by the decision.

Interacting is the name given to the nonstructured approach to group decisions most commonly seen. Two techniques receiving acclaim are the Delphi approach and NGT—Nominal Group Technique.

Personal goals may also profit from a systematic approach to decision making. Almost all of the success manuals and studies of happiness place primary emphasis on being specific and crystal clear about goals. The very essence of success in any endeavor is knowing exactly what you want.

In this chapter, eight guidelines for effective decision making were cited. They are (1) marshal the facts, (2) consult your feelings, (3) use wise timing, (4) don't infer too much, (5) get on the right wavelength, (6) keep the decision flexible, (7) follow through, and (8) have courage.

Answers for Exhibit 4.4

1	?
2	T
3	?
4	T
5	?
6	?
7	?
8	?
9	T

Review Questions

1. What is Murphy's Law of Management?
2. What is the difference between problem solving and decision making?
3. Apply the preventive problem-solving model to your next term paper.
4. What are the steps in problem analysis?

5. Distinguish between the Delphi technique and Nominal Group Technique as a means of generating group consensus.
6. Name one thing that a manager does (as a manager) that does not involve making decisions.
7. Use the potential problem analysis format to plan your next trip home.
8. Contrast how U.S. and Japanese executives might approach a decision to produce new products.
9. Why do executive decisions tend to be somewhat conservative?
10. Use Napoleon Hill's formula for financial wealth to achieve the grade you desire for this course.

The Planning Process

To forget his corporate troubles, Quixley decided to go hunting. It was a beautiful day, and the walking and fresh air were clearing away all thoughts of business. Soon Quixley sat down to rest. He leaned against a rock in the warm sunlight and soon fell asleep. He was awakened by a low growl. He opened his eyes slowly and realized what a precarious position he was in.

A giant grizzly bear had trapped Quixley in a box canyon. The bear was just behind a large rock at the only opening to the canyon . . . and he was growling in a rather hungry manner.

Quixley did not panic. With the coolness of top management he evaluated the situation and the alternative actions and made his decision. He would kill the bear by ricocheting his one remaining bullet off the rock next to the bear.

With speed and efficiency, Quixley computed the distance to the rock, the appropriate angle of refraction, the velocity of the projectile, and the exact point at which the bullet would strike the bear.

With his planning completed and reviewed, Quixley checked his computations, reviewed his procedures, raised his rifle, sighted carefully, squeezed the trigger, and missed the rock completely.

In the end, the bear had his dinner and Quixley forgot his worries about the office.

Failing to plan means planning to fail. Whatever the activity
. . . whatever the stakes . . . the person who refuses to plan is agreeing to trust all outcomes to the probabilities of chance. Regardless of
the confidence and efficiency of its staff, the company is in trouble that
launches the production of a new product that nobody wants or needs.
If you are on the wrong road, it does not matter how fast you are going.
J. Paul Getty said, "I think business has to be guided by military history. You've got to plan campaigns and strategies. You've got to plan for
all the things that can go wrong."

Planning is the primary task of management. It must occur before any
of the other managerial functions because it determines the nature of
those functions. Planning is more than forecasting. It involves the process of choosing an objective, charting a course, and moving along that
course to the attaining of the objective. Planning frequently takes more
time than wishing—but it has a much better chance of success. It is the
means by which successful managers bridge the gap to the future.

Planning makes things happen that would not otherwise occur. In addition, planning prepares us for those unexpected inevitabilities that
fill the days and keep life interesting. Good planning will not stop the
occurrence of a tornado. But it will allow you to remark calmly from
your tornado shelter, "It sure sounds bad out there, doesn't it?"

Since Henri Fayol's[1] pioneering treatise on management in 1916,
planning (or *prevoyance*, as he called it) has involved two considerations: (1) assessing the future and (2) making provision for it. All planning, whether it be for the next twenty-four hours or the next century,
should include these two factors. Decisions about future activities can
be no better than the assumptions or premises upon which those decisions are made.

John McHale emphasizes the far-reaching implications of today's decisions in his striking statement, "The future of the future is in the present!" Progress and even survival in the years to come will be largely determined by decisions made during these days.

Billy E. Goetz simplified the definition of planning. "Planning," said
Goetz[2], "is essentially choosing." Planning might also be defined as
evaluation in advance. To be more complete, planning can be described
as the process of making assumptions about the future, gathering facts
and opinions in order to visualize and achieve the proposed activities.
This process involves establishing objectives, policies, procedures,
methods, and rules. Harold Koontz and Cyril O'Donnell[3] have spoken of
the "primacy" and "pervasiveness" of planning. They say, "Planning

[1] Henri Fayol, *General and Industrial Administration*, trans. by C. Starrs (London: Sir Isaac
Pitman & Sons, 1949).
[2] *Management Planning and Control* (New York: McGraw-Hill Book Company, 1949), p. 2.
[3] *Management: A Systems and Contingency Analysis of Management Functions*, 4th ed.
(New York: McGraw-Hill Book Company, 1976), p. 131.

logically preceeds the execution of all of the managerial functions." And "planning must filter through the entire scope of management, from top to bottom." Any person who would take the position that planning is unimportant has obviously not planned his position very carefully!

Strategy is a term that is increasingly being used to cover the overall general plan of an enterprise or a major portion of it, or of a major project within it. The main thrust of strategy is in the description of a type of planning program that gives overall direction to company efforts. Two types of strategies are usually referred to: grand strategies and competitive strategies. The emphasis in grand strategies is on the pattern of basic objectives and goals and the major policies and plans for achieving them. The purpose of grand strategies is to determine and communicate a picture of the kind of enterprise that is envisioned. Competitive strategies, as the name implies, describe the "game plan" that is designed with an eye to outdoing the actions of the competition. The planner may know what the competition plans to do. If so, the competitive strategy is one step simpler. If the competitor's intentions are not known, the planner must first develop a set of plans for the competitor's likely moves and then proceed to counteract and overcome those moves in his or her own competitive strategy.

Planning as a Process

In Chapter 4, planning was introduced as the preliminary state in decision-making. In order to appreciate the significance of planning at every point in the executive's responsibility, it is useful to break down this managerial function into sequential steps. At least, that is the plan this chapter plans to follow.

As a manager gains practice in planning the activities of a job, the sequence—which is closely akin to the scientific method—becomes almost second nature. It should be mentioned at the outset that the step-by-step, linear nature of most explanations is deceptive. Although it is helpful to explain a process in simplistic terms, life events usually occur at the speed of lightning and with anything but simplicity. In the real world, steps of a process will often happen simultaneously. In such a case, confusion is inevitable unless the manager has made the proper process so much an automatic reaction that things *feel* wrong if a step is ignored.

The student will be wise to use the following steps of the planning process as soon as possible in real-life situations. Memorizing the list will be only an artificial and meaningless learning experience. On the other hand, the student who systematically plans an upcoming social engagement or other activity is in a position to make the planning process *live* in the real world. If you think the planning process can be of value to you *only* after you become head of Consolidated Amalgamates . . . go back and read the first part of the chapter again. But if you plan to be a planner, read on.

1. Choose Objectives

Objectives are merely goals or end points of planning. They set the direction for all other managerial planning. One of the most common causes of failure is the lack of a clear-cut and carefully considered statement of objective. It is quite common to confuse the method with the objective. When this is done, the emphasis is on the wrong phase. Suppose you are in Chicago and you need to be in New York. What is your objective—New York or a trip from Chicago to New York? The *trip* is only your method. New York is the goal. Being clear about this, you will not become involved unnecessarily in choosing scenic routes or highways or byways or overnight stops. Your objective is New York and the route and carrier that will get you most efficiently to that objective are the ones you want. What differences can you suggest if the trip itself had been your objective? How would values and emphases be different?

Another common mistake is to confuse objectives with motives. Though it seems a lot of concern about a word, managers soon learn the difference. What differences can you see between organizations that are *motivated* by profits, and those for which profit is the *objective?*

The Roman philosopher Seneca once observed, "When a person knows not what harbor he seeks, any wind is the right wind." As part of a career plan, every person should spend some time carefully charting personal objectives. People who are able to tell you exactly where they want to be, what they want to be doing, or how much money they plan to be making in five years are much more likely to get somewhere than the individual who drifts aimlessly through life.

There are many objectives for business endeavor. Profit making in the long run is an explicit and central aim of all privately organized business enterprises. Even "nonprofit" agencies try to make a kind of profit —i.e., to operate without a loss within their budget of available financial resources.

However, profit only is a limited objective and must be combined with other goals. Ultimately, business must justify its existence by being of use to society. Either a valuable product or service is produced, or the organization becomes parasitic on the society.

There are some judgments that can only be made well by the human manager who has the ability to weigh all advantages and choose the trade-offs that are most agreeable. With any plan that is chosen, there are courses that are automatically forfeited—if you go right, you cannot go left. In most major business decisions, there are desires for the things that can result from both the right and the left. We want higher profits . . . but we also want cleaner air. We want short-term gradual growth. We want well-paid, satisfied employees . . . but we need to cut the costs of production.

The planning plight of the manager is to find the balance . . . to weigh all the data and choose the best possible mix of give and take, now and later, people and profits, that will accomplish the objectives of the organization. In the midst of such frustrating riddles, the manager must find consolation in the awareness that, if all the decisions were easy ones, the company would not need the manager to make them. Some decisions will be right. Others will be half-right. But all decisions will incorporate the unique human ability to sense the situation, absorb the statistics, and find the trade-off that is most acceptable.

Peter F. Drucker[4] has identified eight key areas in which objectives of performance should be set: (1) market standing, (2) innovation, (3) productivity, (4) physical resources, (5) financial resources, (6) profitability, (7) human organization, and (8) social responsibility. These categories grew out of Drucker's consulting experience with General Electric. The company was attempting to measure its managers only on results that focused on return on investment. Very quickly it became apparent that a clever manager could obtain high profit ratings by neglecting long-term considerations. Neglecting innovations, employee attitudes, and other long-term considerations can add money to short-term profit figures. Usually the resulting problems did not appear until the clever manager had been promoted for the appearance of success. Somebody else had to solve the problems created by the quick-and-dirty tactics of the first manager. The resulting procedure of measuring managers in eight areas assured that the total company picture was being "profited."

The conclusion of the experience was stated by Drucker in his book, *The Practice of Management:* "Objectives are needed in every area where performance and results directly and vitally affect the survival and prosperity of the business."[5]

At the same time, it is easy for a manager to have too many objectives to give proper attention to any. Experience has shown that a manager who has objectives in too many areas will not be as successful as one who focuses on the truly important aspects of a job.

[4] *Management: Tasks, Responsibilities, Processes* (New York: Harper & Row, Publishers, 1974), p. 120.
[5] *The Practice of Management* (New York: Harper & Row, Publishers, 1964), p. 63.

Personal Objectives

The identification of major objectives is equally as important in planning personal success as for business achievements. Similarly, an individual managing his or her personal life can face difficulties by identifying too few or too many objectives. In a sense, Drucker's advice to General Electric is equally appropriate for you. Spend some time in identifying several of the key areas that are important to achieve your definition of success. Several comprehensive studies of what makes people happy or successful emphasize the importance of making progress toward reasonable or achievable goals and having a balance between personal and professional interest. Figure 5.1 suggests one format for identifying key personal goal areas.

Most studies of happiness have concluded that personal happiness comes from having specific objectives and making progress toward achieving those goals. In a comprehensive study involving 52,000 readers of *Psychology Today*, Shaver and Freedman conclude, "Happiness is the matter of setting personal standards, not chasing after other people's."[6] In a real sense, good management, whether personal or organizational, involves making progress toward specific and reasonable objectives.

Directional Planning

Michael McCaskey has made a valuable distinction between planning with goals and planning without goals.[7] He says that some types of work do not lend themselves to a traditional compulsiveness for establishing

[6] Phillip Shaver and Jonathan Freedman, "Your Pursuit of Happiness," *Psychology Today*, April, 1979, p. 35.
[7] M. D. McCaskey, "A Contingency Approach to Planning: Planning with Goals and Planning Without Goals," *Academy of Management Journal*, June, 1974, pp. 281–291.

Figure 5.1		Personal Goals	
	Key Areas		Objectives
	1	Career	
	2	Financial	
	3	Mental	
	4	Physical	
	5	Religious	
	6	Friends	
	7	Family	

exactly what will be accomplished before any move has been made into the effort itself. McCaskey wisely points out that some efforts do not reveal their most valuable traits until we get into them. His cure for this problem is "directional planning," through which the planner decides to move into a certain domain of investigation . . . to move in a certain direction first and then narrow the objectives as more becomes known about the situation.

It is certainly of value to be reminded that the compulsion to "have a plan" should not be allowed to keep us from doing the best that we can. And yet, the "directional planning" advocated by McCaskey could harden into concrete as quickly as any other approach. The message for managers is to keep your options open and avoid being run by your plan. Being alert to the unknowns, the wise planner will want to "plan

Table 5.1
Contrast Between
Planning with Goals
and Directional
Planning

Planning with Goals	Directional Planning
Characteristics	
teleological, directed toward external goals	directional, moving from internal preferences
goals are specific and measurable	domain is sometimes hard to define
rational, analytic	intuitive, use unquantifiable elements
focused, narrowed perception of task	broad perception of task
lower requirements to process novel information	greater need to process novel information
more efficient use of energy	possible redundancy, false leads
separate planning and acting phases	planning and acting not separate phases
Contingent Upon	
people who prefer well-defined tasks	people who prefer variety, change, and complexity
tasks and industries that are quantifiable and relatively stable	tasks and industries not amenable to quantification and which are rapidly changing
mechanistic organization forms, "closed" systems	organic organization forms, "open" systems
"tightening up the ship" phase of a project	"unfreezing" phase of a project

in" flexibility rather than lock out serendipitous discoveries. McCaskey's characteristics of "planning with goals" (closed) and "directional planning" (open-ended) are presented in Table 5.1 on page 95.

Managing with Objectives

Management by objectives (MBO) is a system of setting up organizational objectives which then become the beginning, middle, and end of the operation. The objectives tell everyone *where* they are going; departure from the optimum path to those objectives causes corrective action to be initiated. Comparison with those objectives becomes the ultimate criterion for success. The use of MBO as an evaluation technique is briefly discussed in Chapter 8.

Figure 5.2 is an adaptation of a sample MBO worksheet for monitoring organizational progress and success by objectives. The importance of objectives to the management task is demonstrated by a story about the famous ancient galley ships. One of the slaves asked his partner, "How come we are all down here rowing our heads off and that guy up there just sits around and takes it easy? Why doesn't he work like the rest of us?"

His friend had the answer. "Oh, he's working, too. . . . It's his job to remember where we are going."

And so it is with managers—the objective setters.

Figure 5.2
Typical Management by Objectives Worksheet.

MBO TASKS   YEAR 19_____   QUARTER _____

OBJECTIVE _____

Key Tasks to Achieve Objectives	Responsibilities (whose)	Measurement	Due Date	Completion

Analysis of Quarter's Progress:

2. Communicate Objectives

Although individuals may not always wish to share their personal objectives with everyone, it is imperative that an organization communicate its objectives effectively to every contributing member.

One of the major, continuing tasks of the manager is to weave the diverse goals of the company's various positions into a unified effort. The manager does not want individual workers to forget or forsake their individual objectives. Rather, the manager must set in motion processes that will unify the efforts of (1) *top management*, with its emphases on the big picture, the big profit, the powerful public, and stockholder satisfaction; (2)*production people*, with their targets of making more faster and cheaper and with more contented "makers"; (3) *marketing personnel*, whose eyes are ever looking toward quotas, bonuses, and percentages; (4) *finance folk*, with their love of dividends, interest, and, above all things, balance; (5) *supervisory personnel*, who are looking up to satisfy management and down to keep the workers working; and (6) the *workers*, who manage only their own efforts in an effort to satisfy supervisors, make a living, and make it to Friday. The company, whether large or small, is filled with objectives. Most of them are worthy, but all are not necessary for all employees. Managers must capitalize on many separate, personal objectives to accomplish their own goals.

Just as a chain is as weak as its weakest link, a business objective ceases to exist if it is hidden safely away in a leatherbound volume in the office of the vice-president in charge of planning. Unless employees can describe quickly and simply their personal-business goals for the next twelve months, it is likely that they have no objectives at all. In one sense it might be said that "If an objective is not on the tip of a person's tongue, it is probably not a controlling factor in setting daily priorities."

The concept of management by objectives[8] is one popular means of ensuring that all employees understand what they are working toward. It is based on the assumption that everyone knows what the objectives are. There are three main ingredients of the management-by-objective approach.

1. *Managers should be measured by what they accomplish rather than how they spend their time.* Many companies are still fearful that removal of the time clock will mean a removal of discipline. They tend to evaluate workers on traditional criteria, like "are they loyal? friendly? trust-

---

[8] The idea of MBO is generally credited to Peter F. Drucker, op. cit., (1964) and Douglas McGregor, *The Human Side of Enterprise* (New York: McGraw-Hill Book Company, 1960). George Odiorne, *Management by Objectives* (New York: Pitman Publishing Corp., 1965) helped popularize the concept.

worthy? brave?" A more rational approach would utilize the power of internal motivation and simply ask, "Do they get results?"

2. *Managers should know what their objectives are.* Though it seems very foolish, many managers are completely unaware of the standards that are being applied to their performance. Sometimes their work resembles a game in which the rules for winning must be figured out while play is in progress. If you lost the ball for that maneuver last quarter, then it must be a no-no for this quarter, too. On the other hand, Sue received a promotion for doing the exact same thing. Could the rules be different for you than for Sue? Consider the ulcers that would never even exist if managers were told what their objectives are . . . exactly and completely.

3. *Managers (and subordinates) should have a voice in setting their own objectives.* One of the simplest ways to assure that managers understand what is expected of them is joint goal-setting. Interestingly enough, research has shown that people tend to set their goals higher than superiors would set them. The superior who sets the objectives for subordinates and never informs them is not only violating the rules of good communication and common courtesy, but is missing a chance to get the greatest amount of work out of the staff.

It is not enough for the organization to have general goals for the entire organization. The process of setting objectives must be broken down to include every individual in the group. There must be established, understood objectives for every function (and functionary) within the group . . . at least according to general directions, if not specific outcomes.

3. Identify Premises

Premises are simply assumptions on which plans are based. It stands to reason that once objectives are stated (once the ideal future status has been described) the next step is to hold that ideal up to all that is known about the future. This is not crystal-ball time. It is time for the gathering of all data about trends and rates for the purpose of isolating potential problems. One of the great values of effective planning is that it forces the planner to analyze assumptions and eliminate, as much as possible, the elements of chance.

Premising is the assessment of the future. Management should give some consideration to factors or premises which are controllable, such as salary levels and program responsibilities, and uncontrollable factors, such as economic conditions and political climate.

Forecasting, or premising, will obviously include such financial factors as supply and demand. It also should be extended to include long-range premising for several years into the future. More and more organizations are learning from bitter experience that wise planning will extend, at least in a limited sense, ten to twenty years into the future. And yet, as late as 1973, a study made for the Planning Executives Institute and involving a sample of nearly 400 firms disclosed that 86 per cent of the firms having long-range plans used a time period of three to five years, and only one per cent planned for longer than ten years. And 19 per cent of the firms surveyed had no long-range plans at all.[9]

Long-range planning may also involve a long-range view of short-term plans. Some decisions that seem short-range at the time they are made later prove to have far-reaching consequences. While the span of risk is lessened with short-term planning (i.e., the short-term planner has a better chance of being right), all plans must be evaluated in terms of immediate and long-term implications.

Decisions about future activities can be no better than the assumptions or premises upon which those decisions are made. In fact, long range planning does not deal as much with future decisions as with the impact of the future on today's decisions.

In assessing the short-range future, you sometimes can assume that the future will be very much like the past. Thus, plans may be built on the implied assumption that the economy, political environment, employees attitudes, human motivations and a host of other variables will remain almost constant. For considerations beyond one year, this can be a very dangerous assumption.

Long-Range Planning and Premises

It is becoming quite common for companies and organizations to form long-range planning departments or committees. The existence of such groups gives evidence that astute managers are concerned about strategies for survival and growth in a complex, changing future. Unfortunately, this concern cannot be met with complete knowledge about what the future holds for an organization or an individual.

The reliability factor in which future planning can be predicted is a matter of degree. In planning the day's activities, we are accustomed to predicting the next 24 hours with a reasonable degree of certainty. Although forecasts with a more distant horizon present a noticeable degree of uncertainty, families, firms and other groups frequently plan as far as a year ahead. As a matter of common sense, only the most primitive organizations do not attempt to project activities and expenditures for at least a twelve-month period. Although an unexpectedly sluggish economy may occasionally cause income to run below original esti-

[9] R. M. Fulmer and L. W. Rue, *The Practice and Profitability of Long-Range Planning* (Oxford, Ohio: The Planning Executives Institute, 1973), p. 18.

mates, the annual forecast or budget still has a powerful impact on regulating the activities of any group.

Forecasting is the basis for Long Range (or strategic) Planning. Sometimes it can be confused with the LRP itself. This is an unfortunate oversight, since the forecast is merely one *component* of the strategic plan . . . never the whole plan. To obtain a forecast from which to plan, most long-range planners rely upon an extrapolation, or conjecture of the recent past, plus a knowledge of current activities in their attempt to gain reliable results. The past and the present are necessary parts of all planning. It is, however, a grave mistake to assume that change will always take place at the same rate that it has during the past. The simple projection of current trends may cause the planner to overlook the impact of developments not evident in any of the trends usually considered.

The problem of considering an anticipated development is especially important when planning beyond the five-year period. In this time frame, planning becomes futuristic and new techniques must be considered.

Of late, a small but growing group of individuals, often known as futurists, have advanced the idea that humans have the unique ability to guess what the future holds and to make the future what we want it to become. To exercise this responsibility, scientists in future-oriented organizations have been developing and refining techniques to anticipate future developments and to assess the consequences of these developments. Usually, futurists want to be far more than prophets or soothsayers. Their aim is not to predict the future in terms of specific events and innovations—although they may use scientific methods of forecasting. Rather, they prefer to analyze an assortment of possible futures in order to decide on the policies they prefer while considering what chance happenings could make each particular future come true. In the long run, the accuracy of the forecast itself is trivial compared with its importance in *making* the future.

Futurists focus their vision five to fifty years ahead, leaving immediate problems to the budgetmakers and other planners. Beyond fifty years remains the domain of science fiction writers. The critical period in between—a time frame in which power will shift from our generation to the next—may become a popular hunting ground for scientists in government, industry and associations.

Several hundred major corporations have turned to futurist consultants, or have set up their own groups, to consider the future well beyond their usual planning span.

The Delphi Technique has been tested and found to be an extremely effective method of forecasting future events in both business and governmental organizations.

This technique was first developed as a means of integrating the opinions of experts without sacrificing or compromising individual suggestions and ideas, as is so often the case when committees compile long-range forecasts.

The technique originally was used by the military to answer such questions as, "What would be the effect of a nuclear attack on major U.S. cities?" It has since been adapted to deal with the topics relating to product lines, cultural constraints on business enterprises in foreign countries, possible educational innovations, scientific breakthroughs, population control, automation, and space progress, among others.

Delphi forecasting makes use of a process sometimes called "cybernetic arbitration." The Delphi method systematically solicits, collects, evaluates and tabulates expert opinions. According to the person most responsible for its development, Olaf Helmer, it is "applicable whenever policies and plans have to be based on informed judgment . . . thus, to some extent, virtually to any decision-making process."[10]

Instead of using the traditional approach of achieving a consensus by open discussion, the Delphi Technique eliminates committee activity. It does so in order to reduce the influence of certain psychological factors such as an unwillingness to abandon publicly expressed opinions, equalize the persuasive power of an articulate, powerful or loud advocate, and limit the band-wagon effect of majority opinion. This technique replaces direct debate by a carefully designed program of sequential individual interrogations (best conducted by a series of questionnaires) interspersed with information and feedback, or results gained from earlier parts of the program.

Delphi in Action

To illustrate the Delphi process, let's notice the steps in an inquiry concerning the future of automation. Each member of a panel selected by the RAND Corporation was asked to estimate the year when a machine would become available that could comprehend standard IQ tests and score slightly above the genius level. Initial response consisted of a set of estimates spread between 1975 and 2020.

In the follow-up questionnaire, a summary of the distribution of responses was given to each respondent by stating the median and, as an indication of the spread of opinion, the inter-quartile range (that is, the interval containing the middle fifty per cent of the responses). Respondents were then asked to reconsider their previous answer and revise it if they wanted to. If an estimated answer was outside the inter-quartile range, the respondent was asked to briefly explain the reason for this deviance.

The effect of replacing the responsibility for justifying extreme posi-

---

[10] Olaf Helmer, *The Uses of the Delphi Technique in Problems of Educational Innovations*, RAND Corporation #3499, December 1966.

tions had the effect of causing a respondent without reasons or strong convictions to move the estimate closer to the median. Those who felt they had a good argument for a "deviant" opinion tended to keep their original estimate and defend it.

In the third round the responses, which were now spread over a smaller interval, were summarized again. The respondents received a concise summary of reasons presented in support of the extreme positions. They received a request to revise their second round responses after taking the suggested information into consideration. The respondent whose answer was still outside the new range was required to explain why he was unconvinced by the opposing arguments.

In the fourth and final round, criticisms of the reasons previously offered were resubmitted to the respondents so that they would have one last chance to consider revising their estimate in view of counter arguments. The average (median) of these final responses was taken to represent an estimate of group consensus. In the case of the high-IQ machine, the median turned out to be the year 1990, with the final interquartile range being from 1985 to 2000. In this instance, the procedure caused the median to move to an earlier date than was generated in the first round, presumably under the influence of convincing arguments. It also caused the inter-quartile range to shrink considerably.

As a matter of record, the time-lag between rounds averages between two hours when all respondents are linked by a computer or in a single site, and two months when the process is administered by mail.

A convergence of opinion has been observed in the majority of cases when the Delphi Technique has been used. To be certain that a desire merely to conform with the majority did not exist, tests have even been conducted where respondents were asked to reflect upon their answers and to rethink the decisions, without receiving a report on group response. Even in these cases, estimates in the second round are closer together than they were in the original statement. In other words, both the opportunity to reflect on a previous answer, and information about what other people think serve to bring estimates together. In those cases where consensus has not evolved, opinions seem to polarize around two distinct answers. Thus, two schools of thought emerge which indicate that opinions are based on different sets of data or different interpretations of the same data. In this case, the Delphi Technique serves its purpose: crystallizing the reasoning process while identifying and clarifying the major alternatives.

A manager must also check out intangible considerations, such as the company's reputation within its field and its public image. Effects of company policy on the environment and the quality of life must be considered right along with products and profits.

Certain factors cannot be predicted or controlled. These lie outside the realm of probability but not outside the responsibility of the planner. The contingency provisions of a plan are just as important as the specifications for things that are known. If the plan will not support the added costs of meeting the unexpected, it is an incomplete plan.

4. Survey Resources

Up to this point, the plan has dealt with the ideal. It has been appropriate to ignore the special deficiencies of the situation. The challenge has been to think in the blue-sky, no-holds-barred arena. This is necessary lest important aspects of objectives be overlooked or ruled out. Some company planners find that the setting of objectives and the identifying of premises are steps in which outside consultants can be of special value. Outsiders don't know all the inside excuses for not trying certain programs. A fresh viewpoint may open new doors in planning.

The surveying-resources step is the time when the blue-sky plans are brought down to earth. Those things that have been proposed are reconsidered in light of the actual situation. Limitations of staff, money, facilities, time, and so on may necessitate a return to the drawing board. The limitations should be questioned heartily, however, to ensure that they are true limitations and not traditional excuses.

Sometimes it is necessary simply to start all over again because it becomes obvious that there are not sufficient resources to achieve the proposed goals. Even so, the first cycle of setting those optimum goals is not lost. If we must accept less than the ideal, it is always good to understand that we are doing so. Otherwise, "the best we can do" may erroneously become equated with "the best that can be done." This approach will provide a more positive and optimistic approach to management. And, at least, everyone will be clear about the ultimate direction of the organization.

5. Establish Policies

Policies are sometimes defined as a substitute for common sense. No doubt you have heard employees say cynically, "There's no reason for it . . . it's just our policy!" Sometimes the statement is true. More often, the policies have been established on a deliberate, logical, intelligent basis to keep some naive employees from hurting someone by trying to think a problem through.

A policy can be a shortcut for thinking. Policies might be viewed as a broad pathway within which the worker moves toward an objective. When considering alternatives, a worker can automatically exclude those matters that are outside the area designated as acceptable by organizational policy. Policies may not be the most direct means to the goal. On the other hand, the most direct means might be too expensive, unethical, or unpopular.

Some policies are imposed by external sources. For example, governmental regulatory agencies often formulate a sizable portion of policy for business and industry. Within the area left to the discretion of the manager, choices must be made between policies that are deliberately created and those created by precedent.

It is safe to assume that whenever a policy is not thought out and established, a situation requiring action will arise and this action will become the precedent for future decision. Deliberate policy making means that company policy and action will not be determined by pressure situations. Although managers cannot possibly conceive of every situation and make policies to govern them, they should realize that decisions made under the stress of the situation may be colored by personal feelings or the personalities of the people involved.

It is important to realize that policies cannot be created to answer every potential problem situation. They should be written in general language that can be easily applied to specific situations. As suggested previously, policies are merely guides to thinking that still allow for discretion on the part of the person on the firing line.

6. Choose Alternatives and Take Action

Billy Goetz has said that "a planning problem arises only when an alternative course of action is discovered."[11] Planning is not necessary unless there are alternatives. Experienced managers have learned that the process of looking carefully at all possible alternatives can cause a decision to "make itself." Too often, the destiny of an individual or an organization is sealed without recognition of all the options that were open.

In his famous poem "The Road Not Taken" Robert Frost suggests,

> I shall be telling this with a sigh
> Somewhere ages and ages hence:
> Two roads diverged in a wood, and I—
> I took the one less traveled by,
> And that has made all the difference.[12]

Although there may be regrets about roads not taken, the regrets are not likely to be as severe as if the other fork is given no consideration at all.

[11] Goetz, op cit.
[12] *Poetry of Robert Frost* (New York: Holt, Rinehart and Winston, Inc., 1969).

When all possible courses of action have been identified, the astute manager evaluates these against the objectives for both feasibility and consequences. In other words, some of the alternatives it will be possible to see through, some will be too expensive, and some will be less desirable or efficient than others.

The worst decision is to decide not to decide. Managers who allow decisions to be made by default are failing in their responsibility as managers, and an organization will soon recognize that it could run better with more courageous leadership.

Only occasionally is there an obvious best course of action—in which case there is almost no decision to be made. A decision exists only when a choice must be made that is not ideal and only slightly better than some other option. If decisions were simple there would be no need to pay dearly for confident and skillful decision makers.

Although it is desirable to maintain as much flexibility as possible, the manager must be willing to make a firm commitment. In one of his fables, Aesop tells the story of a donkey that starved to death because it was an equal distance between two bales of hay. The donkey wanted to make the very best choice, but it deliberated until it was too late to choose either alternative. A manager who refuses to weigh alternative strategies and take a decisive stand may be demonstrating many characteristics of the donkey family.

7. Create Procedures and Rules

As opposed to a more general or companywide format of policy making, procedures and rules are precise means of making a step-by-step guide to action that operates within a policy framework. Procedures, then, are the established subpolicies of an organization.

Established procedures may be viewed as a chronological sequence of steps to be taken in order to accomplish a specific objective. They attempt to guarantee that the best—or at least acceptable—decisions will be applied to problem situations. Procedures are policy decisions made in advance. They are often worked out carefully with the help of industrial engineers or time-and-motion specialists. Procedures may be established because the organization can save considerable money by eliminating unnecessary duplication of effort, as with prior-approval purchase procedures. Additionally, many operations have to be performed consistently, and a procedure is developed so that everyone knows and can use the same approved method.

The creation of exact procedures has become more important with the increased popularity of the computer. Individual employees can no longer "do their own thing"—if their creative expression is to be understood by some narrow-minded automatic data processor.

Besides the procedures we have learned for communicating *with* computers, there is today a greater general knowledge about systematic procedure that has been learned *from* computers. Indeed, living in this era almost guarantees some awareness of the computer programmer's basic philosophy that "even the most complicated operation can be reduced to a series of *yes-no* questions."

Additionally, the creation of procedures may help in facilitating the training of new employees. An orderly statement of *"what to do if"* can spare new employees the expensive and frustrating trial-and-error method of finding the acceptable way of performing a task. Instead they may be instructed in a procedure that has been worked out by someone with considerably more knowledge and experience.

In the same way rules are guides to action rather than to thinking. They differ from procedures in that there is no time sequence and in that rules typically stand alone rather than as part of a sequence. We can hardly picture two football referees conferring to decide on an appropriate penalty for an ungentlemanly act by a player. Rather, the rules are set in advance.

8. Establish Budgets

It is difficult to separate budgeting as a planning function without also recognizing the role that it has in control. Unfortunately, most people in organizations (and out of them) find it easier to plan their budgets than to execute them. Budgeting has been defined as telling money where to go rather than asking it where it went.

Cynics sometimes view budgeting as an orderly way of going broke or a mathematical expression of what was feared. One of the best and most simple definitions states that *budgets are expressions of expectations in numerical terms.* Budgets are generally financial, though this is not necessarily true. They may be expressed in labor hours, square footage, or number of hamburgers per minute.

In entering the budgeting process, it is important to recognize the dangers that may render the activity cumbersome, meaningless, and unduly expensive.

First, in the determination to stay within budget limits, a manager may lose sight of a primary allegiance to the objectives of the company. For example, a research director may not be willing to provide necessary information to the advertising manager, fearing that successful advertising and sales might disrupt the neat and tidy research operation.

Another danger is that a manager who operates within the budget may be *assumed* to be operating efficiently. But budgets come with little pockets for hiding inefficiency because they typically grow from precedent. The fact that an expenditure has been made in the past does not provide evidence of a need. Budgets should be reviewed carefully each year to be sure that a manager is not hiding inefficiencies behind a padded budget.

Overbudgeting

There is always the danger of overbudgeting. This does not mean simply budgeting more money than is required; it also means spelling out minor expenses in such detail as to deprive a manager of the necessary freedom in operating the department. An extreme example would be an executive who has no money left for postage in late November . . . but still has $15,000 for paper clips.

A final and perhaps most important danger is the inflexibility that budgeting often creates. Managers, especially top managers, need to be aware that budgets are merely statements of expectations and are not carved on tablets of stone. Most budget items will vary, depending on the volume of business or the number of employees involved in an operation.

Evidence of the value of holding strictly to budgets was given by a very successful restaurant owner. In explaining the secret of his success, he said, "It's simple—I just stick to the budget. I buy my steaks for one dollar and sell them for five dollars. And it is amazing how four per cent can add up."

9. Establish Timetables

Although it is important to know how much a particular process or project will cost, there is seldom a situation in which time is not also one of the important ingredients to be considered. The fellow who coined the phrase "Time is money" probably failed to realize the timelessness and impact of this three-word financial statement.

Managers have long recognized that in giving a subordinate an assignment, it is desirable to indicate when the assignment will be due. Universal use of the designation *ASAP* makes "as soon as possible" almost meaningless. Completion dates are the most important part of any schedule; however, it is also wise to designate some mileposts along the way.

The concept of *milepost budgeting* has begun to gain wide acceptance in many organizational settings. This concept merely indicates that at the end of given amounts of time, certain portions of a project will have been completed. Similarly, mileposts are created for convenient intervals throughout the year or the life of the project. In this way, a manager does not suddenly realize at the end of the year that major objectives are only half realized.

Smokey and the Bandit, II (Universal Pictures, 1980). [Copyright © by Universal Pictures, a Division of Universal Studios, Inc. Courtesy of MCA Publishing, a Division of MCA INC.] Organizations do not always fit the task.

10. Decide on Standards

As a final step in the planning process, it is important for the manager to realize that the plan will become the standard by which performance is measured. Consequently, plans should be stated in a measurable manner. Sometimes a separate step of establishing standards for measurement and evaluation purposes is appropriate.

The decisions that planners make today will influence the kind of future the organizations will have. With corporations (as with individuals) "the future of the present is in the past and the future of the future is in the present."[13] It is imperative that managers be cognizant of the continuing value of the hours spent at the drawing board.

[13] Suggested by John McHale, *The Future of the Future* (New York: George Braziller, Inc., 1969).

Ten Reasons for Failure

The results of a wide survey of decision-making and planning practices in over 350 European and American corporations carried out by Kjell A. Ringbakk[14] indicate that most plan failures can be traced to one of the following factors:

1. Corporate planning is not integrated into the total management system.
2. Planning is not systematic; there is a lack of understanding of the different dimensions of planning.
3. Management at all levels is not engaged in or involved in planning.
4. Responsibility for planning is vested solely in planning departments.
5. Management assumes that because it is planned, it will come true.
6. Too much is attempted at one time.
7. Management plans its work but fails to work its plan.
8. Extrapolation and financial planning are confused with planning.
9. Inadequate information inputs are used.
10. Too much emphasis is placed on any single aspect of planning.

Summary

Speaking about the importance of careful planning, Bernard Baruch once observed, "Whatever failures I have known, whatever errors I have committed, whatever follies I have witnessed in public and private life, have been because of action without thought."

Planning is the primary task of management. It must occur before all other managerial functions because it determines the nature of those functions. Planning makes things happen that would not otherwise occur. Henri Fayol's word *prevoyance* involves the two considerations of planning: (1) assessing the future, and (2) making provision for it.

In order to understand better the managerial role in planning, this chapter has described the sequential steps in the *planning* process. Although the steps do not necessarily occur in a linear fashion, they must all be included or a planning effort has provided itself with an Achilles' heel.

    1. *Choose objectives.* One of the most common causes of planning failure is the lack of a clear-cut and carefully considered state-

[14] "Why Planning Fails," *European Business*, July 1970.

ment of the objective. It is also common to confuse the method with the objective.

2. *Communicate objectives.* Unless employees can describe quickly and simply their personal-business goals for the next twelve months, it is likely that company objectives have not been clearly communicated to them and that, in reality, they have no meaningful objectives at all.

3. *Identify premises.* Premising is the assessment of the future. Consideration must be given to factors that are uncontrollable, such as economic conditions and political climate.

4. *Survey resources.* When the resources are surveyed, the blue-sky plans are brought down to earth. Proposals are reconsidered in light of the actual situation.

5. *Establish policies.* A policy is a shortcut for thinking. Policies are stated to solve problems in advance and communicate foundation facts upon which subsequent decisions should be made.

6. *Choose alternatives and take action.* The manager must be aware of all the alternatives. Some will be impossible, some too expensive, and some less desirable or efficient than others. Once the information is gathered, there is no turning back. Action is the only next step for the success-oriented manager.

7. *Create procedures and rules.* The procedure is a step-by-step guide to action that operates within a policy framework. Rules differ from procedures in that there is no time sequence and in that rules typically stand alone rather than as part of a sequence.

8. *Establish budgets.* Budgets are expressions of expectations in numerical terms. Though generally stated in financial terms, budgets may be expressed in personnel-hours, square footage, or a host of other modes.

9. *Establish timetables.* Completion dates are the most important part of any schedule; however, it is also wise to design some mileposts along the way.

10. *Decide on standards.* Planning and control are often viewed as Siamese twins. It is impossible to have real control unless there has been real planning.

The entire case for planning can be summed up in Edison Montgomery's statement, "Successful planning—i.e., a clear definition of goals, determination of methods to move all parts of the organization toward them, a careful review of progress—is the keynote of success in an organization."

Review Questions

1. What is the primary task of management? Explain.
2. What is "management by objectives"? What are the main characteristics of this approach?
3. Define *policy*. How are policies imposed?
4. What is the difference between procedures, rules, and policies?
5. The objective of many college students is to receive a degree. Do you have any other objectives for your college activities?
6. How could a professor in a graduate seminar practice management by objectives?
7. Illustrate how improper premises can destroy good plans.
8. Use the planning process identified in this chapter to plan an important date.
9. In some bureaucratic organizations, budgeting is accomplished by merely adding 10 per cent to last year's allocations. What dangers are associated with this practice?
10. Explain the statement "The future of the future is in the present."

6

Organizing for Action

"Come in, Phipps. What is it you wanted to see me about?"

"Well, sir. It's about that big machine you have put me on . . . you know, the one that heats the parts to three hundred degrees before they can be bent into shape."

"Please, Phipps. I don't need to hear about the machine. Just tell me what the problem is."

"Well, sir. There's actually no problem. I just got to thinking that if I didn't have to call my supervisor each time for him to call in the Thermometer Division to verify the three-hundred,-degree temperature . . ."

"Get to the point, Phipps. I have to see a lot of people today."

"Sir, my calculations indicate that it would save the company seven million dollars per year for the machine operators to check the temperature themselves. We could save the supervisor's time and almost eliminate the whole Thermometer Division."

"Sounds like a worthwhile idea, Phipps. Write it out in triplicate on form three nine four nine four and submit it to the Office of New Idea Deliberation. You should hear from them through channels."

"Sir, if they take their usual time, the company will lose two million dollars while they are deciding. What this company needs is a little productive disorganization."

"That will be all, Phipps."

In almost every school class or job situation there are those people who spend so much time "getting organized" that they never get the job done. We live in an organization-conscious society. Almost nobody opposes the idea of getting organized. Yet in many situations (both personal and group situations) the organizational patterns we utilize are inappropriate, overbearing, or soon forgotten.

Origins of Bureaucracy

Almost all of us know, or think we know, the term *bureaucracy*. The word comes from an organizational approach that appoints a bureau to handle each facet of the total job. The most common complaint about the highly organized bureaucracy is that there is too much red tape (i.e., too many steps involved in getting things done). Indeed, some workers in overorganized concerns soon begin to feel that the process is more important than the product.

Max Weber, a German social scientist and philosopher of the early twentieth century, considered bureaucracy to be one of the three main factors in understanding the behavior of any organization. Weber listed societal taboos, human leadership, and bureaucracy as the big three. Weber's characterizing of bureaucratic function occurred before the proliferation of processes that we know today. Therefore, he gives a strangely positive description of bureaucratic functions:[1]

1. Regular activities aimed at organizational goals are distributed as *fixed official duties*.
2. All activities follow the organizational principles of *hierarchy*.
3. Operations receive equal treatment under a consistent *system of abstract rules*.
4. Officials operate as *formalistic personalities* without becoming emotionally involved.

These organizational characteristics were very desirable at the time of Weber's writing. In more recent years, an overdose of bureaucratic abuses has caused us to resist noninvolved administrators and rules that cannot bend. We must give thought to a world without law before we complain of the irritations of our present laws.

Governments take a lot of abuse for their cumbersome bureaucratic organizational patterns. Even so, the nonprofit organization is not the only one that can become paralyzed by red tape. Any company can lose sight of the reasons for its rules. Its organization can take over and become more important than the outcome. The company is foolish indeed that is not continually reviewing its ways of getting things done. To some extent, every employee should be part of a continuing committee

[1] *Theory of Social and Economic Organization* (1921), trans. and ed. by A. M. Henderson and Talcott Parsons (London: Oxford University Press, 1947).

for review and refinement of the way people and activities relate to each other in the company. Every organizational plan should have built into it the provision for its own reorganization.

Today, we can see only that society has gone overboard with these functions. Italy's government reportedly has 24 bureaus established to study ways of cutting out its many unnecessary bureaus. It is the bureaucratic tendency to "swell" that makes it so hard to control. Profit-making companies also get entangled in their own procedures and structures. A good organization builds into its systems methods of examining and regularly pruning itself of unnecessary operations.

Organization is necessary and desirable. It is the only way to be sure that all participants will come out "even" in the desired result. No one questions the importance of organization. But, as with communication and other management tools, *poor organization is worse than no organization at all.*

Organization ≠ Efficient Organization

Peter F. Drucker has said that "an institution is like a tune; it is not constituted by individual sounds, but by the relations between them."[2] To carry Drucker's analogy even further, we could compare an organization to an orchestra. The problems of bureaucracy can hamper the individual expression of the various musicians who make up the philharmonic. Many of the members of the orchestra play different instruments and have different roles from their colleagues. And yet, the area in which they can be free to do their own thing certainly must be restricted if the total sound is to be accomplished. The conductor and the organizational plan (the score) have the overview and direction needed to bring the group *together* in its announced objective. In the same way, of course, our friend Phipps (introduced in the prologue of this chapter) may be trying to institute organizational or procedural changes that would involve far-reaching implications understandable only to Phipps' superiors.

The word "organization" may convey at least three meanings. First, it may refer to the activity of management in *arranging people, tasks, and resources* in the most orderly and efficient manner. "Organization" may also name the *arrangement itself*, the outcome of the organizing activity. The word is also used, especially in the adjective form, to describe any number of business, behavioral, and humanist concepts. In simplest terms, then, *organization is the process of people working with each other toward their common goals.* If we want to include in our usage the idea of

[2] *Concept of the Corporation* (New York: The John Day Company, Inc., 1946), p. 26.

A S.W.A.T. Team Goes into Action in Two-Minute Warning (Universal Pictures, 1976). The organization must fit the task.

success in this process, then we are obliged to use a term such as "efficient organization." Having an organization no more assures success than having a personality assures popularity.

In a recent work,[3] Drucker suggests three ways in which work has been organized traditionally. The first is to organize according to the progression of the work. In building Solomon's temple, some workers quarried rock and felled timber; others cut the raw materials to specifications; others hauled them to the construction site; and still others assembled the processed pieces to complete the temple.

The second traditional method is organization based on moving the work to where the required skills and tools are located. The modern assembly line follows this pattern. And a university, where students move from class to class, also bears a resemblance.

The third approach uses a team of persons with differing skills and

³ Drucker, *Management*, pp. 529–40.

tools, all moving to the location of the work, which itself is stationary. This team approach dates back to prehistoric hunting parties, but is only now being seriously considered as a legitimate industrial practice.

Project management most frequently associated with aerospace and defense industries illustrates the contemporary team approach. When a new contract is secured for the development of a major piece of equipment, Lockheed or McDonald-Douglas is likely to appoint a project team that has ultimate responsibility for the successful completion of that contract. When contract specifications have been met, the team is dissolved and the individual members are reassigned to other projects.

The Team vs. the Function

The first two forms identified by Drucker are functional organizations. They have been used as common approaches to formal organization since the early part of this century. Frequently, an organization will have both functional and team characteristics. Despite the project orientation of Lockheed, most of the divisions are permanent groups, which will have permanent executives assigned to direct the marketing, engineering, personnel, and other major functions. These concepts will be developed more fully throughout this chapter.

Organization, basically, is simply people working together toward a common goal. *Efficient organization* goes a step further and involves the grouping of people and processes for the prevention of waste. The difference between *organization* and *efficient organization* can easily be seen in the garbled message received from the top management of a struggling company. "ABEEGHLLNOTT" said the message, which the boss' secretary had organized alphabetically. The workers in the plant somehow failed to appreciate the orderly arrangement of letters. They came back for a more efficient organization of the letters of the message. When the proper relationship of the letters was established, the message was clear: "GET ON THE BALL." Organization exists whenever all the parts are present—efficient organization exists when the most productive interrelationships of the parts are established. Productivity and the satisfaction of accomplishing mutual objectives depend on the skill managers have in organizing people into workable systems of authority.

The Basic Elements of Organization

William G. Scott has identified four factors which he describes as the pillars upon which classical organization theory is built: (1) division of labor, or specialized effort; (2) scalar and functional processes, or the chain of command; (3) span of control, or span of management; and (4) structure.⁴ To these we should add size and complexity. These factors make up business organization as we know it.

Division of Labor

Division of labor seems to be the most basic of the four pillars of organization. All the other pillars are related to this one. The scalar and functional concepts grow out of specialization and the splitting up of functions. The organizational structure is naturally dependent upon the direction that specialization takes in the activities of the group. Finally, span of control problems are tied to the number and complexity of specialized functions under the jurisdiction of the manager.

Division of labor into specialized process units was historically the most obvious step toward organizing a job. It took place even before the development of large-scale manufacturing. In the latter part of the tenth century, the textile industry in England was divided into small units for spinning, weaving, dyeing, and printing textiles.⁵

Early classic studies by Adam Smith in 1776 and Charles Babbage in 1834 described the division of labor in one of the earliest mechanized manufacturing tasks: the making of pins. They described the production as being broken down into a series of steps and spread out among several workers. Smith is given the credit for creating the phrase "division of labor."⁶

Smith described a small shop with ten workers. Some of these were doing two or three steps, but no one was making a pin from start to scratch all by himself. The group was turning out forty-eight hundred pins in a single day. Smith added that if each person had performed all the steps to make a single pin, the workers could not each have turned out more than twenty pins in a day. Some of the workers would probably have made about one pin per day by this method.

According to Smith, there were three reasons why the division of labor increases the quantity of work. First, the skill of the worker increases. Second, little time is lost in passing from one type of work to another. Third, division of labor encourages the invention and use of special machinery that also adds to increased productivity.

The Negative Side of Specialization

The economic virtues of the division of labor were emphasized throughout the writings of the managers experimenting in the 1800's. Little attention was paid to the possible ill effects on the individual worker's creative satisfaction or emotional well-being. More recently,

---

⁴ *Journal of the Academy of Management*, April 1961, pp. 7–26.
⁵ Alan C. Filley and Robert J. House, *Managerial Process and Organizational Behavior* (Glenview, Ill.: Scott, Foresman and Company, 1969), p. 213.
⁶ Ibid., p. 215.

the behaviorists have been critical of classical division of labor. They argue that if a job is broken down into smaller and smaller operations (i.e., turning wing nut 3A one quarter-turn to the right), the worker will suffer from boredom, monotony, and dissatisfaction . . . thus lowering productivity in the long run. Division of labor has often been accused of degrading individuals by making them into machines. Every day, they repeat the same movements with monotonous regularity without being interested in them or understanding their purpose or value in the big picture.

One study that is often cited regarding this dehumanization of division of labor was conducted by C. R. Walker and R. H. Guest.[7] They studied an automobile assembly plant to discover the social and psychological problems of mass production techniques. They found that many workers disliked many things associated with their specialized jobs. Things such as mechanical pacing, repetitiveness of operation, and lack of a sense of accomplishment led to low morale. Their studies further showed that a positive relationship existed between the number of operations performed and the overall interest that the employees had in their jobs.

In 1976, Guest and a Dartmouth colleague, Stanley Udy, conducted an almost exact replication of the original study. The result of this re-investigation can be summarized as follows:

> We found that nothing substantially had changed over twenty-five years in the way people feel about the intrinsic nature of assembly line work itself. It is dull, pressure-ridden and frustrating; this in spite of the presence of other factors in the total quality of one's work life that have improved measurably. . . . There were improvements in technology, in greater benefits . . . and in more enlightened management policies.[8]

In an effort to deal with these criticisms of the division of labor approach, some organizations have developed special strategies. Job enlargement, rotation, and participation have proved effective in many cases.

Job enlargement is just the opposite of dividing work. It involves an attempt to structure the varied tasks so that an employee has more different operations to perform. This obviously requires more training, but the assumption is that the worker's efficiency is increased because the boredom level is lowered.

Probably the most famous study in job enlargement took place at the Endicott plant of IBM.[9] A parts manufacturing unit at the plant was reorganized in an attempt to improve worker morale.

---

[7] *The Man on the Assembly Line* (Cambridge, Mass.: Harvard University Press, 1952).
[8] Robert H. Guest, "The Man on the Assembly Line Revisited," Thirty-sixth Annual meeting, The Academy of Management, Kansas City, August 12, 1976.
[9] Ernest Dale, *Organization* (New York: American Management Association, 1967), p. 132.

This movement to reverse the trend toward specialization may have begun at IBM when Thomas J. Watson, Sr., then president of the company, found a young woman standing idle by her machine waiting for the setup man to make an adjustment. She knew how to adjust the machine, but it was against the rules for her to do so. As a result, Watson decided to let her and the other operators make their own adjustments. The idea proved to be a good one, both from the aspect of morale and also with regard to production and quality. IBM has made a continued attempt to expand the job responsibilities and interest of these line workers. After the reorganization, the job of a machine operator included setting up the job, sharpening the tools, inspecting the work, and operating the equipment.

The conclusions and findings of the Endicott study suggest that the job enlargement strategy increased worker morale, lowered production costs, increased the interest of employees, and improved the quality of the output. It was also possible to eliminate an entire level of management in the organizational structure because not as much supervision was required.

Job enlargement has an optimum level. There is a limit to the extent to which many employees are willing to accept enlarged spheres of authority and responsibility. Workers have shown increased absenteeism when there was excessive job enlargement.

Job rotation is the process of moving an individual from one job assignment to another. As jobs are switched periodically, the boredom and disinterest may be reduced. Workers are also able to get a more complete view of the importance of each job to the whole. This strategy is perhaps easier for management because jobs do not have to be redesigned. It also allows management to select the best time to rotate a person.

The participation approach refers to the strategy of giving workers the opportunity to participate in the making of the decisions that will affect them. This calls for a redistribution of authority that allows subordinate managers more voice about their own jobs. The rationale is that people will be more inclined to accept decisions that they have helped to make. The McCormick Company and the Glacier Metal Company of Great Britain were pioneers in the use of the participation strategy, using committees to make decisions concerning job design, promotion, salary, retirement plans, and appeals procedures. Of course, it is understood that management must be willing to relinquish a portion of its authority in return for the employee satisfaction that can result from employee participation.

Some helpful guidelines for the design of individual jobs would include:

1. The job assigned to an individual or a group should constitute a

distinct phase of the work process—a phase that enables employees to see a distinct result from their work.

2. The speed and rhythm of the job should always depend only on the performance of the person or group that performs it; and the worker should be able to do it a little faster at times and a little slower at other times.

3. Each job should embody some challenge, some element of skill or judgment.[10]

Scalar and Functional Processes

Scalar and functional processes rest upon the assumption that there is a chain of command throughout the organization. This pillar of organizational theory assumes the existence of someone at the top of the organizational ladder who can exercise the ability and the authority to make final decisions. Once this ultimate sort of responsible position is established, the other positions on the ladder may be understood as designates. These are the people *by whom* the top person makes decisions on various matters.

Delegation is one of the most necessary and often abused skills of managers within the scalar process. A manager neither can nor should perform every job for which he or she is responsible. It would seem easy and simple to turn over the tasks to subordinates. But delegation is almost never simple. It is, in fact, a skill that separates the pros from the amateurs in management.

The problems of delegation arise when a manager either wants to do the work personally or is unwilling to let go and trust the subordinate who has been designated. It is not uncommon for employees to complain, "My boss wants to delegate the job but not the authority to accomplish the job." There are two sides to this statement. First, the boss *should* provide adequate clout to the person who was asked to do a job. On the other hand, it is impossible for the boss ever to surrender the ultimate responsibility. Whatever happens (whether the boss or a delegate does the job), the final outcome is the boss's responsibility.

Responsibility should be assigned as far down the organizational structure as possible. That is, they should be delegated to the lowest level in the organization at which there is sufficient competence and information for effective task performance. According to this theory, when people join an organization they accept the obligation to peform position responsibilities as part of the employment contract with the organization. This obligation makes them accountable to higher authority for the quality and quantity of their performance. However, to make it

[10] Peter F. Drucker, *The Practice of Management* (New York: Harper and Row, Publishers, 1954), pp. 295–296.

possible for them to carry out their responsibilities, it is also necessary that they be delegated formal authority equal to their tasks.

Delegation Is Difficult

A manager delegates duties, assigns responsibility (but never ultimate responsibility), and grants authority. Duties define the task that the worker is to do. Responsibility is the obligation to give account for the accomplishment of the job. Authority gives the worker power to act officially within the scope of the delegation. When a job is delegated, the manager is implying the following statement: "I trust your judgment. The action you will take (even the mistakes you are likely to make) will be acceptable to me. I'll be willing to accept responsibility for it all." Unfortunately, the implications of delegation are not always understood by both parties. Perhaps employees should make sure that they and the boss have a clear understanding of the extent of delegation. Crystal-clear communication at the outset may eliminate some serious misunderstandings at a later date. Theodore Roosevelt once said, "The best executive is the one who has enough sense to pick good men to do what he wants done, and self-restraint enough to keep from meddling with them while they do it."

Harold Koontz and Cyril O'Donnell[11] have listed some personal attitudes that can lead to effective delegation. An effective delegator has (1) *receptiveness*—is willing to give other people's ideas a chance; (2) *willingness to let go*—is not afraid to release decision-making power to subordinates; (3) *willingness to let others make mistakes*—is a patient counselor but not a hovering hawk; (4) *willingness to trust subordinates*—knows that people must either be trusted or traded; and (5) *willingness to use broad controls*—knows how to stay in touch without taking back the job.

Unity of command means just what it says, but it is tough to make it stick. Idealistically, management would like to think that employees receive a unified statement from all management. But realistically, it is obvious that the orders received by an employee are often contradictory or conflicting. Usually, the orders delivered with the greatest force are obeyed. The result is that the loudest, not the wisest, boss usually is obeyed.

The practice of establishing project or product managers is increasing the incidence of interdepartmental conflicts. The project managers for Zesto Shampoo, Zingo Soap, and Zap Toothpaste must each cooperate with the respective production, marketing, and financial managers of their parent company Zudds Limited. Each manager is in charge of a

---

[11] Harold Koontz and Cyril O'Donnell, *Principles of Management*, 6th ed. (New York: McGraw-Hill Book Company, 1976), pp. 382–383.

particular product but not in charge of the functional departments that serve the product's needs.[12]

The interdependent nature of most organizational departments makes necessary some method of cooperation among managers. A century ago, Henri Fayol recognized the need for some method of bypassing the strict chain of command. He suggested an organizational arrangement that enabled individuals to work together across departmental lines. His method is known as the "Fayol Bridge."[13]

The need for crossing organizational lines is greater in companies that are *decentralized*. Decentralization is a philosophy that decisions need not, and in fact should not, always be made at the top of the organization. The use of product or project managers usually shows evidence of decentralization of authority. General Motors, with its large product divisions, is a classic instance of federal decentralization. The Buick division, for example, operates in relation to GMC headquarters in much the same way that a state operates in relation to the federal government. Basic policy is set at the national level, but day-to-day operations are generally left to the states or divisions.

The importance of communication bonds grows by leaps and bounds with every delegation or effort at decentralization. The reporting process can enable work to be accomplished across departmental and managerial lines. As long as everybody is up to date on who is supposed to do what and how it is being accomplished, delegation can proceed on a healthy basis. Later, an entire chapter will be devoted to the communication process. For now, it should suffice to say that clear communication is half the battle of organization and delegation—in fact, it's the first half!

Structure

The grouping of employees and their activities into departments makes it possible to manage the ever-increasing complexities of an enterprise. Otherwise a point would soon be reached when it would be physically impossible for the manager to oversee the entire operation. The structure he chooses for the organization will determine the methods and speed by which the company can move. If all the decisions reside at the top, things will move slower, be less interesting for the workers in the ranks, and be just the way the boss wants them. If, on the other hand, the boss is willing to adopt a structure that redistributes the decision-making responsibilities, this can change the entire complexion of the company. There are unlimited varieties of organizational structure. But the choice should be made with care. Structure can set the pace for the company.

[12] For a discussion of product and matrix management see Robert M. Fulmer, "Product Management: Panacea or Pandora's Box?" *California Manager Review*, Summer, 1965.
[13] *General and Industrial Management* (New York: Pitman Publishing Corp., 1949).

Departmentation is a long word for "how will we divide up the workers?" The earliest methods of departmentation were based on the nose count—armies and factories alike were divided into numeric groups regardless of the characteristics of the group members. Thus the ancient armies had men who were called captains of tens, captains of fifties, and captains of hundreds (or centurions). As time went by, it became obvious that there were more productive ways of grouping workers.

Workers began to be grouped according to their *function*. It is logical to put the workers involved in selling, production, and financing into departments where they can work together toward common goals. The advantage of functional departmentation is that it is logical and time-proven. The disadvantage is that when the special interest groups are grouped together, the difficulty of maintaining a "company" viewpoint is increased. Thus, the worker's loyalty can be misplaced in the department rather than in the company as a whole.

Departmentation by *geographical* area is rather common when a company does business over a large area. We are accustomed to hearing of regional offices, local sales representatives, and company buyers. This approach is strong when its purpose is to provide better sevice or coverage. Its dangers lurk in the problems of communication and supervision.

The grouping of activities on the basis of *products or product* lines is steadily growing in importance. Thus General Motors can neatly divide into Chevrolet, Buick, Frigidaire, and so on. This departmentation strategy allows the efficient delegation of large lumps of authority and responsibility.

Departmentation may also be approached according to the *customer* involved, the process, or the type of equipment. Personnel and equipment are brought together in order to serve the special needs of consumers (as with the pharmaceutical sales representative who specializes in ear, nose, and throat doctors) or the special types of equipment used (as in the crop-dusting division of a large agribusiness).

As with most alternative systems, the very best method is to use some hybrid system especially designed for the company in question. A mixture of departmentation approaches is used in most large companies. What departmentation strategy has been used to establish the position of the southeastern regional managers of the ten-person sales force and ten-person leasing force of the lift-truck division of a large heavy equipment producer?

The advantages and disadvantages of functional organization generally come in matched pairs. Job definitions are clear, but a worker often has no idea what part each job plays in the overall effort of the company. Job stability is a prominent asset, but the price paid for it is job rigidity. Functional structures tend to make adaptation difficult.

Workers specialize in their functions and become competent, but they are not usually encouraged to prepare themselves for anything else in the future.

The organizational chart is the skeleton of the organization. No one wants to live with the skeleton alone, but everyone recognizes its importance in supporting and giving form to the body. The organizational chart is widely used and appropriate for making organizational principles work. It is a way of spelling out the relationships upon which progress depends.

Charts should be kept current and should be more than a managerial pipe dream. If the chart is to make some future achievement more graphic, this purpose should be stated. The organizational chart and the status quo should be identical, or one of them should be changed.

Organizational levels of authority are established by the application of the scalar process. The resulting chain of levels is usually called a hierarchy or a *chain of command*. The primary value of these levels is in determining power relationships. They give social status to their occupants, influence patterns of association, provide authority, and affect the way workers perceive their own roles.

Individuals may function in any one of several levels of management. The level determines the style in which they will operate. If at the *trustee* level, they will function as members of the board of directors, providing policy and making decisions that will be carried out by all levels below. Below the trustee management level is the level of *general* management, the top executive level. This group has responsibility for the direction of the entire organization. Being far removed from the point of operations, the executive vice-president or general manager lives in a world of words and paperwork decisions. *Departmental* managers are at the highest level of management that deals with actual business functions, such as production, sales, finance, and industrial relations. These managers can be oriented either toward the brass or toward the workers. It is unusual for a departmental manager to look both up and down with equal interest. *Middle* management is a nice way of saying, "He or she is no longer a supervisor, yet is not running the company." Middle management covers all managers below departmental and above supervisory. They neither make major decisions nor carry them out. Because of their ambiguous halfway position, middle managers depend heavily on lateral communication and supervisory influence to get their jobs done. *Supervisory* managers are the last ones on the ladder who can delegate work. They are the firing-line managers who bear the ultimate responsibility for job accomplishment. Traditionally organizations have neglected the management training of these up-from-the-ranks managers who have the last managerial word before the rubber meets the road.

The Sears Studies

James C. Worthy studied the morale of over 100,000 employees at Sears, Roebuck and Company during a twelve-year period.[14] He was concerned with determining the morale of Sears' employees with respect to six major factors of their work environment: (1) the company in general, (2) the local organization, (3) the local management, (4) immediate supervision, (5) fellow employees, and (6) job and working conditions.

The reults of the Worthy research program are basically the following:

1. The more complex the organizational structure, the greater the probability that poor management-employee relationships will result.
2. Dividing work into fewer and fewer units and dividing departments into subdepartments often result in low output and low morale. Those groups that are most consistent in contributing to the organization (e.g., salesmen) and display the highest morale complete tasks in their entirety.
3. Minutely defined work requires close and constant supervision at the work level to maintain production. A consequence of closely supervising employees is rigid control systems that negatively affect morale and productivity.
4. Highly specialized work does not allow personnel to operate except in closest coordination with others, and the system is often so complex that this coordination cannot occur spontaneously.
5. The overly complex, overly functionalized organizational structure typically requires the type of leader who uses pressure as a supervisory device.

Next, Worth compared and contrasted various organizational structures. The implication of his analysis is that organizations with fewer levels and wider spans of control yield a less complex organizational system. The wide span of control literally forces management to delegate authority. In addition to delegation, the flattening technique (widening span of control) requires a better-trained management team, shortens communication networks, and shortens the administrative distance between levels of management.

Span of Control (Management)

The span of control (or span of management or supervision), refers to the number of persons a manager directly manages. Classical theory puts limits on the span, because every manager has a limited amount of

---

[14] Organizational Structure and Employee Morale," *American Sociological Review*, April 1950, pp. 169–179.

knowledge, energy, and so on. He or she cannot be all things to all people. The idea of a limited span developed from experience. It has always been a problem. The Bible tells how Moses had to reduce his span of management from several thousand to approximately twelve.[15]

In modern literature the development of the concept that supports a limited span of management is generally attributed to the work of three management pioneers: Sir Ian Hamilton, A. V. Graicunas, and Lyndall F. Urwick.

Hamilton's conclusions are drawn from his experiences as a military officer. He begins his line of reasoning with the statement that the average human brain finds its optimum work level when handling three to six other brains. His observation that a noncommissioned officer is not fully occupied when directing only three soldiers and that a lieutenant general finds it difficult to direct the activities of six divisional generals is recognition that the number of persons under the direction of one supervisor should be greater at the lower levels of the organization than the number supervised at the top of the organization. General Hamilton recommended that "the nearer we approach the supreme head of the whole organization, the more we ought to work toward groups of three."[16]

A. G. Graicunas, a Lithuanian management consultant, developed a formula for determining some of the relationships inherent in a given span of management.[17] If, for example, one supervisor (*S*) has two subordinates (*A*) and (*B*), a direct relationship may occur between the supervisor and *A*, and the supervisor and *B*. But there are times when the supervisor talks to *A* with *B* present or to *B* with *A* present; thus, two *group relationships* are possible. Further, *cross-relationships* may exist between *A* and *B* and between *B* and *A*. These 3 sets of relationships— direct, group, and cross—combine to form 6 possible interactions among one supervisor and two subordinates. When a third subordinate, *C*, reports to *S*, the potential number of interactions rises to 18. A fourth subordinate raises the theoretical interactions to 44. The fifth results in an even 100 relationships, and the executive with eight subordinates in the center of a web of 1,080 potential relationships.

Graicunas' mathematical analysis of the potential relationships in a given span of management is significant for two reasons. First, his theory emphasizes the complex social processes that occur between a superior and subordinates and among the subordinates themselves. Second, the application of his formula stresses the amazing rate at which the complexity of these social processes increases with each additional subordinate. Fortunately, the relationships envisioned by Graicunas do not

[15] Revised Standard Version, Exodus 18:13, 14, 17, 18, 24–26.
[16] *The Soul and Body of the Army* (London: Edward Ronald Publishers, Ltd., 1921), p. 221.
[17] Relationship in Organization," *Papers on the Science of Administration*, ed. by Luther Gulick and Lyndall F. Urwick (New York: Columbia University Press, 1947), pp. 183–187.

occur on a daily basis, or for that matter may not occur at all; but the warning is clear—somewhere there is one additional subordinate who proves to be the straw that breaks the managerial camel's back.

Lyndall F. Urwick, a noted management consultant, credits Sir Ian Hamilton with being the first to call attention to the concept of a limited span of management. Urwick encouraged Graicunas in developing his mathematical analysis of relationships. Urwick himself offered as a reason to support a limited span the observed psychological phenomenon that people have a limited span of attention—a limit to the number of items that may be attended to simultaneously. Other limitations in human spans, such as the amount of energy available to a supervisor in the performance of the job, may be advanced. Time may also be a limiting factor. Colonel Urwick recognized the variable complexity of a supervisor's job as a function of the work being performed in the following statement of principle: "No superior can supervise directly the work of more than five or, at the most, six subordinates whose work interlocks."[18]

Other writers believe that the span of control should not be limited to a definite number in any case but that it should depend on the situation and the type of supervision required. They would restate the principle as follows: "There is a limit to the number of persons who can be effectively supervised by a single individual." For example, the National Industrial Conference Board lists the following factors to be taken into account in determining the optimum span for a given instance.[19]

1. The competence of the superior and the subordinate.
2. The degree of interaction between the units or personnel being supervised.
3. The extent to which the supervisor must carry out non-managerial responsibilities, and the demands on personnel time from other people and units.
4. The similarity or dissimilarity of the activities being supervised.
5. The incidence of new problems in the supervisor's unit.
6. The extent of standardized procedure within the organization.
7. The degree of physical dispersion of activities.

Some experts believe that the optimum span of control is usually much broader than Urwick or Hamilton specified. Others, though, reject the basic assumptions of these theories. They say that whether the ratio is

---

[18] "The Manager's Span of Control," *Harvard Business Review*, May–June 1956, pp. 39–47. Colonel Urwick's article is an excellent discussion in support of a concept of limited span of management. The principle stated above first appeared in Urwick's *Scientific Principles and Organization*, Institute of Management Series No. 19, (New York: American Management Association, 1938), p. 8.

[19] Harold Stieglitz, "Optimizing Span of Control," *Management Record*, September 1962, pp. 25–29.

one-to-three, one-to-six, or one-to-1,000 is immaterial, because the most important ratio is one manager to one group of employees.

In actual practice, most spans of management are found to be much larger than the recommendations of theorists. They may range from one to 100, with spans most often between five and 15. The Woodward research[20] reported average spans in their three industrial groups as follows:

Type of Operation	Persons Supervised
Small batch production	23
Large batch and mass production	49
Long-run continuous process production	13

Size and Complexity

Organizational size affects more than the number of parking places that must be provided. There is mounting evidence that the size of a company affects its human relations variables. Larger size is associated with lower employee satisfactions and increased absenteeism. The more workers absent, the more complicated is the task of coordinating the overall effort. When the coordination suffers, there are resultant pressures, problems, and changes in productivity. The net result is a vicious circle of interlocking depressing conditions which arise as an organization becomes large.

This variation is usually based on the size of the *local* work force. Therefore, a 100-person company that is part of a 10,000-employee conglomerate would have size effects more like a 100-person company than a 10,000-employee company. As far as employee attitudes and morale are concerned, the size of the company may actually be measured in the number of parking places available at work.

C. Northcote Parkinson has provided a way of looking at organization size in his *Parkinson's Law*, which suggests that administrative size grows at a fixed annual rate which is totally unrelated to the actual work load.[21] Executives simply see their status in terms of the number of workers under them. If they can put more and more people there, it is a sure indication of success. The irony and the sting of Parkinson's Law are in its truth.

Complexity. The implications of an organization's complexity have been shown to be far-reaching. Tom Burns and G. M. Stalker investigated 20 varying companies in Great Britain and found that they

[20] Joan Woodward, *Industrial Organization: Theory and Practice* (London: Oxford University Press, 1965).
[21] Northcote Parkinson, *Parkinson's Law* (London: John Murray, Publishers, Ltd., 1958).

adapted to industrial complexities in one of two ways: (1) mechanistic and (2) organic systems.[22]

Mechanistic systems were developed along the lines of: (1) specialized, functional division of labor; (2) coordination among supervisors within functional departments; (3) clear-cut job definition; (4) vertical authority hierarchy; (5) encouragement of organizational loyalty and conformity.

Firms which had *organic systems* were typified by: (1) organizational goals seen as the end, functional goals as the means; (2) lateral coordination as well as vertical; (3) flexibility in job guidelines; (4) direction given as consultation rather than group loyalty. Burns and Stalker conclude that neither system is inherently better, but each works better in some situations.

Whatever form of department is used by a company, the chances are good that some change will be required in the immediate future. In one study,[23] more than two-thirds of the nation's largest 100 industrial firms reported major organizational realignments. Because of the need for organizations to be able to respond to change, business firms are beginning to accept the need for adapting their organizational structure on a regular basis. Hower and Lorsch describe a trend away from the rigid bureaucratic form of organization to a more dynamic, flexible form. The characteristics of the old, mechanistic structure are contrasted with the newer organic form in Table 6-1.

The need for flexibility in organizations is increased by a recent change in emphasis from training and changing the individual to attempting to change and train the organization. This is generally refered to as organizational development, and will be discussed in a subsequent chapter.

The Lawrence and Lorsch Study

Probably the most thorough study of the effects of complexity was conducted by Paul Lawrence and Jay Lorsch.[24] Their search focused on three industrial areas: plastics, consumer foods, and containers. They then divided the companies into three environmental areas: sales, production, and research and development. Managers in each of these specialties were surveyed in regard to four attitudes.

---

[22] Tom Burns and G. M. Stalker, *The Management of Innovation* (London: Tavistock, 1961), pp. 5 ff.

[23] D. Ronald Daniel, "Reorganizing for Results," *Harvard Business Review*, November, 1966, p. 96.

[24] Paul R. Lawrence and Jay W. Lorsch, *Organization and Environment* (Homewood, Ill.: Richard D. Irwin, Inc., 1969), p. 190.

Table 6.1
Organizational
Characteristics of
Organic and
Mechanistic
Structures*

Organizational Characteristics Index	Types of Organization Structure	
	Organic	Mechanistic
Span of control	Wide	Narrow
Number of levels of authority	Few	Many
Ratio of administrative to production personnel	High	Low
Range of time span over which an employee can commit resources	Long	Short
Degree of centralization in decision making	Low	High
Proportion of persons in one unit having opportunity to interact with persons in other units	High	Low
Quantity of formal rules	Low	High
Specificity of job goals	Low	High
Specificity of required activities	Low	High
Content of communications	Advice and information	Instructions and decisions
Range of compensation	Narrow	Wide
Range of skill levels	Narrow	Wide
Knowledge-based authority	High	Low
Position-based authority	Low	High

* Adapted from Ralph M. Hower and Jay W. Lorsch, "Organizational Inputs," in John A. Seiler, *Systems Analysis in Organizational Behavior*, Richard D. Irwin, Inc., and The Dorsey Press, Homewood, Ill., 1967, p. 168.

1. *Functional goal orientation.* Were sales people more likely to have chauvinistic attitudes toward other departments?
2. *Time orientation.* Did any of the groups tend to seek short-range goals rather than long-range, or vice versa?
3. *Interpersonal orientation.* Did the managers put more emphasis on task completion or human relations?
4. *Formality of structure.* Was the classical theory of organization or innovative approaches followed more closely?

The degree of variation in attitude which was observed between the three management groups was termed *differentiation*.

The study found that the different climates of the industries in question strongly influenced differentiation. In the container industry, for example, all three areas of management were found to be *homogeneous*, or predictable and stable. Therefore, little differentiation between departments was observed. In the plastics industry, the production climate was homogeneous, while the research and development field was uncertain because of the dynamic condition of the science involved. The plastics industry, then, was said to have a *diverse* climate. This diversity produced higher differentiation in these firms.

The resolution of differentiation, or *integration*, was an important factor in each climate. Among container firms, integration was most important between production and sales and between production and research and development. With plastics, the primary integration was research and development with sales, and research and development with production. Formal hierarchy structure was found to be adequate in integrating homogeneous firms, but special teams were needed to coordinate when diverse climates were involved.

Simply stated, Lawrence and Lorsch's study showed that the best organizational structure is determined by the contingencies, or environmental variables, affecting the firm.

Organization: The Best Way?

Throughout this chapter we have looked at the research and experience of managers who have attempted to find optimum approaches for organizing the activities of a particular group. Unfortunately, there is no utopian or ideal approach to organization. Tall or flat, functional or product, mechanistic or organic, every approach to organization can be ideal given a particular set of circumstances.

Throughout the world of scholarship about life situations, there are theories and iron-clad mathematical formulas for what ought to be done. Occasionally, the real-life success demonstrates to embarrassed theorists that every situation possesses its own unique variables that may in fact reverse the commonly applicable laws. The lesson for all of us is that research about organization (or anything else) should be the servant of people and not their master. In the final analysis, the number of employees that can be efficiently supervised depends on the skill of the supervisor. *General* rules can help in *general* planning, but for *specific* situations, we need *individual* adaptation.

The Classics Revisited

The major topics discussed in this chapter are typically associated with the classical approach to organization. This classical theory began to develop in the 18th century and came into its greatest influence during the middle of the 20th century. The prime objectives of classical theory (control, discipline, uniformity, and productivity) have been successfully achieved. Organization theory must now continue to be successful if we are to survive our successes.

To be realistic, we need to recognize the limitations of the theory. Classical theory was not built with human relations in mind. Because human factors have begun to receive their rightful importance in the past few decades, new theories have had to be incorporated into classical thinking to keep the theory relevant. It would be shortsighted to condemn the entire classical heritage because it ignores our modern precepts about humanity. Americans have not found it necessary to conduct a revolution every few years as political thinking has changed. Rather, there has been continuous, productive incorporation of the new ideas into the establishment. That is the approach which must be used with management theory.

The most obvious strength of the classical theory is its task emphasis. Lack of psychological support is its big weakness. But these emphases are not mutually incompatible. In other words, few employees will be psychologically comfortable if the job does not get done. But neither will the job get done for long if human factors are totally cast to the wind. Management has to evaluate the tasks being done and give an honest, open hearing to the various theories. The determining factor should be the applicability of the theory to the job. In many cases, the classical model will continue to function well. Assembly-line production, for example, requires the close coordination which the model offers.

Summary

Because we live in an organization-conscious world, there is an ever-present danger of organizational patterns getting out of hand. To some extent, every employee should be part of a continuing committee for review and refinement of company organization—the way people and activities relate to each other in the accomplishment of company goals. The wise student sees a meaningful distinction between *organization* and *efficient organization.*

William G. Scott has suggested the four pillars of organization: (1) *Division of labor* is the most basic of the four pillars. It has been criticized for stifling individualism while increasing production. To counteract this, some organizations have developed special strategies, like job enlargement, rotation, and participation. (2) *Scalar and functional processes* refer to the chain of command within an organization. This pillar relies on the processes of chain of command, delegation, and unity of command. (3) *Structure*, or the grouping of employees and their activities, makes the management of complicated enterprises possible. Four important considerations of organizational structure are departmentation, organizational charts, organizational levels, and organizational size. (4) *Span of control* refers to the number of persons a manager directly manages. Many studies have been done to try to determine scientifically the optimum number that can be supervised. In the final analysis, of course, the research can only make suggestions, for each case must be decided on its own individual merits.

This chapter also considered the impact of size and complexity on organizational decisions. As is usually true, the ideal approach cannot be determined without looking at all the factors in the situation.

Review Questions

1. Name William G. Scott's four pillars of classical organization theory and briefly define each.
2. What is unity of command?
3. What is an organizational chart?
4. What is span of management or span of control? Is the concept valid?
5. What is meant by delegation?
6. Is *organization* a noun or a verb?
7. Illustrate each of Scott's pillars of organization theory in a university setting.
8. What kind of problems would exist in a university if specialization of labor was not practiced?
9. Why might labor organizations object to strategies such as job enlargement and job rotation?
10. What problems relating to unity of command do college students have?
11. Illustrate the major types of departmentation, using a college or university illustration.
12. Explain why the span of control is typically smaller in graduate classes than it is with freshman courses.

7

Concepts of Control

"I remember as a boy going to visit old Jones out at his shack by the lake. He had no deed to that property, but everybody just figured that he wasn't doing any harm by living out there with his old hound dog. Fact is, you could just about sum up old Jones' life by saying that he never did much harm.

"I can still hear him telling how he had been a great general in the Spanish-American War. Of course, I was just a boy and would sit wide-eyed for hours and take in his tall tales. All his statements seemed quite logical to me then, and as I look back I realize that old Jones taught me some of the most basic principles of management.

"'If you're going to do anything, do it right,' went one of his lectures. 'You have to have control. Whether it's a whole army or just a pet dog, you got to have perfect control.'

"Jones turned to his mangy hound, 'Now, Rounder, I want you to roll over two times,' he ordered sternly.

"Rounder stretched sleepily and walked across the room and slid under the bed.

"'. . . or get under the bed,' continued Jones. 'Now where were we, boy . . . ?'"

One of the most universally accepted pieces of advice from old, experienced managers is "Plan your work—work your plan." The advice could hardly be stated in more simple fashion. Yet contained within those last three words is an apt summary for this chapter. Indeed, the volumes that have been written on managerial control are trying to lay down principles and appropriate generalizations by which aspiring managers can "work their plans."

The control process is such an automatic thing in daily life that we sometimes have difficulty recognizing the necessary components of this necessary process. In completely automatic fashion, our bodies maintain thermostatic control and monitoring of our temperature. In cold conditions, the body closes the pores and conserves valuable heat. In hot weather, the body perspires and utilizes a simple evaporation process to keep its normal temperature. The average person rarely even thinks of these operations unless the measures become extreme and produce fever or chills.

Control techniques are essentially the same whether they are operating on body temperature, cash flow, office procedures, morale, product quality, or anything else. The parts of the control phenomenon are roughly the same in every case. And they are equally likely to be overlooked or taken for granted when they are operating at an efficient level. The topic of control seems to occur to us more readily in the presence of a squeaking wheel than a well-oiled machine. If all our plans were executed flawlessly and the unexpected were not quite so frequent, there would be no need even to be concerned with the topic of control. There would also be very little spice to life. Though we might long for an existence in which everything goes according to plan, the truth is that people thrive on challenge. To manage well (and avoid ulcers) the wise person learns to appreciate the opportunity to match wits with problems . . . either before or during their occurrence.

Control is not a popular topic—either with the controllers or the controllees. The term has lurking within it the suggestion that everything is not as it should be, and that suggestion always produces a guilty party on the angry defensive.

The Control Process

The basic control process, wherever it is found and whatever the object of its constrictions, can be boiled down to three steps: (1) establishing standards, (2) measuring performance against these standards, and (3) correcting deviations from standards and plans. To put these familiar three terms in down-home terminology, control is (1) sayin' how things oughta be, (2) seein' how things is, and (3) straightenin' out what's crooked.

Standards must be established before any evaluation can be made. Evaluative results must be stated in relation to something or they are meaningless statistics. Standards may be expressed in terms of money, time, quotas, or almost any commodity that is measurable and understandable. "Striving for excellence" makes nice pep-talk terminology, but it results in rather vague goal setting and even more confusing attempts at evaluation.

There are several ways that standards may be set. Statistical standards, sometimes called historical standards, are based upon an analysis of past experience. Meeting the standards of past performance is a poor motivator and proves very ittle even if accomplished. What is the value of meeting, or even exceeding, a standard from the past? One of the things about competing with yourself is that you always win . . . or is it that you always lose? Most of the time when we assume that we are setting standards on statistical bases, there is actually another very important element entering in without our awareness: the judgment of the standard setter.

Judgment or hip-pocket, seat-of-the-pants, gut-level appraisal by the person in charge is probably the most common method of standard setting. And in some ways it has never been excelled. Normative data are a useful adjunct in setting standards of performance in regard to profitability, market position, employee attitudes, and, to some extent, public responsibility. However, the final word about what shall constitute satisfactory performance emerges from the melting pot of the manager's mind. There is probably a close correlation between the manager's subjectivity/objectivity ratio and success. He or she can become neither a puppet of the statistical indicators nor a selfish dictator. The balance with which the manager utilizes data and intuition is the measure of worth.

Engineered standards are based upon the objective, quantitative analysis of specific situations. These are computed or deduced on the basis of observation of workers in action. However, it doesn't take long for the workers in the factory to learn that it is wise to take it easier whenever the person with the stopwatch comes snooping around. The lower you can "engineer" those engineered standards, the better you're going to

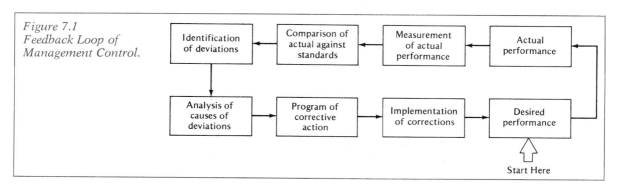

*Figure 7.1
Feedback Loop of
Management Control.*

look on the day-to-day production reports. Students may sometimes be observed cleverly manipulating the engineered standard with regard to test grading systems.

Measurement of performance is essential if the standards are to serve any purpose. It would be nice to think that the measurement could be conducted before the fact by the powers of anticipation, enabling the planner to adjust and avoid the problem. However, in most cases we do it, measure it, and then fix it. Our greatest difficulty with efforts at evaluation can usually be traced back to the previous step: we failed to say exactly what we were about in measurable terms. This situation can result in a lot of futile research, rubber-stamp evaluation projects, and changing of objectives after the results come in.

Phases of Control

The control activity can enter the picture at one or more of three points: before, during, or after. There are more elaborate terms for these phases, but the heart of the matter is that you can choose to *prevent* the problem, *deal with* the problem, or see that the problem *doesn't happen again.*

Precontrol is a term often used to refer to those activities performed to keep a problem (or less than ideal situation) from happening. We are familiar with the term "preventive maintenance," referring to fixing things before they have a chance to break. Industry has learned that a $1.00 fanbelt can be replaced *before* it really needs replacing to assure a $1,000 loss of time does not occur when that fanbelt *does* wear through.

Concurrent controls take place while the activity continues. Every motorist has endured the irritation of one-lane traffic while the highway is under repair. This maintenance-as-usual approach is certainly more to be desired than the alternatives. The cost of building maintenance-free roads would be prohibitive, and the inconvenience of closing the roads completely or letting them remain unrepaired would be unacceptable.

Post controls are theoretically the poorest approach, and in practice the most common. It is costly and wasteful to repair, renovate, or rebuild. Careful review of mistakes and revisions for the future is a praiseworthy practice, but, *when there is an option*, the wise manager chooses to eliminate the need for post control through application of pre- and concurrent monitoring and control.

Correction of deviations is a common offender in the problems of effective managerial control. The sooner a correction can be made in an incorrect procedure, the sooner the original goal can be reached. A moon rocket that leaves the earth off course by only a few degrees will be likely to miss its target by several thousand miles. The manager may be able to correct a problem by redrawing the plans or by modifying the goal. It may be necessary to reorganize functions, reassign duties, add staff, retrain, or fire. Or the problem may be solved through better directing or fuller explanation of the mission.

The individual style of control that will be utilized by a manager cannot be prescribed. The ways of reacting to control problems are varied and would only lose potency if adopted by the wrong persons. Nothing is more confusing or comical than an easygoing supervisor who decides that it is time to get tough.

Although specific styles of personality cannot be prescribed for aspiring controllers, there is a definite value in considering several factors that should be considered in any control situation:

1. Are the controls being brought to bear on the situation or the personalities involved?
2. Do the measures adopted follow logical processes—have they been objectively arrived at after the consideration of all alternatives?
3. Do the controls treat the symptom or the cause of the problem?
4. Does something need changing if repetition of the same problem is to be avoided? Does the problem lie in the mangement system or in unavoidable conditions?

The dictionary defines *standards* as units of measurement established by authority to serve as a model or criterion. Three important facets are included in such a definition. "Units of measurement" points to the necessity of establishing a measurable quantitative description of the objective sought. "Established by authority" refers to the standard's reason for being—to communicate and assure some delegated task. And the standard's service as a "model or a criterion" describes its usefulness in communicating the difference between "what is" and "what ought to be."

Types of Control

There are many systems designed to assist in controlling functions. Some are simple, some are complex, but all seek to isolate those steps that will eliminate surprises. *Production control* is concerned with the timing and paths of any production from peanut butter to Broadway hits. *Inventory control* monitors and adjusts quantities of things from peanuts to grease paint. *Quality control* tests and adjusts qualities of things like crunchiness and pazazz. These types of control are presented and expanded in Chapter 18, but this chapter will mention the categories briefly.

Production Control
Production control consists of six functions:

1. *Routing* determines the operations to be performed, their sequence, and the path of flow of materials through a series of operations.
2. *Loading* is the function of assigning work to a machine or department in advance.
3. *Scheduling* of production determines the time at which each operation is to take place.
4. *Estimating* involves determining in advance the probable cost of producing a job on which the sales department wishes to make a bid.
5. *Dispatching* is the process of actually ordering work to be done.
6. *Expediting* is a follow-up activity that checks whether plans are actually being executed.

Inventory Control
Inventory control deals with (1) raw materials, (2) work in progress, and (3) finished goods. Inventory controllers must answer the following questions:

1. What is the optimum amount of inventory to carry?
2. What is the economic lot size for an order?
3. What is the record system for showing the status of inventory on hand?

Quality Control
This form of control is concerned with keeping the quality of a firm's production above the standards that have been established by the customer or by the company's own engineers. Specific tests are conducted to determine if the product is the correct size (often within $1/1000$ of an inch) or is strong, hard, or durable enough to do its job.

While each stage of a missile assembly is tested several times, the manufacturer of lawn mower parts cannot personally examine each item. Consequently, samples of production are drawn at regular intervals to provide data on the level of quality. Statistical methods and probability theory are necessary tools for this activity. Quality control specialists want to be sure that the sample they are evaluating is typical of the total production run.

Financial Control
Almost everything is related to financial control. Either financial control is the object of the business activity or it is a major determiner of the activity. Even in the nonprofit organization, budgeting limitations are of utmost significance. The manager who does not control the financial aspects of an area of responsibility is in for a sudden fast ride at the

end of a tiger's tail. Budgets, profit-loss, and return on investment are areas that seem to be able to get farther out of hand faster than any other aspect of business.

Budgets

Any manager or company that makes vague and generic financial plans should not plan to be "financial" for long. The word *budget* has developed a rather negative connotation for most folks. This has occurred because the budget has often been the reason that things could not be done. In recent years, some companies have tried a little positive thinking by referring to their *profit plans* instead of budgets. Whatever the name, financial planning and anticipation of expenditure are meant to be the slave of business, not the master. Putting plans down on paper in exact amounts, and leaving no blank spaces for maybe's, allows a manager to know exactly where he or she is going. Numbers force a kind of orderliness that makes possible the minimizing of disconcerting surprises.

The budget for most organizations of any size is really a summary statement of several subbudgets. Contained within the financial statement are the final figures from other budgets. Five of the most common budgets are (1) revenue and expense budgets, (2) time, space, material, and product budgets, (3) capital expenditure budgets, (4) cash budgets, and (5) balance-sheet budgets. The master budget gathers together all other budgets for the involved departments.

As discussed in the chapter on planning, there are a few pitfalls in the budgeting process that must be avoided lest the tail begin to wag the dog. Budgeting is a tool with which the organization hopes to accomplish its goals. Whenever meeting the budget becomes more important than the goals of the enterprise, things are out of order. Overbudgeting, for instance, can burden workers with such meaningless detail that they cannot concentrate upon goals. Accounting for paper clips is an activity of dubious value for a man making $100,000 decisions.

One of the really interesting processes to witness is the swivel-hipped rationalizing of a supervisor who is making out the budget. The process is especially interesting when the supervisor wants to include money for some expenditure that he or she feels is valuable but that is definitely taboo according to the budgetary rules. It would seem a strength for managers to be able to tell the truth. When the responsibility for accomplishing some task is delegated but the authority over budget is not, what needs to be changed?. . . The people, the budget, the policy, the . . . ?

The inflexibility of budgets has often earned enemies for the plan-ahead system. Projecting costs that will not actualize for two or three years can prove rather limiting. Particularly in government agencies, there is annual frustration over the need to guess the financial needs of the future. Inflexibility can be extremely disabling for a manager in a rapidly changing, highly competitive world. Even so, it is much too easy to say that flexibility should be a characteristic of a good budget, for in one sense the primary purpose of a budget is the elimination of flexibility. Perhaps the irritations of budget inflexibility are more the fault of slipshod data-gathering.

The budget can be a potent controller of business activity. The challenge confronting the budget maker is the making of plans that will control without constricting and serve as a monitor without becoming a monster.

Break-even Analysis

The break-even chart is similar to the variable budget chart. Both are discussed in greater detail in Chapter 18. Though the two are often confused, they have quite different purposes. The variable budget chart sets percentages instead of dollars to keep amounts flexible. The break-even chart sets specific amounts of time, money, products, or other commodities. The beginning point for the break-even analysis is the amount at which all expenses are paid and the profits start to come in. Beyond that point, the income increases proportionately with each sale. A publisher might say, "As soon as we sell five thousand copies of this book, we will have paid all the cost of development and production. After that, everything else is clear profit." If, however, a writer must receive royalties on the book, a break-even chart could demonstrate the way both royalties and company profits continue to grow as income increases.

The break-even analysis chart can function as a control device through its emphasis on the marginal concept. The chart graphically portrays the effect of increased sales or costs or profits or expenses. The chart says "See . . . it's simple . . . more productivity! more profit!"

Ratio Analysis

In the comparison of growth *rates*, the ratio analysis is often helpful. Rather than concentrating on absolute figures and amounts, ratio analysis centers on relationships. This can make amazing differences in either direction, making the company's *true* growth appear or occasionally making the facts more impressive.

While Table 7-1 shows several key financial ratios and over-all industry norms, ratio analysis needs to be used carefully. Capital investments in the steel and petroleum industry are much higher than in cosmet-

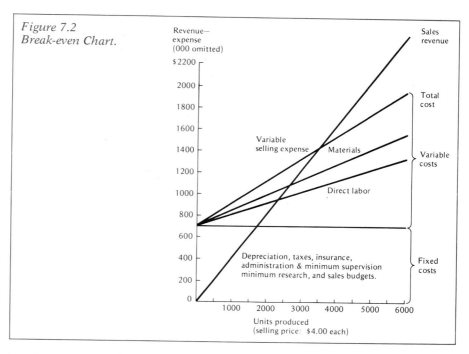

*Figure 7.2
Break-even Chart.*

ics. Inventory turnover is much higher for grocery products than for jewelry. Ratios need to be considered in reference to industry norms and historical patterns for a particular organization if they are to have real precision.

Return on Investment

Imagine Harold and Maude are two real estate people who work for the same agency. Harold and Maude both work forty hours per week for a year. Harold makes twenty sales and Maude makes one sale. Which of the two received a better return on his or her investment of time? The answer can be rather urprising and illustrative of the return-on-investment concept. Maude received a high return on her investment of time because her one sale was a $10 million shopping center and land development deal. Harold, who sold twenty residences during the year, made $18,000 in commissions. Maude invested the same number of hours, made only one sale, and took in a $120,000 commission.

With almost any endeavor, it is necessary to invest time, money, or effort in order to make a profit. The return-on-investment chart is being used increasingly to evaluate possible alternative routes, communicate proper values to subordinates, and control the investment processes.

Table 7.1   Checklist for Financial Ratio Analysis

Name of Ratio	Formula	Industry Norm (assumed merely as illustration)
1. *Liquidity Ratios* (measuring the ability of the firm to meet its maturing obligations)		
Current ratio	$\dfrac{\text{Current assets}}{\text{Current liabilities}}$	2.6
Acid-test ratio	$\dfrac{\text{Cash and equivalent}}{\text{Current liability}}$	1.0
Cash velocity	$\dfrac{\text{Sales}}{\text{Cash and equivalent}}$	12 times
Inventory to net working capital	$\dfrac{\text{Inventory}}{\text{Current assets}-\text{Current liabilities}}$	85%
2. *Leverage Ratios* (measuring the contributions of financing by owners compared with financing provided by creditors)		
Debt to equity	$\dfrac{\text{Total debt}}{\text{Net worth}}$	56%
Coverage of fixed charges	$\dfrac{\text{Net profit before fixed charges}}{\text{Fixed charges}}$	6 times
Current liability to net worth	$\dfrac{\text{Current liability}}{\text{Net worth}}$	32%
Fixed assets to net worth	$\dfrac{\text{Fixed assets}}{\text{Net worth}}$	60%
3. *Activity Ratios* (measuring the effectiveness of the employment of resources)		
Inventory turnover	$\dfrac{\text{Sales}}{\text{Inventory}}$	7 times
Net working capital turnover	$\dfrac{\text{Sales}}{\text{Net working capital}}$	5 times
Fixed-assets turnover	$\dfrac{\text{Sales}}{\text{Fixed assets}}$	6 times
Average collection period	$\dfrac{\text{Receivables}}{\text{Average sales per day}}$	20 days
Equity capital turnover	$\dfrac{\text{Sales}}{\text{Net worth}}$	3 times
Total capital turnover	$\dfrac{\text{Sales}}{\text{Total assets}}$	2 times

When management uses return-on-investment thinking to control over-all performance, it does not consider profit as an absolute but rather in relation to what was required to make the profit. They recognize that if the highest gross income were the supreme accomplishment, it would be easy to accomplish . . . perhaps by selling below cost. But, of

Table 7.1 (Continued)

Name of Ratio	Formula	Industry Norm (assumed merely as illustration)
4. *Profitability Ratios* (indicating degree of success in achieving desired profit levels)		
Gross margin	$\dfrac{\text{Gross profit}}{\text{Sales}}$	30%
Net operating margin	$\dfrac{\text{Net operating profit}}{\text{Sales}}$	6.5%
Sales margin	$\dfrac{\text{Net profit after taxes}}{\text{Sales}}$	3.2%
Productivity of assets	$\dfrac{\text{Net income less taxes}}{\text{Total assets}}$	10%
Return on capital	$\dfrac{\text{Net profit after taxes}}{\text{Net worth}}$	7.5%
Net profit on working capital	$\dfrac{\text{Net profit after taxes}}{\text{Net working capital}}$	14.5%

course, the name of the game is profit-net income. And profits are computed *after* all the bills are paid.

The DuPont Company has been using the return on investment scheme of evaluation and control since 1919.[1] Figure 7.3 shows the relationship of factors affecting return on investment.

This chart allows the controller to see things as they really are instead of as they may appear from the sales manager's reports. The center of the trouble can be spotted easily. Whether too much inventory is being built up or the cost of selling the product is getting out of hand, the manager can pinpoint the problem and bring about corrective action. Otherwise, that dreaded day may come when sales are at an all-time high and the business goes bankrupt. This financial deception has also been known to occur in personal budget situations as well as in the corporate realm. Return on investment is a viable process for the budget control of college students as well as conglomerates.

Direct Management Control

Systems for control are necessary. There is, however, one school of thought that feels that the major responsibility for control should rest not upon an inanimate chart or timetable but on a living, breathing manager. Let the manager employ whatever control he or she thinks is needed to meet a personal responsibility.

[1] *How the DuPont Organization Appraises Its Peformance,* Financial Management Series No. 94 (New York: American Management Association, 1950).

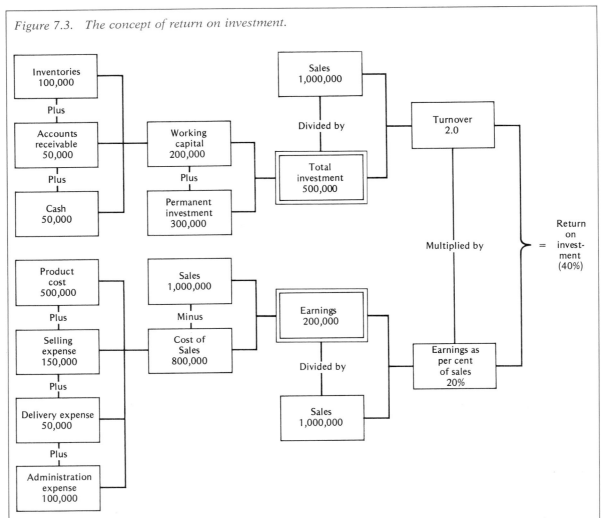

Figure 7.3. *The concept of return on investment.*

Essentially, ROI is determined by dividing total investment into earnings to determine a percentage rate of return (200,000 ÷ 500,000 = .40). This more complex method provides a fuller explanation of how this figure is determined. Incidentally, a ROI of 40% is fantastic. You might want to buy stock in this firm. What other conclusions can you draw about it?

This attitude of direct control embraces the idea that personal responsibility for problems can be fixed if the administrative approaches are "fixed." There is still a need for proof on the part of those who propound that all control problems can ultimately be traced to the controller. On the other hand the direct control philosophy is based on four valid assumptions: (1) that trained managers make fewer errors, (2) that managerial activities can be reduced to quantitatively measurable units, (3) that principles of management exist that can serve as a clear standard for comparison with the status quo, and (4) that the expertise with which a manager is following good management rules can be reliably measured.

Control of control by controlling the controllers has several advantages. First, it is simpler and more direct—each manager must face being called on the carpet for things that are amiss. Second, it is surer —knowing that errors will be uncovered in periodic evaluation discourages procrastination and glossing over. Third, it is fairer—the managers can begin to anticipate and rely on the predictability of the standards by which superiors will judge them.

Direct Control Through Key-Result Areas

One method of evaluating various control areas is through a system called key-area evaluation as we saw in Chapter 5. This system was instituted by General Electric in the 1960's to find a method of comparing differing organization units with one another.[2] Each area was measured according to the way it was accomplishing its stated goals in eight key areas: profitability, market position, productivity, product leadership, personnel development, employee attitudes, public responsibility, and the balance between short- and long-range goals.

This system came about at GE because of the recognition that department evaluation on the basis of the profit motive alone could be quite deceptive. Without much imagination, a department manager could conduct business to maximize immediate, short-term profits, get promoted, and be clear when the long-term problems began to appear. One manager's quick-and-dirty profit approach would bring the department crashing down around his unsuspecting successor. General Electric realized that each of the key areas is closely related to a company's success and ultimate long-range profit-making ability.

Direct Control Through Management Audit

The periodic financial audit by an impartial, outside auditor has become an established practice in most sizable organizations. It is also likely that the future will bring the rather traditional use of a management audit for the evaluation of the nonfinancial factors of progress. Hopefully, the management audit will eventually take on some of the matter-of-fact acceptance of the financial audit (i.e., "Everything is as it should be . . . I'm doing my job . . . nobody is trying to get me . . . why should I worry?")

The tough part of conducting such an audit is in deciding what managerial characteristics to measure and how to measure them. There are some who feel that time is wasted unless the audit probes into management's morals and integrity, its creativity, its "social values," its

[2] Based on Peter F. Drucker, *The Practice of Management* (New York: Harper and Row, 1964), p. 63. Also discussed in Chapter 5 of this text.

human empathy and so on. The old-timers, however, favor a "measurement by the bottom line" philosophy on the assumption that, in business, the only thing that matters is productivity.

Peter F. Drucker[3] has suggested that both these points of view are wrong. Performance *is* the way to measure skill, but some of the more "social" characteristics have enough significance to merit measuring. Drucker suggests, therefore, that the following four areas ought to be measured by productivity specifics:

1. The manager's performance in appropriating capital.
2. Performance on people-decisions (i.e., the development and placement of subordinates).
3. Innovation performance.
4. Planning performance.

In the 1930's, James McKinsey introduced a periodic management self-audit appraisal system.[4] Its purpose was to discover and correct errors of management. Such self-appraisals have become more and more prevalent within the last few years. They range from scientifically constructed and weighted questions to simple questionnaires that appear occasionally in magazines for managers to evaluate everything from deskside manner to coffee-break finesse. A worthwhile self-appraisal should include company policies, organizational structures, personnel practice, physical facilities, managerial methodology, control behavior, and human relations philosophy.

A self-audit can be valuable if performed regularly and impartially. Obviously, these are the two characteristics hardest to control from the management suite. There is rarely the extra time required to complete an involved self-analysis. But even more difficult is the objectivity that must be dredged up to do justice to such an analysis. What type of manager relishes seeking out personal shortcomings and those of colleagues?

The American Institute of Management, a private nonprofit organization, has been active for many years in conducting audits of management based on the system devised by Jackson Martindell.[5] This organization has devised a list of several hundred questions that is used as the basis for reaching a decision on the quality of the management of a particular enterprise. Questions primarily cover ten broad areas concerning economic functions, corporate structure, earnings growth, fairness to stockholders, research and development, composition of the

[3] Peter F. Drucker, "A New Scorecard for Management," The Wall Street Journal, September 24, 1976, p. 16.
[4] R. W. Lewis, *Planning, Managing and Measuring the Business* (New York: Controllership Foundation, 1955).
[5] See Jackson Martindell, *Scientific Appraisal Management* (New York: Harper and Row, 1950), and Jackson Martindell, *The Appraisal of Management* (New York: Harper and Row, 1962).

board of directors, fiscal policies, production efficiency, sales, and executive evaluation.

A total maximum number of points is assigned to each area.[6] The individual questions, grouped by areas, are submitted to corporate officers and to outside sources. The answers are analyzed by members of the Institute in order to determine how many points out of the maximum attainable rating are to be given for each answer. The points are added up to arrive at a total for each of the ten areas. Depending on how the total number of points compares with the maximum attainable, the management audit will show either a high or a low rating.

The problems involved in the self-audit (or even an outside audit for which all information is supplied by the audited parties) are clearly evident. People never seem to testify against themselves . . . even when they would profit in the long run. For this reason, there is an increasing trend toward having management audits performed by outside consultants. Such external management audits performed by expert but non-involved parties are similar to external financial audits performed by outside accountants. They are concerned with the examination of company performance, its position in the industry, its organizational structure, and the control and operations of its divisions and departments.

As business leaders continue to strive for excellence, it is almost certain that some variety of regular and consistent evaluation will come into common use. There will be the old problems of quantifying talent and evaluating intangibles, but something must be done to develop efficient controls on managerial control.

Indirect Control

Some of the factors that management needs to control are open-and-shut cases. If you want 10,000 cream puffs off the bakery line by Thursday, you can monitor your degree of control all the way by keeping one eye on the clock and one on the cream puff counter at the end of the conveyor belt.

Other factors that need controlling just as much are far less tangible, and much harder to put the managerial finger on. Such control objectives require more subtle but equally intensive effort.

Organizational conditioning is the process of uniting the whole "team" behind the organization's objectives and methodology. Many wise companies consider this task to be important enough to justify an on-going program or a department of internal communication. This corporate pep talk must walk a narrow line between propaganda and a weak pep rally. The building of spirit in management and worker personnel is one of the frontiers still wide open to those who claim that the

---

[6] Discussed by Billy Goetz, *Management, Planning and Control* (New York: McGraw-Hill Book Company, 1959), p. 167.

King Kong (Paramount Pictures, 1976). Inflexible control systems can put the squeeze on managers.

challenge has gone out of business. Company success depends upon a cumulative state of mind, yet the methods for appropriately conditioning the organization still await discovery.

Managerial molding, often called socialization of managers, is the specialized conditioning that must take place in the management suites. In the front office, especially, it is critical that all think alike . . . but not too much alike. Creativity must be selected and bred. But too much creativity and too many independent directions can spell disaster for "the company way."

Characteristics of a Good Control System

Harold Koontz and Cyril O'Donnell[7] have listed ten requirements of adequate controls. They point out that although generalizations can be made about the desirable characteristics of a control system, each individual system requires special design. Trewatha and Newport[8] have proposed six characteristics for an effective control system. These sixteen suggestions are combined into a single list below—a list which could beneficially appear on the wall of any manager at any level.

1. *Controls must reflect the nature of the activity.* It stands to reason that the control practices of organized crime would be likely to differ from those used by the Campfire Girls.

2. *Controls should report deviations promptly.* Dangerous trends become as great a concern as actual failures to the manager in control.

3. *Controls should focus on the future.* Even though a necessary margin of error must be recognized, the controlling manager must predict, forecast, blue-sky, and estimate or be left holding the bag that someone has let the cat out of.

4. *Controls should point up exceptions at critical points.* Few managers monitor every activity under their authority. At least, they cannot treat them in the same way. They must manage by exception—dealing only with the nonstandard situations—at the same time it is wise to budget time and effort in the handling of exceptional matters.

5. *Controls should be objective.* Textbook descriptions of business situations sometimes imply that all actions are taken coolly and objectively by realistic, mature people. In reality, many of our critical decisions and rulings are based on subjective, personal reaction.

6. *Controls should be flexible.* The danger in making controls objective is the tendency to remove all flexibility and common sense. Unless the mechanics of adjustment are built into the system, a situation may arise in which the cure is worse than the disease.

7. *Controls should reflect the organizational pattern.* To accomplish their purpose, control data must be specific about amounts and sources of difficulties. In recent years, cost accountants have emphasized the futility of supplying general information for specific purposes.

8. *Controls should be economical.* The choices between the relative economic values of controls are external manifestations of the internal thinking of management. In those organizations that know where they are going, controls are means to an end, never an end in themselves.

9. *Controls should be understandable.* If the control system is not un-

[7] Harold Koontz and Cyril O'Donnell, *Principles of Management*, 4th ed. (New York: McGraw-Hill Book Company, 1968), pp. 643–647; and *Management*, 6th ed. (1976), pp. 652–656.
[8] Robert L. Trewatha and M. Bene Newport, *Management: Functions: Behavior* (Dasins, Business Publication, Inc., 1976), pp. 276-280.

derstandable and readily applied by the involved workers, the control system is a drawback instead of an asset.

10. *Controls should avoid obsolescence.* Build the system's graceful demise into the system. Let it (or any part of it) die when it becomes useless.

11. *Controls should seek employee commitment.* They must be designed in a way to seek understanding, promote participation, and develop a supportive employee attitude.

12. *Controls should seek rapid feedback.* Control systems that get their information too late to avoid problems are systems "out of control."

13. *Controls should indicate corrective action.* An adequate control system must do more than flash a red light. It should disclose where failures are occurring, who is responsible for them, and exactly what preprogrammed responses are most appropriate. The real value of any planning or control function is that it allows optimum decisions to be made before the pressure of the emergency.

Summary

Control techniques are not notices at all when they are functioning at their optimum level. Ideally, controls in business processes will resemble the methodology of the thermostat rather than the slavedriver.

The basic control process, wherever it is found and whatever the object of its constrictions, can be boiled down to three steps: (1) establishing standards or "saying how things ought to be"; (2) measuring performance against standards or "seeing how things really are"; and (3) correcting deviations or "straightening out what's crooked."

Standards for evaluation may be arrived at through analysis of past experience, subjective appraisal by the authority, or engineered standards based on objective, quantitative analysis. Correction of deviative plans should always consider the following questions: (1) Are the controls being brought on the situation or the personalities involved? (2) Do the measures adopted follow logical processes? (3) Do the controls treat the symptom or the cause of the problem? (4) Does the management system need changes to avoid repetition of the problem?

Financial control is the basic control in profit-dependent endeavors. It may be assisted or facilitated by budget refinements, variable budgeting, the break-even analysis, or return-on-investment charting. Nonbudget control tools recently developed include: systems for management control through evaluation of key-result areas, management self-audit, American Institute of Management evaluation, or evaluation by outside consultants of control processes and managerial maneuvers.

Three types of control have generally been recognized: precontrol, concurrent, and postcontrol. When considered in view of time relationship to the event, they might be called *before, during,* and *after* controls.

Thirteen characteristics of an adequate control system were listed: (1) Controls must reflect the nature of the activity. (2) Controls should report deviations promptly. (3) Controls should focus on the future. (4) Controls should point up exceptions at critical points. (5) Controls should be objective. (6) Controls should be flexible. (7) Controls should reflect the organizational pattern. (8) Controls should be economical. (9) Controls should be understandable. (10) Controls should avoid obsolescence. (11) Controls should seek employee commitment. (12)) Controls should seek rapid feedback. (13) Controls should indicate corrective action.

Review Questions

1. What are the three basic steps in control?
2. Why is return on investment a more meaningful measure of financial success than profit?
3. Is ratio analysis an appropriate technique for an assembly-line operation? Explain.
4. What is key-area evaluation? What is its origin?
5. What is a management audit?
6. How can the basic control process be applied to a classroom study?
7. If a professor announces that her previous experience as a teacher indicates that approximately 10 per cent of the class will make *A's,* 20 per cent will make *B's,* 40 per cent will make *C's* and the remainder will make *D's* or below, what type of standard is she employing?
8. Theoretically, how could a class of students "engineer" grading standards on a typical assignment?
9. In December, O. W. Holmes, supersalesman, writes to the personnel manager in his firm: "So that you may have ample information to evaluate my performance, I am attaching a complete list of all the sales calls that I made during the past eighteen months. As you can see, no one could possibly have worked harder than I during this period of time." Evaluate this report from the standpoint of a sound control system.
10. In personnel administration, we learn that new employees are typically given more frequent performance appraisals than seasoned managers. From a control standpoint, why is this a sound procedure?
11. In planning budgets for the forthcoming year, some bureaucratic organizations merely increase the previous budget by 10 per cent. Discuss this procedure from a control standpoint.
12. Rent on Lucy Schneider's psychiatric office is $1.00 per month. She estimates that each emotionally disturbed patient uses up one penny's worth of

tissue. Her fees average 10¢ per patient. Construct a variable budget and estimate the break-even point of this activity.

13. Jack and Jill are each managers of large profit centers. Jack has earned a 20 per cent return on investment in his operation. Jill has earned 15 per cent. Yet the company president feels that Jill has done a better job. Using the General Electric control system, explain how this might be possible.

8

The People Problem – Personnel and Staffing

Dear Mr. Sanders:

Thank you for your letter of application for the position of Public Relations Director with our firm. Upon reviewing the résumé that you enclosed, we were very impressed by the variety and social significance of the positions you have held. We noted with interest your participation in politics and remember well your skillful handling of the successful campaigns of Senator Smithers and Congressman Clumpwater. We have nothing but admiration for your experience as a Peace Corps volunteer, and we remember your skillful arbitration of the national transportation strike and the effective advertising scheme that you developed for Consolidated Conglomerates, Inc. Many of our staff are regular readers of your articles on personnel procedures and innovations in business.

However, we are unable to consider you for the position at this time. The qualifications for the position specifically state that the director must hold at least a bachelor's degree from an accredited university. Because your record shows that you did drop out of college in your senior year, I fear we will not be able to consider you at this time.

> If you should complete your college work in the near future, please notify us so that we may reactivate your application file.
>
> Sincerely,
> Seymour Clod
> Personnel Counselor

There is no more critical activity in the manager's responsibility than staffing. After all is said and done, after all the systems and safeguards have been designed, an organization is only as strong as its people. Good people can make a poor plan succeed, but all the careful coaching in the world cannot produce success if the staff is unable or unwilling to carry the ball.

"I knew that coach was going to be a winner," commented a knowledgeable fan, "because the first thing he did was to build a coaching staff of players who were better than he was . . any one of them could have filled his job."

The coach to whom the fan referred had realized the importance of staffing.

Georges Doriot, former president of American Research and Development, is frequently quoted as saying, "Class A managers hire Class A people. Class B managers hire Class C people . . . so they won't feel threatened." Managers on the move hire people who will rise to the top —pushing them ever upward in the process. The staffing process is not one of filling positions and keeping secure. It is the manager's great opportunity to make a great leap forward. Consider the department head who commented, "The way the work is piling up, I can't take much time out to interview people for the vacant position in my department."

In spite of its importance, staffing is one of the most ignored and most poorly performed management functions. One of the reasons for staffing's low batting average is that it is almost entirely "people work" and is, therefore, harder than paperwork. The functions of evaluating people and their potentials are very hard to reduce to a chart of foolproof steps. Staffing decisions involve subjective judgments and intuitional decisions. After all the tests have been scored and the interviews concluded, the manager must decide on people—not percentile rankings. Organizations that have reduced the staffing procedure to computer decisions are destined to pass up power people, like the amazing Mr. Sanders in the prologue to this chapter.

Human Assets

Rensis Likert[1] asserts that human assets are even more valuable than physical assets and should be carried on the organization's balance sheet. After all, each productive employee represents a considerable investment in recruiting and training. Add to this the cost it would take to find, hire, and train someone else to do the same job and you can begin to see the significance of "human resource accounting." Likert goes so far as to argue that, in economic recessions, firms would be wiser to reduce inventories drastically and sell machinery than to dispose of their most important asset—people. You may not agree with Likert's position, but at least he does emphasize the importance of the staffing function.

After examining the experience of such companies as American Telephone and Telegraph and the R. G. Barry Corporation, which have implemented human resource accounting, James D. Powell, Henry A. Sciullo, and Gertrude Matteson (University of Nevada, Las Vegas) conclude that conflicts between the behavioral scientists who advocate this system and the financial specialists who must develop the necessary accounting documents have retarded acceptance of the technique. They suggest that the current programs have yielded organizational benefits and recommend that companies move cautiously in attempting to adopt human resource accounting.[2]

How does a company measure its people in order to place them alongside inanimate objects on the financial balance sheet? Two approaches seem most likely. One is the *cost approach*, by means of which the company endeavors to measure dollar investments offset by the maintenance of the current staff. It is a way of stating what it would cost the company to lose its staff.

The other approach is to obtain some estimated assessment of the current value of staff members. This is usually accomplished by establishing the individual's current dollar-and-cents value to the company and multiplying it by the number of years the worker is likely to have left in the work force. This approach tends to evaluate on the basis of what it would cost to replace current staff.

Almost everybody can agree with the concept that human elements are the company's most valuable asset. But the intricacies and uncertainties of translating intangible skills and unpredictable futures into definite numbers has thus far kept investigation into human resource accounting to a minimum.

During the past decade, several writers raised the question of a poten-

[1] Rensis Likert, *New Patterns of Organization* (New York: McGraw-Hill Book Company, 1961).
[2] "Human Resource Accounting: Why the Delay?" *Journal of Management*, Fall, 1976, pp. 25–31.

tial shortage of managerial talent. While quality has always been an uncertain commodity, the quantity of available managers has also been a concern. Arch Patton[3] has examined the problem and places the blame on the low birth rate of the thirties, the rapid expansion of corporate size in recent years, the growing complexity of the management task, and the demand on business managers by government and nonprofit organizations. People born during the post World War II baby boom are now beginning to move into management positions. Most of today's college students will find considerable competition for the management positions that become available throughout the next few years. Nevertheless, tremendous opportunity will always exist for the individual who has good training and is willing to work hard.

When the organizational lines have been drawn, the company has a skeleton. The process of staffing seeks to fill in the body around the skeleton. In any job-filling situation, the manager is adding either muscle or flab to the organizational skeleton. Strangely enough, many managers prefer to allow the personnel department to pick their employees. Managers who would not think of accepting a departmental budget without careful scrutiny will blindly accept any warm body that personnel sends up to help spend that budget.

Staffing Activities

Most organizations have a continuing need for new personnel when people change jobs, change companies, or retire. As any organization grows, it requires additional personnel. All new employees must be trained in order to be productive. They must be compensated for their services, or they will seek other employment. In order for them to be compensated fairly, their performance must be reasonably evaluated. And in order for performance to be evaluated, there needs to be a clear understanding of what is expected of them.

The details of these and many other personnel problems, such as administering employee benefits or checking to see that governmental requirements are met, can take almost the entire time of individual operating managers. Consequently, most large organizations assign the responsibility for personnel management to a separate department. This department usually operates with staff authority, advising and providing service to the rest of the organization in this important area. At the same time, each manager maintains considerable responsibility for the staffing functions.

[3] "The Coming Scramble For Executive Talent," *Harvard Business Review*, May, 1976, pp. 155–171.

The people factor tends to complicate the staffing job beyond the reach of checklist systems. Even so, there are some definite, easily recognized steps that should be taken in the staffing process. We will discuss the following steps briefly to give the student a feel for the orderly approach to staffing: (1) determination of needs, (2) selection and recruiting, (3) orientation and training, (4) performance appraisal, (5) compensation, (6) promotion, and (7) termination. These are not the "magic seven steps" of staffing. They are seven areas that should receive attention from the manager who has staffing opportunity.

1. Determination of Needs

Unfortunately, this logical first step, the determination of needs, is very often overlooked by those who are embarking on the staffing opportunity. As with many other management activities, we shoot first and hang up the target later.

After all our rhetoric about every job in the organization being critical and primary, the obvious truth is that we value some positions more than others. We pay more for them, and we take greater pains when it is time to fill them. In view of the wide divergence of importance we place on different jobs, we might expect to find a great deal of work already done in this field, but not so.

Several workable approaches to the evaluation of jobs have been presented, but most of them are waiting for a serious manager shortage to bring them to the top of the priority list. Remember as you read this section that we are talking about evaluating jobs rather than the people who fill these jobs. In a later section, we will discuss the challenge of evaluating people and their performance.

The *comparison method* of evaluating positions that managers fill is basically a subjective guesswork approach. The "known" salaries of top management in the same company, and the "going price" for similar positions throughout the industry are balanced in the mind of the evaluating manager to arrive at a comparative value figure.

The *job-factor* method is more involved and objective but still owes a major debt to the subjective judgment of the evaluator. This approach assigns mathematical difficulty factors to each job or position. This technique has been used for years at the lower level jobs, and has resulted in phenomena such as overtime, "dirt money," and combat pay. However, it is still not widely applied in the upper echelons because the assignment of pay-worthy difficulties pits one evaluator's guess against another's. *Every* manager assumes his or her problems to be the most insurmountable.

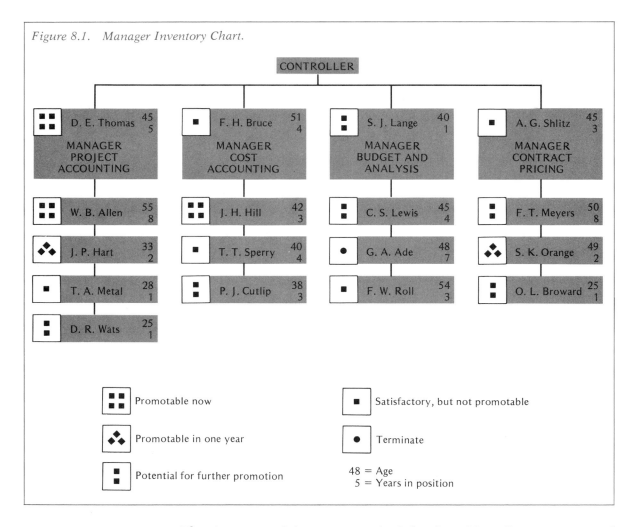

Figure 8.1. Manager Inventory Chart.

The *time-span of discretion* method developed by Elliott Jagues is of great interest. Jagues' efforts to find a *truly* measurable factor to evaluate by have produced the idea that *the longer it takes for a person's shoddy work to surface, the more important his position must be*. Jagues said it more formally:

> The longest period which can elapse in a role before the manager can be sure that his subordinate has not been exercising marginally sub-standard discretion continuously in balancing the pace and the quality of his work.[4]

Jagues' attempt to reach an objective measurement criterion appears to be the most promising yet in this young field of study.

An inventory chart, like the one shown in Figure 8.1, should exist in the desk drawer of every manager with any say so about corporate promotions. It is not the kind of chart that should be on the wall or in the

[4] *Equitable Payment* (New York: John Wiley & Sons, Inc., 1961).

company newsletter, but the frank, honest evaluation of staff promotability needs to be put down in black and white, and not exist merely as a vague feeling in the manager's mind.

The drawing of the organizational chart should certainly involve more than artwork. All those involved should have input in the establishment of the way problems will be approached and the kinds of people and positions that will provide the optimum goal-reaching capability. We might look with skepticism upon the beginning company that "borrowed" the organizational arrangement of some other company because it seemed to work before. Each position should be undeniably necessary. In fact, once the organizational chart is drawn, some time should be given to removing each position one at a time and tracing the systems again. If the company's goal can still be accomplished over the long run, then serious doubt should arise about the necessity of that position. Unless the operation is crippled by the removal of a position, the position should not exist.

The Pepsi-Cola Company has developed an extremely concise and complete method of charting the varying components of positions in their bottling operations. All jobs are placed in rank order from low to high based on management's judgment of importance and complexity and contribution toward company goals. Five categories (knowledge, skill, scope and impact, relationships, and direction over others) are subdivided and scored. The resulting scores provide concrete evidence of job values to the company. Probably for the first time in history there is a reasoned answer to the age-old question, "How come they get more for *sitting* in an air-conditioned office than I get for *working* out here in the sun?"

Job specifications should list guidelines of the education, the ability, and the minimum personal qualities required of the people who will fill the jobs. Such guidelines, however, should never be allowed to harden into concrete, bureaucratic laws that would cost the company an applicant who is qualified and capable but deficient under the letter of the law. It is far better for job descriptions to stress skills and performance criteria rather than personality, experience, and education. These latter factors are useful only if they contribute to performance in a specific way. For example, possession of a college degree is far less important than the ability to read and understand complex reports and directives. Yet it is easier to recognize the completion of a collegiate program than to measure the ability or knowledge that education should provide.

When guidelines regarding qualifications, duties, and responsibilities have been spelled out, the whole staffing task moves into a different dimension. It may seem casual and sophisticated for a recruiter to say, "We want you on our team. There's no telling what we'll ask you to do, but we've got a great bunch to work with. We want people who are ready for anything!" This type of statement can be made only when pro-

Table 8.1
Point Scale
"Pepsi Cola Job
Evaluation"

	Points	
125 A. "Knowledge"	(60)	Education: Some H.S.: 15 pts.; H.S. grad: 30 pts.; some college: 45 pts.; college grad: 60 pts.
	(65)	Experience: 0–1 yr.: 10 pts.; 1–2 yrs.: 20 pts.; 3–4 yrs.; 30 pts.; 4–5 yrs.: 50 pts.; over 5 yrs.: 65 pts.
150 B. "Skill"	(50)	Creativity: None required: 0 pts.; minimal: 10 pts.; medium (empl. should do some thinking): 15 pts.; considerable (job requires many new ideas, etc.): 25 pts.; significantly high (job depends on it): 50 pts.
	(50)	Judgment: Same as above.
	(50)	Foresight: Same as above.
75 C. "Scope and Impact"	(25)	Effect on sales/total business: minimal: 0 pts.; medium: 10 pts.; considerable: 15 pts.; significant: 20 pts.; highly significant: 25 pts.
	(25)	Effect on decisions: Same as above.
	(25)	Company commitments: Can't make any: 0 pts.; plays advisory-indirect role: 13 pts. ($ contracts, etc.); makes commitments: 18 pts. (under $2,000); makes significant commitments: 25 pts. (over $2,000).
75 D. "Relationships" (job coordination operational needs, etc.)	(30)	Internal: None: 0 pts.; other jobs at low level: 10 pts.; middle mgmt. level: 20 pts.; top mgmt.: 30 pts.
	(45)	
	(45)	External: Same as above. (outside co.'s–services–suppliers, etc.)
75 E. "Direction Over Others"	(50)	Direct: None: 0 pts.; minimal, 2 to 5 empls.: 8 pts.; average, 6 to 12 empls.: 14 pts.; aver. plus, up to 25 empls.: 20 pts.; significant, less than 100 empls.: 35 pts.; highly significant, over 100 empls.: 50 pts.
	(25)	Functional: Same as above, but points reduced by one half. (indirect)

500 pts.

spective managers are being hired for their potential rather than their ability to do anything at the moment.

One of the most common causes of job dissatisfaction is uncertainty about what is expected. A job description is no infallible document but it's a mighty secure foundation upon which to recruit and build a job.

In determining needs, it is also necessary to determine the *number* of managers needed and project the *dates* they will be needed. By looking at those who are currently employed, management can to some degree

Table 8.2.   A point System for Job Evaluation

Rate each job using the following job factors, assigning points by picking the statement that most closely describes the requirements for the job.

Points

Job Factors	0	2	4	6	8	10
1. Details to be organized	Few details; little organizing	Well-routinized	Varied work with some need for organizing	Numerous details; organize work of others	Many details that cause problems	Cannot be routinized
2. Supervision of others	None	Two subordinates with routine duties	Small group doing individual work	Large group in routine tasks	Several groups with varied work assignments	Important work that requires individual attention
3. Education and experience needed	High school education; average intelligence; no experience	Minor special training; e.g., typing, operating simple machines	Experience in lower level job; post high school courses	Knowledge of special field	Thorough knowledge;	Knowledge of several fields
4. Time required for training	Very little	One month	Three months	Six months	One year	Two years or longer
5. Resourcefulness	Very little	Requires little interpretation	Independent thinking at intervals	Independent thinking regularly	Much initiative and thought	New issues faced constantly
6. Personality required for dealing with others	Rarely in contact with others	Contact with small group	Contacts with public on routine basis	Employees; customers, public on routine basis	Major contacts with key customers, employees	Ability to get along with others most important
7. Responsibility required	Work under direct supervision of another	Any failure noticed immediately	Handles cash and payrolls; audited frequently	No close check by superior	Responsibility for expensive equipment and large funds	High dedication and trust required

163

ascertain who will be available three or five years in the future. By comparing the present picture with the ideal organizational chart, management might also see the value of reorganization or creation of new positions. When the available in-house personnel have been promoted as far up the line as they should go, it is time to go out and find some new blood. The boundaries and goal posts have been set up, and it is time for the staffing game to begin. The recruiters go forth to find the new talent.

2. Selection and Recruiting

It may, at first glance, seem strange to mention selection first and recruiting second. Selection, however, involves more than picking names from a list of potential employees. A great deal of the selection process is included in the careful description of organizational needs and the delineation of job qualifications. Beyond this, the knowledgeable recruiter will establish in advance the methods of selection to be used. If selection methods are not consciously preset, it is likely that the manager will fall into one of three common traps or selection fallacies.

First, managers may make no provision at all for selection. That is, they do not seek to build a continuing strength into their management force. They ignore the problem and then suddenly wake up one morning to realize that their entire management staff is over sixty or all demanding simultaneous promotion. The top-notch manager has done some careful charting of subordinates. They have been lined up according to age, years of service, and promotability. The manager is like the wise forester who realizes what trees he must plant every year if there is to be a continuing harvest in the future.

Another common pitfall of selection is to assume that "somebody will come along at the right time." This is the kind of slipshod, catch-as-catch-can approach to management that puts feebleminded in-laws in positions of responsibility because they picked the right person for marriage. It is irresponsible to assume that the next person up will be right for a highly specialized task of management. However, the businessperson who picks managers on a "who's available" basis probably has even more serious problems lurking around the corner, for this philosophy of planning is of questionable value.

Many managers in the recruiting situation like to depend on their own personal judgment. They are not swayed by past histories or all this newfangled psychological testing! They can tell by just talking with the candidate whether he or she is right for the job—nonsense! Scientific indicators must not be blindly trusted, but neither should human impressions. The characteristic remark of the personal impression se-

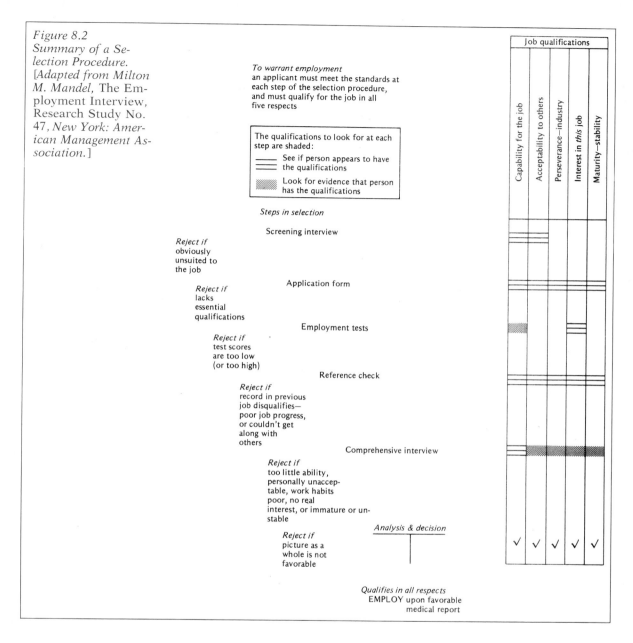

Figure 8.2
Summary of a Selection Procedure.
[Adapted from Milton M. Mandel, The Employment Interview, *Research Study No. 47, New York: American Management Association.]*

To warrant employment
an applicant must meet the standards at
each step of the selection procedure,
and must qualify for the job in all
five respects

The qualifications to look for at each
step are shaded:
——— See if person appears to have
——— the qualifications
▓▓▓ Look for evidence that person
has the qualifications

Job qualifications

Capability for the job
Acceptability to others
Perseverance—industry
Interest in *this* job
Maturity—stability

Steps in selection

Screening interview

Reject if
obviously
unsuited to
the job

Application form

Reject if
lacks
essential
qualifications

Employment tests

Reject if
test scores
are too low
(or too high)

Reference check

Reject if
record in previous
job disqualifies—
poor job progress,
or couldn't get
along with
others

Comprehensive interview

Reject if
too little ability,
personally unaccep-
table, work habits
poor, no real
interest, or immature or un-
stable

Analysis & decision

Reject if
picture as a
whole is not
favorable

√ √ √ √ √

Qualifies in all respects
EMPLOY upon favorable
medical report

lector might be, "I knew that kid was right for the job the moment I laid eyes on him—reminds me of myself at that age!"

The approach to selection should be established at the outset. As time goes on and the enterprise gains experience in its selection process and recruiting and training techniques, it will probably be able to improve and narrow the ratio between the number of selectees and the number of possible openings. Larger and more experienced companies will take the long view of recruiting. They will recruit regardless of economic or political fluctuations. They realize that sporadic hiring of outstanding young prospective managers can sooner or later show up in a poorly balanced age distribution among executives. Therefore, it is wise for a company to set up and stick to a regular recruiting program. In fact, in one sense, it might be said that when things are going badly, recruiting is more important than ever.

The Recruiting Process

The first step in the recruiting process is *screening*. This may take place when the firm's recruiting officer visits university campuses to interview potential candidates. It is extremely important that the recruiting officer be more than an errand runner. Being able to tell the story of the company is important, but far more crucial is the recruiter's understanding of the kind of material the company is seeking. A well-qualified recruiter will develop valuable relationships between the company and the placement counselor and business professors of the college. Clear communication with those who know the applicant's daily performance is one of the most meaningful resources for the selection process.

There are always certain minimum requirements unique to a firm. A good recruiter should be able to eliminate, quickly and accurately, candidates who do not fulfill those requirements. The sooner he spots applicant deficiencies, the better for all concerned—both company and applicant.

Although the specific requirements vary from company to company, almost all companies make specific age rules. This is not because of discrimination against older people. Rather, the companies realize that it takes time to make a manager—even from promising stock. If the applicant is approximately twenty-five to twenty-eight years old, this means that at the age of forty-five or forty-eight he could, theoretically, step into a top executive position and still render the firm approximately twenty years of service before retirement at age sixty-five. Therefore, the upper age limit that most enterprises usually set for management trainees is about twenty-five to thirty.

Writing Right Résumés

The résumé is a job-getting requirement that is often shortchanged by beginning job seekers. The résumé should be thought of as an assist to the interviewer. Putting it together is more than writing down all the facts and figures of one's experience. It is an opportunity to demonstrate for a potential employer the manner in which the prospect can communicate and perform. In writing a résumé, endeavor to see things through the eyes of the interviewer. Emphasize the points that are interesting and significant, but don't clutter the résumé with things that are important to you but meaningless to the interviewer. Be concise—the interviewer is probably going to read this résumé while you are fidgeting. Make it simple. Make it clear. Make it interesting, and, by all means, *remake* your résumé if an interview demonstrates that some point is particularly distracting or confusing.

The recruiter will try to read between the lines when talking to an applicant. In the interview situation, one can often discover significant aspects of personal attitude, drive, initiative, and common sense. If all systems are go, the recruiter will encourage the applicant to become an active candidate for the company's training program. They will discuss starting salaries, benefits, and opportunities for advancement. At this point, the recruiter is walking a dangerous tightrope. The challenge is to sell the company but not oversell it. An oversold employee could soon become dissatisfied once the honeymoon is over and the new job becomes deadeningly daily.

After the résumé obstacle is overcome, the next trauma for the fearful job searcher is the interview. Actually, both the résumé and the interviews should be viewed positively by most people. Instead of worrying because the perfect qualifications cannot be honestly included in the résumé, the applicant should look forward to the interview as an opportunity to show that he or she is *more* valuable than the on-paper version.

It is equally important for the applicant to remember that the interview has value in both directions. It is far better to be disappointed in a job's failure to match up to you . . . than to *get* the job and regret it for many years. The prospect of being rejected is frightening, but it should be seen as an asset when you are rejected from a job you really ought not to have. The only thing worse than "not getting the job" is "getting it . . . and wishing you hadn't."

Interviewer's Rating Scale

1. APPEARANCE: dress, grooming, bearing, health
2. MANNER: poise, self-confidence, executive stature
3. VOICE AND EXPRESSION: clarity, grammar, modulation
4. ORGANIZATION: ability to present case logically and get to point quickly
5. EXPERIENCE: kind of work, indication of interest, ability and leadership, accomplishments
6. REACTIONS: alertness, quickness of responses
7. FORCE OF DRIVE: ability to stimulate others, self-assurance
8. INTELLIGENCE: reasoning ability, smartness, keenness
9. SENSITIVITY: social sensitivity, "good with people"
10. INTEREST: sincerity of ambitions and objectives

NAME

Permanent Address
Chickasha, Oklahoma 73018
Telephone: 405–224–4047

Temporary Address
800 Boyce Avenue
Telephone: 415–328–0423

Job Objective	A position of responsibility in the area of personnel and staffing.
Education	Stanson University, Paloma, California. Candidate for B.A. degree in June, 1983, with 3.4 average. Major in business, minor in economics. For senior year, chosen as one of four student interns in psychology department to teach, grade exams, tutor. Participated in research project (published) with two professors. Financed expenses by part-time work, partial university scholarship.
Summer and Part-Time Work	Last summer, saw industrial side of management by assisting in maintenance of inventories for meat by-products division of major meat wholesale company—processed orders, routed truck logistics. During previous two summers, was stringer for local city newspaper, and did supervisory work for education/training program for inner-city counselors in Los Angeles. For several years, worked part-time for university's placement office to successfully present "career orientation" workshops on campus. In high school and college, tutored students in English, mathematics, other subjects.
Personal Background	Salutatorian in high school, vice president of senior class. Active in school and community service clubs. Member of Student Council, debate and swimming teams. Spent junior year as exchange student at a high school in Canberra, Australia, where developed interest in personnel relations from living with a family whose head was director of executive training at a computer firm.
Hobbies	Coin collector, water skier, travel enthusiast.
References	Transcripts, references, and previous employer evaluation furnished upon request.

Source: Adapted from College Placement Annual, 1980, p 20.

It would be extremely short-sighted to sign contracts after campus interviews. The normal procedure is to advance a successful campus interviewee to a series of home office interviews. Although these interviews are usually supervised by the officer in charge of the training program, a number of corporate executives should be included. It is very important that the prospective boss of the applicant and some of

---

PREPARATIONS FOR THE INTERVIEW

Guidelines

Physical

Women:
- Fully rested
- Appropriate and becoming dress
- Careful grooming
- Clean hair, simple style
- Nails well manicured
- Minimum of jewelry

Men:
- Fully rested
- Clean, well-pressed suit
- Fresh shirt
- Conservative tie
- Hair trimmed
- Nails clean
- Close shave

Mental

- Be familiar with all information on your résumé
- Be prepared to complete an application blank
- Be prepared to take skills and aptitude tests
- Be prepared to answer the following questions:
  - What position are you applying for?
  - What experience have you had?
  - What school subjects did you like?
  - What do you do in your free time?
  - Why do you want to work for this company?
  - Would you work overtime?
  - What foreign languages do you speak?
  - What salary would you expect?
  - Do you have any marriage plans?
  - Do you want to continue your education?

What should you take with you to the interview? You may find it helpful to have a loose-leaf notebook with samples of your work and proficiency certificates for typing, transcription and shorthand, filing, and bookeeping. Be sure to have:

Copies of your résumé (at least two).
Social Security Card or number
Proof of age

Letters of recommendation from employers and instructors or list of references. Always be prepared to take a preemployment test. Take along a good pen, pencil, eraser, eraser shield, pocket dictionary, and a clean notebook. These can be carried in a plastic case or a clean manilla envelope.

---

the staff interview the candidate. *And* interviews should definitely go beyond the small-talk stage.

The final selection decision should be based upon a discussion that includes those who have interviewed the candidate. This final confer-

---

CHECKLIST FOR JOB APPLICANTS

According to a study of 153 companies, the following negative characteristics are frequently responsible for rejection of a job applicant. Such a list also serves to outline what businessmen are looking for when they hire a new employee.*

1. Poor personal appearance.
2. Overbearing, overaggressive—"knows it all."
3. Unable to express oneself clearly—poor voice, grammar.
4. Has not planned for career—no purpose and goals.
5. Lacks interest and enthusiasm—passive, indifferent.
6. Lacks confidence and poise—nervous, ill at ease.
7. Fails to participate in activities.
8. Overemphasized money—interested only in best dollar offer.
9. Poor scholastic record—just got by.
10. Unwilling to start at the bottom—expects too much too soon.
11. Makes excuses—hedges on unfavorable factors in record.
12. Lacks tact.
13. Lacks maturity.
14. Lacks courtesy—ill mannered.
15. Lacks social understanding.
16. Shows marked dislike for schoolwork.
17. Fails to look interviewer in the eye.
18. Limp handshake.
19. Indecisive.
20. Sloppy application blank.
21. Late to interview without good reason.

* These lists were provided by Professor Betty Anderson of Memphis State University.

---

ence is no time for "being nice" or overlooking concerns. A large amount of heartache and money can be saved if it is determined that the new applicant is not quite right for the position.

3. Orientation and Training

The word *orientation* is commonly used in our day to describe a period of introduction. The original implication of the word was to show the newcomer which way was east—or toward the Orient. During orientation we align the newcomer's compass with the old hands' compasses—we get our easts and wests and norths and souths synchronized. Or, in the language of our times, we show the new employee which way is up.

Some of the orientation experience may wisely be included in the interview and selection phases. Interviewers will want to observe closely the ease or difficulty with which the initiate grasps the big ideas of the company. For the most part, orientation includes few things more top secret than data about holidays and vacations.

Most organizations provide an official orientation session. Either a classroom lecture, a movie, or a group conference is used by a member of the personnel department. In many cases, the company puts its worst foot forward—like the television network that conducted its orientation entirely by the lecture method!

Whatever the method, the following types of subjects are usually covered:

1. Company history, products, and major operations.
2. General company policies and regulations.
3. Relation of foremen and personnel department.
4. Rules and regulations regarding:
   a. Wages and wage payment.
   b. Hours of work and overtime.
   c. Safety and accidents.
   d. Holidays and vacations.
   e. Methods of reporting tardiness and absences.
   f. Discipline and grievances.
   g. Uniforms and badges.
   h. Parking.
5. Economic and recreational services available:
   a. Insurance plans.
   b. Pensions.
   c. Athletic and social activities.
6. Opportunities:
   a. Promotion and transfer.
   b. Job stabilization.
   c. Suggestion systems.

Of course, very little of this information can be retained by the new employee. The real purpose is overview, introduction . . . orientation. It should be said that the company's orientation program is only a gesture. The real orientation depends on the personal ambition of the new employee. The wise person comes into the company making friends at every level and asking questions of all. Perhaps more relevant orientation takes place on coffee breaks than in all the personnel presentations that will ever be produced. One company, realizing this, arranged its orientation on a roving conversation basis—providing the newcomer with a schedule of appointments for informal discussion with workers and managers in every phase of the operation.

In chapter 15, we will look at the task of training workers. It will suffice to say at this point that in employee training, as in all education, we learn by experience and there are some lessons that only time can teach.

When some mechanical or physical skill is being taught—or even if the complicated skills of management are involved—the only way we teach effectively is to give the learner the experience . . . actually, in simulation, or vicariously.

4. Performance Appraisal

In 1800, Robert Owen[5] (who was introduced in Chapter 3) used what he called character books and blocks to appraise his workers in his New Lanark cotton mills in Scotland. The character books recorded each worker's daily reports of production. The character blocks were displayed at each worker's work station and showed different colors to demonstrate the worker's values from bad to good. We might be concerned about bruised egos in the plants, but Robert Owen was quite impressed by the way the blocks improved the workers' behavior.

Whether it be colored blocks above the work station or a gold star on the chart, performance appraisal is here to stay. Nobody likes grades in school and many people object to performance appraisal at work, but some method must be used to measure progress . . . and the lack of progress. From management's point of view, appraisal is necessary in order to (1) allocate resources, (2) reward employees, (3) provide feedback for workers, and (4) maintain fair relationships and communication bonds.

The hallmarks of modern appraisal philosophy are (1) performance orientation—to make workers aware of the mistakes they are making; (2) focus on goals—to wake them up to the kind of potential they should be achieving; and (3) mutual goal setting—to make sure they see mistakes as a personal problem. More positively, the idea might be stated as an attempt to focus on goals and objective accomplishment.

In our age of mass communications, it seems that everyone is an amateur psychiatrist. This can be one of the most dangerous factors in the performance appraisal. Unless the manager has the employee's progress in mind, he or she can do irreparable damage. Mature managers think of the performance appraisal as a chance to discuss openly the employee's progress and possible avenues for improvement. Immature managers approach the appraisal session as a long-awaited chance to unload on the subordinate all the ill will and irritation the manager has stored up.

In order to reduce threats during performance appraisal, a number of firms separate the appraisal program from wage increase interviews. The two programs can put the manager into conflicting roles when they

[5] *The Life of Robert Owen* (New York: Alfred A. Knopf, Inc., 1920), pp. 111–112.

are operated together. It is difficult to act in the role of counselor for improved performance while at the same time presiding as judge over the employee's salary increase. Still, this is the most common procedure.

Management By Objectives

One of the most important concepts to arise from the performance appraisal is the idea of management by objectives. MBO was probably first developed by a manager who was tired of evaluation systems like the one shown in Figure 8.3. Instead of grading employees on the basis of whether or not they are "honest, loyal, and true," the manager establishes an objective and clearly communicates it to the subordinate. If the objective is accomplished, the worker is judged to be a success. It is a simple, direct approach to performance. Its only problem is that it

Figure 8.3. Guide to Employee Performance Appraisal.

GUIDE TO EMPLOYEE PERFORMANCE APPRAISAL
PERFORMANCE DEGREES

Performance Factors	FAR EXCEEDS JOB REQUIREMENTS (1)	EXCEEDS JOB REQUIREMENTS (2)	MEETS JOB REQUIREMENTS (3)	NEEDS SOME IMPROVEMENT (4)	DOES NOT MEET MINIMUM REQUIREMENTS (5)
QUALITY	Leaps tall buildings with a single bound	Must take running start to leap over tall buildings	Can only leap over a short building or medium with no spires	Crashes into buildings when attempting to jump over them	Cannot recognize buildings at all, much less jump
TIMELINESS	Is faster than a speeding bullet	Is as fast as a speeding bullet	Not quite as fast as a speeding bullet	Would you believe a slow bullet?	Wounds self with bullets when attempting to shoot gun
INITIATIVE	Is stronger than a locomotive	Is stronger than a bull elephant	Is stronger than a bull	Shoots the bull	Smells like a bull
ADAPTABILITY	Walks on water consistently	Walks on water in emergencies	Washes with water	Drinks water	Passes water in emergencies
COMMUNICATION	Talks with God	Talks with the Angels	Talks to himself	Argues with himself	Loses those arguments

goes counter to most of our preconceptions about the use of employee time. If we see one worker busily slaving away with sleeves rolled up and breathing heavily . . . we naturally assume that this means dedication and a high evaluation. On the other hand, the employee who appears to be relaxing with feet up on the desk is frowned upon. Such judgments make no consideration of production. Yet if we really stop and think about it, why should we care how the worker *looks?* What we should be interested in is how the worker *works* . . . or what kind of results he obtains. By the same reasoning, the boss might say, "Don't give me gold-plated reasons for your heroic failure—I'll be happy with clumsy, unheroic success."

When the performance appraisal can be shifted to and built on the concept of management by objectives, the emphasis has moved to the real goal. Managers will have to be clear, concise, and specific about what they want. Employees will know exactly what is expected of them. And the performance evaluation will be removed from the personal platform. It will be obvious to manager and subordinate if the objective has been reached—the job goal of this dialogue is an exchange of intelligence instead of an exchange of ignorance. Regular, continual feedback is essential if performance appraisal is to be anything other than an annual ceremony. If objectives have been adequately identified, there will be few surprises at the appraisal interview. In important relationships, feedback is provided regularly. Can you imagine one spouse saying to another, "My dear, I see you have been with me for five years. Now, there are a few things about your performance that I would like to dis-

Figure 8.4
Which worker would
you give the higher
performance rating?

cuss with you." The chances are that there would be a resignation before time came for the next appraisal.

The performance appraisal can be a great asset. Or if the manager waters down the evaluation, its significance, or the impact of the employee's input, it can become routine and meaningless drudgery. The fact is that performance *is* going to be appraised, whether formally or informally. It is up to the manager to make the experience meaningful and beneficial.

5. Compensation

It is almost impossible for us to imagine a society in which income is guaranteed regardless of effort. Our entire system of private enterprise is predicated on the premise that people should be paid or rewarded in accordance with what they produce or what risk they take. Although there are forces that work against this concept, we are accustomed to making financial considerations major in our employment planning. Even those who recognize that many things are more important than money eventually discover an undeniable status value in income. Pay is a unique incentive—unique because it can satisfy both the lower order of psychological and security needs and also the higher needs for esteem and recognition.

About 25 per cent of workers in manufacturing work under incentive plans.[6] The main reason for the use of wage incentives is clear: they nearly always increase productivity while decreasing labor costs per manufactured unit. Workers under normal conditions without wage incentives have the capacity to produce more. Wage incentives are one way to release that potential.

The increased productivity brought about by wage alterations can be amazing. Some industries have shown increases of over 100 per cent. It should be admitted that incentive results may also reflect the extra planning and interest when studies are being conducted. Nevertheless, there is no way of arguing with the logic of some brilliant but unknown ancient philosopher who said, "Money talks!" If compensation is a major motivation of any given worker, it stands to reason that a worker's motivation can be proportionately increased if the compensation is increased. When there are many other factors that affect the performance of workers, incentive programs may be a mixed blessing—especially in cases where they have been hastily conceived or poorly implemented.

[6] Keith Davis, *Human Relations at Work*, 4th ed. (New York: McGraw-Hill Book Company, 1972), p. 480.

If the carrot held before the donkey results in movement and bonus plans cause production workers to produce faster, how powerful can compensation be as a staffing and performance factor with managers? The chapter on motivation also discusses the impact of money on the performance of managers and workers. Obviously, there is a quantity-quality variable between production and management. The assembly-line worker is generally judged on *whether* the job is done. The manager's success, on the other hand, is measured more in *how well* challenges are met—often in relation to an abstract standard. There-fore, the principle of supply and demand is very much in operation in the selecting and hiring of the manager. These more subtle skills make managers more costly. And, by the same token, the subtlety of these abilities makes managers even more difficult to compensate and moti-vate with money alone.

The Compensation Cafeteria

The selection of forms of compensation for managers is a major enter-prise decision because it must satisfy the interests of both employee and employer. The employee needs cash income, protection of earning power, a chance to accumulate an estate, and financial security after re-tirement. The enterprise does its best to meet and enhance these differ-ent forms of compensation. Qualified managers must be attracted and retained. Still, the profits of the company cannot be totally sacrificed for the building and maintenance of a showcase staff. Thus, the delicate balance: enough compensation to motivate, but not to spoil!

Companies have developed some very complicated forms of executive compensation. One small company had its owner-president on a $150-a-month salary . . . and an unlimited expense account, including use of a company house and company cars. Other companies have ridden the fringe benefit heavily because executives may prefer increased taxfree services to increased taxable income. Cash income to meet current needs, fringe benefits, group insurance, bonus plans, stock options, and pension and retirement pay must all be added up to determine the "pay" any given manager is receiving. It is not surprising to see compa-nies picking up the tab for club memberships, haircuts, and certain other expenses—where this can be handled without Internal Revenue Service objection.

The relationships between incentive systems and organizational be-havior is both important and complicated. Many questions must be considered. What compensation should be paid? What strings should be attached? In what form should compensation be paid? What gradations are justified? Does seniority automatically deserve increased pay? How do we equate experience and training when setting salary scales or ranges?

Large, publicly owned firms are adopting staggeringly complicated mixtures of compensation methodology. Individual proprietorships and institutional enterprises must be more limited in their methods. In any case, superior managers must be cognizant of the variety of forms in use. And in many cases they will need to create innovative ways of getting and keeping quality staff.

6. Promotion

Advancement to a higher position is one of the most familiar forms of compensation. Usually promotion involves increased pay. Even so, there are many appealing things about promotion that have nothing to do with money. The social, psychological, and personal gratifications that are inherent in promotion can be very meaningful to any worker. A promotion is a direct form of praise—it says, "You have done such a fine job at your present position that we know you will meet this new challenge equally well."

Promotion from within is a term that has come into general use in the last fifty years. Its sound is much more attractive than its reality. The idea suggested by promotion from within is that "This company takes care of its own—stick with us and work hard and you can go all the way to the top." The fallacies of this theory lie in the fact that all people do not possess equal talent for management. The same principle would be in operation if a baseball coach announced the pitchers would be chosen only from among those who had played all the other positions. What kind of proficiency would be built if all rookies went to the outfield, then worked their way up to the infield, eventually became catcher, and finally pitcher? Different skills demand that specialists be brought in. On the other hand, a policy of *no promotion from within* could be equally shortsighted.

The fact is that many organizations that make loud noises about their promotion-from-within policies always maintain an escape clause. The magic words in the policy statement are usually "whenever possible" or "unless we have no one who can qualify." These loopholes allow management the personnel advantage of promotion from within and the realistic opportunity to hire from the outside.

There are many problems in promotion. First of all is the sometimes fallacious assumption that because a worker does one thing well he or she can automatically do the next thing well. The popular Peter Principle[7] is demonstrated many times daily by people who *had to be* pro-

---

[7] This concept was popularized by Lawrence Peter and Raymond Hull, *The Peter Principle: Why Things Go Wrong* (New York: William Morrow & Co., Inc., 1969). It is suggested that in most organizations people are promoted until they reach the level of their incompetence. Peter suggests that greater efficiency could be achieved if everyone in the country were demoted one level. He argues that everyone would then be operating at their top level of competence.

moted. In many cases the demand for more money, prestige, or recognition has propelled workers into positions they do not enjoy or cannot do well. Equally dangerous are the celebrated moves from labor to management, player to coach, teacher to administrator, or enlisted person to officer.

Almost everybody *wants* a promotion . . . but not everybody *needs* or deserves a promotion.

7. Termination

The final promotion takes the worker right out of the firm. Retirement is the arrangement by which the employee earns the right not to work after a certain age. Theoretically, the salary received in the form of retirement payments is money earned during productive years and set aside for deferred payment during the "golden years." It is to be hoped that advancing technology can deal with this problem in a more innova-

Albert Schweitzer (The Bettman Archive). How can you tell when it's time for such a person to retire?

tive way than we have in the past. The crying need is for people to be dealt with on an individual basis. Perhaps retirement criteria can be changed from chronological age to some more meaningful measure. Obviously, different people are ready to retire at different ages and some people are never ready to retire. There are many questions to be answered in this area. Our past performance has proved shortsighted and in many cases . . . heartless. Hopefully, the future holds many valuable and humanitarian innovations regarding the length and quality of work years.

Mobile Managers

More and more workers are working for more and more companies more and more. The mobility of our society has made the resignation a common occurrence. Eugene Jennings has characterized the current generation of rising executives as the mobile managers[8] because the average tenure of college graduates has dropped so dramatically. Occasionally, the letter of resignation is used as a lever to bring about some desired change or to focus attention on some serious wrong. More often, the sentiment expressed is one of "With regret, I must move on to greener pastures." Although high turnover is a legitimate reason for concern and investigation, a resignation should not be thought of as a desertion or a knife in the back. If the employee leaves as an enemy of the company, it is good riddance. This is better than keeping an enemy on the payroll. If the departure is friendly . . . what company doesn't need more friends among its competitors? For years, IBM has smiled over its claim to have trained and launched many of the pioneers in the computer software field. Evidently, IBM has been able to weather the storms and grow because of its contribution to the entire field.

Dismissal is the unhappiest form of termination. Whether it comes through layoff (because the company's not making it) or through firing (because the worker's not making it), dismissal is a sad affair. On the more optimistic side, there are probably innumerable success stories that started when a dismissal shook loose a creative personality from a static position. Sometimes the best thing that can happen to a person is to be "fired with ambition."

Unions

The activities of labor unions are well known to any citizen who pays average attention to the newspaper. We are accustomed to the easy use of terms like *union leader*, *strike*, and *collective bargaining*. The person in

[8] Eugene Jennings, *The Mobile Manager* (New York: McGraw-Hill Book Company, 1967).

the street probably has fairly definite opinions about labor unions. Usually these opinions depend upon whether he or she has most recently crossed the path of union corruption or union benevolence. The concept of the labor union is certainly not a wishy-washy topic with most folks—they either love the union idea or loathe it.

Interestingly enough, something quite different exists in the labor situation than most people are aware of. As the theory goes, the bad old business is giving the poor workers the short end of the deal. So the workers band together for strength and bargain for what they want. Actually, the bargaining is not between labor and management. It is really between the business *managers* and the labor *managers*. In the effort to accomplish their goals labor has taken on a second set of managers to deal with.

Double Jeopardy?

When there are two sets of managers taking care of the works, they have twice as many chances at everything. There is double potential for fair treatment, double potential for being abused, and an even higher probability that the ultimate agreement will be fair to the worker. It is interesting to reflect upon the possibility that any two students reading this book (or any other management text) may some day find themselves on opposite sides of the negotiating table. The principles of effective management are not limited to a good-guys-bad-guys arrangement. The principles of effective management are equally important to the person who manages a cheese factory and to the person who represents the cheesemaker's local in negotiations with the big cheese.

The historic role of unions was to balance the economic power of the employer. The employees, through their elected representatives, negotiate the terms of employment with company officials. The agreement thus reached by "equals" becomes the accepted mode of conduct between the parties for a contracted period of time.

The union is much more than an economic institution. It has political characteristics, seeking to use its political power and public opinion to accomplish its goals. Even collective bargaining is a more complicated concept than it appears on the surface. Broadly speaking, *collective bargaining* refers to a process by which employers and employee representatives attempt to arrive at agreements governing the conditions under which employees will contribute and be compensated for their services.

Labor History

Labor unions have existed in the United States since the Revolutionary War. However, it has only been in the last eighty or ninety years that the union movement has had any muscles to flex. The American Federation of Labor (AFL) was formed in 1886. This group grew to the point where in the early 1930's it was *the* labor organization in the country. Internal conflicts occurred, and in 1935 a number of unions — primarily the unskilled workers and miners — dropped out of the AFL to form their own group, which they named the Congress of Industrial Organizations.

In 1955 the two got back together. The unions reunited and took the name American Federation of Labor — Congress of Industrial Organizations. The name was a little hefty for tattooing on the members' chests, and it is generally shortened to the AFL — CIO. Present estimates place U.S. union membership at a little less than one quarter of the working force.

Labor Legislation

The reason for union growth can be seen in large part in terms of legal strength. Until the 1930's, labor unions could gain little momentum because of the legal bulwarks erected against them. In the first place, business had little to do with unions as long as their right to organize and bargain collectively was a matter of mutual consent and not compulsion. Second, legal injunctions could easily be obtained by business to halt a variety of union activities such as strikes, boycotts, picketing, and efforts to increase membership. And third, business could insist upon making employees, as a condition of employment, agree not to join unions (the yellow-dog contract).

Changes in the federal segment favoring unionization, however, started to come after the impact of the Depression of the early 1930's. The first important change came in 1932. The passage of the Norris-La Guardia Act placed severe restrictions upon the use of court injunctions intended to curb or limit union activities and outlawed the yellow-dog contracts, where, as a condition of employment, workers agreed not to join a union. Then in 1933, the National Industrial Recovery Act gave employees the right to organize and bargain collectively and prohibited employers from using the yellow-dog contract. Union growth, as a consequence, accelerated.

The act was short-lived, being declared unconstitutional on May 27, 1935. Congress passed the National Labor Relations Act, which was signed by the President on June 27, 1935. This act gave employees the right to organize and made it mandatory for employers to bargain collectively with representatives of employees. The legal basis for collective bargaining was laid in the United States. Subsequent federal legislation has added preventive measures in unionized relationships to both employees and employers.

How Unions Are Organized

In almost every case, unions follow the same kind of pyramid formation that companies do. At the grass roots level are the *locals*. These are like small clubs of people in the same kind of work, usually with elected

Table 8.3		
Largest Unions	Teamsters	1,888,895
and Their	National Education Association	1,886,532
Membership	Auto workers	1,358,354
	United Food and Commercial Workers	
	International Union	1,076,000*
	Steelworkers	964,000
	State, county, municipal employees	889,000
	Electrical workers	825,000
	Machinists	664,000
	Carpenters and joiners	619,000
	Service employees	528,000
	Communication workers	485,000
	Laborers	475,000

* Retail clerks and meatcutters merged in 1979 to form the United Food and Commercial Workers International.

Source: Union membership and employment 1959–79 prepared by AFL-CIO Department of Research, February 1980.

local representatives who not only talk and negotiate with local management, but also represent the local interests at the next step up in the labor organization's pyramid.

Nationals are affiliations of locals with similar interests. Theoretically, the need for unions emerges naturally on each local scene, after which the locals form, find each other, and affiliate. In reality, a strong national is likely to evangelize any area where the need for a union is not yet felt.

It is estimated that about twenty million workers are union members. When these workers become united through ever growing super affiliations and "national nationals," it is easy to see how they are able to get what they demand, regardless of the long range consequences for the company or even for the national economy.

Federations are unions of unions. They are built as unions in related work activities thrown in together to add power to the bargaining of each. Sometimes, as in the case of the Teamsters, the variety of occupations included is almost impossible to reconcile along job-relationship lines. Originally a union of those who drove wagons, the Teamsters now represent occupations ranging from medical technologists to policemen.

Craft and industrial unions are groups of workers in the same fields. Many of the craft fields (i.e., plumbers, electricians, carpenters, bartenders) have fluctuating worker demand. When this is the case, the union hall often becomes a sort of placement agency, with union staff dispatching available craftspeople to fill available positions. Industrial unions exert little influence on hiring, but do a great deal of "watchdogging" over all other phases of the operation. Unions may influence the policies of the company with regard to salary, benefits, safety, promotion, seniority, and grievance procedures.

In recent years there has been a growing tendency to develop a strong labor relations division in the personnel department and to make it responsible for handling contract negotiations.

Once contracts are signed, it is of extreme importance for all affected parties to be thoroughly oriented to the new limitations and opportunities. Management, supervisors, and line production staff all need to be familiar with the new rules that will influence every decision they make forever . . . until next year when the contract expires.

Summary

There is no more critical activity in the manager's responsibility than staffing . . . for a business is only as strong as its people. Managers who abdicate the opportunity to fill the ranks with strong employees deserve all the deadheads they inevitably hire.

Seven areas that should receive careful attention from the manager facing the staffing opportunity are (1) determination of needs, (2) selection and recruiting, (3) orientation and training, (4) performance appraisal, (5) compensation, (6) promotion, and (7) termination.

The growth and philosophy of the union movement will certainly have bearing upon the manager's staffing situation sooner or later.

Managers involved in labor relations can serve both labor and management, or serve one and alienate the other, or serve neither and look for a job somewhere else . . . in which case a staffing challenge is created for the old employer as well as the new!

Review Questions

1. What are the historical role and objectives of unions, generally stated?
2. How was the legal basis for collective bargaining laid in the United States in 1935?
3. It has been said that the union contract merely formalizes what should be good personnel practice in the areas covered by the contract? Do you agree? Explain.
4. Discuss "character blocks" and their relationship to performance appraisal.
5. What has restricted the application of accounting for human assets?
6. Identify the major areas that should receive attention from a manager with staffing authority.

7. Using the sample résumé, prepare your own personal résumé.
8. Using the summary of the selection procedure (Figure 8.2), identify which steps were taken before your application or admission to college was accepted.
9. In introducing a new employee to a corporation, there is usually a period of orientation and training. Does your college or university provide a similar service for new students?
10. Is performance appraisal provided for students at your institution?
11. Contrast the problem of terminating employees with the termination of students in an academic institution.
12. If you were successful in organizing a union for oppressed business students, what type of conditions would you include in the contract?

The Question of Authority

9

"Okay Buzzman, what did you want to talk about . . . I don't have all day."

"Well, it is this question of authority, Ridley. I feel that you are not demonstrating the proper respect for authority."

"What's that supposed to mean?"

"It simply means that I would prefer to have more respect for my position and obedience to my orders."

"Look, Buzzman, I am doing my job. Just because I don't bow and scrape and say 'Yes sir, Mister Buzzman, sir,' you think I ain't got no respect for authority. And when you give me an order, maybe I don't always do it right away, but I'll get around to it . . . eventually."

"But, Ridley . . . this is my company. I expect employees to do as I say when I say it and show me the proper respect."

"Now see here, Buzzy, old boy. My job here is far too important to me to be stopping every few minutes to feed your ego starvation for praise and priority."

"Well Ridley . . . if that's the way you feel about it . . . you are fired!"

"You can't talk to me that way, Buzzman, I quit!"

Authority is the key to the management job. When managers have authority, they can get their wishes carried out. After that, success is a matter of whether they were wishing right. Because managers accomplish their goals through other people, a paramount factor in the process is the authority by which the other people are motivated to strive.

People use many types of authority to get results. Like governments, individual managers may exercise authority in a totalitarian manner (i.e., "Don't ask me why I told you to do it—you do it because I am the boss!") and in a democratic manner (i.e., "Gee folks, I'll be glad to be the representative if you want me to—now, what is it *we* really want to do?") Unfortunately, the kind of authority a manager uses may be just the opposite from what is appropriate.

Some of the most fascinating studies of the social sciences have to do with the ways humans get other humans to do things their way. When you were in the primary grades, for example, the explanation of the U.S. political system was simple. The President was the boss and everybody else did what he said. As you grew older and more sophisticated, you realized that intricate power relationships exist not only in national politics, but in every area of society.

Two of the words that are of great importance here are *influence* and *power. Influence* includes virtually any interpersonal transaction that has psychological or behavioral effects. *Power* is the potential for influence characteristically backed by the means to coerce compliance. When we speak of authority, we are referring to legitimate power—there are other kinds.

Kast and Rosenweig[1] have devised a helpful continuum to show how different styles of influence relate to each other. The continuum, which appears as Table 9.1, ranges from emulation, to suggestion, to persuasion, to coercion.

Authority People and Positions

One of the most tragic management situations to observe is the boss who is in a position of authority but has no real influence or authority. In other words, workers reluctantly surrender to the orders, but not to the person giving them. The word *authority* and the word *author* come from the same Latin root word. The obvious root meaning is that the true authority is the originator, the one who knows the way.

It is fairly easy to think of authority in simplistic hypothetical situations: the beloved and trusted leader or the despised drill sergeant. Yet life is rarely a matter of one or the other. More often it is composed of confusing mixtures of complications. The manager has a task to accomplish. . . . It was not her idea in the first place. . . . She even sees some

---

[1] Fremont E. Kast and James E. Rosenweig, *Organization and Management,* 2nd ed. (New York: McGraw-Hill Book Company, 1974), p. 330.

Table 9.1
Spectrum of Means
for Influencing
Behavior*

Influence Spectrum			
Emulation: Striving to equal or excel; imitating with effort to equal or surpass; approaching or attaining equality	*Suggestion:* placing or bringing (an idea, proposition, plan, etc.) before a person's mind for consideration or possible action	*Persuasion:* prevailing on a person by advice, urging, reason, or inducements to do something (rather than force)	*Coercion:* forcing constraint; compulsion; physical pressure or compression

* Fremont E. Kast and James E. Rosenweig, *Organization and Management*, 2nd ed. (New York: McGraw-Hill Book Company, 1974), p. 330.

problems in the task. . . . But her job is to accomplish, not question. . . . The subordinates respect her, but they also occasionally spot her mistakes. . . . They sense that she is not sold on the project. . . . Their performance is tempered by their uncertainties about her conviction. . . . There is, therefore, a question of her authority: Does she really want us to do it? What will she do if we do not do it? Is she questioning the assignment herself? The boss is given part *respectful* obedience and part obedience merely because she is the boss. The authority situation is anything but clear-cut.

A popular wall plaque for offices makes the ominous suggestion that "The boss may not always be right—but is always the boss." Most of these plaques were probably purchased and hung by bosses. There is truth in the sentence, but not the kind of truth that evokes love and devotion for the boss. Despite the importance of authority, managers prefer to avoid using the word because of its discomforting connotation of power and forced obedience. People like to be asked—not told. Many human relations conflicts could have been avoided by a wiser, more considerate use of authority.

The word *authority*, then, coined to refer to emergent organizations in which it was agreed that a person would be the boss because of prowess or preeminence. Yet most authority situations we encounter today are not emerging but existing. We agree to follow rules when we take the job or join the club. The nature of authority is one more of the tiny characteristics that are ignored by the masses but weighed, refined, and exploited by those who would excel.

Two supervisors at the Four-square Box Company are employed in identical positions. They have the same job descriptions and supervise the same number of workers. Everything is the same except the results

—one supervisor gets twice as much work out of her group. What is the difference? It may be a question of how authority is employed . . . a question of influence and power.

Sources of Authority

What is the real source of managerial authority? Why is it that one individual chooses to obey the wishes or commands of another individual? For years, this proposition has been debated by professors of management. The business community, for the most part, was happy for the academic world to "play its little word games."[2] Managers on the firing line were not concerned with *why* they were obeyed as long as they *were* obeyed. It was only as traditional attitudes and values began to crumble that managers had cause to look closely at their true sources of authority.

During most of the history of human development, the dominance of a formal theory of authority had been virtually unchallenged, especially in the fields of religion, government, and business. To dispute the intrinsic worth—and sometimes the divine right—of kings or the sacred prerogatives of the Church was, in the Middle Ages, an offense punishable by death. Similarly, when employers, generals, or schoolmasters gave orders, the average mentality saw no alternative but to obey.

As time passed, there were some attempts to question and hinder the operation of formal authority. For the most part, such rebellions operated against the *way* in which authority was exercised—not authority's right to be the authority. In a few rare cases, there was a frontal attack on the assumptions underlying authority. Instances in which formal authority was successfully contested usually arose out of highly mixed motivations. Such instances constituted significant human achievement won with great difficulty. The Protestant Reformation, the Magna Charta, and even the American Revolution could be cited as examples of the exercise, to a greater or lesser degree, of the right of acceptance. In these instances, individuals or social groups refused to accept the prescription of formal management and insisted on a greater voice in the establishment of policies affecting their own welfare.

In the nineteenth and twentieth centuries instances of the collective questioning of authority became more numerous. In the 1950's and 60's, the trickle of rebellion became a flood. In particular, the fields of civil rights, labor negotiations, military involvement, and university administration have been battlegrounds. Even as the first startling outbreaks

[2] Adapted from Robert M. Fulmer and Charles Wellborn, "The New Morality and New Managers," *Business Horizons*, Winter 1967, p. 98.

of resistance to authority began to subside and give way to a counteremphasis on law-and-order conservatism, it became obvious that the foundations had been shaken. The people had had an overdose of *violent* reaction to authority—and violence would be avoided—but the idea of questioning authority had come to stay. Even though general trends of conservatism across the nation may increase the allegiance to formal authority, the wedge has been driven. There is a new spirit in the population—people are infected with the thoughtful questioning of everything. This increased demand for proof is an integral part of the emergence in our culture of what has been termed the new morality.

Two sources of authority have emerged. Both of them may be in existence simultaneously—in fact, both may be operating in a given company. The two theories of authority that will be examined here are formal authority theory and authority-acceptance theory.

Formal authority theory asserts that obedience or compliance in a given situation is a natural consequence of authority arising out of a superior situation enjoyed because of a position of ownership. In other words, "This is my company and if you don't like the way I want things done, get out."

Cyril O'Donnell has pointed out that, in most cases, the right authority came with the ability to own private property. He traces authority delegations up the organizational chart.

> Thus, the supervisor of cash control obtained his authority from the assistant treasurer, who obtained his from the treasurer, who in turn got his from the president of the company, whose authority was delegated by the board of directors, who obtained theirs from the stockholders, who held theirs by virtue of the institution of private property, as modified by incorporation and other laws. Thus, in a business firm, the ultimate source of authority lies principally in the institution of private property.[3]

As the concept of private ownership has been questioned, so has the style of authority that depended upon it. Nevertheless, authority tends still to originate in the process of ownership or primacy. Even government is privately owned, tracing its *eventual* allegiance to the individuals who pay taxes and cast votes. From the "owners," the authority is formally passed down the line to individual managers.

Pure acceptance theory is difficult to rationalize. Situations that appear to illustrate acceptance could be questioned. The soldier's obedience of commands—because the alternative is the guardhouse or the firing squad—is hardly genuine acceptance. The convict hardly has a choice about accepting the warden's authority. Perhaps the wisest distinction we could make about acceptance theory is with regard to the *attitude* of obedience instead of the decision between obedience and disobedience. That is to say that employees are not likely to choose daily

---

[3] "Sources of Managerial Authority," *Political Science Quarterly*, December 1962, p. 573.

The Ten Commandments (Paramount, 1956). Did Moses rely on formal or acceptance authority?

between obeying the boss and losing the job. Rather more likely is some decision between whether to obey with gusto or to obey with reluctance. In this case, the theorizing shifts somewhat—from specific acceptance of the command to general acceptance or nonacceptance of the *commander*. It appears then that acceptance theorists are not discussing authority at all but leadership—the ability to work well to accomplish a group goal.

Competence Authority

An additional type of authority besides formal and acceptance authority is discussed by some authors. They say that *competence authority* is the type bestowed on individuals who have obvious expertise in their field. Admitting that this kind of authority is closely akin to acceptance authority, Koontz and O'Donnell place under this heading "the individual who has made subordinates of others through sheer force of personality and the engineer and economist who exert influence by furnishing answers or sound advice."[4]

Rather than a separate type of authority, the competence theory seems to this writer to be an excellent illustration of the acceptance theory. The expert is accepted because of unique ability or knowledge. Illustrative of this phenomenon is the story of a service representative who was called in when a highly sophisticated piece of equipment broke down in a factory. The expert walked calmly around the equipment, took out a small hammer and tapped the machine once on the side. Lights blinked, machinery purred and the equipment whirled immediately into action. Factory management was amazed. They were even more amazed when they received a bill for $4,005.00. They asked for an itemized explanation and received the following: "One tap with hammer, $5 . . . Knowing where to tap, $4,000. Thank you very much."

Obviously competence gains acceptance of authority for the expert in any field. An airplane may be full of high-powered executives, but it goes nowhere until a blue-collar worker says that it is safe to fly! Undoubtedly, most cases of authority which we encounter in "the real world" are partially formal and partially acceptance, perhaps even acceptance gained because of competence. The professor of a college class is a good illustration of this relationship. As the duly appointed administrator of a specific class, he or she does hold the *formal* authority over the class situation. Even though all professors share alike in possession of this formal authority, it is immediately obvious that some teachers

---

[4] Harold Koontz and Cyril O'Donnell, *Principles of Management*, 5th ed. (New York: McGraw-Hill Book Company, 1972), p. 63.

are more *accepted* as authorities by their students. This may be for any number of reasons from ease of tests to power of personality. However, the president of the university would like to believe that the professors hold their students spell-bound by the perfection of their professional manner and knowledge. This being the case, we could say that the professor holds both *formal* authority and *acceptance* authority on the basis of competence.

Actually, there is a sort of *de facto* competence authority which has already begun to bear fruit in many organizations. In companies utilizing a program of product management, extensive, multimillion dollar market strategy proposals are developed by a new breed of managers, often in their late twenties or early thirties. While these proposals may need approval at three or four successive levels of management, competent proposals (or those assumed to be competent because of the reputation for competence enjoyed by the proposal's author) are routinely approved.

There is no question that students, workers, soldiers, and government employees have resisted arbitrary imposition of formal authority. This resistance has usually emerged because the particular authority was seen as invalid because it lacked the validity created by competence. "Because I say so" will become increasingly less acceptable as an answer to the eternal question, "Why?" Authority has been historically viewed as the cement that holds organizations together. Tomorrow's managers must clearly utilize a better grade of cement if they are to maintain order and progress! The academic argument that competence is a characteristic of leadership rather than a condition of authority has little practical relevance for the once and future manager. Throughout the future, managers who have reached their level of incompetence can expect great resistance to their plans while the competent, well-tempered executive will find technical and moral justification for his or her proposals.

Authority Relationships

In looking at organizational charts, it is easy to make assumptions about the kinds of authority imposed by these different position relationships. Actually, misunderstandings regarding the extent and nature of authority inherent in a position cause as much friction and loss of efficiency as any other factor. Authority relationships, whether perpendicular or horizontal, can make or break important systems of departmentation and delegation. While there is an obvious relationship between power and authority, this topic is discussed in greater detail in Chapter 14.

This section will describe three types of authority relationships within organizational patterns: line, staff, and functional.

Line relationships are the ones we usually draw when someone asks to see the basic organizational chart of our group or company. It is only later, after they have followed with the further question, "And is this the whole organization?" that we come around to adding on the staff-related aspects of the chart. Some authorities have tried to explain the difference between line and staff positions by this essential-nonessential approach. They have said that line jobs are those that deal with the basic processes of the business (i.e., production, sales, and perhaps finance). On the other hand, staff jobs have been characterized as the frills—those departments that are nice to have if you can afford them. A military line officer is one who is in the specific business of fighting wars. A staff officer might be involved in medical or supply functions. This essential-nonessential definition works well on charts but develops complications in actual practice. For instance, how long will an army fight without its kitchen staff? Or how much could the busy executive accomplish without a corps of special assistants? Line and staff jobs cannot be adequately divided by the essential-nonessential criteria.

The best way to define the two types of jobs is by their relationship to the jobs above and below them. In line authority, one finds a superior and a subordinate with a line of authority running from the former to the latter. The line employee is a link in the chain of command. He or she receives orders from above and gives orders to those below. A superior exercises direct supervision over a subordinate in a direct line relationship.

Staff authority does not permit a manager to give orders to other departments. When the manager of a staff (service or support) department has subordinates, line authority exists between these individuals. When someone is described as being a staff manager, they typically have relatively few subordinates. Staff managers may give out a lot of requests—but few orders. Their task is to assist, advise, and do anything to facilitate the work within their special area—but not by direct command.

An outstanding graphic technique for demonstrating the positions of lines and staffs is the horizontal and vertical placement on the organizational chart. Line positions are usually depicted vertically, one beneath the other. Staff positions, on the other hand, are generally drawn as little boxes out to the side of some line position. The military general's aide is a staff officer and certainly not second in command to the general. Indeed, the antics of generals' aides in securing the best provisions have become legendary. Even without authority, these aides to the brass are able to beg, borrow, and steal the things they need. At any rate, they serve as sterling examples of the fact that tact, diplomacy, and true influence can usually run circles around delegated authority when it comes to reaching a specified goal.

Table 9.2 Comparison of Line, Staff, and Functional Authority

Advantages	Disadvantages
Line Authority	
Maintains simplicity.	Neglects specialists in planning.
Makes clear division of authority.	Overworks key people.
Encourages speedy action.	Depends on retention of a few key people.
Staff Authority	
Enables specialists to give expert advice.	Confuses organization if functions are not clear.
Frees the line executive of detailed analysis.	Reduces power of experts to place recommendations into action.
Affords young specialists a means of training.	Tends toward centralization of organization.
Functional Authority	
Relieves line executives of routine specialized decisions.	Makes relationships more complex.
Provides framework for applying expert knowledge.	Makes limits of authority of each specialist a difficult coordination problem.
Relieves pressure of need for large numbers of well-rounded executives.	Tends toward centralization of organization.

The development of the staff approach can probably be traced simply to the use of assistants to handle the details of a managerial job, to furnish the information needed for decisions, and to offer advice in making plans. It has been said (with some relevance to the staff concept) that "Robinson Crusoe was the only person ever to accomplish his work by Friday."

The staff idea has come into its vogue with the twentieth-century emphasis on planning and control and with the increasing complexities of legal, labor, and tax structures. Obviously, staffs have to be worth their cost or they would eventually die out or pull the company down. Of course, the larger the business and the less definite the staff contribution to overall profit or loss, the greater the staff's chances of continuing year after year even though draining the company's resources.

The difference between line and staff positions may seem unimportant. Yet many a managerial frustration could be relieved by a more exact understanding of the relationships of staff to other departments. Successful administration requires that line subordinates understand and accept policy decisions. Staff subordinates must deal in a more subtle manner with accomplishing goals. As has been stated previously, the line officer has the authority to *tell* subordinates what to do—the staff

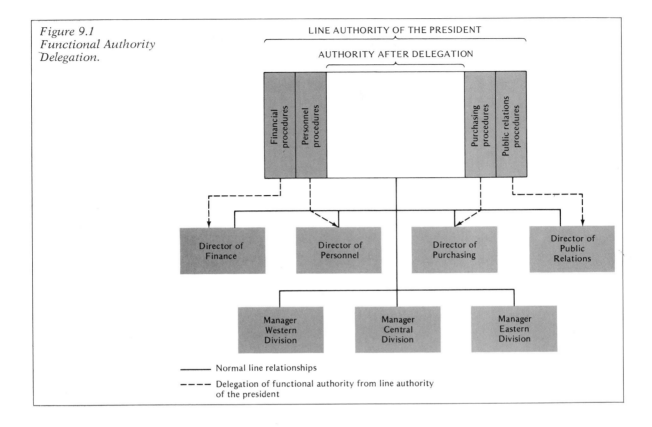

*Figure 9.1
Functional Authority
Delegation.*

LINE AUTHORITY OF THE PRESIDENT

AUTHORITY AFTER DELEGATION

Financial procedures

Personnel procedures

Purchasing procedures

Public relations procedures

Director of Finance

Director of Personnel

Director of Purchasing

Director of Public Relations

Manager Western Division

Manager Central Division

Manager Eastern Division

——— Normal line relationships

– – – Delegation of functional authority from line authority of the president

worker has the authority to *sell* superiors and line workers on ideas. Would it be accurate to say that the line employee works for the company, whereas the staff employee works for someone who works for the company?

Functional relationships between the line and staff divisions of an organization exist whenever one position is given authority to cut across normal organizational lines. Functional authority is sometimes called a slice of line authority that is delimited. The limits to which functional authority may usurp the ordinary chain of command are usually spelled out quite carefully. The president of a company might, for example, decide that there is a need to accumulate certain research data regarding employees. Depending upon the urgency of the data the change may be (1) "The research staff has top priority—give them anything they ask for whenever they ask for it," or (2) "The research staff is seeking data— give them any assistance possible without jeopardizing your regular production quotas." Functional authority functions according to the ground rules established whenever the line organizational procedures

Patton (20th Century Fox, 1970). Do generals and executives have the same kind of authority?

are intentionally short-circuited. Figure 9.1 demonstrates the organization chart representation in which this "cutting across normal lines" is taking place.

The use of functional authority has increased in recent years with the emphasis on the project approach in business and government. In a television studio, for instance, there are continuing line functions (i.e., engineers, camera operators, sound experts, and actors). These may be simultaneously under the direction of the studio supervisor and the project manager of a specific program that is being produced. These employees have two bosses; their actions will be determined according to the arrangement established for this functional situation. In such a situation, it is easy to see why clear lines of authority . . . line, staff, and functional authority—must exist for communication to remain constant.

The question, therefore, is how to determine the right amount of staff services for the organization. Manpower needs for production become fairly obvious, whereas the needs for research or personnel people are harder to determine.

Management theoreticians have attempted to answer this question by analyzing the changes in organizational complexity in growing companies. They also worked with the assumption that a reason for staff coming into existence may, in fact, be the complexity itself. The idea of increasing functional complexity in a growing enterprise is expressed in the classical literature as the law of functional growth:

> The various functions of an organization increase in scope and complexity, as well as the amount of work and the technical requirements for their proper performance, as the volume of business grows. The complexity of functional relationships tends to increase in geometric progression as the volume of work that the organization must handle increases in arithmetic progression.[5]

To draw an analogy regarding this relationship of line to staff increases, let us go to the kitchen of a large convention center. Here we find the head chef planning a banquet. Calculations show that no more kitchen equipment or cooks are needed for a thousand-person banquet than for a hundred-person banquet. But the increased crowd will definitely necessitate more ushers, more parking attendants, more expensive entertainers, and even the installation of a small clinic in case of emergency. The chef's line employees can easily increase their output of stuffed drumsticks, but a large additional staff of helping personnel will be necessary to service the larger banquet crowd.

[5] R. C. Davis, *The Fundamentals of Top Management* (New York: Harper and Row, Publishers, 1951), p. 232.

Dangers in Using Staff

Staff departments are necessary. They can do much to make an organization successful. Even so, staff commitments must be made carefully and monitored wisely lest staff services get out of hand. Melville Dalton[6] has identified several limitations for the use of staff functions. Dalton, a sociologist, lived and worked in industrial settings to observe the behavior of people at work. He was especially impressed with the almost-inherent conflicts that would arise between individuals with line and staff authority. A little red light should come on in the manager's mind whenever staff functions are:

1. Tending to undermine line authority.
2. Allowing both line and staff to shift blame to the other.
3. Developing an ivory tower complex and making impractical recommendations.
4. Causing management complication and disunity of command.
5. Failing to understand the different authority relationships of line and staff.
6. Giving advice that is ignored or rejected by line managers.
7. Unable to keep informed of line conditions.
8. Making recommendations that are indecisive, obscure, erroneous, or unrealistic.
9. Trying to take credit for the success of line managers who follow staff recommendations.

The more we investigate the difficulties and complications of line and staff relationships, the more important appear those two old friends: cooperation and communication. People who understand their jobs and their jobs' relationship to the whole organizational direction can give and take to reach the common goal. There is no foolproof line and staff arrangement. It is up to the manager to keep the workers appropriately together and appropriately apart.

The Future of Authority

It should be recognized that new managers are now being recruited for middle management positions. Those who will fill the executive suites in the next generation are being molded in an environment whose values and attitudes toward authority are significantly different from those of past generations.

A revolution in attitude and authority had occurred. Even if the na-

[6] "Conflicts Between Line and Staff Managerial Offices," *American Sociological Review,* Fall 1950, pp. 342–351, and Melville Dalton, "Changing Line-Staff Relations," *Personnel Administration,* March–April 1966, pp. 3–5.

ture of society changes, business must continue to fulfill its role, although new attitudes, objectives, policies, and practices must be developed to keep abreast of moral, as well as technological progress. Young college graduates will be attracted to business as long as they see indications of its being responsible and responsive, in a flexible manner, to the demonstrated needs of society, rather than to the traditional concepts of corporate roles.

Summary

Authority is the key to the management job. Because managers accomplish their goals through other people, a paramount factor in the process is the authority by which other people are motivated. Despite the importance of authority, many managers prefer to avoid using the word because of its discomforting connotation of power and forced obedience.

During most of the history of human development, the dominance of a formal theory of authority was virtually unchallenged, especially in the fields of religion, government, and business. Gradually, individuals or social groups refused to accept the prescriptions of formal management and insisted on a greater voice in the establishment of policies affecting their own welfare. In the last decade or two, the trickle of rebellion has grown into a flood. We live in a world of changing attitudes toward authority.

Two theories of authority are commonly cited. *Formal authority theory* asserts that obedience or compliance in a given situation is a natural consequence of authority arising out of a superior situation because of a position of ownership. The *acceptance theory of authority* takes the position that the real source of authority lies in the acceptance of its exercise by those who are subject to it. The theory of *competence authority* is sometimes discussed, although this may be in reality one form of acceptance theory.

Three types of authority relationships were discussed: *line relationships*, which may be recognized by the direct passage of command from the superior down through the chain of command; *staff relationships*, which are established primarily to assist or advise some line positions, and *functional relationships*, in which one manager is given delimited authority over another's normal department.

Two prime causes of dissension between people with line and staff authority are differences regarding *responsibility* and differences regarding *importance of function*.

The law of functional growth can help in the understanding of the best ratio of line to staff positions. As a company grows, staff positions will increase faster than line positions. Staff departments can do much to make an organization successful. Even so, staff commitments should be monitored closely lest they get out of hand.

The concept of authority appears to be in for definite changes. Those who will fill the executive suites in the next generation are being molded in an environment whose values and attitudes toward authority are significantly different from those of past generations. The more we investigate the difficulties and complications of authority situations, the more important those two old friends: cooperation and communication. It is a wise boss who knows how to "let the employees have their way."

Review Questions

1. What is the acceptance theory of authority?
2. Is the impact of formal authority declining? Discuss.
3. Define functional authority.
4. Why do competent managers usually have more authority than incapable managers?
5. Does the vice-president of marketing usually have line or staff authority? Discuss.
6. On a university campus, what is the source of authority exercised by the following individuals?
    a. A professor in a three-hundred-student lecture hall.
    b. A football coach.
    c. The leader of a cafeteria boycott.
    d. The president of the debate club.
7. What type of authority relationships exist in the following situations?
    a. University department head to professor.
    b. University professor to student.
    c. Athletic director to professor (in the case of Moose Mulligan, who needs a passing grade to maintain his football eligibility).
    d. Registrar to university professor (concerning reporting of grades).
    e. University professor to university president.
8. What are the dangers relating to authority that exist in setting up a central secretarial pool rather than having individual secretaries reporting directly to the various executives?
9. When a presidential assistant is asked to represent the United States in important military negotiations, what type of authority does the assistant possess?
10. Ensign Quigg, Jr., has been given command of PT Boat 6½. Despite his authority, he notices that several of the men check with a grizzled, uneducated seaman for their assignments. How do you explain this?

11. Do you believe that we can continue to extrapolate the increasing popularity of the acceptance theory of authority?
12. A personnel placement agency has been growing rapidly for the last three years. They now have approximately twenty offices throughout the Southwest. In order to gain some assistance in the staffing function, the president is considering the addition of a personnel manager. What potential problems would you suggest be taken into account before making this decision?

part III

The Human Dimension in Management

10

Know Thyself—The Most Difficult Lesson

Back in the good old days, before thinkers began all the dissension about the world's being round, everybody was quite content with the prospect of an uncomplicated, straightforward, flat world. It seemed the logical thing to do to put something pretty special at the exact center of everything. The Greeks came up with a plan.

Zeus, who was a sort of chairman of the board of Greek deities, turned loose two eagles, one from each end of the earth. The point at which the eagles came together was declared to be the center of the world and the construction site for a great temple. The place was named Delphi (perhaps in honor of one of the eagles?) and the temple was prepared to be the center for all ancient wisdom and learning.

When the time came to choose the maxims that should be carved over the building's doors, a contest was held. A late model chariot and a year's supply of laurels would be awarded to the philosopher who could come up with two maxims that would embrace the totality of human wisdom.

The two winning entries were chosen by state-appointed judges and agreed on by all the sages who amounted to anything. Each of the winning sayings contained only two words (which was probably the briefest government report ever re-

leased). At one end of the temple were carved the words "Avoid
Extremes," expressing the essence of Aristotle's concept of the
golden mean, virtue being a balance between two equally undesirable extremes. The other maxim (which is two letters shorter
and a lot more important to this chapter) was "Know Thyself."

Cervantes once said, "Know thyself . . . for this is the most difficult
lesson of life." The truth of his statement is obvious to anybody who
pays attention to the events that total up to make for life experience. It
is certainly difficult to be objective and unbiased about that noble coun-
tenance that appears in our mirror each morning. Yet, if we can develop
a measure of objectivity, we have grasped the key to success in any kind
of endeavor.

In order to evaluate ourselves, it is appropriate to consider some of
the systems by which people have attempted to explain themselves and
their actions through the ages. It is worth noting at the outset that no
vote will be taken at the end of the chapter to determine which philosopher had the right answer. More than likely, you will not agree 100 per
cent with any of the philosophies cited. But all of them will have valuable ideas to contribute as you think through and establish your own
philosophy of life and concept of self.

The Basic Motives of People

Our motivation for investigating motivation is to motivate. We want to
know the kinds of values and needs that will cause people to take certain actions. Early religious and philosophical investigations into the
nature of man represent attempts to get at the *why* of life's events. Fatal-
ism, rationalism, egoism, altrusim, hedonism, and utilitarianism represent a progression of thinking. Table 10.1 summarizes these major milestones in our progressive understanding of motivation.

Beginning with "people have no control over what happens," the
thought expanded into "perhaps they can, by intelligence, have some
influence." Finally, the thinkers were generally agreed that humans
were making their own determinations. Religion and philosophy
pointed to various motivators of behavior—selfishness, goodness, pleasure, group pressure, and so on. At the same time, the scientific community has established its own explanations for the moving force behind
"the thinking animal."

The *sociological view* suggests that human behavior is a result of the
people and events in our social sphere. The values and customs of a par-

Table 10.1 The Nature of Mankind?		
Fatalism		The fate of people is predetermined by outside forces
Rationalism		People control their own destiny
Egoism		People are driven by selfish interests
Altruism (Auguste Comte)		People are basically interested in helping others
Hedonism (Epicurus)		People strive to maximize pleasure and reduce pain
Utilitarianism (Jeremy Bentham)		People desire the greatest pleasure (happiness) for the greatest number of people

ticular society are said to determine the actions of the people in that society.[1] For example, in our society one motive learned by many children early in life is to be number one, to achieve. If thirty American children are locked in a room for an hour, they will instinctively elect officers. It is obvious that culture influences many of our actions. Can you accept sociological causes as man's exclusive motivators?

The *biological view* of motivation says that our actions hinge on our physical and biological needs and drives.[2] We behave in certain predictable ways when we are hungry, when we're thirsty, and even if we have built up a sleep debt. Beyond these simple biological examples, some investigators have suggested that everyday behavior and misbehavior may depend on chemical or nutrient balances within the body. Perhaps your seemingly unexplainable behavior problems can be traced to the cucumbers on toast you like so much for breakfast.

The *psychoanalytic view*[3] was first stated clearly by Sigmund Freud (1856–1939). His premise was that our motives are mostly unconscious and under the surface. Freud felt that the subconscious held the keys to our true motivation and that most of our conscious reasoning is confused and self-deceptive. The Viennese doctor found, for example, that a patient might be aggressive toward another person because of personality insecurity. A little learning can be quite confusing, and many injustices have been perpetrated in the name of someone's special understanding of underlying factors. Do you ever wonder if what you think is really what you think? Or do you just want yourself to think you think that so you won't have to think about what you really think?

The *behaviorist view* is a fairly recent addition to the explanations of human motivation. Simply speaking, behaviorists do not care about conscious or unconscious motives—their interest is in what's happening. They deal in behavior, and their premise is an undeniable overt *result*. Behaviorists consider time wasted that is spent discussing "why."

[1] J. W. Atkinson, *Motives and Fantasy, Action and Society* (Princeton, N.J.: Van Nostrand Reinhold Company, 1958).
[2] C. Morgan, *Physiological Psychology*, 3rd ed. (New York: McGraw-Hill Book Company, 1965).
[3] Sigmund Freud, *Psychopathology of Everyday Life*, 2nd ed. (London: Ernest Benn, Ltd., 1954).

They want results. The behaviorist school of thought was started by J. B. Watson,[4] who said that humans resemble a modern-day computer and that our behavior is essentially the result of input via eyes, ears, nose, and so on. B. F. Skinner has become famous for his system, which claims that a model society could be created if the behaviorist approach were followed completely. Skinner's novel *Walden II*[5] describes such a society based on state-controlled stimuli that are programmed into us from birth. More recently, Skinner has suggested, in one of the most controversial books of the past few years[6] that our entire culture must be conditioned to behave in such a manner as to allow us to survive. To do this, he says we must go beyond the traditional concepts of freedom and dignity. Most friends of the American entrepreneurial spirit and our system of private enterprise find themselves opposed to Skinner's philosophy. The behaviorist school has its unanswered questions, too, perhaps illustrated by the laboratory mouse who returned to his cage and told his wife, "I have the professor conditioned perfectly now: everytime I run through the maze, he gives me a piece of cheese."

No time is ever lost that is spent in evaluation and correction of our motivations. Truly, the things that propel us determine where we will go, how fast we will travel, and the kinds of obstacles we can surmount on the way. The wise person will develop a *motivation-oriented* approach to problem solving. In management, in communication, and in interpersonal relationships, to understand the motivation is to understand the action that needs to be taken.

We have reviewed briefly four theories of motivation. We have seen that, at one time or another, almost everything has taken the blame for being humanity's primary driving force. For most readers, though, it will be impossible to accept any single factor as the exclusive key to motivation. Neither the *sociological, biological, psychoanalytic,* or *behaviorist* views of motivation can answer all the questions.

In the last few years, motivation specialists have evolved a theory that draws on all facets of people. The *humanistic* theory[7] of motivation gives credit to biological drives but also honors sociological causes. It does not deny that people respond to the behaviorists' stimuli nor that those stimuli might reside in the psychoanalytic subconscious. Abraham H. Maslow sees humanistic psychology as the third major force (along with behaviorism and psychoanalysis) in modern American psychology.[8]

In seeking to help "Know thyself," the humanistic theorists have taken the advice that was carved on the other end of that temple of Del-

[4] *Behaviorism* (Chicago: University of Chicago Press), 1958.
[5] (New York: Macmillan Publishing Co., Inc., 1948).
[6] *Beyond Freedom and Dignity* (New York: Alfred A. Knopf, Inc., 1971).
[7] Abraham H. Maslow, *Toward Psychology of Being* (Princeton, N.J.: Van Nostrand Reinhold Company, 1962).
[8] *Psychology Today: An Introduction* (Del Mar, Calif.: CRM Books), 1970, p. 476.

phi—they have *avoided the extremes* of oversimplification. They have dealt with human motivation as a total, complicated, many-faceted phenomenon. In the next section, we will discuss the work of Abraham Maslow, whose descriptions of the "self-actualizing person" provide a holistic view of that rare individual who has gotten all his parts together.

The Humanistic Approach

Many great discoveries for healthy people have been made by those who work with the sick. Special education has opened many doors for regular education, and physicians to the sick have discovered preventive medicine for the healthy. In the field of psychology, Maslow and others working with brain-damaged and mentally disturbed persons began to draw certain conclusions about mental health.

The tone of Maslow's philosophy is extremely positive. He saw people's needs and drives as good rather than evil. He felt that each person has a natural drive toward health, happiness, and accomplishment rather than a pessimistic, negative desire for failure and self-destruction. Whether Maslow's humanistic philosophy is right or not, it certainly is a much happier way of characterizing people.

Maslow determined five basic needs that he said are sequential in nature. These five basic needs are arranged in a stepladder chart, with the

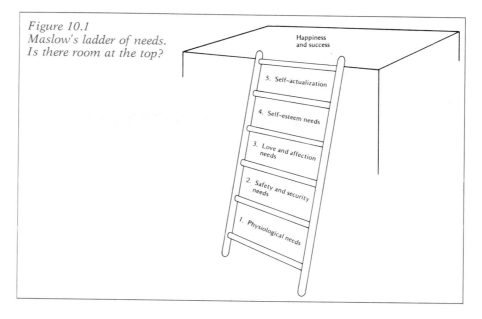

Figure 10.1
Maslow's ladder of needs.
Is there room at the top?

Happiness and success

5. Self-actualization

4. Self-esteem needs

3. Love and affection needs

2. Safety and security needs

1. Physiological needs

most basic needs at the bottom.[9] Everyone has all five of these needs but must have one set met to a minimum or relative degree before he can become concerned with the satisfaction of the next set. Unfortunately, many people in the world are never able to get off the bottom rung of Maslow's ladder.

Maslow outlined the following needs for people. As you read, check to see how far up Maslow's ladder you have progressed.

1. Physiological needs. The first step on the ladder to self-actualization is the satisfaction of the basic physiological needs of food, air, shelter, and so on. If you were lost on a deserted island, you would be more concerned with finding food and shelter than finding the closest opera house or bookstore. And you'd give even your food and shelter to maintain your air supply. There is obviously a priority order to the things we need. Maslow says the physiological needs come first.[10]

2. Safety and security needs. In some societies, the human need for safety and security is never satisfied. People may live under continual threat by political, geographical, or weather factors. Generally, people will try to migrate to satisfy their need for safety. However, if the migration is likely to deprive them of more basic needs, they may decide to endure. Thus, people can reconcile a daily trip to work in dangerous mines or on lofty scaffolding to satisfy their needs for food or shelter.

3. Love and belonging needs. Humans are social animals. They want to be loved and needed by others. They can forestall the satisfaction of gregarious needs long enough to guarantee food, water, air, stimulation, and safety. In our society, the bottom three rungs of Maslow's ladder are almost taken for granted by the majority of people. But the failure to love and be loved is at the heart of many individual and group social problems. There are persons who spend their entire lives searching for love and desiring to belong. The lower needs must be met before an individual begins to pursue actively the need to belong. However, we should not leave the impression that the upper rungs of the ladder are unimportant. Love deprivation can be as devastating as (and can sometimes cause) the lack of fulfillment of the more basic needs.

4. Self-esteem needs. As we near the top of the ladder, the needs get harder to satisfy. In our society there are many activities and products that promise to give self-esteem but are unable to make good the promise. Consciously, we know that the right deodorant and the right car will not make us right with ourselves. But advertisers and socializers still manage to convince us that self-respect lies somewhere in the possession of the big car, the big jewels, or the big title. Maslow's ladder

[9] Op. cit.
[10] Most management treatments of Maslow's theory omit stimulation needs which include sex, exploration and other forms of stimulation mentioned in Maslow's work.

could be of great value if it does no more than to cause us to reflect on the kinds of things and activities that will help us really to like ourselves.

5. Self-actualization. We sometimes speak of some acquaintance as being a "fulfilled" person—one who has a specific goal and seems happily busy getting it. Achieving the top rung of Maslow's ladder is a matter of developing the inner nature or the potential we each have within us. Those who attain self-actualization have conquered the other levels of human need, either by getting the things they need or by altering the preceding needs. In the next section, we will go into greater detail about the characteristics Maslow assigned to the self-actualized person.

It is obvious that there are overlapping needs and drives in the system Maslow suggested. Love can make us forego shelter, food, or life itself. Attainment of a higher rung may mean sacrifice of something we considered absolutely imperative at an earlier, less-mature stage in life. In fact, self-actualization quite often occurs when an individual becomes more concerned with fulfilling others' needs than with pampering himself. Jesus puzzled his Palestinian audiences with piercing and perceptive questions about the priorities of life: "Is not life more than food, and the body more than clothing?" (Matthew 6:25 RSV).

The Self-actualizing Person

Instead of dwelling on the unhappy abnormalities of psychology and motivation, Maslow devoted his energies to painting a portrait of the psychologically healthy individual. To describe the complete person at the top of his ladder, Maslow investigated the characteristics of people he considered to be self-actualized. He studied famous people like Lincoln, Thoreau, Beethoven, Eleanor Roosevelt, and Einstein. He also studied people who were his personal friends and acquaintances.

Maslow found the following characteristics of mentally healthy or self-actualized persons:[11]

1. They can accept the way things really are. It is not unusual to notice in the autobiographies of famous people that turning points in their lives often occurred when they decided to quit dwelling on what "ought to be" or "what should be" and start functioning in the arena of "what is." Maslow's self-actualized people can accept themselves—big noses, flat feet, funny voices, and all. They are folks who realize the futility of forever bemoaning their weaknesses and learn to accent their strong

[11] The following section is adapted from Maslow's own writings footnoted earlier in this chapter. A very excellent summary of his concept is contained in G. L. Hershey and D. O. Lugo, *Living Psychology* (New York: Macmillan Publishing Co., Inc., 1970), pp. 14–21.

points (and sometimes turn their weaknesses into strengths). One man said that Mother Nature handed him a lemon . . . so he decided to make lemonade. Because they can accept themselves the way they are, mentally healthy persons are also willing to take other people just as they come. When you consider the dynamics of our personality conflicts, things could be much smoother and more productive if we would just deal with people the way they are instead of refusing to have anything to do with them until they are the way they ought to be. We should avoid the attitude of the professor who answered a student's question with "If you don't know the answer to that question, I certainly am not going to tell you."

Self-actualized folks are basically acceptors. They can tell it like it is and go from there. They are neither self-satisfied nor content with the status quo. Rather, they are action people and they know that the project must start where the problem is.

2. They are not afraid to get close to others. Another quality of these people, Maslow found, is that they tend to get closer to people. Because they feel secure and happy with themselves, they can afford to have deep human relationships with others. They are not threatened by others. They are not threatened by the experience of revealing their inner feelings to others. Their openness and security causes them to be kind and patient with others. It never ceases to amaze us that the great are human. There is always a good public-interest story to be written when a famous person shares humanity with the masses. Newsmen once noticed that a ten-year-old boy came every afternoon to visit with Albert Einstein. When they asked Einstein about it, he replied, "We have a mutual benefit program: he likes the way I help him with his arithmetic and I like the jellybeans he brings along."

Maslow also found that the interpersonal relationships of mentally healthy people, though deeper, seemed to be fewer. The strong ties were limited to only a few people. Deep involvement with even one person takes considerable time.

3. They are efficient judges of situations. Maslow found that his prizewinning people had "an unusual ability to detect the spurious, the fake, and the dishonest in personality and, in general, to judge people correctly and efficiently.[12]

The result of this heightened perception is that mentally healthy people tend to get more done because they spend less time spinning their wheels or relying on inappropriate easy answers. When a problem arises, they can solve it more efficiently because they can make their decisions in terms of how things really are, rather than how they wish they were.

[12] "Self-actualizing People: A Study of Psychological Health," in C. E. Moustikas (ed.), *The Self: Exclamations in Personal Growth* (New York: Harper and Row, Publishers, 1956), p. 65.

4. They are creative and appreciative. "Self-actualized people have the wonderful capacity to appreciate again and again, freshly and naively, the basic goods of life—with awe, pleasure, wonder, and even ecstasy, however stale these experiences may have become to others. . . . For such people even the casual workaday, moment-to-moment business of living can be thrilling, exciting, and ecstatic.[13]

Mentally healthy persons tend to do things in creative ways. At least, they respond in ways that other people call creative. They are not trying to be creative, they are just giving a natural, logical response to the situation as they see it. The difference, of course, is that creative people respond according to the problem—other folks respond according to the way they have always responded before.

5. They march to a different drummer. Having a good feeling about oneself generates confidence. The most healthy and self-actualized are self-reliant. They make their own judgments. They are, therefore, more autonomous and independent in thought and action. They rely more on their own standards of behavior and values. They are more likely to set the pace than to tag along behind asking, "What is everybody else doing?"

"This independence of environment means a relative serenity in the face of hard knocks, blows, deprivations, frustrations, and the like. These people can maintain a relative serenity and happiness in the midst of circumstances that would drive other people to suicide. They have been described as 'self-contained.'"[14]

6. They are willing to learn from anyone. Because the self-actualized person is confident and honestly aware of her own worth, she is not threatened by the prospect of appearing dull or uninformed. She is far more interested in understanding or getting the information than she is in maintaining any reputation of knowledgeableness. Truly healthy persons are always a boon to the other members of a class: they are willing to stop a lecturer and ask the question that everyone else is afraid to ask. The self-actualized person has her values straight and therefore realizes that it is better to blunder into learning than to learn nothing gracefully.

Rogers' Self-actualized Person

Another psychologist who has worked toward the description of the self-actualized, mentally mature individual is Carl R. Rogers. As a clinical psychologist, Rogers has drawn on years of clinical observation and practice to understand people and their motives.

[13] Ibid., p. 177.
[14] Ibid., p. 176.

The most famous mark of Rogerian psychology is the nondirective approach, in which the counselor endeavors to reflect ideas to the patient without giving answers or oversimplifying. Nondirective counseling is a way of serving as a sounding board to help people understand and solve their own problems.

Rogers, too, outlined certain patterns of behavior that he found consistently in people of exceptional emotional maturity. He said they almost always manifest:[15]

1. willingness to accept experiences for what they are
2. trust and confidence in their own ability and judgment
3. greater reliance on self than on society or friends
4. willingness to continue to grow as persons

In addition to Maslow and Rogers, there have been others who have delved into the delineating of the mentally healthy. From the dominions of psychology and philosophy have come names and terms that suggest entire approaches.

Erich Fromm approached the same idea in a slightly different way. He suggested that a person can be looked at in the same way as a seed.[16] Most seeds are not impressive to look at. Some are so small you need a microscope even to see them. Yet within a seed there is a tremendous amount of potential for growth. If you were to throw a flower seed into an open field and kick some dirt over it, it would probably sprout in a week or two. If you watched the progress of the plant for several weeks, you could observe it developing buds and eventually producing a flower. Then, if you were to look at this plant more closely, you might notice the bloom was rather small with dull-colored petals. You might see insects eating away at it. In general, you could say this plant was stunted, that it had not realized its full potential.

Fromm went on to suggest that if we were to take the same seed and plant it at just the right depth in prepared soil and then provide the right amount of light, water, and plant food, we could see a beautiful plant emerge with full green leaves and flowers of a beautiful hue. Most of us are very much like that first plant in that we seldom achieve much of our true potential. Only a few people ever achieve the true concept of self-actualization. Fromm's major emphasis in theory is called *productive orientation*.

No matter which theory you read, there is an obvious emphasis on the basic need to accept oneself. As Ralph Waldo Emerson suggested in his famous essay on self-reliance, "There comes a time in a man's education when he must accept himself, for better or worse, as his lot upon the earth."

No relationship is as permanent as the one we have with our own per-

[15] *Client-Centered Therapy* (Boston: Houghton Mifflin Company, 1951).
[16] Quoted by Hershey and Lugo, op. cit., p. 153.

sonalities. We can drop out of school, resign our job, or divorce a marriage partner. Still, we are linked to the individual who may really be responsible for our problems.

The Importance of Self-acceptance

In every library, there is a section of "success" books for individuals. These books promise everything from the secret of looking younger and living longer to the magic formula for selling life insurance. Basically, these books are banking on the same truth of humanity—you *can* actually change yourself by changing what you think about yourself.

The illustrations of this phenomenon are plentiful. In athletics, in politics, and in your own experience, skill and understanding are often dethroned by positive attitudes. A team with all-star players and negative attitudes is no match for an average team that *knows* it can win.

It is unfortunate that the self-image is so often sold as the cure-all. For obviously, a turtle cannot jump a fence—no matter how positive the attitude. Truly healthy people are not often given to the practice of psyching themselves up to expect the impossible through self-hypnosis. Rather, they know their strengths and weaknesses, emphasize the strengths, do not fear to try a new method, are not concerned with the shame of failure, can learn from anyone, and attack the problem instead of the problem maker. People with positive self-images are achievement-oriented, and thus they are eager contenders.

There is also evidence that how people feel about themselves is related to how effectively they think. People who do not like themselves tend to have difficulty in solving problems effectively.

People who doubt their own worth tend to think in fairly rigid patterns. They see everything as black or white, rather than with any in-between shades.

On the other hand, those who are confident of their personal worth have less difficulty in dealing with complex or ambiguous situations. People who do not feel good about themselves cannot tolerate ambiguity.

There is evidence to suggest that our motives affect the nature of our thoughts. People who have a high need for achievement and success tend to have many more fantasies about getting promoted or winning in athletic competition than do those who do not have such strong needs to try for the top. David McClelland et al.[17] have categorized these basic

[17] David McClelland et al., *The Achievement Motive* (New York: Appleton-Century-Crofts, 1953); E. G. French and E. H. Thomas, "The Relationship of Achievement Motivation to Problem-Solving Effectiveness," *Journal of Abnormal and Social Psychology*, Vol. 56, 1958, pp. 45–48.

motivational drives into three groups. (1) The *need for achievement* is that inner drive to reach success . . . whatever constitutes success according to the individual's sense of values. (2) The *need for affiliation* involves gregarious natural craving for close interpersonal relationships and friendships with other people. (3) the *need for power* refers to the desire to feel able to change the natural course of events, either directly or by influencing those who influence events. These people have more thoughts about being promoted and rising to the top of their respective heaps.

Charles Taylor and Arthur Combs[18] conducted a study to determine if well-adjusted children could accept as true a larger number of derogatory statements about themselves. One hundred and eighty sixth-grade children from rural Pennsylvania were given the *California Test of Personality*, a paper-and-pencil questionnaire designed to measure degree of adjustment or maladjustment. They were then divided into two groups—those who scored above average on mental adjustment and those who scored below average. Two weeks later, the children were given another mimeographed listing of twenty statements judged to be true of most children but not at all complimentary (e.g., "I sometimes use bad words or swear." "I sometimes am lazy and won't do my work." "I sometimes talk back to my parents."). Each child was asked to indicate which of the twenty statements were true. The results clearly demonstrated that the children who were above average in adjustments were able to accept a significantly larger number of threatening statements than the group who were below average. The conclusion was that well-adjusted children are better able to accept the undesirable aspects of their personalities. An accurate, honest self-appraisal can be an asset to an emotionally mature person, whereas the same honesty would be a danger sign to the less mature.

For many generations, a favorite children's story has been *The Little Engine That Could*.[19] Children like to hear stories about trains, and parents like to be reminded that the main difference between success and failure is a realistic self-acceptance that says "I can do it!" As one apostle of success put it: "Big shots are just little shots . . . that kept on shooting!"

[18] Self-Acceptance and Adjustment," *Journal of Consulting Psychology*, Vol. 16, 1954, pp. 89–91.
[19] David McClelland, *The Achieving Society* (Princeton, N.J.: D. Van Nostrand Company, Inc., 1961) has hypothesized that the desire to achieve as a part of national character can be traced to the type of stories young children are told. Historically, children in rapidly developing nations are told stories in which the hero overcomes obstacles to achieve some significant goal. This may be in the form of historical or fictional heroic characters. In underdeveloped countries, McClelland found a tendency for children to be taught stories emphasizing the virtues of acceptance, endurance, and related concepts.

The Accurate Self-image

Nobody questions the value of a healthy self-image. But if you have done much thinking about the kind of person you really are, then you have discovered one of the great hurdles of knowing yourself. Human beings have great difficulty being objective about themselves. This is because we have only two eyes and they happen to be located in almost the same place. We cannot see ourselves physically because of physical limitations, and it is just as difficult to take a good, unbiased look at our emotional selves because of the emotional defenses we all maintain.

The famous Scottish poet Robert Burns learned the lesson of the accurate self-image one Sunday in church. He was fascinated by the grand

My Fair Lady. A flower girl is introduced to royalty (Warner Brothers, 1965). How important is self-image to social success?

ladies and gentlemen in their splendid outfits. One woman, who had the most elaborate hat of all, made a very dramatic entrance and sat down directly in front of Burns. Her monstrous hat completely obscured the poet's vision. As the service continued, Burns became absorbed in watching a louse, which crawled out from under the hat, made its way up over a ribbon and a bow and a flower. Finally, as the louse reached the summit of a great plume that dominated the hat, Burns opened his hymnal and, on the inside cover, penned the words of "To a Louse." This famous poem describes the lady's blindness to her real image. She sat in her pew quite confident that all the women were envying her and all the men desiring her. Burns was only thinking how dirty her hair had to be. He ended his poem with the now-famous words

> Would some power the giftie give us,
> To see ourselves as others see us,
> It would from many a blunder free us.

It is not unusual to find convenient blind spots in our self-perception. Only rarely do we meet individuals who, like Maslow's self-actualized persons, know and speak freely about their strengths and weaknesses.

Most success stories add weight to the arguments of the positive thinkers. Much has been written to encourage aspiring achievers to set their self-expectations high. Many suggest that we should all demand 110 per cent of ourselves. Obviously, nobody really does 10 per cent better than it is possible to do. But we can do 10 per cent better than we have done or even thought we could do.

We speak of teams "playing over their heads" and people "out-doing" themselves. These are phrases that attempt to explain a simple fact: the team or the person has merely exceeded expectations. The moral of these familiar experiences is that we need to be more willing to accept our own potential greatness.

Most psychologists agree that the average person uses only 10 to 15 per cent of the brain's potential. Under extreme circumstances humans can run faster, jump higher, and lift more weight than would "normally" be thought possible. Like Olympic athletes, we should always be trying to push ourselves just beyond previous attainments. If we say that we cannot do a thing, we're probably right. But if we maintain that we *have* the ability, the battle is half won.

Most of us tend to be too humble about our abilities. Our cultural taboo against the braggart has caused many of us to talk down the skills and abilities we honestly know we have. We are afraid to appear confident and self-assured. One of our greatest needs is the realization that lying about our abilities can be just as socially and psychologically damaging as bragging. Perhaps we should give heed to the renowned existential philosopher Dizzy Dean, who says, "If you've done it, it ain't bragging!"

The concept of humility is often misinterpreted. For example, the Apostle Paul wrote to first-century Christians in Rome not to think of themselves "more highly than [they] ought to think" (Romans 12:3). Many people have quoted this verse as proof that we ought to be self-effacing. However, Paul continues by saying that we should recognize that "God has given to every man a measure of grace." Paul's meaning, therefore, was not endorsement of the practice of running down everything we do. Rather, he was saying, "Be honest about the gifts God has given to you."

A few years ago, Notre Dame's star center, Frankie Szymanski, became quite well known for his humility. Despite the fact that he had made most of the All-American teams and was outstanding on both offense and defense, he was never known to brag or speak highly of his football prowess. On one occasion, Frankie appeared in a South Bend court as a witness. The attorney asked if he was on the Notre Dame football team. Frankie replied that he was. Next, the lawyer asked what position he played. "Center," replied Szymanski, without looking up. "How good a center are you?" demanded the attorney.

The shy young man squirmed in his chair but in confident tones answered, "Sir, I am the best center in the history of Notre Dame."

Coach Frank Leahy, who was in the courtroom, was shocked by such a statement from the usually modest player. After court was adjourned, the coach asked him why he had made such a statement.

Szymanski blushed and responded, "I hated to do it, Coach, but after all *I was under oath!*"

The young man from Notre Dame knew his ability. He had had the opportunity to test himself on the gridiron. But physical abilities and limits are much easier to test and evaluate than the elusive inner strengths. Each of us has the problem of finding out what we really are. What methods are there for self-analysis? How can we overcome our natural lack of objectivity? How reliable are those honest and frank evaluations so willingly provided by our friends? Was the old commercial speaking the truth when it said, "Your best friend won't tell you"?

A growing number of psychological profile tests are available to act as a mirror for those open enough to want to know themselves. Although hard-and-fast conclusions cannot always be drawn from these tests, they do provide some insight into personality characteristics as well as presenting a typical format for psychological tests. Most colleges and universities now have testing services that offer a wide variety of psychological and vocational aptitude tests for students. Usually a trained counselor is available to help interpret test results and give the student personal insight. Many industries are finding it a good investment to pay large sums of money to have employees given psychological inventories. Not only is the business able to locate potential problems, but the employees' value to the firm is increased as they are aided in

The Winning Team. Ronald Reagan as Grover Cleveland Alexander (Warner Brothers, 1952). Are great athletes usually humble?

knowing themselves better. Students should certainly avail themselves of the opportunity to receive professional psychological services offered by learning institutions. An accurate understanding of one's strengths and weaknesses can provide a boost not only to scholastic work but also amidst the slings and arrows of interpersonal relationships.

Me and You, Babe

One of the ways we get to understand ourselves is by comparing our friend in the mirror to people we see about us. Of course, it is rather difficult to do a thorough comparison with each of the hundreds of individuals we contact. As a result, we tend to generalize or stereotype people into major groups. At the very mention of the word, you can summon up a mental image of a used car salesperson, a business executive, or a defensive lineman. There are certain traits that do appear more often in some groups than others. Our biggest mistake is not in noticing these similarities, but in assuming the presence of one trait because of the presence of another. Are all Texans big and boastful? Are all redheads short tempered? What absolutely fair generalizations can we make about women drivers, Republicans, or church goers?

We must use generalizations. Without them we would never get all our thinking done. At the same time, we must remember that categorizing is a shortcut process and subject to error.

The Typists

Though every age has been peopled with simple, one-of-a-kind beings, there have always been some folks around who wanted to make life simpler. From antiquity, scholars have been intrigued by the idea that people fall into natural categories. In this section, we will briefly review some of the theories about the necessary pigeonhole arrangement for sorting the whole population, with no leftovers.

Hippocrates

The great Greek physician Hippocrates came up with an extremely simple arrangement. People are of four basic types, he said, the *sanguine* (optimistic), the *phlegmatic* (sluggish), the *choleric* (grouchy), and the *melancholic* (who live down in the dumps).[20] Things did not go well for this theory when people thought about their ever-changing moods. They soon realized that everybody had each of these characteristics sometimes. If everybody was in every category, then things were right back where they had started . . . except that Hippocrates was almost as famous as Dr. Spock.

Jung

Modern thinkers, too, have repeatedly sought the all-inclusive type of theory. Carl Jung, one of Sigmund Freud's students in the emerging sci-

[20] A. Q. Sartain et al., *Psychology: Understanding Human Behavior*, 3rd ed. (New York: McGraw-Hill Book Company, 1967), p. 44.

Table 10.2		Thinking	Feeling	Sensation	Intuition
	Introvert	A philosopher like Immanuel Kant	Introspective people who express their confidences in diaries and secret poetry	An oil painter like Firmin-Auguste Renoir	A mystical dreamer—maybe an artist or an unappreciated "genius"
	Extrovert	A scientist like Charles Darwin	Fashion-conscious people interested in social causes and cultural affairs	An outgoing seeker of "sense" experience, as a gourmet or an art lover	A promoter who has a keen nose for new enterprises showing promise for development

ence of psychoanalysis, proposed his own two-part theory of personality. He proposed that people's feelings fell into two general types:[21] *extrovert* and *introvert*. The mixture of these two ingredients determines the kind of overall personality.

If *extrovert* feelings dominate our thinking, our decisions and actions are determined primarily by objective relationships and not by pure opinion. The extrovert's attention and interest are centered on the immediate surroundings and the business at hand. He or she is objective—a reality-oriented individual who is much more a doer than a thinker.

The *introvert* feelings produce more of an inward, thoughtful personality. What the introvert does is usually guided by personal ideas and philosophy. Because of a lack of flexibility, Jung's introvert tends to be subjectively oriented instead of objectively oriented. It is more important that things be done "the right" way than that they simply be done.

Under introversion and extroversion, Jung described four basic functions. He called these our ways of approaching the universe. These four channels of input are (1) *thinking*, which includes factual and logical reasoning; (2) *feeling*, which relates to personal interpretation on the subjective level; (3) *sensation*, in which one deals with perceptions—with things as they are perceived, without interpretation or evaluation; and (4) *intuition*, based on an unconscious inner perception of the potentialities of things.

As you read about Jung's two-type theory and think about your own characteristics, a few problems become immediately apparent. For instance, each of us has both introvert and extrovert feelings at one time or another. R. Stagner[22] has suggested that most folks fall more into an *ambivert* category, as seen in the chart. Even with all his subtypes, Jung

[21] From Dolande Jacobi, *The Psychology of C. G. Jung*, rev. ed. (New Haven, Conn.: Yale University Press, 1951), p. 15.
[22] *Psychology of Personality*, 2nd ed. (New York: McGraw-Hill Book Company, 1948) p. 242.

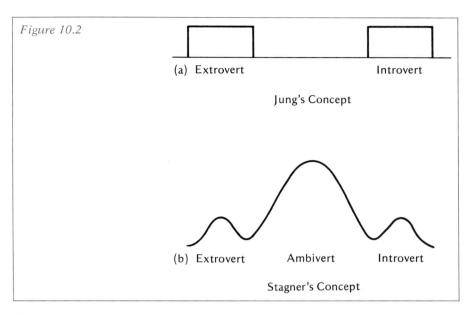

Figure 10.2

(a) Extrovert   Introvert

Jung's Concept

(b) Extrovert   Ambivert   Introvert

Stagner's Concept

dealt with only a few aspects of personality and failed to consider many others.

Sheldon

The most modern scholar to add to the theories of physiognomy (the science of interpreting personality from physical features) has been William H. Sheldon,[23] whose system uses three main tags. For purposes of explanation, Sheldon's types are described in the following manner.

The *endomorph* is the bulky, but beloved jolly-old-Saint-Nick type. Sheldon says the endomorph tends to be rather thick, or even fat, in proportion to height. This is the kind of person who will eventually be told by a doctor to give up those intimate little dinners for four—unless there are three other persons present. If the body type is predominantly endomorphic, said Sheldon, the personality and temperament will be *viscerotonic*. That is, the person will seek comfort, love fine food (and eat too much of it), and be a jovial, affectionate, well-liked person. If Sheldon's endomorph is a reliable phenomenon, then it must be true that everybody loves a fat man . . . Idi Amin notwithstanding.

Category number two of Sheldon's absolute types is the *mesomorph*. This is the person who would kick sand on Charles Atlas on the beach. The mesomorph is strong, tough, and athletic. He or she is usually well built and well proportioned and has just the physique that all the other "morphs" are wishing for. One college student had no trouble remem-

[23] W. H. Sheldon and S. S. Stevens, *The Varieties of Temperament* (New York: Harper and Row, Publishers, 1942).

bering the mesomorph—"this is the one you don't meso-round with." According to Sheldon's theory, someone with physical mesomorph characteristics would be expected to have a *somatotonic* temperament. This sort of person is fond of muscular activity and tends to be aggressive and self-assertive. The mesomorph can probably run faster, jump higher, smile brighter, and poll more votes than the other two morphs put together.

Sheldon's remaining category of folks is called the *ectomorph*. These guys are not likely ever to be draft choices for defensive line positions in pro football, but they may well own the team. The ectomorph is the kid who had two nicknames in school: "Skinny" and "Brains." They tend to be long, thin, and poorly developed. Though a "98-pound weakling" physically, the ectomorph leads the league in the intellectual department. This temperament is *cerebrotonic*, which is characterized by excessive restraint, inhibition, and avoidance of social contacts. The shy, absent-minded, but brilliant college professor is a stereotype.

Sheldon developed a mathematical formula for describing an individual's peculiar combination of these three basic body types. An individual's *somatotype* is composed of three numbers each on a 7-point scale. The first refers to endomorphic traits. The second indicates mesomorphy. And the last number tells how ectomorphic the individual is. Therefore, a perfect endomorph will have a somatotype of 7-0-0, a perfect mesomorph would rank 0-7-0, and the extreme ectomorph would (like James Bond if he were skinny) be numbered 0-0-7. Most physiques are a mixture of the three components. Abraham Lincoln was a 1-5-6; Jackie Gleason is, roughly, a 6-4-1; and Muhammad Ali a 2-7-1.[24]

The following exam was developed by the editors of *Psychology Today* to help individuals identify their own personal blend of characteristics associated with the major physique types. Take the test and see if your personality traits correspond with your own physique (see Figure 10.3).

Most people, of course, have some less distinctive somatotype, like 1-2-3 or 4-6-4. Although there are 343 possible somatotypes, less than 100 different ones were catalogued in a survey of forty thousand human physiques.

To investigate his ideas about temperament and physique further, Sheldon asked observers to assign temperament ratings to his subjects. He found a remarkable correlation between physical traits and personality traits. Fat persons *did* prove to be slower reacting, and muscular persons *did* definitely enjoy exercise more than the others.

The question remains: Does a man eat a lot because he is fat or is he fat because he eats a lot? Are your personality traits the cause of or the

[24] Suggested by J. B. Cortes and F. M. Gatti, "Physique and Propensity," *Psychology Today*, October 1970, p. 44.

Figure 10.3   Self-description Test

To find out if you are by temperament an endomorph, mesomorph or ectomorph, select adjectives that best describe you. See key at end of chapter.

Below are some statements that I would like to have you complete about yourself. Fill in each blank with a word from the suggested list following each statement. For any blank, three in each statement, you may select any word from the list of twelve immediately below. An exact word to fit you may not be in the list, but select the words that seem to fit *most closely* the way you are.

1. I feel most of the time _____, _____ and _____.

calm	relaxed	complacent
anxious	confident	reticent
cheerful	tense	energetic
contented	impetuous	self-conscious

2. When I study or work, I seem to be_____, _____ and _____.

efficient	sluggish	precise
enthusiastic	competitive	determined
reflective	leisurely	thoughtful
placid	meticulous	cooperative

3. Socially, I am _____, _____ and _____.

outgoing	considerate	argumentative
affable	awkward	shy
tolerant	affected	talkative
gentle-tempered	soft-tempered	hot-tempered

4. I am rather _____, _____ and _____.

active	forgiving	sympathetic
warm	courageous	serious
domineering	suspicious	soft-hearted
introspective	cool	enterprising

5. Other people consider me rather_____, _____ and _____.

generous	optimistic	sensitive
adventurous	affectionate	kind
withdrawn	reckless	cautious
dominant	detached	dependent

6. Underline *one* word out of the three in each of the following lines which most closely describes the way you are.

   a) assertive, relaxed, tense   d) confident, tactful, kind
   b) hot-tempered, cool, warm   e) dependent, dominant, detached
   c) withdrawn, sociable, active   f) enterprising, affable, anxious

Temperament Test. (*Reprinted from Psychology Today, October 1970. Copyright ©* Communications/Research/Machines, Inc.)

result of your physical inheritance? In basic psychological terminology, does heredity or environment dominate in the shaping of personality?

When Sheldon found it necessary to somatotype people to compensate for mixtures, he lost the basic intent of reducing people to minimal common groups. There is no doubt that every person has a somatotype all his own and that the full range of combinations would extend far beyond the reaches of Sheldon's 343.

People Can Change

Some facts of life are so basic to our experience that we often overlook their importance. One of these foundation facts of society is that people can change. Not only can people change, but they are sure to change in one way or another. This is even true of people who appear to be thinking and acting in the same way day after day. They are changing, too— becoming daily more entrenched in their habits than before.

Management, education, medicine, and almost every occupational endeavor can trace their very existence and purpose to the fact that people are going to change. For years, aspiring teachers were told that they would be like potters and their students like clay—and that the molding, shaping process was the essence of education. Unfortunately, this is an oversimplification, for clay responds only when the potter is working on it. People, however, grow, change, and develop whether there is guidance or not. Perhaps teachers, managers, and all leadership professionals should think of their subordinates as living plants rather than dead clay. Plants will grow no matter what, but with careful and patient nurture and guidance they can grow into things of beauty and usefulness.

Summary: The Healthy Self-image

Philosophers and psychologists have sought the one basic motivator of mankind. It has variously been said to be biological, sociological, psychoanalytic, and so on. The behaviorists' solution for this dilemma has been that the result, not the cause, is the thing that should be reckoned with. Combining the other theories of motivation and emphasizing the qualities of the mentally healthy person is the *humanistic* approach to motivation.

Abraham H. Maslow arranged human needs in a sequential ladder chart. Maslow said that the needs that motivate people come in the following priority order: (1) physiological needs; (2) safety and security needs; (3) love and belonging needs; (4) self-esteem needs; and (5) self-actualization.

Maslow, Carl Rogers, and others have recognized the self-actualized person and enumerated some of the characteristics of mentally healthy and emotionally mature individuals:

1. They can accept the way things really are.
2. They are not afraid to get close to others.
3. They are efficient judges of situations.
4. They are creative and appreciative.
5. They march to a different drummer.
6. They are willing to learn from anyone.

The work of Maslow, Rogers, and many others is unified in its support of the healthy self-image as a key to happiness and success. Self-confidence and honesty about their abilities have been found to characterize people who have been successful in every type of endeavor.

The removal of fantasy from our expectations is the initial step toward achievement. Accepting yourself does not guarantee that you will be the greatest. It does, however, mean that you will be likely to manifest the patience and determination to rise at least to your rightful level of achievement. A healthy self-image will not enable you to walk on water, but it will let you have a lot more fun swimming.

Key to Self-description Test (*page 225*)

Key to Temperament Test. Count the number of adjectives that you selected in each of the three categories. For example, if your totals are 10/6/5, you have predominantly endomorphic traits. A 6/10/5 means you are high in mesomorphic traits.	**Endomorphic**	**Mesomorphic**	**Ectomorphic**
	dependent	dominant	detached
	calm	cheerful	tense
	relaxed	confident	anxious
	complacent	energetic	reticent
	contented	impetuous	self-conscious
	sluggish	efficient	meticulous
	placid	enthusiastic	reflective
	leisurely	competitive	precise
	cooperative	determined	thoughtful
	affable	outgoing	considerate
	tolerant	argumentative	shy
	affected	talkative	awkward
	warm	active	cool
	forgiving	domineering	suspicious
	sympathetic	courageous	introspective
	soft-hearted	enterprising	serious
	generous	adventurous	cautious
	affectionate	reckless	tactful
	kind	assertive	sensitive
	sociable	optimistic	withdrawn
	soft-tempered	hot-tempered	gentle-tempered

Individual differences are a characteristic of life that we all understand and accept. Even so, for convenience we find it necessary to recognize stereotypes and generalizations about individuals and groups. As long as our stereotypes and categorizing are fair, open-ended, and tentative, they can be highly useful. The danger occurs when we begin to classify illogically and unfairly, assume the presence of one character trait because of the presence of some other trait, or allow generalizations to harden into "facts" of life upon which we base actions.

Through the ages, various observers have endeavored to derive some reliable means of grouping people by physical traits (physiognomy). Hippocrates suggested four types: the sanguine, the phlegmatic, the choleric, and the melancholic. Jung described the traits of the introvert and the extrovert (and later thinkers suggested that Jung should have included an ambivert). Sheldon classified people physically as endomorphic, mesomorphic, and ectomorphic. He said that temperament corresponds to physical characteristics and named the corresponding temperaments, *viscerotonia*, *somatotonia*, and *cerebrotonia*.

Like Sheldon, the other typists have all had eventually to increase the number of categories they had proposed. The theories may have originally been suggested as tentative classification systems, but they were soon forced into the untenable position of proving their infallibility. Types are now regarded as extreme forms of personality traits—very handy for conversation but scientifically unreliable.

Review Questions

1. Name Maslow's five basic needs. How far up the ladder do most people progress?
2. Is self-acceptance important? Why? How is it related to self-image?
3. Explain the golden mean concept.
4. According to Maslow's hierarchy, what level of need is represented by each of the following statements?
    a. I must climb the mountain because it is there.
    b. Gentlemen of distinction drink Whipple Wine.
    c. Bob's bomb shelters are best.
    d. The Tri-Peu fraternity wants you as a brother.
    e. I'd give $1,000 for a cold beer right now.
5. Make a list of the four people you respect most. How many characteristics of the mentally healthy or self-actualized person do they possess?
6. Relate the development of an early education program such as Headstart to Erich Fromm's parable about a flower.
7. Why do outstanding athletes frequently appear "cocky"?

8. Ayn Rand argues that there is no such thing as altruism. Although she would be willing to give her own life to save her husband's life, she argues that this is purely a selfish act. Can you explain her reasoning?
9. What are the two major classifications of Carl Jung's theory of personality?
10. Using William H. Sheldon's theory, classify the following individuals:
    a. Woody Allen
    b. O. J. Simpson
    c. Santa Claus

11

Working with Others

Poor Honos McGee! It was the worst day of his life when they elected him representative of the union. He tried too hard to please everybody. And every time he'd negotiate the big bosses into a raise, the union boys would fuss at him for not getting enough in the bargain. If he bargained for something that benefited one man, some other joker would stay mad for a month. Finally, Honos hit on a plan—he would get a committee together to go with him when he bargained. Everyone agreed it was a fine idea. Well, the committee argued long and hard and they stuck to their demands. Finally, the teamwork paid off. The committee returned victoriously to the union hall.

"Well, men," reported Honos McGee proudly, "the new contract says that from now on we only have to work on Wednesday. What do you think of that?"

The answer came from the back of the room: "You don't mean every Wednesday, do you?"

It has been cynically estimated that one third of all the people in the early morning traffic are headed for a committee meeting. Such a statistic would be difficult to substantiate (unless a sizable Substantiation Committee were appointed), but it does often seem that we live in a committee-cluttered culture.

Almost everyone has chuckled bitterly over the observation that "A camel is a horse put together by a committee." We know that there is some truth in the allegation that the best way to kill an idea is to appoint a committee. And yet we persist in making committees and establishing groups for specific purposes.

The appointing of committees, however, may not be half so naive or bumbling as it might appear. A committee is very often set in motion with a charge to do one thing, when the manager fully anticipates that some totally different—but equally important—job will be accomplished. For example, many a committee is formed, not to make decisions, but to involve influential people. The Federal government has made extensive application of this "task force" approach, which is based on the idea that the best way to keep people from disagreeing with a final decision is to "pull them into" the committee procedings that lead up to that final decision. They may not affect the decision at all, but they will feel more responsible for it if their names are listed among the committee dignitaries.

The committee obviously doesn't find its strength in quick and decisive decision making . . . but in longer-lasting decisions. Committees and other group-exchange methods *are* effective for communicating and sharing ideas and growth processes.

Besides those groups we appoint, there are those that seem to result from spontaneous generation. Any person trying to reach an objective and take a group with him can testify to the puzzling nature and bullheaded resistance of groups. The Clean Air Society is opposing the Homefires Federation and the Senior Citizens are down on the United Young. We can't seem to live peaceably with our groups. Yet they are important enough to us so that we continue to form and nourish the group concept.

Why do we persist in making things hard for ourselves? Do we want the decisions to be harder to reach? Wouldn't everything move faster if one person could make all the decisions? Why do we listen to the groups? Why must problem solvers and managers spend so much time batting a question about? Don't they usually end up with an idea that one of them had back at the beginning?

No. Contrary to what the most verbal critics of the group process say, the combined efforts of a group can far exceed the efforts of any or all of the group members working separately. Sometimes, of course, groups don't work together—in that case, they are not worth the red tape it would take to disband them. On the other hand, when a group of people work well together, they very often bring about a total result that is greater than the sum of the group's parts. Or, in the words of a great lettuce salesperson: two heads are better than one.

Synergy is a popular term for the concept that where creativity or problem solving are involved, one plus one *can* equal three or more. Perhaps you have heard that ordinary table salt is a combination of sodium, a highly poisonous alkali, and chlorine, a highly poisonous gas. Two substances, poisonous alone, are combined to create a useful and beneficial commodity. The balance resulting from differences produces a more valuable final product. In other words, groups have properties of their own that are different from those of individuals.

In 1885, the World Series of Mule Team Competition was held in Chicago. The winning team of mules was able to pull 9,000 pounds. The second-place team pulled slightly less. Someone came up with the idea of hitching both the first and second teams to a load. Together the teams pulled a 30,000-pound load. This excellent example of synergy was duplicated in Death Valley when a young foreman named Stiles noticed that a team of twelve mules was hauling loads twice the size that eight mules could have. This set him to thinking and experimenting. A twenty-mule team wound up pulling ten tons—about half the capacity of a modern railroad freight car. This was the origin of "Twenty Mule Team Borax," which became a household word and an international trademark. It was also synergism in action.

It is worth mentioning at this point that not all synergy is positive. The combined negative attitudes and bickering of *dissatisfied* group members can add up to greater trouble than any one of the members could have caused individually. Negative synergy in action is sometimes called a panic or a riot.

This chapter will discuss characteristics of groups and outline group processes and pitfalls for the purpose of assisting the reader to work with groups. As with most rewarding activities, group work presents many difficulties and unanswered questions. The only way to endure the frustration is to realize that success comes to those who can draw on the strengths of other people.

Groups: How You Spot One

Most sociologists agree that a group does not truly exist until the members are involved together in doing something. Unity of purpose makes a group exist. Reach your destination on the train, and you leave the group of commuters pursuing the same goal. Or . . . fall asleep at the symphony, and you are not a part of the listening group.

There are many definitions of what constitutes a group. Almost all writers stress that members must be psychologically aware of each other's existence and function . . . if only in a general sense.

The definition used in this chapter includes the characteristics assigned by most other definitions. A group can be defined as two or more individuals: (1) interacting with some or all group members on an individual or network basis; (2) sharing one or more goals; (3) governed by a normative system of behavior and attitude; (4) maintaining stable role relationships; and (5) forming subgroups through various networks of attraction and rejection.[1]

Interaction in a group does not have to be on a simply one-to-one basis. Many modern groups routinely do "different things together." They interact through networks and remain completely anonymous to each other; yet they have a potency to make the most intimate small groups envious.

Shared goals are characteristic of groups that *are* groups. Whether it be a football team, a production group, or everyone who votes yes on the bond issue, the togetherness transcends introductions, intimacy, or time spent in each other's physical presence.

A *behavior system* can also make a clear distinction between a group and a random closeness of people. Even a mob deserves its "mob" designation because there is a certain unity in its antisocial acts. In the less drastic forms, groups submit to rules and norms to gain group membership.

Stable role relationships are characteristic of groups. Whether there are formally established offices or an undefined "pecking order," groups of humans dependably organize themselves in roles and work within that framework. Interestingly enough, much group activity results from efforts of group members to advance or change their assigned roles. Translation: progress happens when someone wants the boss' job!

Subgroups tend to follow automatically in the wake of group activity. The subtle movements within the outwardly visible roles can produce the bitter realities of group politics. The office "grapevine" and the "straw boss" are examples of subgroups that form informally. More structured groups have formally appointed units, divisions, offices, and task forces.

The manager's awareness of the characteristics of these groups is highly significant. Groups are more than "bunches of individuals." They demonstrate synergistic reactions in almost every activity. The manager's response to a group must take account of interaction of group members.

It has been only in the last half century that meaningful, specific research has been conducted on the group process. In the 1920's Elton

[1] G. E. Myers and M. T. Myers, *The Dynamics of Human Communication* (New York: McGraw-Hill Book Co., 1973) pp. 125–127.

Mayo and his associates at the Harvard Business School made studies that demonstrated the importance of groups in the company's profit-loss column. Their experiments showed that industrial workers tend to establish informal groups that affect both morale and productivity.

Kurt Lewin was the founder of the group dynamics movement. Lewin was a professor of social psychology at the University of Iowa in the 1930's. His experiments in industry showed that leadership attitudes had a direct correlation with worker morale and productivity. These findings were, no doubt, much more popular with labor than with management.

In recent years, the University Center for Group Dynamics at the University of Michigan, the National Training Laboratories in Bethel, Maine, and other research groups have made contributions to the understanding of what happens when a group attacks a problem . . . and vice versa.

Perhaps we ought to make a distinction in our thinking between a group and an organization. The difference is one of common purpose and cooperative effort. If three alley cats have their tails tied together and are thrown over a tree limb, there is definitely a group in existence, but it is unlikely that much organization will be demonstrated. Chester I. Barnard, the esoteric president of New Jersey Bell Telephone, defined an organization as "a system of consciously coordinated activities or forces of two or more persons rather than an abstract legal entity."[2]

In an earlier chapter, we dealt more specifically with the matter of organization. The following information regarding groups and the process of cooperative effort provides a valuable foundation for the study of organization. One of the common mistakes of management is the blind attempt to impose organization without understanding the group in question.

Groups: Why They Form

The following factors contribute to the function of groups. The physical, economic, sociopsychological, and other causes of group formation should be of great interest to those charged with leadership.[3] In almost every case, the reason for group formation is directly related to the group's goal and enthusiasm.

Location is the most obvious cause of group relationships. Those who live and work in close proximity tend to become grouped. However, in

[2] *Functions of the Executive* (Cambridge, Mass.: Harvard University Press, 1938), Chapters 6, 7, 9.
[3] These topics are suggested by John M. Francevich et. al., *Managing for Performance*, (Dallas, Texas: Business Publications, Inc., 1980), pp. 254–257.

some respects location is not an altogether independent cause. Although it is true that we usually form friendships with those we see often, it is also likely that some common interest or task has brought us together in the first place. What do you suppose would happen if a large company decided to homogenize its employees—labor, management, secretaries, and bosses—in one big room to do their jobs? Would work groups form according to location in the room? Or would time and convenience eventually put all the sales reps in one corner, all the copy writers in another corner, and all the fork-lift drivers somewhere else? Obviously, work groups form because of location. However, our location is likely to result from some other factor.

The growing sophistication of transportation and communication has also reduced the incidence of location-resultant groups. The conference call and the jet day-trip have made geographic nearness less of a factor in group closeness.

Economic reasons often cause group formation. Obviously, the AFL-CIO was not formed because all its members lived on the same block or liked to bowl together. Some work groups form because of individuals believe that they can derive more economic benefits by collective bargaining. The stockholders' meeting and the economic boycott may bring together people who would otherwise never meet.

Sometimes management offers a financial bonus to the department or shift that exceeds its monthly quota by the greatest amount. In such a case, individual financial gain is dependent on group performance, and the quality of togetherness and innovation can become absolutely inspiring. A favorite device of novelists is to describe the plight of two natural enemies who, through some quirk of fate, find themselves dependent on each other for survival or gain.

Groups formed for economic reasons demonstrate one characteristic of all groups: group members do not necessarily agree on every point, but they have absolute unity on the thing that makes them a group. Staunch Republicans may prefer many different brands of coffee, but there is little doubt about how they will vote in the next presidential election.

Sociopsychological needs are factors in group formation. Workers in organizations are motivated to form work groups so that their needs can be more adequately satisfied. The security, social esteem, and self-actualization needs can be satisfied to some degree by workers if they belong to groups.

Security needs are most likely to cause group formation when individuals lack sufficient power to effect a change on their own. The beginnings of the labor union movement resulted from the fact that there were far more workers than jobs. With ten people waiting in line for your job, you were somewhat hesitant to make demands of the boss. Workers joined forces to bargain for security and discovered power. As labor power has grown over the years, many security needs have been produced . . . and many headaches for management. As the balance of power shifts, would it be surprising to see management groups formed to guarantee security from union domination? What forms might such an emerging group take?

Social needs form some part of almost every group-forming instinct. The group phenomenon itself is social—that is, most of the things that can be said of any group are true of society in general. People need others to feel fulfilled—even Robinson Crusoe approached his island captivity with a mental model of a group-created society. It is almost impossible to imagine the nature of a human totally denied the privilege of group exchange. In fact, one of the harshest punishments that can be given is to be put in solitary confinement for a period of time.

The desire to belong and to be a part of a group is perhaps more critical in some cultures than in others. An interesting discussion of the social needs of Americans is given by Edgar Schein.[4] He examines the effects of prisoner treatment on group accomplishment. Schein refers to the unusually low incidence of escape attempts and the numerous instances of apparent collaboration by American prisoners of war in North Korea. Schein suggests that one of the reasons for this situation was the manner in which the prisoners were treated.

The North Koreans were careful not to allow social groups to form or continue. In the North Korean POW camps, officers were separated from enlisted men. Groups were systematically broken up and prisoners were regularly transferred between barracks. The fact that informal organizations could not be formed on a continuing basis could explain the low escape rate. The men were unable to develop the organization necessary to hatch an escape plan. In addition, prisoners were unable to develop the necessary trust in each other that was so essential for an escape. Without mutual trust, the escape capability was eliminated and the overall morale among POW's was very low.

Does Schein's discussion have implications for today's managers— perhaps that promising employees should be transferred often to keep them from escaping to other companies? Although "escape attempts" are not very troublesome to most businesses, worker satisfaction can be. It is important that work-social groups be permitted (and in some cases encouraged). Small-group research findings indicate that employees who are isolated from each other because of plant layout find their jobs less satisfying than those group members who are able to socialize on the job.[5]

The *esteem* of one's peers is often the cause of grouping. We like to per-

---

[4] "The Chinese Indoctrination Program for Prisoners of War," *Psychiatry*, Vol. 19, May 1956, pp. 149–172.

[5] Elton Mayo, *The Human Problems of an Industrial Civilization* (Boston: Graduate School of Business Administration, Harvard University, 1946), pp. 42–52.

ceive ourselves as successful and prestigious. Some employees are attracted toward joining a group or having a position that, according to their perception, has a higher social standing. The esteem needs are the most intangible of the motivations of group formation. Even so, they are just as important to the individual feeling the need as are the other needs that have been discussed. Above certain salary ranges, the negotiations for jobs very closely turn on the elements of status and prestige that go with the position. Many a thankless job has been passed off to a person who highly valued a title, a corner office, or an assigned parking place.

Self-actualization needs often lead to the formation of professional organizations and other groups that facilitate communication among workers in the same job. There is a feeling of personal growth and accomplishment that comes from the exchange of shop talk and professional jargon. The line is hazy between groups formed to meet needs for esteem and those formed to meet self-actualization needs. Many professional organizations are chartered under the flag of professional growth and maintained for the satisfaction of economic, security, or status needs.

To deal with any group without first investigating the reasons for its formation is equivalent to chopping down a tree by starting on the limbs. Now that we have looked into some of the reasons groups form, we will consider some of the stages of group growth.

Groups: How They Grow

As groups grow in maturity, they pass through recognizable stages of proficiency. They don't just get older, but, if they are growing, a bond of trust and understanding is easily seen to characterize them. Some groups, of course, never progress at all. They maintain the wasteful individual approach to every task. When a number of people fail to develop their team capability, the tragedy is double. Not only are they wasting time and money by inefficiency, they are missing the self-actualizing experience of working effectively with other people. It is precision teamwork—not eleven individual antagonists—that makes football an exciting spectator sport.

Mutual acceptance is a sort of initiation step for group memebership. The newcomer must *earn* real acceptance. Reputation may have preceded arrival, or co-workers may be disposed to positive attitudes. But any initial good must be strengthened by positive experiences in actual practice. In a sense, each new employee's first task is to get past the honeymoon period and establish respect, trust, and acceptance based on personal performance.

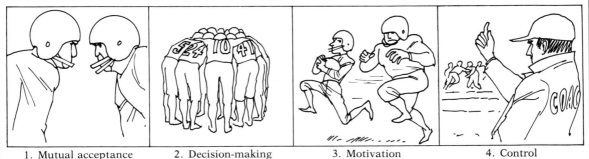

| 1. Mutual acceptance | 2. Decision-making | 3. Motivation | 4. Control |

Figure 11.1. Stages in group development.

Decision-making privileges are withheld from new people on the job. While they are still learning their way around, it is unlikely that the group will seek their participation or advice. This natural tendency is unfortunate, since the newcomer probably has some real positive contributions to make. Objectivity, for example, is a positive factor in decision making. Many groups lose the valuable input of newcomers because a loss of objectivity often comes with orientation.

Motivation is a leadership quality. As workers begin to identify with and "internalize" the organization, they move into the stage of maturity when they can sincerely prod other workers to work toward group goals for the common good. This *control* becomes internal as workers reach maturity. If the executive ranks still have to punch a timeclock, the organization is in serious trouble. Self-control is the watch word of mature group participation . . . in business or on the athletic field. More will be said about this concept when we explore the importance of worker maturity in Chapter 14.

Groups: How They Group

Groups overlap. One person may occupy many diverse group roles simultaneously. Consider Elbert Zinger, who is (1) Grandpa Zinger to his children and grandchildren; (2) Representative Zinger to the folks in his political district: (3) Chief Zinger to the boys at the volunteer fire department; (4) Major Zinger to his army reserve unit; and (5) Exalted Grand-Stomper Zinger to the boys down at the Brotherhood of Buffaloes Lodge.

Like each of us, Elbert Zinger is an active participant in many diverse groups at the same time. Leonard R. Sayles[6] has suggested a classification system to describe groups. He has named four groups of grouping groups.

[6] *Research in Industrial Human Relations* (New York: Harper and Row, Publishers, 1957), pp. 135–145.

The *command group* is a place where orders are given. Such a group is usually characterized by a formal organizational chart and a chain of command. The military is the most familiar example of the command group. Many businesses are also command groups with activities taking place on the orders of a superior. The "orders" may take the form of a request but the command still exists because of the rank relationship of the group members.

The *task group* usually exists for a specific project or task. Many businesses are finding that smaller, less formal task forces are faster moving and more productive than traditional command groups. The activities of task groups or staffs create a situation in which group members are able to communicate and coordinate with each other regarding the best way to attain the goal. In the command group, the emphasis is on following directions. In the task group, the emphasis is on the task and its completion.

The *interest group* emphasizes the group itself. It may have a chain of command; it may have a task to accomplish; but its reason for being is the shared interest of all its members. Examples of the interest groups might include older workers demanding pensions, minority groups demonstrating for their rights, and business groups banding together for the purposes of influencing legislation or public opinion. This type of group may exist for a shorter period of time than the other categories because of the likelihood that its objective will be accomplished or abandoned.

The *friendship group* exists because its members like to be together. They may have met at work or through other types of groups, but there is no motivation for their activities other than enjoyment of being together. Friendship groups may have things in common—political, ethnic, age, or hobby interests. Or friendship groups may form because of dissimilarity—as with discussion groups and town meetings.

Sayles groups people according to the purposes of their togetherness; but groups can also be classified according to their different patterns of behavior and process. Groups may be categorized by their (1) degree of formality, (2) intimacy of their emotional involvement, (3) principal goal, (4) size, (5) complexity, and (6) degree of voluntarism.[7]

Being aware of each of these characteristics can help the manager observe, analyze, and deal with groups. The characteristics do not equate with value judgements—that is, volunteer workers are not better or worse than paid workers—but they do suggest keys to managerial group planning—that is, volunteers require a different style of motivation than do the paid help.

As is often said regarding categories, these groupings of groups are not infallible. They overlap and they intertwine. But they do help us in

[7] Based on Robert M. Fulmer, *Practical Human Relations*, (Homewood, IL, Richard D. Irwin, Inc., 1977) pp. 81–84.

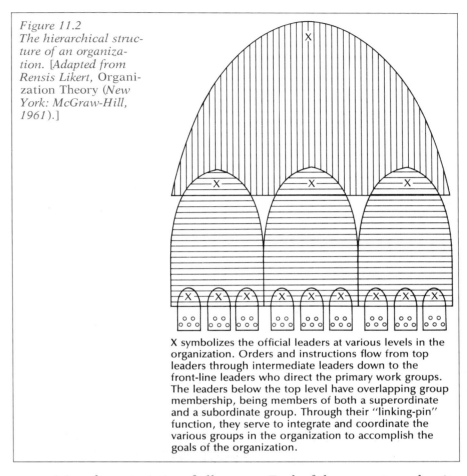

Figure 11.2
The hierarchical structure of an organization. [Adapted from Rensis Likert, Organization Theory *(New York: McGraw-Hill, 1961).]*

X symbolizes the official leaders at various levels in the organization. Orders and instructions flow from top leaders through intermediate leaders down to the front-line leaders who direct the primary work groups. The leaders below the top level have overlapping group membership, being members of both a superordinate and a subordinate group. Through their "linking-pin" function, they serve to integrate and coordinate the various groups in the organization to accomplish the goals of the organization.

recognizing characteristics of all groups. Each of the group types has its advantages and disadvantages. It is comical to imagine a "family of soldiers" or a bowling team with a strict-command group organization. Whatever the group style, we cannot hope to manage it effectively until we understand its goals and emphases.

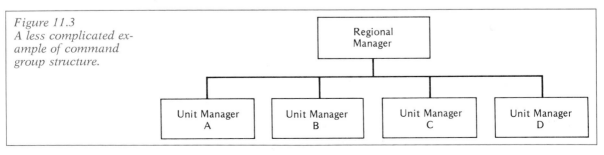

Figure 11.3
A less complicated example of command group structure.

Group Members: How They Rank

Just after the great revolution in Russia, it was decided that if the socialist ideology were to be followed all the way, the Russian army should abandon traditional rank and uniform distinctions. In the spirit of community, insignia were removed and generals looked just like privates. History recounts that total chaos took over. Orders were mistrusted and ignored. The ideal of equality was abused, and soon the army had to return to an organizational system that everyone could understand and respond to.

The members of groups assume positions of importance. If such ordering of position is not imposed on a group, some division of responsibility will automatically emerge. Beyond that, a pecking order of group members may emerge *even if* an organizational order is imposed.

The Leader

There is sometimes considerable difference between electing someone to be president of the class and recognizing by ballot someone who is already leading the class. Groups will always have leaders. Whether or not those leaders will occupy the official leadership positions is another question.

The concept of the informal leader should be familiar to managers. It is true that the management always has the authority. However, the importance of locating and recognizing the group's natural leader cannot be overemphasized. It is through leadership—not through legislation or regulation—that acceptance may be gained for change.

The formal leader possesses the power to discipline and/or fire members of the work group. On the other hand, the informal leader emerges from within the group because he or she meets some need of the group. This leader may be the one who initiates action, provides direction, and compromises differences toward the accomplishment of goals. Usually leaders will be effective communicators; it is imperative, however, that they represent the values of the group. They are able to perceive these values, organize them into an intelligible philosophy, and verbalize them to nonmembers.

A major responsibility in working with groups is the recongnition of leadership forces. It has been said that there is really only one person to be reckoned with in a mob. Efficient group management means finding and dealing with the leadership forces. When this is accomplished, the group's direction will flow more naturally.

There is a scale of dominance that almost always demonstrates the difference between the appointed authority figure and the natural leader of the group. The authority figure is task oriented—he wants to get done with the job he was sent out to do. The natural leader, though conscious of the task, is group oriented. Her prime concern is the welfare of her group. The authority figure attempts to dominate and impose. The natural leader deals rather in consensus and compromise. The authority figure tends to use negative motivation, and the punishment approach may earn him the reputation at being a hatchet man. Quite the opposite, the natural leader is striving in behalf of the group and may be seen affectionately as *our* person in the negotiations.

The Status Seekers

Some of the most frequent offenders in the "leaders who don't lead" category are those who have sought their positions merely for the status of being leader. Both in social realms and in business strata, there are those who are primarily interested in *proving themselves.* Their proof may be satisfied by the attainment of membership, as in some exclusive clubs, churches, and social groups. They may gain satisfaction from the mere trappings of success—i.e., the corner office or the one with the most windows, the carpeted floor, or the highest salary. "Having a key to the executive washroom" may be an extremely unsatisfactory kind of motivation. However, even that value can be used to effect desired group outcomes.

The Followers

The father of a first-grader was filling out a questionnaire. To the question "Is your child a leader?" he replied, "No, but she *can* follow directions." The next evening, he received a note from the child's teacher. "Just thought you would like to know," the note said, "that in a class with 29 leaders, it is a delight to look forward to working with one follower."

The value of good and dependable followers is much touted but little supported. Astronauts and movie stars always publicly thank the crews that made their accomplishments possible . . . and then accept the reward themselves. We talk about "too many chiefs and not enough Indians," but we give the fancy feathers to the chief. If our society is going to be as dependent as we say on the followers and faithful backup crews, then we ought to reward the worthy behind-the-scenes workers. Every group process must have efficient and faithful workers. The wise manager will recognize and cultivate loyal workers. The foolish manager will spot these workers and promote them to leadership positions—even if they lack the potential for this responsibility.

Interacting with the Chiefs and Indians of any managerial situation requires several kinds of communications. *Cohesion communications* refers to the "inside language"—the chitchat, gossip, ribbing, and other personal exchanges that make participants feel part of the group. *Maintenance communications* involve the various exchanges which are necessary to live and work together, keep the peace, and maintain discipline. *Task communications* relate directly to the job being done. In some scenes, the task language may be a highly technical cohesion language of its own.

Tragedies of managerial group interaction can often be traced to the mistake of limiting all communications to one of the above three. A manager who is "all business" is certainly in for some human relation problems.

Group Control

Although none of us is willing to admit being a manipulator of people, we all want to know how to get what we want. Getting groups to go in one direction or another is a ticklish enterprise. There are three most frequent forms of group control. These three social processes bring about compliance with group norms.

Group pressure is the most powerful motivator of people in groups. Social approval or disapproval can be discovered lurking behind most of the decisions we make.

The process of group pressure has been clearly (and somewhat humorously) demonstrated in a series of experiments by Solomon E. Asch.[8] Asch recruited groups of college students to conduct "an experiment in visual judgement." He told them they would be comparing the lengths of lines printed on index cards. The subjects had only to tell which of the lines on card number two matched the one on card number one.

Actually, Asch was not interested in visual perception—but in individual perception of group agreement or disagreement. Prior to the actual observation of the cards, the experimenter rigged the results. He informed all but one member of the group that they should choose a line that *did not* match the first line. When the experiment began, all eyes were on the uninformed group member. How would this person respond to being the only one right?

[8] "Opinions and Social Pressures," *Scientific American*, Vol. 193, November 1955, pp. 31–35.

National Lampoon's Animal House (Universal Pictures, 1979). Is the process of group formation similar regardless of the objective?

The results of the Asch experiments showed that when a subject was confronted with only one other group member who saw things differently, the individual continued to stick to the correct answer. But as the number of wrong-answering group members increased, the guinea pig was less likely to stick to the right answer. Some people were influenced by group pressure to give incorrect responses 31.8 per cent of the time!

The experiment illustrates how group pressure and support can affect participation. If an individual stands alone, he or she is inclined to succumb to popular opinion. However, if an attitude or opinion is supported by even one group member, it is easier to resist pressure to change.

The lesson for group leaders is obvious: never allow the intimidation of majority opinion to stifle creativity or railroad unjustified conclusions.

Group enforcement, although an avenue of group control, is actually an extension of group pressure. It is the application of discipline by the group to one who has not complied with generally accepted group procedure.

A soft approach to group enforcement would be a discussion between the leaders and the troublemaker(s). If this does not correct the situation, more rigid actions, such as public rebuke, ostracism, or excommunication, may follow. Other, more severe techniques, such as sabotaging the nonconformer's performance, have also been used in some organizations.

Group pressure may exist only in the mind of the worker. That is to say that much of our action is prompted or molded by fears of what others might say even though others do not, in actuality, care. Group enforcement, on the other hand, is real and unmistakable. In this sense, at least, it is a simpler foe to encounter.

Personal values compose a third method of group control. Ideally, we would like to think that group members have fully developed philosophies and will always be true to these principles. In reality, group pressure and enforcement seem often to overcome personal values. In addition to the group's ability to overcome personal value systems, the group often is the creator of value systems in its members. The opinions and goals of the group may then become accepted by the individual as morally and ethically correct.

Groups: How They Flow

After all is said and done about categorizing groups, one basic question remains. It is the question that determines the ultimate value of the group. No one wants to employ an unproductive group, no matter how congenial and polite its members may be. The primary evaluation question for groups is not "How did the group play the game?" but "Did the group accomplish its task?" After a losing season, few alumni groups ask "Did the coach teach good manners on the field?"

Two further aspects of group dynamics can contribute to group success. They are the group's communication network and cohesiveness. These two aspects must, like other group characteristics, be determined by the unique group situation.

Communication network studies have been conducted in most traditional organizational arrangements. Harold H. Kelly's[9] work demonstrated the flow of information in the traditional pyramid organization.

J. L. Moreno[10] has used the sociogram to gain knowledge about group

---

[9] "Communications in Experimentally Creative Hierarchies," *Human Relations*, Vol. 4, February, 1951, pp. 39–56.

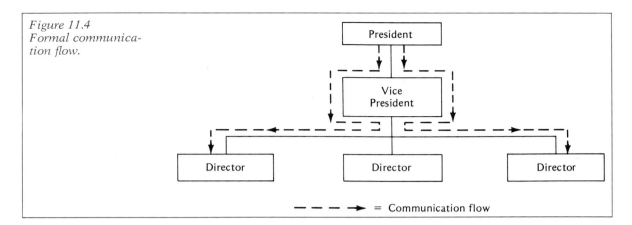

Figure 11.4
Formal communication flow.

President

Vice President

Director Director Director

– – – → = Communication flow

relations. A sociogram is a diagram that illustrates the interpersonal relationships existing within a group. The system can be used to depict feelings of preference, rejection, or any intergroup arrangement. A sociogram may be simple (as in Figure 11.5) or it may demonstrate a complicated system of relationships.

Alex Bavelas[11] made a study of the communication networks that exist in groups (Figure 12.4). He was interested in the efficiency with which groups complete their tasks. It was determined that when simple problems had to be solved, the wheel network was the fastest and most efficient arrangement.

Bavelas' findings indicate that less rigid forms of communication can lead to effective problem solving. Obviously, any communication network is improved by the elimination of unnecessary transfers of information. *And* the best group communication network is the one that *works* best for your group.

Cohesiveness is another important group concept. Formally, cohesiveness is the attraction of members to the group in terms of the strength of forces on the individual member to remain active in the group and to resist leaving it. Informally, we might say that cohesiveness designates the mysterious ability of the group to demonstrate unified action.

Experiments by Stanley E. Seashore[12] showed that employees who are members of a highly cohesive group will receive the type of support that reduces typical work-place anxieties, and the group will serve as an anxiety-reducing mechanism. Seashore also found that the greater the cohesiveness of the group, the greater the influence group goals have on the performance of individual members.

After researching the behavior of a number of management groups in many large corporations, Douglas McGregor, a pioneer in the study of

[10] "Contributions of Sociometry to Research Methodology in Sociology," *American Sociological Review*, Vol. 12, June 1947, pp. 287–292.
[11] "Communication Patterns in Task-Oriented Groups," *Journal of the Acoustical Society of America*, Vol. 22, 1950, pp. 725–730.
[12] *Group Cohesiveness in the Industrial Work Group* (Ann Arbor: University of Michigan, Institute for Social Research, 1954).

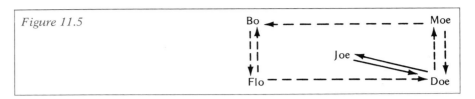

Figure 11.5

groups, drew up a list of characteristics of a successful, creative group. His observations were based on rather elite groups, but the same characteristics can be noted in most groups which meet their goals, and with which members are generally satisfied.

1. The atmosphere tends to be informal, comfortable, relaxed.
2. There is a lot of discussion in which virtually everyone participates, but it remains pertinent to the task of the group.
3. The task or objective of the group is well understood and accepted by the members. There will have been free discussion of the objective at some point until it was formulated in such a way that the members of the group could commit themselves to it.
4. The members listen to each other! Every idea is given a hearing. People do not appear to be afraid of being foolish by putting forth a creative thought even if it seems fairly extreme.
5. There is disagreement. Disagreements are not suppressed or overridden by premature group action. The reasons are carefully examined, and the group seeks to resolve them rather than to dominate the dissenter.
6. Most decisions are reached by a kind of consensus in which it is clear that everyone is in general agreement and willing to go along. Formal voting is at a minimum; the group does not accept a simple majority as a proper basis for action.
7. Criticism is frequent, frank, and relatively comfortable. There is little evidence of personal attack, either openly or in a hidden fashion.
8. People are free in expressing their feelings as well as their ideas both on the problem and on the group's operation.
9. When action is taken, clear assignments are made and accepted.
10. The chair of the group does not dominate it, nor on the contrary does the group defer unduly to the leader. In fact, the leadership shifts from time to time depending upon the circumstances. There is little evidence of a struggle for power as the group operates. The issue is not who controls but how to get the job done.
11. The group is self-conscious of its own operation.[13]

---

[13] D. McGregor, *The Human Side of Enterprise*, (New York: McGraw-Hill Book Company, 1960). Reprinted by permission of the publisher.

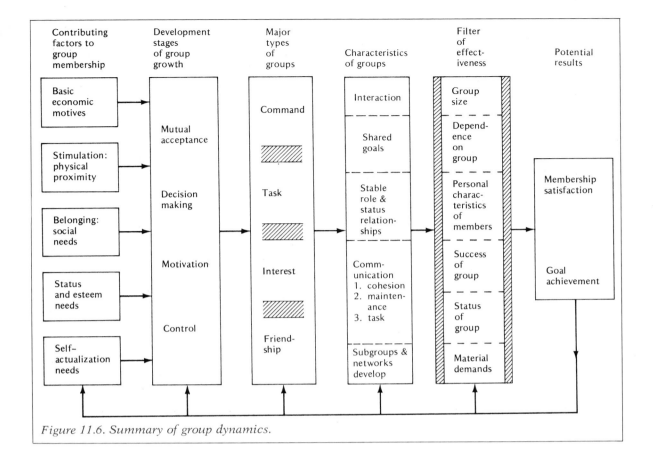

Contributing factors to group membership	Development stages of group growth	Major types of groups	Characteristics of groups	Filter of effectiveness	Potential results
Basic economic motives	Mutual acceptance	Command	Interaction	Group size	Membership satisfaction
Stimulation: physical proximity	Decision making	Task	Shared goals	Dependence on group	
Belonging: social needs	Motivation	Interest	Stable role & status relationships	Personal characteristics of members	
Status and esteem needs	Control	Friendship	Communication 1. cohesion 2. maintenance 3. task	Success of group	Goal achievement
Self-actualization needs			Subgroups & networks develop	Status of group	
				Material demands	

Figure 11.6. Summary of group dynamics.

Summary

Contrary to the multitude of critics of the group approach, the combined efforts of a group can far exceed the efforts of any or all of the group members working separately. *Synergy* is a popular term for the concept that where creativity or problem solving are involved, one-plus-one *can* equal three or more.

It has been in the last half century that meaningful research into the dynamics of the group process has been conducted. The work of Elton Mayo, Kurt Lewin, and others has contributed to the data available.

Factors that often lead to the formation of groups are locations or physical proximity, economic motivations, sociopsychological needs, security needs, social needs, esteem needs, and self-actualization needs.

Groups pass through recognizable stages of proficiency. These stages may be described by the terms *mutual acceptance, decision making, motivation,* and *control.*

Groups can be efficiently classified according to their organizational orientation. The command group follows orders. The task group usually exists for a specific project or task. The interest group exists because of a common interest or need of all its members. The friendship group exists because its members like to be together socially. Each of these group types has its own advantages and disadvantages.

Various roles are likely to emerge in any group. These roles include formal and informal leader, status seekers, and followers.

The three most frequent forms of group control are group (social) pressure, group enforcement, and personal values.

The group's communication network and cohesiveness also contribute to group success or failure. The final evaluation question for any group deals with product—not process. Figure 11.6 may be helpful in organizing the concepts of group dynamics that have been presented.

Review Questions

1. What is synergy?
2. Who was Kurt Lewin?
3. How did the administrators of the North Korean POW camps prevent the formation of social groups? What was the result? How might the POW's have combated the procedures?
4. Identify four types of groups. Which type best represents your class?
5. What factors lead to the formation of groups?
6. Apply the concept of synergy to preparation for an exam.
7. Do any of the factors that typically contribute to the formation of a group apply to the formulation of your class?
8. Does Edgar Schein's discussion of POW's indicate that promising employees should be transferred frequently to prevent them from escaping to other companies?
9. Assume that you have assembled a group of supercriminals to become the world's leading team of bank robbers. Describe the phases of group development that your organization might experience.
10. Within a college or university environment, identify the major types of groups suggested by Leonard R. Sayles.
11. Identify a group in which status is nonexistent or unimportant.
12. Draw a sociogram for the first fifteen minutes of your next class.

12

Communication – The Idea Transplant

"It's a high fly ball to short center field! Clanahan is rushing up to make the catch. But wait . . . Carl Klutz is coming in from left field waving his arms and calling for the ball. And now Scooter Scurvy, the speedy shortstop, is there too. All three men are calling for the ball. . . . All three are. . . . Here comes the ball. . . . The catch will be made by. . . . OH NO! . . . Sports fans, you are not going to believe what those three numbskulls just did!"

"I don't know, gentlemen. I just don't know what to do. I have been in this business for twenty years. We have never had anything like this happen. We have always taken pride in the way this company has gone beyond the call of duty to take care of its employees. But now, all of a sudden, it seems as if the whole bunch has gone just plain crazy. They will not listen to reason. They are making demands. They refuse to sit down and discuss the issues. They want every demand met or else . . . and yesterday, when I went out to try to talk sense with them, they shouted me down every time I opened my mouth. There's just no talking to them!"

"Turning to the international scene, the news is not so good. The summit talks adjourned today after nearly two weeks of dispute over the question of which country should be the first to speak. All four powers remain adamant. To the casual observer,

> the controversy may appear childish. However, we understand that diplomatic protocol assigns great meaning to seemingly unimportant details."
>
> "Look! I did not come to you for advice about patching up my marriage. I came because it takes a lawyer to get a divorce and that is exactly what I want. . . . No, I am not interested in sitting down to talk anything out with anybody. Believe me, I have wasted far too much of my life already on him. He won't listen to reason, and the constant arguing and bickering is just about to drive me out of my mind. Talk? No, I don't want to talk to him . . . that is just the point!"

Good communication, like clean air, is usually taken for granted until its absence begins to make life unpleasant. Of course, we can always count on some sage diagnostician to step forward and explain what went wrong. The wise one carefully surveys the wreckage of a life or an enterprise and delivers the verdict: "What we have here is a problem in communication."

The expert can't go wrong by suggesting communication breakdown as the cause of failure. At work, at play, across the nation, and around the world, it is that same elementary failure to make the message clear that keeps lousing up the best laid plans of mice and men and women.

Communication activities fill the business day. An analysis of time spent in communication shows approximately 10 per cent spent in writing, 15 per cent reading, 35 per cent speaking, and 40 per cent listening.[1] The same pattern would hold true for most people—with by far the majority of time spent in oral communication.

In his management classic, *Functions of the Executive*, Chester I. Barnard says, "A business organization consists of persons who are both able to communicate with one another, willing to serve, and united to accomplish a common purpose or goal."[2] Thus it would appear that communication is a key to management effectiveness. Oral and written communications, formal and informal, go through many channels and in various directions. Management needs to communicate policies, instructions, objectives, and goals so that all employees will understand and accept them. There is no management magic to hold and control people better than understanding. The final test of all communication is whether it produces the desired results quickly and correctly.

Communication is an idea transplant. The center fielder may have the right idea about who should catch the fly ball. But unless he can trans-

---

[1] Harold P. Zelko, "Art of Communicating Your Ideas" (New York: Reading Rack Service, Inc., 1968), p. 3.

[2] (Cambridge, Mass.: Harvard University Press, 1938), p. 226.

plant this idea into the minds of teammates, he may be through in baseball. Almost every area of human endeavor revolves around the efforts of people to get ideas into the minds of their peers.

The information explosion is not making the matter any simpler. Every day there are more new ideas to be communicated. Sometimes we might feel that we suffer from a sort of communication indigestion. In this era of mass communications, the bombardment almost never stops. A barrage of printed, projected, and performed messages flows over us at home, at work, at school, and everywhere in between. Each day, the average person receives between three hundred and two thousand advertising messages.[3] As fast as we learn to tune out one irritating medium, the experts come at us from another direction. They seem to be determined to put their thoughts into our heads. Their cause may be toothpaste sales or voter registration . . . but their game is communication.

And then, of course, *you* communicate to get what *you* want. You show and tell . . . smile and frown . . . demonstrate . . . and gesture . . . all for the purpose of making your meaning clear. No person is an island, and communication is the bridge that connects people to people.

Yet, even beyond the people-to-people version of communication, we are continually sending and receiving—even *within* ourselves. An artist communicates with herself (and with others) as she pours her inner feelings into some tangible form. An experienced sailor communicates with "feelings in my bones" to get a forecast of tomorrow's weather. And are you not communicating with your own experience when you interpret the signs of the times, the trends of the market, or the handwriting on the wall?

The Process

For the purpose of explanation, we can reduce the components of the communication process to a fairly simple diagram (see Figure 12.1).

The person with the *idea* (1) decides to share it. Next, the idea is *encoded* (2) into some form of written, spoken, or otherwise communicable language, which is capable of being *transmitted* (3) by symbols, sounds, or expression. Unfortunately, there is almost never a closed circuit from transmitter to *receiver* (5). In between are lurking all types of *interferences* (4) that stand ready to garble the message. Environmental noise and other distractions can change the original transmission.

[3] J. F. Engle et al., *Promotional Strategy* (Homewood, Ill.: Richard D. Irwin, Inc., 1971), p. 81.

Figure 12.1
The communication
process.

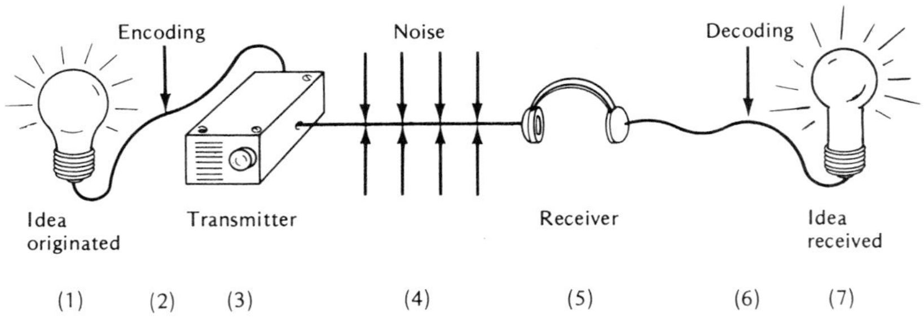

Encoding   Noise   Decoding

Idea   Transmitter   Receiver   Idea
originated   received

(1)   (2)   (3)   (4)   (5)   (6)   (7)

When the message is received via the eyes, ears, or emotions of the second person, it passes to the brain, where the language is *decoded* (6). The resulting impressions make up the *received idea* (7). Unfortunately it is only in a neatly charted theory that idea (7) is exactly like idea (1). In actual practice, there are pitfalls at every step along the way to prevent clear communication. As Lewis Carroll, the author of *Alice in Wonderland*, observed, "One of the greatest miracles in the world is the process of conveying meaning accurately from one mind to another." Yet we attempt this miracle anytime we attempt to communicate with friends, supervisor, or subordinates.

Even though this chart is oversimplified, it does provide a foolproof and dependable method for evaluating any attempted communication. We may safely say that any communication is successful to whatever extent idea (7) resembles idea (1). That is, if the idea received is identical to the idea sent, we can be sure that *two* skillful communicators were involved. It takes two to make a meaningful message, for either side of the process can break down and distort the original idea. Effective communication is the joint responsibility of teacher *and* student, management *and* labor, husband *and* wife. There must be perception and interpretation by the other person. It is the understanding of the message that determines the effectiveness and the reaction to this meaning. The recipient must want to receive the message. We therefore realize that communication is the *exchange* of meaning between two or more persons and is not merely transmittal.

No communication is ever as simple as the seven-step diagram would imply. There is no conceivable situation in which two or more people are communicating and only one mode of communication is in action. Any good public speaker, for instance, monitors with his own ears and tempers his remarks with impressions received by observing the audience reaction.

It is the rule, rather than the exception, for multiple modes of communication to be operating simultaneously. For example, you can *listen* to a lecturer, *write* your class notes, *react* mentally to the idea being presented, and *respond* physically by smile or frown or nod. At least four modes of communication in action . . . and you never stopped chewing your gum!

The Pitfalls

At every step in the process of communication there are potential traps. It is important for any communicator to be aware of the places that things may go wrong. The ounce-of-prevention-pound-of-cure adage has never been more meaningful than when applied to communication theory and practice.

One of the most common pitfalls for communicators is the assumption that because a message was sent, a message must have been received. Thus we may hear someone ask, "How could you not know about it? I sent you a memo!" Mistaking the communication act for actual transfer is a common fallacy. It has been said that "The greatest enemy of communication is the illusion of it."

Whenever you send out a message, it ought to be armed for battle. You should prepare it to encounter the dangers of inaccurate transmission or reception; the additions and omissions resulting from competing communications, and the outrages of faulty translation on the receiving end.

Every time you endeavor to communicate with another person, at least six different messages can come to life:

1. the message you intend to send
2. the message you actually send
3. the message the other person receives
4. the other person's interpretation of what was received
5. the other person's response
6. the difference between the response expected and the response received

Life would be simple indeed if communication were merely a one-way process, with messages received exactly as they were intended. Such a situation could eliminate the many irritations and uncertainties that often plague us as a result of communication breakdown. However, total one-way communication would also tend to eliminate things like education, conversation, and progress. For all the problems communication brings with it, it is still more desirable than loneliness.

No Panaceas

Everybody knows that communication is a problem. And we all would have to agree vaguely that in one way or another we eventually pay for poor communication practice. A college student may pay dearly for expressing the correct answer in some incorrect or unclear manner. A manager of business or people can eventually begin to feel the dollar-

and-cents effect of poor communication. Mark Twain once remarked that the difference between the right word and almost the right word can make a considerable difference . . . like the difference between lightning and a lightning bug.

Because poor communication is such a universal irritant, it is not surprising that a new system is born every day. Of course, each new method proclaims itself to be the long awaited cure-all . . . the panacea for all our plaguing pitfalls and misunderstanding.

With regard to this steady stream of "final words" on the communication process, it is quite safe to make the following generalization: each communication has its own personality, its own peculiar blending of people, places, and predicaments that demand more than a form letter or a canned answer. In other words, "Dear Occupant" may streamline your company's mailing tasks and make your computer whirr with delight, but it is also going to leave your customers feeling a little cold.

This is not to say that the form letter or the prepared text are never to be used. It is rather to suggest that a look of skepticism is the appropriate response when anyone comes to you with a new form or system that is reputed to be the "surefire method to stop all this misunderstanding we've been having." Listen politely and *do* evaluate the proposed device —it might have some real value. But keep a little sign in the upper left-hand corner of your brain that says, "No person can effectively communicate *for* another person."

In your own communication efforts and in the communicating of people under your supervision, there is great benefit to be derived by learning to ask simple questions about the specific communication situation at hand. These questions deal with the basics of the situation. What is the idea? Who is the one to whom the idea is directed? What channels will carry the message most clearly to that person? What factors are likely to distort the message en route? How can I avoid those distortions? How will I be able to tell if they have received the correct idea?

Media to Carry the Messages

Marshall McLuhan's statement that "The medium is the message"[4] has been quoted often (and occasionally with understanding). Even without delving deeply into the McLuhan philosophy it is possible to see that the mode of communication does greatly influence the message received.

[4] Marshall McLuhan, *Understanding Media* (New York: McGraw-Hill Book Company, 1964).

An engraved invitation has a different message-carrying character than a spoken message. A whisper commands a mystery that a shout can hardly muster.

Each mode of communication is subject to the quantity-quality gap. We tend to surround one thought with many words, skim our reading matter, and listen only to every fifth word we hear. Our problem is not to learn to perform these communication modes, but to perform them more effectively. We can all relate to the note of explanation found on an office desk: "I know that you believe you understand what you think I said, but I am not sure you realize that what you heard is not what I meant."

Human modes for processing information of a communication include many more than we usually consider:

1. Thinking. The thinking process is often overlooked in lists of the modes of communication. Most people will immediately identify the sending modes. A few are alert enough to add the receiving modes. But almost never is the internal mode of communication considered. Ironically, thinking is perhaps the most pervasive of all the modes of communication, for it is a participant in all the other modes.

Even though thinking is a necessary component of all modes of communication, it can also stand proudly by itself. Ask your local psychiatrist or *guru*. He or she will assure you that we should all spend more time communicating with ourselves. Meditation can be a power-packed experience when it introduces us to our true selves, perhaps for the first time.

2. Action. For many years, Ted Williams held the record for receiving the largest fine ever charged a professional baseball player for arguing with an umpire. Interestingly enough, Williams never spoke a single word in that confrontation. The entire content of his message to the umpire was communicated in a single gesture.

Actions speak louder than words. A lantern in the steeple of Boston's Old North Church gave an important message to Paul Revere. Facial expression and body language can communicate just as effectively (and sometimes more interestingly) than spoken or written words. The tragic thing about action is not that it is so powerful a mode of communication but that, even realizing its power, people tend to ignore it for the more traditional modes.

3. Observation. Freud suggested that people all tend to practice selective perception, seeing only those incidents or parts of incidents that they want to see. One of the hurdles of attaining emotional maturity is learning to perceive all that is happening around us—even those things that might be offensive to us personally.

The past experiences of an observer have a tremendous impact on the accuracy of perception. Our communication effectiveness is colored by the choice of ourselves as a median. Ben Jonson said of an acquaintance, "What you have to say about Aristotle tells me very little about Aristotle, but a great deal about you." Emerson made the same point even more forcefully: "What you are sounds so loudly in my ears that I cannot hear what you say." The communicator should be alert to the possible distortion in his message created by the previous impressions he has made.

All failure to observe correctly cannot be traced to the intentional ignoring of offensive data. Sometimes things happen too fast or in some chaotic circumstance that can confuse or distort what is seen. Lawyers are familiar with the phenomenon of honest witnesses giving conflicting testimony about the same incident.

4. Speaking. The average rate of speaking is 125 words per minute, though some people have gusts up to 200. In almost every case, the objective could be accomplished with fewer words. Using fewer words would not only waste less time, it would offer less opportunity to confuse the issue. Almost everyone has at least one acquaintance who is incapable of giving a brief answer. Ask for the time and you receive the entire history of the person's watch and the company that made it.

Proficient businesspeople develop their speaking habits carefully. They (consciously, at first) develop a talent for keeping the other person talking. Perhaps they are hoping to get as much information as possible without surrendering their own thinking. By design or accident, they are applying an old axiom: "You ain't learnin' nothin' when you're talkin'."

5. Listening. Table 12.1 identifies Ten Commandments for Good Listening. These rules will probably be of little value to you in your normal day-to-day life . . . unless you are involved with people.

Carl Rogers[5] has fathered a whole area of listening psychology, suggesting that many troubled persons can discover and treat their own problems with the help of a good listener. This nondirective form of counseling attempts to guide by giving only replies that confirm that we are listening and interested but not giving advice. The listener's replies are not reactions, but rather a restating of whatever the speaker has just said. The counselor merely repeats in different words, perhaps followed by "Is *that* what you are saying?" This type of psycho-help has come to be called "um-hmm psychology" because the counselor occasionally says only "um-hmm" throughout an entire therapy session.

[5] Carl Rogers, *Client Centered Therapy* (Boston: Houghton Mifflin Company, 1953).

The Son of the Sheik. (Warner Brothers, 1926). Is nonverbal communication effective?

Theodore Reik's *Listening with the Third Ear*[6] makes the point that we all need to listen for what the speaker is *trying to say.* There is often a lot of chaff and protective cover around the real message. It is by empathizing, by "listening with the third ear," that we can hear the message that lies between the lines.

6. *Writing.* Although writing composes a relatively small percentage of our total communicating time, it is one of the most important modes. The fact that writing constitutes a *permanent record* makes all the difference. We can always call up a few more spoken words to clarify unclear talk, but writing usually has to make its way without the benefit of an interpreter.

For some reason, business writers have a hard time writing in simple, straightforward terminology and style. Big words and fancy phrases give an illusion of intelligent communication. However, the only person who can write straight to the point without beating around the ambiguity bush is the person who understands (1) the topic and (2) the reader.

[6] (New York: Farrar, Strauss and Giroux, Inc., 1948.)

Table 12.1 *Ten Commandments* *for Good Listening*	1. Stop talking. You cannot listen if you are talking. 2. Put the talker at ease. Help him feel that he is free to talk. 3. Show her that you want to listen. Look and act interested. Do not read your mail while she talks. Listen to understand rather than to oppose. 4. Remove distractions. Don't doodle, tap, or shuffle papers. It might be quieter if you would shut the door. 5. Empathize with the talker. Try to put yourself in his place so that you can see his point of view. 6. Be patient. Allow plenty of time. Do not interrupt her. Don't start for the door or walk away. 7. Hold your temper. An angry person gets the wrong meaning from words. 8. Go easy on argument and criticism, which will put him on the defensive. He may clam up or get angry. Don't argue: even if you win, you lose. 9. Ask questions. This encourages her and shows you are listening. It helps to develop points further. 10. Stop talking. This is first and last, because all other commandments depend on it. You just cannot do a good listening job while you are talking.

The Gettysburg Address contains 266 words. The Ten Commandments have only 297. Yet a government OPA order to reduce the price of cabbage required 26,911 words.[7] When you know what to say, it doesn't take many words to say it.

7. Reading. One study has concluded that the average business manager spends approximately four and a half hours reading reports, memoranda, and other official information per day. College students have been known to stare at the printed page even longer than that. Interestingly enough, a minimum of attention to reading skills can double the average reader's speed. Increased reading proficiency could add two or more hours to almost anyone's day.

We have to read—it is no longer a matter of choice. Every profession is subject to a mushrooming body of critical professional knowledge. Regular reading is the only way to keep up and get ahead. Several years ago a highly successful advertising campaign was built on the statement "Send me a person who reads." The magazine ads documented the fact that those people who are most successful in almost every profession are the ones who read most extensively.

No employer expects employees to know everything that they have ever read. Rather, a person is hired who demonstrates the ability to implement the ideas read. Long lists of suggestions on good reading habits could be given. However, one important procedure can make a big difference: tie what you are reading to what you already know. Com-

[7] Quoted in Dennis Murphy, *Better Business Communication* (New York: McGraw-Hill Book Company, 1957), p. 15.

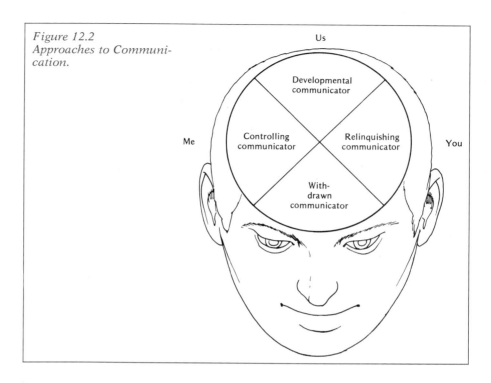

*Figure 12.2
Approaches to Communi-
cation.*

pare . . . evaluate . . . question . . . identify . . . relate . . . make
your reading encounter (and either conquer or submit to) what you already know.

Philosophies of Communication

There are four philosophies of communication by which we can group
communicator characteristics. They are hypothetical descriptions for
the convenience of observing the cooperation quotient of varying styles
of communication. It would be rare to find a person who always communicates according to any single philosophy—most of us tend to
apply different philosophies in different situations.[8]

The Developmental Communicator. To begin on a positive note, we will
discuss the developmental communicator. This approach, as the name
implies, is not predetermined and unalterable. This does not assume
that one is always right. This style implies a willingness to contribute

[8] These philosophies are drawn from Malcom E. Shaw, *Developing Communication Skills*
(West Point, Conn.: Educational Systems & Designs, Inc., 1968), pp. 30–31.

ideas and suggestions. It also strives for the development of joint understanding of problems or tasks.

Two-way communication is the strength of the developmental communicator. This communicator is looking for new approaches and encourages exploration and experimentation. The developmental communicator believes and demonstrates that two heads are better than one. With this person, one plus one can add up to three or more.

Research conducted by Alex Bavelas and Dermont Barrett[9] suggests that developmental communication is extremely desirable from the morale standpoint and for the solution of problems, although having negative factors relating to speed and accuracy.

The Controlling Communicator. On the opposite end of the philosophical spectrum, controlling communicators do not like to consider alternatives. As far as they are concerned, there are no alternatives to their ideas. They are not interested in experimentation because they assume that their own ideas and approaches are best. One-way communication suits their purposes because backtalk can only slow them down as they try to impose or sell their own point of view.

Many administrators are not interested in two-way communication. Much of management thinking has strong overtones of authoritarianism and paternalism—many of our management stereotypes are still pictures of one person *telling* others what they ought to do. The mathematical equation of the controlling communicator might be stated one plus one equals one (or less). If it could be guaranteed that the controlling communicator could always be infallibly correct, then this philosophy of communication would certainly be the most productive. Unfortunately, it always comes as quite a shock to most administrators when studies indicate that humans (including managers) score very low on the infallibility scale.

There are, however, situations in which the controlling approach is appropriate. If the supervisor has complete knowledge of the situation and with the necessary experience or knowledge can make a judgment, the controlling approach to communication may result in speedy, efficient action. In an emergency or crisis situation, the controlling approach is extremely appropriate. Anyone who has the presence of mind and the knowledge to give directions during a fire would be behaving in an appropriate way by attempting to control the situation. Additionally, controlling communication may be appropriate when joint commitment or motivation is unimportant. If an office is being closed early during the holiday season, it shouldn't take much discussion or joint problem solving for people to accept management's decision. On the

[9] "An Experimental Approach To Organizational Communication," *Personnel*, March 1951, pp. 366–371.

Smokey and the Bandit, II (Universal Pictures, 1980). [Copyright © by Universal Pictures, a Division of Universal Studios, Inc. Courtesy of MCA Publishing, a Division of MCA INC.] Developmental communication.

other hand, when the resistance to change is high, controlling techniques are rarely effective.

The Relinquishing Communicator. Relinquishing communicators are certain of one thing—the other folks have more to communicate. They are self-deprecating and unrealistically humble. They make few contributions of their own ideas and always try to shift the burden to other people. They are willing to consider alternatives, but not probe them with enthusiasm. They are willing to let others experiment and happy to see it their way without question. A relinquishing communicator and a controlling communicator can get along very well, but they will never rise above the total potential of the controlling communicator. In such a situation, we might characterize the process by the equation: one plus a shy one may still equal one.

When there is a controlling supervisor, it is difficult for the subordinate to react in any manner other than relinquishing. He or she may respond by giving developmental clues, but the supervisor will generally set the tone of the communication.

In some instances, it is appropriate to relinquish influence when the other individual has most of the information, experience, facts, or expertise. For example, if you have retained a competent, responsible attorney or management consultant to deal with a particular technical problem, it makes a great deal of sense to bow to this experience and knowledge. In an emergency situation in which someone else has already assumed the leadership, there is little reason to challenge this authority and to engage in a developmental process of communication.

The Withdrawn Communicator.   The withdrawn communicator is interested in maintaining the status quo. This person assumes that nothing can be done to improve the situation and that if new unknowns are mixed in, things could get a lot worse.

Withdrawn communicators avoid interaction and neither contribute nor solicit contributions from others. (It should be noted at this point that the withdrawn communicator may often *appear to be* contributing heavily to the group thought process. However, the end product of the communication process will usually demonstrate that the withdrawn communicator is very proficient in the questionable skills of eloquently and verbosely contributing absolutely nothing.) There are few situations in which the withdrawn pattern of communication is desirable. Perhaps when there is a legal, moral, or ethical issue at hand, you may not wish to get involved. In a managerial situation, the manager is not a manager if he or she withdraws from the challenge at hand.

The four philosophies of communication may be charted in a circle to illustrate their relationships to each other. The circle may be divided into four quadrants, to indicate the four individual approaches to another person. Table 12.2 shows these philosophies of communication.

Table 12.2	**Style**	**Approach**
	1. Controlling	"I want to have the most influence." (me)
	2. Relinquishing	"I want to give you the influence." (you)
	3. Developmental	"I want to use my influence and yours to solve a problem." (us)
	4. Withdrawn	"I want to stay uninvolved and neither exert nor respond to influence."

Transactional Analysis

One of the oldest psychologist jokes in existence is the cartoon showing one counselor meeting another on an elevator and saying, "You're O.K., how am I?" In Chapter 10, we stressed the importance of our self-perception and the attitude we have about others in mental health. The same concepts are extremely important to the success of our communication. An important theory of behavior called transactional analysis (TA, for short)[10] helps us understand our behavior and communication in relationship to others. Many of the ideas of this theory were originally developed by Eric Berne, a psychiatrist who is best known for his book *Games People Play*.[11] More recently, one of his associates, Tom Harris, has developed transactional analysis more fully in his book *I'm O.K.—You're O.K.*[12]

TA philosophy is a tool for helping us to understand what happens when any two persons interact. The theory describes the actions of various personalities with which all of us can identify at one time or another. According to this theory, everyone has three typical modes of behavior. They are called the parent ego state, the adult ego state, and the child ego state. Future references to these will be merely as Parent, Adult, and Child with capital letters to distinguish them from actual parents, adults, and children.

The Child.   The Child in you is that body of experience stored in your brain while you were small. These include the feelings of frustration, inadequacy, and helplessness that were an inevitable part of your childhood. In addition, your brain contains the early experiences of joy, curiosity, imagination, and spontaneity born from new discoveries that were also a part of your childhood. For these reasons, the Child is often called the "felt concept of life." You can spot your Child when you find yourself whining, sulking, throwing a tantrum or abandoning yourself to the joy of a pleasurable new experience.

To be more precise, the Child ego-state can be divided into two components. The *free child* is the part of you that can be carefree and spontaneous. The *hurt child* is the insecure part of your behavior that indicates that everyone else may be O.K. but you aren't. The child frequently feels freer to express emotion than the parents or adults. The free child feels the positive excitement of childhood, and the hurt child feels or demonstrates the negative behavior traits of immaturity or insecurity.

The Parent.   Your Parent comes from your observation about the way your mother and father or other "big people" in your early life behaved. Usually, it is based on events that occurred during your preschool years.

[10] This section was suggested by Lyman K. Randall, *P-A-C at Work* (New York: American Airlines, 1971), pp. 1–47.
[11] (New York: Grove Press, Inc., 1964.)
[12] (New York: Harper and Row, Publishers, 1969.)

Because of your smallness and dependency as a little person in a world of "giants," your overriding assumption was that "they" were right. Thus, the Parent is often referred to as the "taught concept of life." Your *critical parent* is the part of you that lectures, moralizes, points a finger righteously or accusingly, and lays down the law. Your *nurturing parent* is the part of you that can comfort, encourage or offer reassurance or assistance to others.

The Adult. The Adult is that part of you that figures out things by collecting and looking at the facts and so on. Naturally, you will see a similarity to this and "developmental" communicator. You may think of this ego state as your computer, which you use to estimate probabilities and to make decisions based on facts. For this reason, the Adult is sometimes called the "thought concept of life." Whenever you explain the reasons for your actions or just suggest alternatives to a proposal rather than reacting emotionally, your Adult has taken charge.

TA has also provided helpful names for some of the other characteristics of the human interaction situation. *Strokes* are those special rewards that all of us are looking for. They may be delivered in words of praise, compliments, or smiles if they are positive. Negative strokes come to us in the form of critical comments, avoidance, failure to return phone calls, or hateful remarks.

Games are little tricks or routines we use to get strokes. We play roles, adapt emotions, and act in ways that experience has shown us will get the kind of strokes we like. Dorothy Jongeward suggests some of the reasons people play games:

1. If people are *bored*, they are more prone to play games, since games are a way to fill up time.
2. The *need for strokes* leads to games. People get strokes from games even though these are negative strokes.
3. Games *reinforce the psychological positions* and strengthen the "I'm not O.K." and/or "You're not O.K." feelings which individuals have.
4. Games *help people avoid or regulate* intimacy.
5. Scripts (the roles we adopt) encourage games.[13]

Scripts (as suggested above) are the roles we adopt. In childhood, many individuals develop scripts or roles that they decide will probably describe their future lives. Some people assume scripts that call for success, achievement and happiness. Others choose scripts that will place them in losing, discouraging or failure-prone situations. You might enjoy trying to remember what your favorite stories were during child-

---

[13] Dorothy Jongeward, *Everybody Wins: Transactional Analysis Applied to Organizations* (Reading, Mass.: Addison-Wesley Publishing Co., Inc., 1973), p. 34. Quoted by Mildred Pryor.

hood. Achievement-oriented people are more likely to have enjoyed stories like "The Little Engine Who Could," "Heroic Cowboy," athletic achievements or mystical heroes such as Thor or Bat Man. People with negative self-images may identify with Charlie Brown, who frequently complains, "I can't do anything right."

Table 12.3 presents some applications of the TA awareness to industrial (or business) relationships. Managers may use this insightful philosophy to change themselves or to more skillfully motivate their subordinates.

The Three Faces of Me. Because everyone has these three ego states, according to this theory, it is easier for you to recognize the P-A-C in others once you have been able to identify your own Parent-Adult-Child.

In TA, a *transaction* is an exchange of words and related behavior between two people. When we see each person involved in the exchange as having a Parent, an Adult, and a Child, we are able to draw an accurate diagram of what happened in the transaction—thus the term *transactional analysis.*

Whether we realize it or not, our behavior toward or reactions to other people are largely based on assumptions we make about ourselves in relationship to them. These assumptions are called *life positions.* They can be classified into one of the following four categories:

Table 12.3 *Motivating with TA*	Suggestions, based on TA concepts, for improving skills in motivating others: 1. Select, teach, and use a motivational terminology in your daily conversations with your staff. The TA approach can be used. 2. Identify the model executive style you want to develop (change your script), and practice daily at being that kind of person. The adult approach proves to be a highly effective leadership model today. 3. See yourself as a teacher-manager, or, in TA terminology, a supportive Parent. 4. Demonstrate a growth and change attitude in dealing with your people. 5. Learn to tune in and relate to the different ego states of your staff and know when you switch from your Parent to your Adult to your Child. 6. Learn to enjoy dealing with the emotional or Child roles played by others. 7. Use positive strokes where possible. 8. Personalize your approach by being yourself and learning to use your Adult self in most business situations. 9. In being this mature Adult, practice being firm, yet fair, in dealing with management situations in a cause-and-effect manner rather than in a childish way. 10. Give and ask for specific commitments or personal contracts in dealing with your staff.

1. *I'm not O.K. and you're O.K.* This is a life position held by many people. It is a conclusion based on early negative feelings about oneself. It dates back to a decision made when you saw and felt a clear distinction between yourself and the "big people" around you. They could do many things that you could not. This individual will defer or relinquish rather than feel able to contribute to a conversation or a problem-solving situation.

2. *I'm O.K. and you're not O.K.* This is a distrustful life position. It usually results from people being mistreated by grownups when young. They looked forward to growing up and being able to exercise control and power over others. When they communicate, they will probably try to control the situation and dominate the conversation.

3. *I'm not O.K. and you're not O.K.* This is a despairing outlook on life. It is totally negative in its perspective. The person with this approach is likely to be withdrawn and resentful.

4. *I'm O.K. and you're O.K.* This is a rationally chosen life position. It

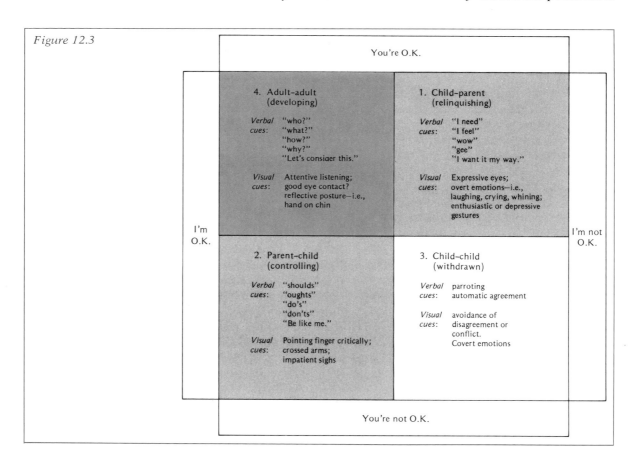

Figure 12.3

is obviously an Adult decision and is likely to be made by a self-actualizing person who may also be a developmental communicator.

We illustrate each of these positions in combination with the styles and characteristics of communication for each in Figure 12.3.

In analyzing our communication activities, we should keep in mind the various ego states and the impact they have on interpersonal relationships. If a subordinate or associate attempts to communicate with us in an inappropriate manner by acting as though he or she were the Parent or the Child, transactional analysis can help us move the discussion back into an Adult perspective. Telling people that they should or must (Parent-initiated "oughtmanship") improve something will probably stimulate their Child and generate resistance. For example, telling a group of employees, "You must improve your customer service and reduce cost," will be likely to generate anger, anxiety, guilt, or fear (Child reaction). On the other hand, the more relevant data you give them about cost and service performance problems, the more likely you are to engage their Adult in problem solving.

The Ups and Downs of Communication

In a busy organization, communication must flow both up and down the organizational pyramid. Unfortunately, there are some organizations in which the edict givers at the top assume that they can speak and expect the organization to understand completely and comply perfectly. The study of participatory management investigates the values of and methods for facilitating two-way communication.

The methods for receiving input from the ranks must be efficient—since there are so many troops and so few generals. And yet, the troops always have a perspective that the generals need to hear. Upward communication not only allows the rank-and-file to feel a part of the decisions (which facilitates a cooperative response), it also allows the generals to know whether or not the instructions or requests are being accurately received by those who must do the work. Flippo and Munsinger[14] have listed some of the devices which managers can put into action to facilitate efficient communication both up and down the organization pyramid.

1. The *chain of command* is usually assumed, by managers at the top, to provide a clear channel for communication up from the ranks. It rarely does so, because of intimidation of workers at the bottom.

[14] E. B. Flippo and G. M. Munsinger, *Management*, 3rd ed. (Boston: Allyn and Bacon, Inc., 1975), p. 390–392.

2. A *grievance procedure* is a systematic method by means of which someone who has a claim against the organization is enabled to have it heard.
3. A *complaint system* usually functions through question boxes or suggestion boxes. This can be a wide-open channel of communication, if management is far-sighted enough to reward divergent ideas.
4. *Counseling* services may be the ounce of prevention that will help the organization avoid the more costly pound of cure.
5. *Questionnaires* about morale and other topics can be valuable as long as the questionees continue to see evidence that the input has power to influence the future.
6. The *open-door* policy is often talked . . . seldom applied. The supervisor must be a secure individual who is able to keep from betraying confidence and candor.
7. An *exit interview* enables the company to gain valuable ideas and attitudes from departing employees—probably the surest form of straight talk.
8. The *grapevine* provides accurate information, as long as it can be separated from gossip and other embellishments.
9. *Labor representatives* can tell the organization a lot about itself, and will rarely try to spare the company's feelings. They have also been known, however, to be a bit biased in perspective.
10. An *informer* has low respectability, but is sometimes necessary in order for the company to find out what would otherwise not be revealed.
11. *Special meetings* will often provoke the spilling of problems that are seething. *Regular* meetings on the more constructive side can also be helpful.
12. An *ombudsperson* represents the little people against the system, and tries to usher them through unfamiliar channels and snip red tape whenever possible.

Communication Systems

Even though the importance of communication remains undisputed, there is remarkable carelessness about the methods employed to get necessary information to the corners of most organizations. The problems exist in both human and mechanical information processing— though it is stylish now to have a staff to monitor and control mechanical communications.

The human communications—on the other hand—are often left to the individual skills of middle and upper managers. Rather than solving

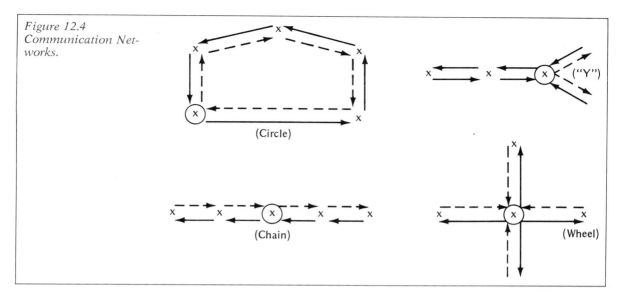

Figure 12.4 Communication Networks.

(Circle)

("Y")

(Chain)

(Wheel)

the communication problems, managers may actually contribute to them. The higher a manager rises in the company the fewer peers he has to communicate with laterally. There is, however, also a direct increase in the volume of communication as the manager rises higher and higher. There is more input from above and more questions from below . . . and less time to consider either at length.

To compound the confusion of human communication, there is the ironic situation that we often assign organizational status on the basis of the amount . . . rather than the quality . . . of messages a person can receive or send.

As suggested in the previous chapter, there are four basic networks that usually characterize the manager's communication system with subordinates.[15] These are shown in Figure 12.4. The chain indicates that the message goes from one "link" to the next until it gets to the person who must take action. It is slow, inefficient, and not very popular with anybody along the chain. But in most cases, it is considered "the system"—a necessary evil.

The circle network allows all involved communicators to exchange ideas freely. It is more democratic, much more popular with its participants, but also more likely to "waste" time in discussion and arriving at a consensus.

The *wheel* is a popular form of spreading the word . . . especially with the person who happens to be the hub. The wheel keeps every message about everything going through the leader, which can create confusion and dissatisfaction for those isolated on the circumference of the activity.

The *Y* network is like the chain except that more than one chain

[15] Alex Bavelas, "Communication Pattern and Task Oriented Groups," *Journal of the Acoustical Society of America*, Volume 22, 1950, pp. 725–730.

comes together at the leader. Both the *Y* and the wheel can be very ego satisfying for the leader, but totally frustrating for those who are waiting for the information to pass through the bottleneck called the manager.

Each network arrangement has its advantages. Each has its weaknesses. No wise manager will always use any one of them, or try to use all of them at any one time. They are models for analyzing the communication situation in order to arrive at the particular channeling ideal for making the information flow to its intended destinations with as little interference as possible.

The C's of Communication

One of the most helpful checklists for refining a spoken or written communication is called the Five C's of Communication. If a message rates high in each of the following categories, it is likely to be successful in transplanting its idea from one mind to another.

1. *Clarity.* When Murphy's Law of Management ("If anything can go wrong, it will") is applied to the communication process, it can be freely translated, "If anything about your message can be misunderstood, it will be."

A message needs to be as straightforward and as logically stated as possible. Very often lack of clarity is due to an attempt to include too many ideas in the same sentence, as in the communications in Table 12.4.

Approximately 600,000 of the 750,000 words in the English language are of a nontechnical variety, and most of these words have more than one meaning. The 500 most commonly used words in our language have more than 14,000 different dictionary definitions.[16] It is easy to see why clarity can be a problem.

Some organizations have adopted the KISS formula. If a message seems unnecessarily complicated, the initials *K-I-S-S* are written across it and it is returned to the sender for rewording. *KISS*, of course, stands for "Keep it Simple, Stupid."

2. *Completeness.* In our efforts to simplify and clarify, we may fall into the trap of incompleteness. It is important to develop skill in role playing for the final evaluation of a message you are preparing to send. That is, increase your ability to pretend you are the recipient of the message —read it or hear it through that perception set.

Part of a message is sometimes more harmful than no message at all. Sol Herk, a Danish pilot, heard a radio message that said, "Herk, your

---

[16] "Communications," *Kaiser Aluminum News*, January 1965, p. 9.

Table 12.4 Examples of Unclear Writing	(Taken from actual letters received by a County Department)

1. I am forwarding my marriage certificate and six children I have seven but one died which was baptized on a half sheet of paper.
2. Mrs. Jones had not had any clothes for a year and has been visited regularly by the clergy.
3. Please find for certain if my husband is dead. The man I am living with can't eat or do anything until he knows.
4. I am very much annoyed to find you have branded my son illiterate. This is a dirty lie as I was married a week before he was born.
5. In answer to your letter, I have given birth to a boy weighing ten pounds. I hope this is satisfactory.
6. I am forwarding my marriage certificate and three children, one of which is a mistake as you can see.
7. Unless I get my husbands money pretty soon, I will be forced to lead an imortal life.
8. You have changed my little boy to a little girl. Will this make any difference?
9. I have no children as yet as my husband is a truck driver and works day and night.
10. I want money as quick as I can get it. I have been in bed with the doctor for two weeks and he doesn't do me any good. If things don't improve, I will have to send for another doctor.

plane is on fire!'' The pilot reacted instantaneously to this limited information. He bailed out of his plane, which then crashed into a mountainside. As the explosion subsided and Herk drifted gently toward the earth, he saw that he was going to come down on the runway of a small airport. From his parachute vantage point, Sol Herk watched airport personnel putting out a minor fire in the tail section of a small private plane that belonged to *John* Herk.

3. *Conciseness.* When Neil McElroy was president of Procter and Gamble, he refused to read any memorandum that was longer than one page. According to McElroy there was nothing to be said about soap that should take more than a page. As Secretary of Defense under Eisenhower, McElroy followed the same policy. Employees of other large organizations have not been so fortunate as to work under an executive like McElroy. After years of hacking through etymological thickets in the U.S. Public Health Service, an official named Philip Broughton hit upon a surefire method for converting ignorance into seeming communication success. Broughton's system employs a lexicon of thirty carefully chosen "buzz-words" (see Table 12.5). Combinations of such buzz-words are impressive. However, most communications are enhanced when a few well-chosen words replace a verbose, carelessly worded effort.

The problem with rambling, lengthy messages is rarely the vastness of the topic. More often, it is the failure of the communicator to delineate the specific message he wants to transfer.

A male chauvinist once observed that a well-worded message is some-

Table 12.5

Column I	Column II	Column III
0. integrated	0. management	0. options
1. heuristic	1. organizational	1. flexibility
2. systematized	2. monitored	2. capability
3. parallel	3. reciprocal	3. mobility
4. functional	4. digital	4. programming
5. responsive	5. logistical	5. scenarios
6. optional	6. transitional	6. time-phase
7. synchronized	7. incremental	7. projection
8. compatible	8. third-generation	8. hardware
9. futuristic	9. policy	9. contingency

The procedure is simple. Think of any three-digit number, then select the corresponding buzzword from each column. For instance, number 257 produces "systematized logistical projection," a phrase that can be dropped into virtually any report with that ring of decisive, knowledgable authority. "No one will have the remotest idea of what you're talking about, but the important thing is that they are not about to admit it."

what like the length of a miniskirt: long enough to cover the subject but short enough to be interesting.

4. *Concreteness.* Communicators usually revert to abstractions and generalizations when they are unsure about actual, concrete facts. Abstractions are certainly valuable in dealing with abstract concepts. However, we are wasting valuable time and talent when we push real things into abstract or idiomatic terminology to make an impression.

Choosing concrete terminology is even more important as we have more and more interaction among nations. A term that is acceptable in one culture may have a totally unacceptable meaning in another culture. For instance, an American minister visiting in New Zealand was asked to speak at the evening service. In his opening remarks, he expressed his regret that his wife could not be present. He explained that she was a little "under the weather." The New Zealanders were horrified, for in their culture "under the weather" means "dead drunk."

5. *Correctness.* Flawless use of communication technique is all in vain if the message is incorrect. Everyone remembers the story about the little shepherd who *very effectively* cried "Wolf!" He accomplished his immediate purpose of getting attention from the townspeople. However, the fact that his message was entirely false had far-reaching consequences for that shepherd boy. In the same way, an incorrect or exaggerated communication may serve our immediate purpose but cost us more in the long run.

In the early years of space exploration, a satellite costing millions of dollars had to be destroyed in flight because of a miscalculation. The miscalculation was attributed to the omission of one apostrophe in several pages of computer instructions. Little things mean a lot!

Incorrect messages are not always caused by intentional misrepresentation of the truth. Minor exaggerations and unfounded generalizations and assumptions have a way of growing into major communication barriers. As one experienced communicator observed, "I find it much easier to tell the truth all the time—that way, I don't have to remember so much."

Summary

Communication practice involves every phase of human life. The quality of communication technique can often make the difference between success and failure. There are no panaceas to cure all our communication problems. However, it is possible to increase the effectiveness of our sending and receiving skills.

To make our idea transplants as successful as possible, we should endeavor to develop a continuing awareness of (1) the basic process of encoding-sending-receiving-decoding, (2) the natural pitfalls of each step in the communication process, (3) the modes or channels of communication, and (4) the four philosophies of communication cooperation.

Transactional analysis utilizes simple terminology to explain complex communication transactions. In communicating with others, people are either operating from the Adult, Parent, or Child ego states. The interaction between these positions, as well as the life scripts and games that are played, determine the effectiveness of communications in personal and professional situations.

Systems of organizational communication often used are the chain, the circle, the wheel, and the Y.

The Five C's of Communication are helpful in evaluating any message. Effective communicators will develop a second sense for asking of each message: Is it clear? Is it complete? Is it concise? Is it concrete? Is it correct?

Review Questions

1. Discuss the role of "noise" in the communication process.
2. What does the phrase "idea transplant" mean?
3. What are the major ways that people communicate?
4. What is the "adult" approach to life suggested by transactional analysis?
5. Identify the "C's" of communication.
6. Evaluate Marshall McLuhan's observation that "The medium is the message" in light of a boss' consideration of whether to send a letter or a telegram of congratulations when a valued employee becomes a father for the first time.

7. William Buckley is widely known as an articulate spokesman for the politically conservative point of view. Yet some people claim that they do not understand Buckley. Using the components of the communication process, try to identify the problem.

8. If you attend a debate between a liberal sociology professor and a conservative professor of management on the contributions of private enterprise to the American way of life, what type of "noise" may interfere with the communication?

9. After arriving in a large midwestern city for a major political appearance, a presidential candidate refused to use the cars which had been generously provided for his group by a friendly automobile dealer. Could his decision have anything to do with communication?

10. Describe how each of the modes of communication may be used in a classroom situation.

11. Is sound an important aspect of communication?

12. Identify the type of classroom situation in which you would expect the following philosophies of communication to be utilized by a professor.
    a. Developmental.
    b. Controlling.
    c. Relinquishing.

13. Identify the type of ego state usually demonstrated by the following individuals.
    a. Your father.
    b. Your best friend.
    c. Your spouse or steady.
    d. Your professor.
    e. Your minister.

14. Using the "C's" of communication, evaluate this chapter on communication.

15. What similarities exist between a business organization and a good marriage?

16. What ego state is demonstrated by the following statements?
    a. Because I say so, that's why!
    b. I've just got to have a C in this course or I won't graduate.
    c. "Grow old along with me! The best is yet to be. . . ."
    d. I will resign unless you let me leave early.

13

The Mystique of Motivation

Granddad never liked sitting through the Sunday morning sermon. On one memorable day, the ordeal was doubly trying for the poor man, who found himself seated next to a misbehaving child.

The brat seemed to be doing his best to disturb the entire assembly. He was standing up, sitting down, wiggling, talking, and making a terrible commotion.

Everyone was embarrassed for the mother of the naughty boy. Granddad sat watching the boy's antics for a while until an idea struck him. He leaned over and motioned for the boy to come closer. Everyone around watched as Granddad whispered in the boy's ear. As the youngster's eyes lit up, Granddad pulled a shiny, new pocketknife from his vest pocket and showed it to the boy.

The people watched in amazement as the boy sat up straight and motionless through the rest of the service. As the final "Amen" was spoken, the boy ran up the aisle and out the door.

Grandmother had seen the whole thing and commented affectionately, "Dear, I think it was wonderful for you to give that youngster some incentive to behave in church. But I wonder why he left without claiming the prize you promised him."

"What prize?" growled Granddad, "I just told the little brat that if he didn't sit still I would cut his ears off."

Motivation is a fact of life that becomes apparent in the earliest childhood experiences. Even before babies learn that a push or a throw can motivate a wagon or a ball; even before they discover that legs can make them go . . . in the first weeks of life they discover that a cry can move a mommy.

As babies grow, they develop their skills of motivation. They develop a knack for evaluating a situation (even subconsciously) and using some motivational device for each occasion. Unfortunately, children may not pick the most efficient or socially acceptable approach to moving others. When this happens, a child either gets something that was wanted or something that was not wanted. Either way, he or she learns from experience. In this manner, children refine and perfect the system by which they will live. In this way, children develop the characteristics that will make up their personalities.

Our personalities are conglomerates of our behavior patterns. Our behavior patterns hinge on the methods of motivation we have learned to use. Our personalities, therefore, are built upon the concepts of motivation we hold.

A management personality, too, is determined by the managers' perception of the people around them. Their attitudes about the things that "make people go" will determine not only their methods but the results. It is unfortunate that we so often fail to progress beyond a simplistic, childlike conception of human motivation. The roots of human behavior are always numerous and intertwined. It is only the most astute manager who wisely becomes a near-fanatic on the subject of motivation. Such people have realized and begun to act upon the basic concept of motivation: that *why* is sometimes as important as *whether*.

Already we have looked at some basic concepts of human behavior. In this chapter we will review briefly some of the outstanding theories of human motivation. These are, in fact, theories about the nature of people. We will begin by looking into personality, behavior, and motivation.

Personality, Behavior, and Motivation

The term *personality* is often misused to describe a characteristic, as in the sentence, "She's got lots of personality!" Actually, what is meant here is that there are some characteristics about her that make her very appealing. Everyone has personality—it is impossible to be without it . . . and be a person. Personality is the wholeness of a person, the conglomerate of forces within the individual. We derive our ideas about the personalities of others by totaling up behavioral evidence.

Components of Personality

Your personality is a composite of the behavior you demonstrate every day. Interestingly enough, personality is dynamic . . . always changing, adapting, being influenced by various factors. Physical size, shape, and sex, for instance, can play a vital role in determining the kinds of personalities we display. The various groups in which we hold memberships can greatly influence our personalities. Group membership in family, school, or religious associations can alter the entire direction of a life. Quite often we show different faces because of the requirements of the roles we play or the situations we are in. The same man may behave quite differently in the roles of husband, father, manager, or Little League coach. We accept without question the idea that there is a time and place for everything. And what we are really saying is that we are quite willing to emphasize different aspects of our personalities on different occasions and for different purposes.

Although each of these determinants can have a major influence on personality development, it is necessary to recognize their interdependence rather than considering them as isolated factors. In other words, it is incorrect to view a single influence as the maker or breaker of an individual's personality. Instead, the personality of an individual is conditioned by many intertwined variables. We might blush in pride to be told that we possess dynamic personalities. Yet such a statement would technically indicate only that our patterns of behavior (*personality*) are continually being influenced and changed (*dynamic*).

If behavioral actions may be called the building blocks of personality what element can be established as the basis for behavior? Motivation is considered by many to be the key to behavior. Without taking a stand that *something* can motivate, instigate, or initiate change, we would be left with a world of chance happenings. Perhaps we balk at the idea that all behavior is caused. Maybe we want to hold out a few areas of life that cannot be controlled by motivation manipulation. Nevertheless, it is only our defensive, insecure selves that avoid the concept of controlling people by controlling their motivations. When our more aggressive selves swing into action—when we want to bring about change—our thinking moves automatically to motivational considerations: "I wonder *why* he said that?" "What should I do to get him to change his mind?" "Everyone has a weakness." "Every man has his price."

If such motivational talk is frightening to some, if it brings on visions of 1984, "Big Brother," and "thought control," then a word of consolation is easily found. The very complexity of the human personality indicates that human motivation will never have simple formulas that can be controlled by some devious computer. It may be exciting to forecast the day when we will all be motivated to thoughtless action by some omniscient computer that has our number or knows our weakness. But it is far more realistic to expect people to go on making generalizations

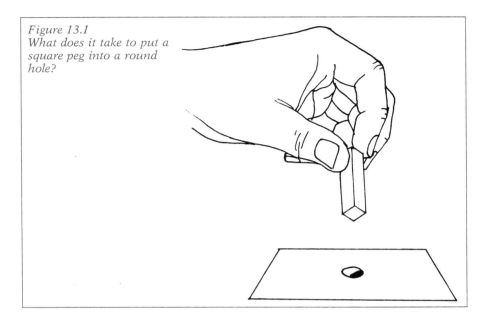

Figure 13.1
What does it take to put a square peg into a round hole?

about motivation rather than computer programs for national thought control. Not only would a different program be required for each of us, but it would have to be under continuous revision to keep pace with our ever-adjusting constellations of motivations.

Pick a Theory, Multiply by X or Y

Each of us has personal feelings about the kinds of factors that may be counted upon to motivate human beings. Perhaps your theory agrees perfectly with that of one of the experts. Or you may have a totally different arrangement of values that you attribute to people. At any rate, when all the philosophizing is said and done, we each will undoubtedly apply our theory of motivation to those whom we wish to motivate.

The manner in which we will attempt to apply our theories is always determined by the concepts we happen to hold about people. Douglas McGregor[1] has given names to the theories most often held about people and motivation. McGregor calls his two groups Theory X and Theory Y.

A manager who fits into the Theory X group leans toward an organizational climate of close control, centralized authority, autocratic lead-

[1] *The Human Side of Enterprise* (New York: McGraw-Hill Book Company, Inc., 1960).

ership, and minimum participation in the decision making process. Such a manager accepts certain assumptions. Theory X assumptions, according to McGregor, are

1. The average person dislikes work and will avoid it as much as possible.
2. Stemming from this, according to Theory X, most people have to be forced or threatened by punishment to make the effort necessary to accomplish organizational goals.
3. The average individual is basically passive and therefore prefers to be directed, rather than to assume any risk or responsibility. Above all else, security is important.

A Theory Y manager operates with a different set of assumptions regarding human motivation. This manager feels that an effective organizational climate has looser, more general supervision, greater decentralization of authority, less reliance on coercion and control, a democratic leadership style, and more participation in the decision process. The assumptions upon which this type of organizational climate is based include the following:

1. Work is as natural to mankind as play or rest and therefore is not avoided.
2. Self-motivation and inherent satisfaction in work will be forthcoming in situations where the individual is committed to organizational goals. Hence, coercion is not the only form of influence that can be used to motivate.
3. Commitment is a crucial factor in motivation, and it is a function of the rewards coming from it.
4. The average individual learns to accept and even seek responsibility, given the proper environment.
5. Contrary to popular stereotypes, the ability to be creative and innovative in the solution of organization problems is widely, not narrowly, distributed in the population.
6. In modern business and organizations, human intellectual potentialities are just partially realized.

Of course, the question arises as to which management philosophy and organizational climate produce the best results. One is inclined to say Theory Y because on the surface it is humanistic and less harsh than Theory X. It is also more optimistic about human motives at work. However, sentiments alone are not sufficient when one is judging the effectiveness of an organizational climate or leadership style. Thus, we must evaluate organizational climate separately in each situation. For now, let us say that under some conditions Theory X works best and under other conditions Theory Y works best. Perhaps the optimum the-

The D.I. (Warner Brothers, 1957). Motivation: Theory X or Theory Y?

ory would be called Theory Z[2] and would take into account the manager's need to employ both approaches at one time or another. Obviously, the wisdom to discern the right time for the right managerial motivation move is the quality that distinguishes the real manager from the boss' in-law who is just starting at the bottom for a few days.

[2] The concept of Theory Z has been suggested by several writers. Perhaps the most significant is Lyndall F. Urwick, "Theory Z," *Advanced Management Journal*, January 1970, pp. 14–21.

Achievement Motivation

Not only are motivational characteristics difficult to pinpoint for individuals . . . they are equally deceptive when attributed to nations. From time to time, attempts are made to characterize the United States according to the things that motivate it.

As suggested in Chapter 11, David McClelland believes that the emerging, "go-ahead" nations are those that are motivated by achievement. Achievement motivation, says McClelland, has declined in the United States from the days of the optimistic Horatio Alger stories and the Davy Crockett hero tales. Some writers feel that any such progression is gain and that a realistic approach is far better than motivation by fantasy figures and striving for unreachable goals. McClelland believes that achievement motivation can be taught and that a new generation indoctrinated with such a keen hunger for accomplishment would be just the shot in the arm the nation has been needing.

More recently, McClelland and his associates have identified a motivation pattern that their research indicates most good mangers share. Good managers are not motivated merely by a need for achievement or the need to get along with subordinates. Rather, they tend to share a need to influence the behavior of other people for the good of the whole organization. In other words, good managers want power.[3]

The Content Theories—"the answer's in there somewhere"

Classical Theory—Frederick W. Taylor

In early 1900's, a young man worked himself up through the ranks from machine operator to supervisor to become the internationally known "father of scientific management." We met him in Chapter 3. His name and his theories about human motivation are classic.[4]

Taylor's reasoning was simple: if energetic workers who naturally work hard find that they earn no more than the lazy employee who does as little as possible, they will soon lose interest in producing as much as they can. Taylor's solution seemed automatic—make it possible for people to earn more by producing more.

To solve the motivation problem, Taylor brought in two magic objects—the stopwatch and the piecework bonus pay system. The stopwatch was for the scientific evaluation of each job. Taylor felt that unclear job requirements caused unpredictable job performance. He

---

[3] David C. McClelland and David H. Burnham, "Power is the Great Motivator," *Harvard Business Review,* March–April, 1976, pp. 100–110.

[4] *Scientific Management* (New York: Harper and Row, Publishers, 1919).

reduced each job to a series of timed and tested movements. Taylor set scientific time limits for the performance of each duty and was therefore able to establish production expectations for each job.

Once the production quotas were set, it became possible to recognize the "doers" and the "loafers" on the production line. Taylor introduced a new reward system for work above and beyond the call of the quota. Piece rates had already been introduced in a number of plants. By this method, employees were paid by the piece—that is, the more they produced, the more they were paid. Taylor's new plan was unique in that it greatly increased the reward for high productivity. People were paid at one rate for each piece produced up to the point where they met the standard. However, once they surpassed the quota, they received a higher rate not only for each additional piece but for all the pieces produced that day. Many workers were able to double their wages under Taylor's new system.

You may recall how, at the Bethlehem Steel Company, Taylor was able to increase the average number of tons handled per person per day from 12½ to 47½ reducing the average cost of handling a ton from 9.2¢ to 3.9¢, while increasing the workers' average daily earnings per worker from $1.15 to $1.85.

The classical theory of motivation makes the assumption that money is the best motivator. It assumes that people consciously choose the course that is most profitable financially. The power of money as a motivator has never been established with full agreement. Some managers agree with Taylor that every person has a price. Others feel that although money *can* motivate some individuals, there are other people who have risen above the power of the dollar. Most research conducted into the motivation by money indicates that financial opportunity can definitely bring about some improvements . . . especially in the jobs with lower socioeconomic rankings. But money simply cannot be the whole answer, for there remain the examples of the great philanthropists and public servants. We can never accept money as the sole motivator as long as the human heart pays tribute to people like Albert Schweitzer, who forsook financial security for a greater satisfaction.

Taylor's classical theory of human behavior and motivation tried to make money the simple solution. As we suggested earlier, there are no *simple* solutions. Money *is* a motivator . . . one of the most significant motivators . . . but the classical theory fails to specify other important considerations that affect individual motivation to work.

Need Theory—Abraham H. Maslow

Taylor's philosophy was simple enough—people could be made to do things if they were given more money. Most of us never reach the point when we do not want more money, but we all have felt at one time or another that there has to be more to life's work than regular paychecks.

In Chapter 10, we learned that Abraham H. Maslow's observations and studies led him to construct a continuum of the human needs that motivate. Maslow's philosophy makes allowances for the individual differences in motivational factors.

Gandhi said of his starving fellow citizens, "To the millions who have to go without two meals a day the only acceptable form in which God dare appear is food." Studies and common sense tell us that when we need food we can think of nothing but food. Yet even a starving person can forget hunger if the supply of air is suddenly cut off. We have an evident priority arrangement of needs. When one need is fulfilled, we become concerned in a more sophisticated drive.

Maslow's need theory, which was first publicized in 1943,[5] postulated that the satisfaction of one need advanced the individual to a subsequent need. Most business writers mention five levels of need satisfaction in discussing Maslow's theory.[6]

Maslow's theory has a great deal to say to the manager who bears responsibility for motivating other people. Even without accepting the theory in its totality, a manager must admit some gradations of needs among workers. The wise manager will study his people and know their needs. This should enable him or her to make them not only more productive workers but more content and appreciative individuals.

In 1957, D. T. Hall and K. E. Nougaim[7] initiated an elaborate five-year study of young management-level employees of American Telephone and Telegraph. For five years, these people each participated in annual three-hour psychological interviews. The motivation strength and need satisfaction of each was assessed from this interview data. The findings of Hall and Nougaim contain several meaningful suggestions for managers of managerial-level workers:

1. For all managers, the need for achievement and esteem increases over the years that they are with a company.
2. Managers who have met high standards of performance will be rewarded with promotions and pay increases or in overall terms, with success.
3. Successful managers achieve a great deal and are given increased managerial responsibility. Therefore, by their fifth year their achievement and esteem satisfaction become significantly greater than those of their less successful colleagues.
4. Possibly as a result of greater achievement and esteem satisfaction, successful managers become more involved in their jobs. By the

[5] "The Theory of Human Motivation," *Psychology Review*, July 1943, pp. 370–396.
[6] Based on Douglas McGregor, *The Human Side of Enterprise* (New York: McGraw-Hill Book Company, 1960).
[7] "An Examination of Maslow's Need Hierarchy in an Organizational Setting," *Organizational Behavior in Human Performance*, February 1968, pp. 12–35.

fifth year, work is significantly more essential to their overall need satisfaction than it is for the less successful group.

5. With increased job involvement, managers are more likely to be successful in future assignments. Thus they are caught in an upward spiral of success.

Two-Factor Theory—Frederick Herzberg

Several years ago Frederick Herzberg, who was then a psychologist at Case Western Reserve University in Cleveland, conducted an interesting series of experiments in motivation[8] with two hundred engineers and accountants. He asked these employees to describe the conditions that had, in the past, made them feel especially good or especially bad about a job.

The resulting data caused Herzberg to describe the two vital factors in every job. First, there are the characteristics of any job that Herzberg called *maintenance factors*. These include some of the necessities of any job—adequate salary, adequate working conditions, job security, and fringe benefits. Herzberg said that these things were necessary before the worker could even begin to be motivated. An adequate salary is of prime importance when it is lacking, but of low motivational value when it does exist. Herzberg concluded that there were ten maintenance factors, namely:

1. Company policy and administration.
2. Technical supervision.
3. Interpersonal relations with supervisor.
4. Interpersonal relations with peers.
5. Interpersonal relations with subordinates.
6. Salary.
7. Job security.
8. Personal life.
9. Work conditions.
10. Status.

Beyond the maintenance factors, Herzberg established the *motivational factors*. These were the things that could really bring about worker dedication to a job. Herzberg listed six truly motivating factors, each of which could fit neatly into the top levels of Maslow's ladder of needs. The six motivational factors (or satisfiers) were

1. Achievement.
2. Recognition.
3. Advancement.

[8] *Work and the Nature of Man* (New York: World Publishing Company, 1966), and Frederick Herzberg, Mausner, and Snyderman, *The Motivation to Work*, 2nd ed. (New York: John Wiley & Sons, Inc., 1959).

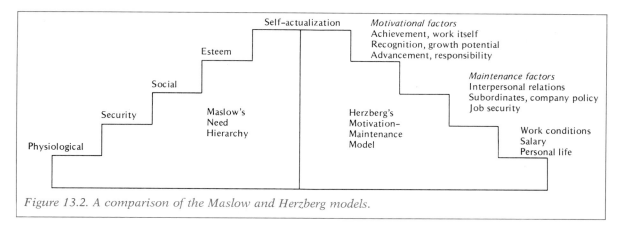

Figure 13.2. A comparison of the Maslow and Herzberg models.

4. The work itself.
5. The possibility of growth.
6. Responsibility.

It became obvious quite early in the investigation that the things that workers can really sink their teeth into deal not with peripheral matters but with the *job itself*. In fact, this phrase ("the job itself") has come to represent to many the real message of Herzberg's theory: if you want to motivate the worker, don't put in another water fountain; provide a bigger share in *the job itself*.

When the theory of Herzberg's two factors is charted next to Maslow's hierarchy of needs, there are several obvious likenesses. Herzberg's maintenance factors are roughly equivalent to Maslow's lower level needs . . . things a worker must have to begin with. Herzberg's motivational factors lie in the upper levels of the Maslow chart. Figure 13.2 demonstrates the similarities of the two theories, both of which emphasize the *sequential* nature of various motivational forces.

R. J. House and L. A. Wigdor[9] reanalyzed the data reported by Herzberg and also reviewed the results of thirty-two studies, all of which dealt with the two-factor theory. The listing of satisfiers and dissatisfiers that emerged from that compilation should be of interest to those seeking to try Herzberg's idea and enhance *the job itself*.

M. Scott Myers, who was manager of personnel research for Texas Instruments Incorporated, using essentially the same techniques as Herzberg, suggested three summary questions that should be committed to memory by every manager with any responsibility for employee motivation:

1. *What motivates employees to work effectively?* A challenging job which allows a feeling of achievement responsibility, growth, advancement, enjoyment of work itself, and earned recognition.
2. *What dissatisfies workers?* Mostly factors which are peripheral to

[9] "Herzberg's Dual-Factor Theory of Job Satisfaction and Motivation," *Personnel Psychology*, Winter 1967, pp. 369–389.

Table 13.1 Reanalysis of Satisfier-Dissatisfier Data		Reported as	
Factor		**Satisfier**	**Dissatisfier**
Achievement		440	122
Recognition		309	110
Work itself		175	75
Responsibility		168	35
Advancement		126	48
Policy and administration		55	337
Supervision		22	182
Working conditions		20	108
Relations with superior		15	59
Relations with peers		9	57

Total number of respondents for each factor: 1,220.

Source: R. J. House and L. A. Wigdor, "Herzberg's Dual-Factor Theory of Job Satisfaction and Motivation," *Personnel Psychology*, Winter 1967.

the job—work rules, lighting, coffee breaks, titles, seniority rights, wages, fringe benefits, and the like.

3. *When do workers become dissatisfied?* When opportunities for meaningful achievement are eliminated and they become sensitized to their environment and begin to find fault.[10]

Human Relations Theory—Rensis Likert

The top three needs of Maslow's hierarchy approach a topic that some have felt could encompass all of motivational theory. Social needs, ego needs, and self-fulfillment needs fall into what might be called the human relations theory of motivation. This theory does not concern itself with the lower-level physiological and safety needs. Rather, its view is that the motivation operates primarily in the satisfaction of higher level needs.

The best explanation of human relations theory has been given by Rensis Likert,[11] who prefers to place the emphasis in motivation upon the motivator. Managers are encouraged to use many factors that will motivate. Such forces include economic motives, security motives, ego motives, curiosity, and the desire to be creative. The difference in human relations theory is the emphasis upon the manager rather than the employee. Money and security become *tools* of the motivator rather than motivations in themselves.

Likert further asserts that organizational units with a high level of production are characterized by favorable attitudes on the part of each member. Production workers like their co-workers better and get along

[10] "Who Are Your Motivated Workers?" *Harvard Business Review*, January–February, 1964, p. 73.
[11] Rensis Likert, *New Patterns of Management* (New York: McGraw-Hill Book Company, 1961).

The Slipper and the Rose: The Story of Cinderella (Universal Picture, 1976). Opportunity for advancement: How important for motivation?

better with their superiors, in their work, and with the organizational establishment. In short, it is the people who relate well to people who are most effectively motivated toward desired goals. According to human relations theory, the appropriate method for leaders to use in motivating their workers is to encourage widespread participation and involvement in decision making—make the worker a part of the company effort and he or she will work better toward it.

Human relations theory is almost the exact opposite of Taylor's classical theory. Taylor's philosophy said, "Don't leave anything to the workers except a simple, uncomplicated single-task command." Human relations theory says, "Bring workers on board; make them members of the team; show them that they are significant—that will motivate them the way nothing else can."

Theories always make everthing so simple! No doubt most managers would like to make workers feel the team spirit. Unfortunately, there is a limit that large-operation reality seems to place on the feeling of close-

Table 13.2
Major Theories
of Motivation

Theory	Author or Major Proponent	Basic Concepts
1. Classical	Frederick W. Taylor	People will be highly motivated if their reward is tied directly to performance.
2. X and Y	Douglas McGregor	Conditions suggest some individuals dislike work and will avoid it whenever possible. These individuals do best under close supervision (Theory X). Others can be self-motivated and find inherent satisfaction in work if the right kind of environment is provided (Theory Y).
3. Need	Abraham H. Maslow	When basic physiological needs are satisfied, higher order needs become dominant and must be included in motivational plans.
4. Two-Factor	Frederick Herzberg	Maintenance factors (working conditions) can make an employee unhappy but will not motivate him or her. Motivational factors are higher level needs such as recognition, the work itself, and the possibility of growth.
5. Human Relations	Rensis Likert	The manager is the key factor in motivation. He or she must make workers feel that they are members of the team and personally important.

ness among all employees. With human relations theory, as with the others, there is an element of truth and a world of incompleteness.

Table 13.2 provides a convenient, concise comparison of the basic concepts of the content theories.

The Process Theories—"There's a stimulus to evoke any response"

Science-fiction writers love the process theories of motivation because, pressed to their ultimate extremes, process theories could conceivably usher in chilling scenarios of mass manipulation of whole civilizations by propaganda or chemical subversion. The reality is not so ominous as the fiction. The theories of managing people by manipulating environmental processes are fascinating, but hardly verge on world conquest.

It All Started with Pavlov

There is scarcely a field of human endeavor that has not been influenced by Pavlov and his dogs. Pavlov was a 19th-century psychologist who did elaborate experiments that studied substitution of motivation stimuli. Knowing that dogs tend to salivate at the sight of food, Pavlov began ringing a bell at the time the dogs would see the food. Eventually the sound of the bell alone would cause the dogs to salivate, even if no food were present. The substitution of stimuli was demonstrated, and the world proceeded to apply (sometimes appropriately) Pavlov's discovery.

Though the world of dog training was little affected, almost every other field seems to need a methodology for substituting stimuli to get desired results. In fact, the greatest benefit of Pavlov's research has probably been the simple *awareness* of stimuli. Modern managers are far less likely to assume that workers are evil or lazy when they do not perform. Instead, they run immediately to find out which thing might be changed to motivate the worker toward the desired response. There has been a *conditioned response* of our modern society to look for conditioned responses!

Conditioning is a term applied to the act of changing the thing that evokes the desired response. Pavlov conditioned the dogs to respond to the bell instead of the food. "Classical conditioning" is the name given to Pavlov's approach—one that puts the new stimulus before the natural stimulus, and gives the subject no control over the stimulus. As this research continued, *instrumental conditioning* emerged. Instrumental conditioning places either a reward or a punishment after the fact, and allows the subject to have some control over which will be received.

Today, we are willing to allow classical conditioning to continue to be used in laboratories for research purposes. But when it is practiced in the real world on real people, we grow suspicious. A person who uses classical conditioning techniques on employees tends to be called a manipulator . . . one who seeks to "trick" people into doing what is wanted. On the other hand, we praise the applications of instrumental conditioning in employee situations. If the worker is "in on" the adjustment of stimuli and response, we like it, and we call the administrator of the effort a manager who understands the dynamics of human motivation. In short, we are quite comfortable with the concept that environmental stimuli can be changed to change the results. But we remain suspicious of any attempt to covertly or uncontrollably tamper with the way things are. We like to be motivated—we abhor being tricked.

Skinnerian Scare

Since Pavlov's initial discoveries, the world of the behavior modifiers has grown considerbly. It is interesting to note that almost all modern professionals who deal with people continually debate about the means that ought to be employed. There are the behaviorists of the field, who say, "Don't waste time talking about historical factors and other stuff— just tell me the results you want, and I can engineer a situation that will produce those results." To which nonbehaviorists answer, "There is more to this thing than mere results. The reasons are important. We don't just want results—we want results that *emerge* from within, rather than those that are *imposed* from without."

B. F. Skinner, a Harvard psychologist, has become the focal point of much animosity toward the unknowns of conditioning in modern society. Skinner's theory carries the name *operant conditioning*, referring to his standard practice of making the subject *operate* in a certain way to receive a certain reward.

Skinner's belief in an absolute conditioned approach is threatening to some. His idea is that people are what they are because of environment, not because of any internal drives, needs, or other unexplainable influences. Skinner scares us by saying that every behavior can be explained if all the stimuli are recognized. He says that behavior has no mystery, and can be empirically observed and analyzed, and, consequently, manipulated. He attacks many of our American cultural values by such a test-tube approach to change. The conflict aroused by his theories has occasionally been more exciting than the theories themselves.

It is important for a student, whether he or she agrees with the operant behaviorists or not, to understand the terminology that has come into common usage in the motivation field. When an *operant response*, the desired behavior, is followed by a pleasant incident, it causes the subject to associate that pleasant experience with the desired response. Since we all seem to prefer pleasure to pain, the subject repeats most often that which brings pleasure.

A *positive reinforcer* is a reward that is given to encourage the repetition of a desired response. A glass of water is a positive reinforcement when we are thirsty. Consequently, we are likely to seek water whenever we are thirsty. A *negative reinforcer* strengthens any behavior that reduces or ends it. For example, when we take off a shoe that is uncomfortable, the reduction in discomfort is reinforcing. Again, we are more likely to repeat this behavior when a shoe is uncomfortable.[12] A *neutral reinforcer* neither encourages nor discourages. Neutral reinforcers are often mixed with positive reinforcers when there is a need to "spread out" the reinforcement requirement.

[12] B. F. Skinner, *About Behaviorism*, (New York: Alfred A. Knopf, 1974) p. 46.

Reinforcement may be *continuous*, happening each and every time the correct response is given, or *partial*, happening only sometimes. If you are training your dog to do a trick, you naturally begin with continuous reinforcement—pats on the head and dog biscuits every time the dog does the right thing. But eventually you will need to taper off—to give the dog biscuits only occasionally. The dog, however, keeps doing the trick because every performance has the potential of being dog biscuit time. The objective of the conditioner is to instill the desired response, and also to keep the positive reinforcement at the lowest level necessary to maintain performance.

Partial reinforcement may be given on a *ratio* or *interval* basis. The ratio approach means that the reward is given every 2nd, 5th, or 10th time the desired action is performed. An interval reinforcement is given repeatedly as long as the desired action is continued.

Whether the reinforcers are served up by ratio or at given intervals, they may have *fixed* or *variable* characteristics. A fixed-ratio approach is good at speeding up performance, as when a sales rep receives a bonus for every tenth order written. The variable-ratio technique has continuing ability to motivate, as when an employee gets a bonus when the boss has a good day.

The following rules have been suggested by Stephen Jablonsky and David De Vries for gaining maximum motivation through operant conditioning:

1. Avoid relying on punishment as a primary means of motivation.
2. Positively reinforce desired behavior and, if possible, ignore undesired behavior.
3. Minimize time-lag between operant response and reinforcement.
4. When using a variable-ratio schedule, apply reinforcement frequently.
5. Determine the response level of each individual and utilize shaping to obtain the final complex behavior.
6. Determine environmental factors that are considered positive and negative by the individual.
7. Specify the desired behavior in operational terms.[13]

Preference-Expectation—adding Vroom to Skinner

Preference-expectation theory is in many ways more an explanation of the motivation phenomena than a prescription for action by leaders. This theory, advanced by Victor H. Vroom in 1964,[14] describes the man-

---

[13] Stephen Jablonsky and David De Vries, "Operant Conditioning Principles Extrapolated to the Theory of Management," *Organizational Behavior and Human Performance,* April 1972, pp. 340–58.
[14] *Work and Motivation* (New York: John Wiley & Sons, Inc., 1964).

ner in which two variables (preference and expectation) work on each other to determine motivation.

Preference refers to the multiple possible outcomes that a worker might have for any activity. If, for instance, she works faster at her machine and makes more pieces, there are several things that might happen. She may receive higher pay, win the production trophy, get a promotion, or make her friends jealous. Or nothing may happen . . . or something may happen that is totally unanticipated. Of all these alternative outcomes, the worker, no doubt, has her preferences . . . probably the outcomes that promise what she is wanting.

However, the worker's preference alone will not explain the different levels of motivation demonstrated by different workers. The other half of the formula involves the worker's *expectation* that the desired outcome can actually happen. No matter how much he may want a raise for working harder, it is unlikely that he will work very hard if he knows that no raises have ever been granted in his company. No matter how great the worker's wishes, it is expectation that tempers enthusiasm.

A person may place high value on bringing about a certain outcome, but if she does not believe that any act of hers will affect what happens, she will not be moved to act. The more she anticipates that the highly valued result depends on *her own actions*, the more her motivation to act increases. Who works harder—the self-employed person or the person who sees her task as an insignificant, meaningless cog on a gigantic wheel?

The preference-expectation relationship formula recognizes the all-important individual differences factor. The theory helps to explain some of the intricacies and interweavings of the motivation phenomenon. Actual application of the theory, however, would require a greater than normal knowledge of the preferences and expectations of the individual concerned.

Porter and Lawler's Expanded Contingency Model

Three years after Vroom's ideas were published, Edward Lawler and Lyman Porter offered an expanded version of the Vroom model.[15] Their addition was the concept that continued performance depends on the worker satisfaction, and that satisfaction is determined by how closely the actual rewards given compare to what the worker feels is deserved. If the reward for performance equals or exceeds what is perceived as being fair, the satisfaction will motivate repeated action. If the reward falls short of perceived equity, however, dissatisfaction will occur and prevent motivation to continue the efforts.

Some writers have maintained that there is really no connection be-

[15] The Effects of Performance on Job Satisfaction," *Industrial Relations*, October 1967, p. 23; also, Lyman W. Porter and Edward E. Lawler, III, *Managerial Attitudes and Performance* (Homewood, Ill.: Richard D. Irwin, Inc., 1968).

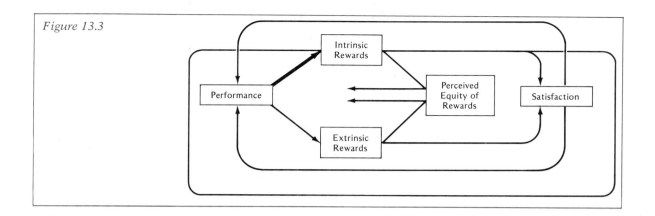

Figure 13.3

tween worker morale or satisfaction and their performance. Vroom himself saw only vague connections between them. Lawler and Porter, however, see rewards and their perceived equity as the "missing link" between performance and satisfaction. As shown in Figure 13.3, the Lawler-Porter model draws a significant distinction between intrinsic and extrinsic rewards. Their distinction correlates with Herzberg's motivation/maintenance model. The intrinsic rewards, fulfilling higher-order needs, are pictured as being much more likely to produce satisfaction and further motivation than the extrinsic rewards, which meet lower needs. Lawler and Porter suggest that intrinsic rewards, which an individual attains, are possible only if the job structure is varied and challenging. The extrinsic rewards, given by the organization, only weakly relate to motivation in this model. Of course, any reward must be desired by the individual in order to have satisfaction value.

One important part of the Lawler-Porter theory is its analysis of the effectiveness of extrinsic, or maintenance, rewards. Their picture of the role of equity perception gives the manager a good indication of how to go about maximizing the effect of such rewards as salary and fringe benefits. Recent motivational approaches, including some job enrichment programs, have neglected this vital relationship between the reward and the worker's evaluation of that reward.

Money and Motivation

Money is a magic word in our culture. It shouts from advertisements and stands behind many of the conclusions we jump to about people. But if we look carefully enough at our preoccupations with money, we begin to realize that it is not the money we worship but the things it represents to us. We *say* money, but we really mean security, independence, status, and accomplishment. If these things are what we really seek and somebody wants to motivate us, would he not be wiser to skip the money step and make more direct offers of security, independence, status, or accomplishment?

Years ago it did take money to have the things we wanted. Today, however, a new suit and a shiny car are no longer accurate indicators of status or independence. In fact, the greater the outward evidences of financial success may be, the greater the likelihood that the person is dependent and far from free. Today it is virtually impossible to have a bankroll that can survive the costs of an expensive period of hospitalization. However, the lowest paid employee can enjoy essentially the same health care security as the president of the company. Fringe benefits have removed much of the soul-buying power of the dollar. When employers began to supply the security and status that money could buy, the money lost some of its motivational clout.

Some experts have said that the bedrock appeal of money is its ability to control the environment. The simple fact in our society is that we can pretty much control our environments by promises, signatures, and monthly payments. What then is the motivational effect of money (i.e., more pay for more work) on a people who need it less every day?

The idea that money is a strong motivator is deeply rooted and still controls the first responses of managers who are having trouble motivating workers. Some people (i.e., those with a background of successfully accomplished goals) still believe that money *can* control their environments. These people do respond well to monetary incentive plans in sales and managerial jobs. And there may be some question as to whether, at upper economic levels, money has not ceased to *represent* status and actually *become* status. If this is the case, it is not the money that motivates, but the status need.

At the lower end of the totem pole are the hourly-wage folks . . . the production workers. William F. Whyte[16] estimates that only 10 per cent of the production workers in the United States respond to a finanacial incentive plan by producing to capacity to increase their earnings. The studies of Whyte and the investigations of Abraham Zaleznik, C. R. Christensen, and Fritz Roethlisberger[17] emphasize the limitations of money as a means of motivating production workers and stress the importance of the work group as a motivating force.

The production worker is not generally driven by money motivation. He is not highly skilled, and his background has not generally been victory after victory, but rather tie after deadlock after standoff, with life. The lack of progress may be due to lack of ability, lack of physiological drive and stamina, poor environmental factors, inability to acquire

[16] *Money and Motivation* (New York: Harper and Row, Publishers, 1955).
[17] *The Motivation, Productivity, and Satisfaction of Workers* (Boston: Harvard Business School, 1958).

training in youth, or many other possible constraints. Socioeconomic forces may have limited expectations to a low level.

The production worker is meeting his basic needs for health and safety, but may have little opportunity or expectation of ever meeting higher needs like self-actualization. To some extent the only opportunity to achieve esteem and recognition lies in the work group rather than in the work. There is greater self-fulfillment in being one of the team than in tightening wing nut 3A one quarter-turn.

Conformity is the price of memebership in the group. Only scabs or rate breakers would try to buck the group's production rates by working faster or harder. The worker who, for some reason, is motivated to rise above majority performance must be prepared for an unpopular social position. Social disapproval is one of the most potent motivational means known to people; only one thing is more powerful—social approval.

In conclusion, it may be said that in a few instances in which money seems to buy better performance and higher production there is some question about the real motivator involved. Is the money moving the workers, or has the money come to represent status, achievement, or independence?

Morale and Productivity

Morale is a word with many connotations. Definitions range from the absence of conflict to a feeling of happiness, good personal adjustment, good attitudes pertaining to work, or the extent of ego involvement in one's job. Regardless of the words we use to explain morale, its presence or absence is not only noticeable but crucial. Some companies have a feeling . . . an air about them . . . an attitude of personal commitment that is seen in their employees. The feeling seems to be "The company goal above all else." In other situations a negative attitude rules and the feeling is "Forget the company; just take care of number one."

Good morale is a significant indicator of company health and promise. Bad morale eventually affects products, profits, and priorities. Both good and bad morale tend to perpetuate themselves. If everything is positive, then workers will keep the cycle going and even be able to see things as better than they actually are. On the other hand, bad morale causes a downward spiral that is very difficult to arrest or reverse. A manager who gives minimal attention to worker morale is making a poor selection of priorities.

Robert M. Guion offers a definition of *morale* that includes most, if not all, of the other definitions usually given: "Morale is the extent to which an individual's needs are satisfied and the extent to which the individual perceives that satisfaction as stemming from his total job situation."[18]

Guion's definition places important emphasis on the "total job situation." There are four relatively independent areas that may either contribute to or detract from job satisfaction. They are intrinsic job satisfaction, satisfaction with the company, satisfaction with supervision, and satisfaction with rewards and the opportunity for upward mobility.[19]

A number of companies are using job enrichment to produce excellent results in the improvement of worker morale. It is not feasible with all jobs, it can be mismanaged, and some people appear not to want it, but it does offer a strong probability of favorable results. Following is an example.[20]

> In the Treasury Department of American Telephone and Telegraph Company, educated and intelligent women handled correspondence with stockholders. They worked in a highly structured environment under close supervision in order to assure a suitable quality of correspondence. Under these conditions, quality of work was low and turnover was high.
>
> Using a control group and a test group, the jobs of the test group were enriched as follows: (1) the women were permitted to sign their own names to the letters they prepared; (2) the women were held responsible for the quality of their work; (3) they were encouraged to become experts in the kinds of problems which appealed to them; and (4) subject matter experts were provided for consultation regarding problems.
>
> The control group remained unchanged after six months, but the test group improved by all measurements used. These measurements included turnover, productivity, absences, promotions from the group, and costs. The quality measurement index climbed from the thirties to the nineties! American Telephone and Telegraph Company also has achieved excellent results in other job-enrichment efforts. In the directory-compilation function, name omissions dropped from 2 to 1 percent. In frame wiring, errors declined from 13 to 0.5 percent, and the number of frames wired increased from 700 to over 1,200.

The worker's attitude toward the work obviously affects the kind of job that will be done. We each know that from personal experience without the benefit of sophisticated psychological test efforts. The real question that each manager must answer is not whether it would be nice for workers to be happier in their jobs but whether it will be worth it. A few years ago, an auto manufacturer initiated a new approach. Factory workers would no longer mass-produce their product, but

[18] "The Industrial Psychologist," *Personnel Psychology*, Spring 1966.
[19] Robert L. Kahn, "Productivity and Job Satisfaction," *Personnel Psychology*, Autumn 1960, pp. 275–287.
[20] Robert N. Ford, *Motivation Through the Work Itself* (New York: American Management Association, 1969).

would work individually and in small groups as craftspeople. It was an interesting experiment. The workers reported increased job satisfaction, but the product cost too much to produce, and the company eventually went out of business. Motivation is of importance . . . but perhaps some things are more important.

Summary

Each individual's personality is determined by beliefs about the motivation of associates. Attitudes about the kinds of things that "make people go" will influence not only our methods but our results. What we call personality is a conglomerate, the whole picture of all the behavior patterns we see characterizing a person. Our patterns of behavior (personality) are continually being altered and changed (dynamic) by many varied and intertwined influences.

A manager will apply the theories of motivation according to an individual concept of the nature of people. Douglas McGregor's Theory X and Theory Y characterize the basic assumptions of whip-crackers and trust-givers. Actually, the optimum theory is probably Theory Z, which would include both the other approaches at one time or another.

It is natural to expect the literature of management to be full of generalizations about human motivation. In this chapter, we looked briefly at both the *content* and *process* approaches to human motivation. The content approach began with Frederick W. Taylor's classical theory of motivation, which proposed ways to allow workers to earn more by working more. Abraham H. Maslow announced a hierarchy of needs that humans experience more or less in sequence. The meaning for motivators is clear: find out where the workers stand on the scale, and motivate them with the next highest need. Human relations theory says that true motivation operates primarily in the satisfaction of the higher level needs for ego and social fulfillment. Frederick Herzberg's two-factor theory establishes two areas: *maintenance factors*, which are necessary to avoid dissatisfaction; and *motivational factors*, the higher needs by which workers can be effectively motivated.

The process approach to motivation assumes that human behavior can be controlled by altering environment . . . the process within which he works. It began with Pavlov's dogs, was developed in modern times by Skinner, and is explained somewhat through the preference-expectation theory: Victor H. Vroom's attempt to reduce motivation to a basic equation: preference times expectation equals motivation. Porter and Lawler expanded this idea.

Although it is generally assumed that money is an efficient motivator, the research tends to indicate that it is not. In fact, the few cases in which money does seem to motivate are probably only situations in which the money *represents* something that can motivate. William F. Whyte estimates that only 10 per cent of the hourly-wage production workers in the United States repond to a financial incentive plan by producing to capacity to increase their earnings. Group membership, approval, and feeling of worth seem to be far stronger producers of morale and higher production than money. As a motivator of workers, morale has far out-distanced money. Perhaps a summary statement might be, "If you want to motivate workers, don't put in another water fountain; give them a bigger share in the *job itself*.

Review Questions

1. What was Frederick W. Taylor's approach to motivation?
2. Is there a relationship between Abraham H. Maslow's higher order needs and Frederick Herzberg's motivational factors? Discuss.
3. Is an autocratic manager likely to view workers from a Theory X or a Theory Y perspective? Discuss.
4. Does money play any role in motivating people? Explain.
5. Do many workers repond to a financial incentive plan?
6. In the opening vignette of this chapter, to what level of Maslow's hierarchy was the old man appealing?
7. Identify the nations that you think are most characterized by what David McClelland refers to as achievement motivation.
8. Would the world be a better place to live if everyone possessed achievement orientation?
9. To what level of Maslow's hierarchy did the following individuals or concepts apply?
   a. Esau (Abrahams's grandson).
   b. Albert Schweitzer.
   c. Harry's Bomb Shelters, Inc.
   d. The key to the executive washroom.
   e. The Tri-Peu fraternity.
10. Which of the following factors would Herzberg say really motivated people?
    a. Company-sponsored bowling team.
    b. Cafeteria decorated by Peter Max.
    c. Gold star for superior performance.
    d. "Acting manager for a day."
    e. Tenure.
11. Does a winning football team contribute anything to the scholastic productivity of students on a campus?
12. Is there any theory that helps explain why you do better in courses that you enjoy? Discuss.

14

Learning to Lead

"Pardon me, old-timer, but I was just wondering if you've been sitting there on the front porch very long."

"Yep! I reckon I been sitting here about ten years now. I sit here every day . . . just sort of watching folks pass by."

"That's good because I want to ask you if you've seen a group of Marchers go by here."

" 'Bout twenty-five of them?"

"Yes! Twenty-six exactly!"

"All dressed alike? Wearing funny little hats like that one you got on?"

"Yes! That's the group. Have you seen them?"

"They passed through here yesterday about this time. They were heading east and making pretty good time."

"Thanks, old-timer. I guess I'd better get a move on if I'm going to catch up with them."

"Hold on a minute, young fellow. Why do you want to find those folks, anyhow?"

"Why, I've got to catch up with them soon, old-timer. I'm their leader!"

Leadership is the ability to persuade others to seek certain goals and the technique of taking them there. *Leadership* is certainly not a new or unfamiliar word to us, and it is, therefore, fraught with great potential for misunderstanding. In spite of a historical interest in leadership, man actually knows very little about what differentiates a leader from a nonleader. Almost any conclusions we may draw about leaders by studying some famous leaders are soon contradicted as we study another famous leader. As Warren Bennis has summarized the situation:

"After at least 50 years of research and theorizing, we can say only one thing with any confidence: There is no proveable generalization about leadership."[1]

One of the overlooked factors of the leadership phenomenon is that true leadership is dependent on the voluntary response of those being led. Possession of a management title does not automatically imply leadership. Many managers—but seldom the best ones—have little leadership ability. And some leaders do not fit into management positions.

Because the manager seeks to be a leader, it is important that we consider in this chapter the qualities that may contribute to leadership. Leadership is part of management but not all of it. If an individual is a strong leader and a weak manager, then people will be faithfully following to the wrong destination. On the other hand, a strong manager must be a strong leader. A manager without the skills of leadership is like a lifeguard who is afraid of water. It does not matter how much you know if you are unable to put your knowledge to work.

Leadership Versus Popularity

One unfortunate misconception that has prevailed is that leadership and popularity are the same quality. How many times leaders are chosen on popularity regardless of their ability to envision goals and guide groups. This is as short-sighted as assuming that the best machinist will automatically be the best supervisor of machinists. It is also quite common for people in leadership positions to make the wrong decision by seeking to maintain personal popularity with staff or even with the competition. It is short-sighted indeed to evaluate a leader on the basis of popularity. This is why it is difficult to judge the effectiveness of U.S. presidents while in office. It is only in the cool light of historical perspective that we can weigh the evidence without the distraction of vocal public opinion. It should also be mentioned regarding popularity and leadership that lack of popularity is no more a proof of good leadership than is abundance of good will. Many managers confuse rudeness and unpleasant behavior with efficiency and leadership.

The best way to appraise the quality of a leader is to look at his or her

[1] Bennis, *The Unconscious Conspiracy* (New York: Amacom, 1976), p. 175.

followers. How many and what kind of followers are there? How strong is their commitment? Are they reaching the group goals? More than anything else, this final question will tell the story. If the group goals are wisely chosen and efficiently reached, leadership practices are in effect.

Leadership is often confused with aggressiveness and enthusiasm. Aggressiveness and bubbling oratory may be part of good leadership . . . or they may not. At times the appropriate leadership action is to stay in the background keeping pressures off the group, keeping quiet so others' ideas may emerge, and calming the excited group members in time of panic. It has been said that a good leader leads from three positions: at the front of the group, pointing the way; in the middle, encouraging the majority; and at the rear, picking up stragglers.

How Leadership Works

Several scholars have given time to trying to explain the phenomenon of leadership. How is it that some people are not only willing but eager to go before the group as leaders and that the others are equally glad not to be leaders? What is the basis upon which a person possesses the power to "let others have the leader's way"?

As suggested earlier, the term *power* is of great significance in true leadership analysis. It is of little consequence who has the *title*—it is the one who has the *power* who will see things go the way he or she wishes. The old phrase "the power behind the throne" has many modern applications in the analysis of leadership. John French and Bertram Raven have described five different channels through which power may be awarded.[2]

1. *Coercive Power.* This is power based upon fear. A subordinate perceives that failure to comply with the wishes of a superior will lead to punishment (e.g., poor work assignment, a reprimand). Coercive power is based upon the expectations of individuals that punishment is the consequence for not agreeing with the actions, attitudes, or theories of a superior.

2. *Reward Power.* This is the opposite of coercive power. A subordinate perceives that compliance with the wishes of a superior will lead to positive rewards. These rewards could be monetary (increases in pay) or psychological (a compliment for a job well done).

3. *Legitimate Power.* This type of power derives from the position of a manager in the organizational hierarchy. For example, the president of a corporation possesses more legitimate power than the vice-president, and the department manager has more legitimate power than the first line supervisor.

[2] "The Basis of Social Power," in Dorwin Cartwright and Alvin Zander (eds.), *Group Dynamics*, 2nd ed. (Evanston, Ill.: Row Peterson & Co., 1960), pp. 607–623.

4. *Expert Power.* An individual with this type of power is one with some expertise, special skill, or knowledge. The possession of one or more of these variables gains for the possessor the respect and compliance of peers or subordinates.

5. *Referent Power.* This power is based on a follower's identification with a leader. The leader is admired because of one or more personal traits, and the follower can be influenced because of this admiration.

Daniel Katz and R. L. Kahn[3] suggest that the real indicator of the extent to which any given person is a leader is the amount of influence wielded beyond the authority inherent in the office. It is a famous saying that "The boss may not always be right, but is always the boss." However, if the group's obedience is only a result of blind respect to the boss' position, there is a low level of leadership in existence. The ideal situation is when the individual who has the natural recognition and respect of his group is coincidentally appointed to or placed in the position of official leadership. It takes more than a title to make the boss a leader.

Leadership Theories

For almost as long as there have been leaders, there have been people who wondered about and studied the phenomenon of leadership. Through the generations, many theories have arisen to attempt to explain the specific qualities that differentiate the leaders from the majority. In recent years the multitude of theories have been grouped under three headings. We will look briefly at these three ideas about the components of leadership: the trait theory, the behavorial theory, and the situational theory.

Physical traits probably received the earliest acclaim as the determinants of leadership. No doubt the authority of many an early leader did have to rest upon the simple fact that he was the strongest . . . if the group did not go his way, many of the group stood to get their skulls cracked. But physical strength could not stand long as an explanation of leadership. Regardless of strength, every person has unprotected times and is vulnerable to assassination. Even the "fastest gun in the West" could not take the silent majority where they didn't want to go by the pure power of physical strength.

Once it became apparent that might did not make right, a different style of physical traitism came into the limelight. Leadership was thought to be inherited through physical lineage. The concept of the royal family became deeply rooted in our thinking. Although this theory did not receive much opposition from the royal families, the common people eventually began to see flies in the ointment. With Robin Hood running circles around royalty, folks began to wonder about the old

[3] *The Social Psychology of Organizations* (New York: John Wiley & Sons, Inc., 1966), p. 302.

idea of the genetic passage of leadership talent. The royalty myth had its leadership monopoly cut off (along with many of its heads) in the revolts of the common people all around the globe.

Today our thinking is strong on "All people are created equal," and it would be difficult indeed to find many folks to follow a leader simply because he or she was taller, faster, stronger, blonder, or the seventh son of a seventh son.

Mental traits are more likely to attract the people of our time than physical powers. We like to hear that our leaders not only read two thousand words per minute but also surround themselves with "brain trusts." Politicians make definite gains by appropriately affiliating with the leaders of the educational community, as long as they don't wind up sounding like pointy-headed pseudointellectuals.

Leaders do tend to have a somewhat higher intelligence than the average of their followers.[4] The difference is not enough to prove the mental trait theory, but it usually exists. The leader's job requires the analytical ability to see the broad problems and complicated relationships with which he deals. His communication skills must be effective enough to convey ideas, motivate others, and understand what others are saying.

After surveying the literature, Ralph Stogdill[5] concluded that leadership ability *is* associated with the judgment and the verbal facility of the leader. Edwin E. Ghiselli[6] also concluded, after conducting research, that an individual's intelligence is an accurate predictor of managerial success within a certain range. Above and below this range the chances of successful prediction significantly decrease. Most of us would agree that a leader must be smart, but common sense tells us the smart people are not *necessarily* leaders. In fact, a person can seem too smart to be accepted as a leader.

Personality traits probably come closer than any of the other trait theories to including the determiners of leadership. This is true because we include so many things in personality. Almost any of the interrelationships of physical, mental, and social traits tend to fall under the broad classification of personality. It is, in fact, undeniably true to say that a leader's personality is the key to success. The problem comes when we try to group the types of personalities for two leaders of completely opposite personality types who tend to succeed because their personalities are right for the group they lead.

Leaders tend to have broad interests and activities. They are emotion-

---

[4] T. A. Mahoney, T. H. Jerdee, and A. N. Nash, "Predicting Managerial Effectiveness," *Personnel Psychology*, Summer 1960, pp. 147–163; and M. L. Rock, "Profile of One Company's Management," *Personnel*, November–December 1958, pp. 52–53.

[5] "Personal Factors Associated with Leadership," *Journal of Applied Psychology*, January 1948, pp. 35–71.

[6] "Managerial Talent," *American Psychologist*, October 1963, pp. 631–641.

ally mature so that they are neither crushed by defeat nor smitten by victory. They have a high frustration tolerance. Their antisocial attitudes, such as hostility to others, are minimal. They are self-assured and have reasonable self-respect.

Leaders have strong personal motivation to keep accomplishing things. They continually seek to satisfy the ultimate need for themselves and their groups. They work hard more for the satisfaction of inner drives than for external rewards. They tend to accept responsibility eagerly.

Successful leaders realize that they get their job done through people. Therefore, they develop social understanding and appropriate skills. They develop a healthy respect for people, if for no other reason than that their success as leaders depends on the cooperation of people. They approach problems in terms of the people involved more than in terms of the technical aspects involved.

The *trait approach* to leadership explanation has many things to recommend it. The traits *do* exist—in many cases they have become the identifying mark of leaders. And yet, there is some area of uncertainty as to whether the trait made the leader a success or the leader's success made the trait noticeable. Generally speaking, those who have sought to isolate leadership traits have contradicted each other. Indeed, Eugene Jennings has concluded,

> "Research has produced such a variegated list of traits presumably to describe leadership that for all practical purposes, it describes nothing. Fifty years of study have failed to produce one personality trait or set of qualities that can be used to discriminate between leaders and nonleaders."[7]

Yet, in spite of this failure of the formal researchers, there seems to be an almost inherent human tendency to look to traits as the identification criterion for leadership. Ask the person on the street why he or she votes for one person over another, and you will get an answer in terms of traits. As Warren Bennis has put it, "There is, above all, a craving for that integrity and simplicity which mark the truly great—a Lincoln, an Einstein, a Holmes, a Schweitzer."[8]

The Behavioral Theories

Some writers on the topic of leadership have chosen the leader's way of doing things as the quality that distinguishes this special person from peers. They feel that although physical, mental, and personality traits are rather homogeneous throughout the population, the ways of accomplishing objectives in a leadership manner are peculiarly characteristic of those we call leaders. In this section we will survey some of the be-

---

[7] "The Anatomy of Leadership," *Management of Personnel Quarterly*, Autumn, 1961, p.2.
[8] Bennis, *op.cit.*

havioral characteristics that have been pointed out as possible indicators of leadership ability.

Benevolent autocracy is a nice term for describing an all-powerful ruler who listens considerately to employees' opinions and then makes a personal decision. It sounds somewhat suspect in our culture to suggest value for any system that limits or moves away from the "will of the people." Yet some writers have come forward to say that our emphasis upon democratic processes should not push us into applying democratic principles where they do not belong and cannot function efficiently.

Robert N. McMurry[9] believes that the cold realities of the "real world" of business and competition make systems of democratic leadership unworkable. McMurry would probably agree that too many brainstormers spoil the decision. Anyone who has ever tried to accomplish any objective with a committee would certainly see the positive value of a benevolent autocrat who could take the foundering project in hand and move decisively toward the accomplishment of the goal.

The benevolent autocrat is interpreted to be a powerful and prestigious manager who can be communicated with and is personally interested in subordinates' problems. This type of manager is perceived as being able to take prompt remedial action for activities within his jurisdiction.

McMurry argues that a benevolent dictatorship is not only a faster-moving but a more effective system for managing an enterprise. Of course, many leaders who never heard of Robert McMurry have quite naturally adopted the benevolent-autocrat approach because of their attitude toward the people they lead. These leaders function on the assumption that they understand and that subordinates do not. They are willing (and in some cases eager) to hear and consider employee ideas and concerns. But when the chips are down this leader may be more autocratic than benevolent.

There is evidence that neither benevolent autocracy or democratic leadership can be declared categorically superior. Each appears to work for some leaders. The person and the *situation* tend to determine the behavioral pattern that can best succeed. Possibly the term *benevolent* should be the center of any dispute. Are leaders benevolent as long as their decisions agree with yours? And do they become pure autocrats when they listen to your advice and make the opposite decision?

The *continuum theory* is closely related to the benevolent-autocrat theory. It suggests that the types of leadership attitudes toward subordinates may be accurately charted along a continuum. At one end of the system would be the total authoritarian. The benevolent autocrat

[9] "Keys for Benevolent Autocracy," *Harvard Business Review*, January–February 1958, pp. 82–90.

Figure 14.1
What are the draw-backs of the benevolent autocratic approach to management?

would fall somewhere near the middle. At the other end of the line are the democratic/laissez-faire leaders. One interpretation of the continuum theory is that the two extremes represent opposite centers of concern—the authoritarian leader being job-centered and the democratic leader being people- or employee-centered.

The differences in the two behavioral styles are based on the leader's assumptions about (1) human nature, (2) authority, and (3) the source of power. The authoritarian style of leader behavior holds to theory X (that workers are innately lazy and unreliable). They will tell the employees what to do and how to do it. In fact, if time would allow, they would prefer to do all the jobs personally. Democratic leaders assume that theory Y is more correct. They see humans as basically self-directed and creative at work if given a free rein. They prefer to set the objective for employees and allow them leeway to accomplish it according to their own creativity. At the extreme lower end of the continuum —even less structured than the democratic style—is the laissez-faire style. This approach permits the subordinates to do whatever they want to do—even determine their own policies, procedures, and objectives.

The research of Rensis Likert[10] and his associates at the Institute for Social Research at the University of Michigan has provided statistical

[10] *New Patterns of Management* (New York: McGraw-Hill Book Company, 1961).

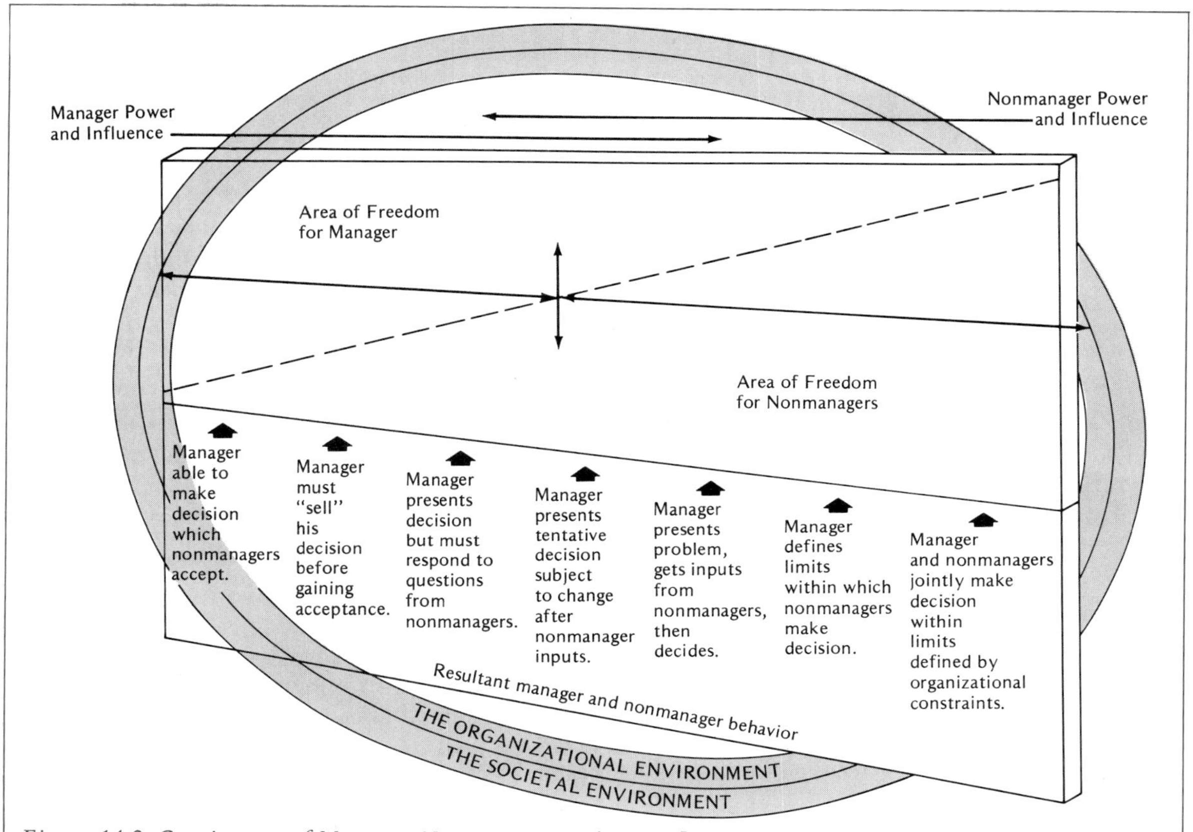
Manager Power and Influence
Nonmanager Power and Influence
Area of Freedom for Manager
Area of Freedom for Nonmanagers
Manager able to make decision which nonmanagers accept.
Manager must "sell" his decision before gaining acceptance.
Manager presents decision but must respond to questions from nonmanagers.
Manager presents tentative decision subject to change after nonmanager inputs.
Manager presents problem, gets inputs from nonmanagers, then decides.
Manager defines limits within which nonmanagers make decision.
Manager and nonmanagers jointly make decision within limits defined by organizational constraints.
Resultant manager and nonmanager behavior
THE ORGANIZATIONAL ENVIRONMENT
THE SOCIETAL ENVIRONMENT

Figure 14.2. Continuum of Manager-Nonmanager Behavior. [Reprinted with permission from Robert Tannenbaum and Warren H. Schmidt, "How to Choose a Leadership Pattern," Harvard Business Review, *vol. 51, no. 3 (May–June 1973), p. 167.]*

data relating to the behavioral style of management leadership. Data were obtained from thousands of leaders in industry, hospitals, and government. Likert found that the categories tended to fall into place along a continuum according to the degree of *job-centered* or *employee-centered* interest of the leader.

Robert Tannenbaum and Warren H. Schmidt[11] depicted the full range of leadership styles on a continuum. This description also ranges from authoritarian to democratic extremes, and each degree is described in terms of the manager's behavior.

Charts are sometimes deceptive. They tend to indicate static status for moving forces. This fallacy is especially present in the continuum. Rather than ever being pinpointed in a given spot on the continuum, leaders are actually moving in one direction or another. A continuum can be of value to us as long as we look at it in terms of *direction* and

[11] "How to Choose a Leadership Pattern," *Harvard Business Review,* March–April 1958, pp. 95–101, and May 1973, pp. 162–180.

relativity of qualities. Leadership styles alter from time to time. A style that is the strength of one manager might constitute the downfall of another.

The *Ohio State University studies* of leadership behavior, which began in 1948, attempted to identify leader characteristics through the development of a questionnaire. The Leader Behavior Description Questionnaire was designed to evoke information about *how* a leader carries out activities.

These investigations are now often referred to as the two-dimensional theory because two dimensions of leadership behavior were identified through statistical analysis. The two dimensions, consideration and initiating structure, were used to describe leadership characteristics in organizational settings.[12]

Initiating structure is task-oriented. It emphasizes the needs of the organization. At the same time, *consideration* is more relationship-oriented and tends to emphasize the needs of individual employees. High scores on consideration were earned by managers who had developed a work atmosphere of mutual trust, respect for subordinates' ideas, and consideration of employees. High scores in initiating structure indicate strengths in planning, communicating, and scheduling.

The cooperative scores that could be achieved by the multitudinous scoring combinations led to the term *two-dimensional theory*. The Ohio State researchers were the first to publicize widely a graphing system of management ability that was represented on two axes rather than on a single continuum. Four quadrants were developed to represent various combinations of the two dimensions.

After comparing the leadership scores and the proficiency ratings, the researchers compared the leadership scores and performance measures —unexcused absenteeism, accidents, formally filed grievances, and employee turnover. A number of other studies have supported these findings. Other research findings, however, present contradictory evidence.[13] Despite these differences, the Ohio State researchers stimulated interest in the systematic study of leadership.

The importance of the Ohio State studies can hardly be overstated. Many subsequent studies owe their foundation and instigation to the work of Stogdill and Coons. For example, the well known managerial grid concept was built on the foundations laid at Ohio State as were the situational leadership concepts proposed by Hersey and Blanchard.

The *managerial grid theory* was made popular by Robert Blake and

[12] R. M. Stogdill and A. E. Coons, *Leader Behavior: A Description and Measurement*, Research Monogram 88, Bureau of Business Research, Ohio State University, 1957; and R. M. Stogdill, *Individual Behavior and Group Achievement* (London: Oxford University Press, 1959).
[13] See A. C. Filley and R. J. House, *Managerial Process and Organizational Behavior* (Glenview, Ill.: Scott, Foresman and Company, 1969), pp. 405–407.

Table 14.1 Ohio State Leadership Quadrants	−Structure+	
Consideration +	High Consideration and Low Structure	High Structure and High Consideration
−Consideration	Low Structure and Low Consideration	High Structure and Low Consideration

Jane F. Mouton.[14] They extended the two-dimensional chart concept and even gave descriptions of the kind of managers who might be found at five points on the grid: at the four extremes and in the very center. Blake and Mouton took concern for people and concern for production as the two axes of their grid. Managers may be located on the grid according to their ranking in each of these two areas.

Five specific leadership styles were described with the understanding that any individual might rank in any of the other seventy-six positions. These positions might be described by the following attitudes:

1,1 = Impoverished—"Don't make waves; do as little as possible to keep the boss happy."

9,1 = Task—"The job's the thing. Accomplish the objective even if all the troops are lost in the battle."

1,9 = Country Club—"Why should I worry about progress? My people know what they are doing and are very happy."

5,5 = Middle of the Road—"People and production . . . they are both important."

9,9 = Team—"Yes indeed! This is the finest staff anybody could want to work with. They really work as a team to accomplish team goals!"

Blake and Mouton suggest four types of activities that might benefit leaders in their continuing campaign for improvement: (1) *laboratory-seminar groups* to create awareness of managerial qualities and leadership needs; (2) *teamwork* in specifying the desirable characteristics and working together toward perfection; (3) *intergroup action* among teams for discussion, analysis, and generalizations about growth experiences; and (4) *goal setting* for specific, measurable progress in leadership development.

Blake and Mouton's outstanding contribution to the investigation of

[14] *The Management Grid* (Houston, Texas: Gulf Publishing Company, 1964).

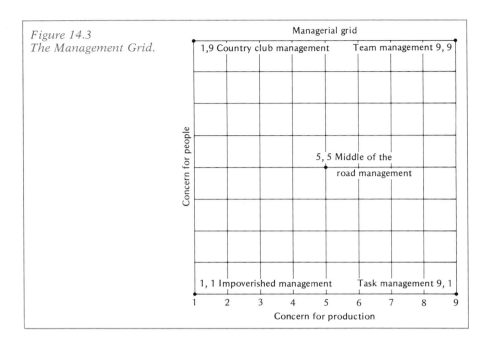

Figure 14.3
The Management Grid.

Managerial grid

1,9 Country club management   Team management 9, 9

5, 5 Middle of the
road management

1, 1 Impoverished management   Task management 9, 1

Concern for people

Concern for production

leadership has been the introduction of an excellent packaging concept —a method for explaining and developing training programs to focus sensitivity training and organizational development on the leadership concept. Their grid made a slippery concept much easier to handle.

The group dynamics studies of Dorwin Cartwright and Alvin Zander[15] were based on the findings of numerous studies at the Research Center for Group Dynamics. They claim the discovery of two different measures of leadership behavior. According to Cartwright and Zander, all group objectives fall into one of two categories: (1) the achievement of some specific group goal, or (2) the maintenance and strengthening of the group itself.

This category arrangement is quite similar to the job-centered—people-centered classification mentioned earlier. The leader most concerned with goal achievement initiates action, keeps members' attention on the goal, clarifies the issue, and develops procedural plans. On the other hand, the group-centered leader keeps interpersonal relations pleasant, arbitrates disputes, provides encouragement, gives the minority a chance to be heard, stimulates self direction, and increases the interdependence among members.

[15] *Group Dynamics: Research and Theory,* 2nd ed. (Evanston, Ill.: Row Peterson, 1960).

From Immaturity to Maturity

After studying business organizations to determine the effect management practices have on individual behavior and personal growth, Chris Argyris concluded that the "healthy" personality develops along a continuum from "immaturity" to "maturity." In moving from infancy to a fully-developed adult, Argyris asserted that an individual would move through a series of seven important changes. They are summarized in Table 14.2.

Although this growth continuum is a natural for all individuals, Argyris believes that many organizations are kept from developing into maturity by restrictive organizational practices. It can be argued that the concept of keeping people immature is built into the nature of formal organizations. For example, high school students are frequently subject to more rules and regulations than their younger counterparts in elementary school. In a business setting, management attempts to enhance efficiency and productivity by making workers "interchangeable parts." Argyris believes that task specialization often results in over-simplifications so that a job becomes unchallenging. Traditional, task-oriented leadership that evokes traditional managerial controls may restrict the initiative and creativity of workers.

While experienced managers may disagree with the practicality of some of Argyris' concepts, most of us will agree with his analysis of the continuum from immaturity to maturity. The importance of recognizing both worker and manager maturity will be further illustrated when we discuss some of the situational leadership concepts that follow.

The Situational Theories

Situational theories of leadership behavior were almost an automatic result of the years of theorizing and searching for traits. The more theories that appeared, the more obvious it became that no single trait

Table 14.2 Argyris's Immaturity-Maturity Continuum	**Immaturity characteristics**	**Maturity characteristics**
	Passivity	Activity
	Dependence	Independence
	Capable of behaving in few ways	Capable of behaving in many ways
	Shallow interests	Deep interests
	Short-term perspective	Long-term perspective
	Subordinate position	Superordinate position
	Lack of self-awareness	Self-awareness and control

Source: Adapted from C. Argyris, *Personality and Organization* (New York: Harper & Brothers. 1957). pp. 50–51.

(or even pair of traits) could adequately identify leadership capability or paths of training. Situational theory says, in effect, that leadership ability is dependent upon the individual's adaptive ability—the feeling he may have for sensing, interpreting, and treating the specific situation.

Symbolically, the situational approach to leadership is expressed as $L = f(LP, GP, S)$, that is, leadership equals the function of the leader's personality, the group's personality, and the situation. As soon as each of these qualities can be definitely quantified and computerized, it will be possible to produce leaders in a test tube. However, that day will be a long time in coming because of the dynamic and deceptive nature of personalities and situations.

The work of Fred E. Fiedler[16] has focused upon adaptive situational leadership style. With a considerable body of research evidence behind him, Fiedler had developed a situational model of leadership. Three important leadership dimensions are specified because they are assumed to be situational factors that influence the leader's effectiveness. The dimensions identified are as follows:

1. *Leader-member relations* refers to the degree of confidence the subordinates have in the leader. It also includes the loyalty shown for and the attractiveness of the leader.
2. *Task structure* refers to the degree to which the followers' jobs are routine as opposed to being ill structured and undefined.
3. *Position power* refers to the power inherent in the leadership position. It includes the rewards and punishments that are typically associated with the position, the leader's official authority (based on a ranking in the managerial hierarchy), and the support that the leader receives from superiors and the overall organization.

In effect, Fiedler has come up with a theory of leadership that takes into account the leader's personality and the behavioral characteristics of the group being led. Perhaps he has begun a great body of research that will ultimately prove that leadership is one of those specifics about which we cannot generalize.

The Hersey-Blanchard Model

Paul Hersey and Kenneth H. Blanchard[17] have attempted to integrate several existing bodies of research into a model for leadership styles appropriate to differing situations. Their "Situational Leadership Theory" is based upon an interaction among 1) the amount of direction (task behavior) a leader gives, 2) the amount of socio-emotional support (re-

---

[16] *A Theory of Leadership Effectiveness* (New York: McGraw-Hill Book Company, 1967).
[17] Management of Organizational Behavior, 3rd ed. (Englewood Cliff, N.J.: Prentice-Hall, Inc., 1977), 360 pp.

lationship behavior) a leader provides, and 3) the maturity level that followers exhibit on a specific task or function.

This model is clearly built on research at Ohio State that showed authoritarian leader behavior (task-emphasis) and democratic leader behavior (relationship-emphasis) were not "either/or" styles. Some leaders mainly directed activities, while others concentrated on providing socio-emotional support for their followers. Still others used both styles at once. Some used neither.

Maturity, the third variable, is built on the work of Argyris. Maturity is the capacity to set high but attainable goals, plus the willingness and ability to take responsibility, and utilize education and/or experience. People tend to have varying levels of maturity depending on the specific task, function, or objective that they are attempting to accomplish.

According to Hersey and Blanchard, as the level of maturity of the follower continues to increase in terms of accomplishing a specific task, the leader should begin to reduce task behavior and increase relationship behavior. As the follower moves into an above average level of maturity, the leader should decrease both task and relationship behavior. At this maturity level, there is a reduction of close supervision and an increase in delegation as an indication of trust and confidence.

When attempting to improve the maturity of followers who have not taken much responsibility in the past, a leader must be careful not to increase socio-emotional support too rapidly. Using a behavior modification concept, the slightest appropriate behavior must be rewarded as quickly as possible. First, there should be a reduction in direction. If adequate performance follows, an increase in socio-emotional support should follow as positive reinforcement. This does not mean that the individual's work will have less direction but that the direction will be internally imposed by the follower. At this stage, the follower is positively reinforced by the trust and confidence of the leader and can begin to generate internal satisfaction for interpersonal and emotional needs.

When followers begin to behave less maturely for whatever reason (i.e. personal problems, change in work equipment, etc.), it is appropriate and necessary for the leaders to adjust their behavior backward to meet the maturity level of the followers.

Figure 14.4 shows that the different patterns of leader behavior can be plotted on two separate and distinct axis. By adding a continuum of four levels of a maturity, appropriate leadership style can be determined by tracing a line up from the maturity line at the follower's determined level until it interesects with the bell curve.

High task/low relationship behavior (S1) is referred to as "telling" because it is characterized by one-way communication.

High task/high relationship behavior (S2) is referred to as "selling" because most of the direction is still provided by the leader.

High relationship/low task behavior (S3) is called "participating" be-

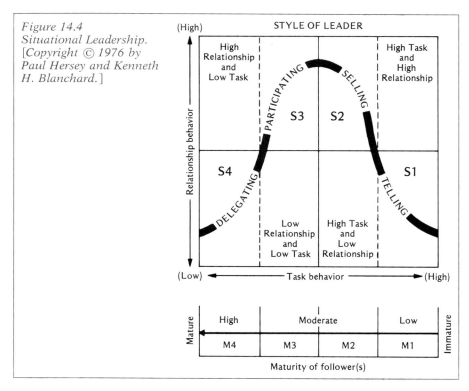

Figure 14.4 Situational Leadership. [Copyright © 1976 by Paul Hersey and Kenneth H. Blanchard.]

cause decision making is now shared in a two-way communication.

Low relationship/low task behavior (S4) is called "delegating" because the followers, having a high level of maturity, are both willing and able to take responsibility for directing their own behavior.

Effective leaders must know their staffs well enough to meet their everchanging abilities and demands. Over time, norms, customs and mores affect patterns of both group and individual behavior. One style of leadership appropriate for the group may not be appropriate for all individuals in the group. In either case, changes in leadership style must be gradual. The process by its very nature can not be revolutionary but must be evolutionary, the result of planned growth and the creation of mutual trust and respect.

Determinants of Leadership Effectiveness

We would not be considering the entire picture of leadership if we spoke only about the leader's characteristics. There are several other outside influences that have the power to hinder or enhance the leader's performance and effectiveness.

The *size of the organization* within which the leader must function plays a definite part in the extent to which the leader will succeed. There is an almost unvarying correlation between organizational bigness and organizational slowness. An elephant carries more weight than a monkey, but an elephant can almost never leap from one tree to another. In the same way, there are many efforts that a monolithic company can accomplish that a small company would never dare to undertake. This is not to say that organizational bigness is bad. Rather, it points to the necessity of both large and small enterprises.

Larger corporations that wish to foster leadership should be continually searching for ways to counteract the sluggishness of communication and decision-making processes. Such formalization of organizational policy and procedure seems to follow inevitably with size increases, but it is not to be accepted without a fight! In fact, one of the primary tasks of corporate management is to maintain the advantages of bigness while innovating to combat the disadvantages.

Perhaps the managers of every company should do some serious thinking about whether or not they actually want their employees demonstrating leadership talents. In all likelihood, many managers who would say they want leaders might realize that they would much prefer to avoid the complications and uncertainties that inevitably follow as leaders arise in the ranks. Once managers have clearly defined the problems and are assured in their own minds that they do desire to foster creativity and leadership, then they are in a position to initiate organizational policies or company practices that will create a favorable climate for leadership. Organizational size can be a definite deterrent to leadership effectiveness—but it can be overcome. As suggested in Chapter 6, the challenge of management and leadership becomes more complex as the workforce (especially the local workforce) increases.

The *degree of interaction* that takes place in the organizational setting also influences the extent to which leadership talents may function or flourish. Some operations have a greater need for total interaction than others. In many cases, modern technology demands the input from many experts throughout the company. As this need for interaction, cross-checking, and collective thinking increases, the organizational structure should be adapted to permit the continued free flow of information and ideas.

Some interesting experiments[18] have been conducted to demonstrate various principles of interaction and communication. It has been found that the most efficient small-group-interaction arrangement is to seat group members around a central leader. The leader serves as a hub for the interaction with all communications passing through. Problem

---

[18] Reported by Harold J. Leavitt, "Inhuman Organizations," *Harvard Business Review*, July–August 1962, pp. 90–98.

solving is much more direct with this hub system. You may wish to review some sketches of communication networks in Figure 12.4 on page 271.

Next in efficiency were those groups arranged with one person in the center and two on either side. The least efficient group was seated in a circle. When selecting a leader, the hub group unanimously selected the person in the center; the leader for the two-one-two group was selected by a substantial margin; and in the circle there was no clear choice of a leader. However, we find that a circle structure, although the least efficient, results in a group whose members are happier than the members of either of the other two groups. Of greater significance is the fact that the circle was able to incorporate new ideas for the solution of the problem much more readily than either of the other groups and was also able to solve modified or new problems more readily.

The lessons we derive from these interesting experiments with interaction can be quite valuable. First, the one-big-happy-family approach tends to keep employees happier, though less efficient in communication and problem solving than the hub approach. (Perhaps here we are simply considering the democratic versus the benevolent-autocrat systems from a slightly different viewpoint.) A second lesson that may be learned from these experiments is that leaders should decide which is more valuable to them: contented interactors or productive contributors to the hub.

The *personalities of the leader and the group members* of an organization must also be considered in a determination of the extent to which leadership may function. Most obvious personalities are those at the top of the heap. Z. A. Poitrowski and M. R. Rock's[19] work shows that the successful executive is a strong, dominant person motivated primarily by a desire to control the environment in such a way that both personal and organizational goals are met. It is difficult to imagine such a personality being subjugated into a nonleadership position. It is always interesting to observe corporate leaders who are attending management training seminars. Even when participating in seemingly insignificant games and simulations, these people are driven to win, to accomplish, to overcome. Leadership and achievement orientation are in the personality, not in the situation.

Sometimes, however, it is impossible for the leader to use the type of leadership that personal philosophy and personality would prefer. The personalities of the followers or the situation may force an autocratic manager to allow union representatives to participate in negotiation sessions. Or consider the case of Douglas M. McGregor, father of the Theory Y concept and one of the first exponents of the human relations approach. After a distinguished professional career, McGregor became

[19] *The Perceptanalytic Executive Scale* (New York: Grune & Stratton, Inc., 1963).

president of Antioch College. In reflecting upon this experience, he wrote:

> I believed, for example, that a leader could operate successfully as a kind of adviser to his organization. I thought I could avoid being a "boss." Unconsciously, I suspect, I hoped to duck the unpleasant necessity of making difficult decisions, of taking the responsibility for one course of action among many uncertain alternatives, of making mistakes and taking the consequences. I thought that maybe I could operate so that everyone would like me —that good "human relations" would eliminate all discord and disagreement.
>
> I couldn't have been more wrong. It took a couple of years, but I finally began to realize that a leader cannot avoid the exercise of authority any more than he can avoid responsibility for what happens to his organization.[20]

Effective organizational structure and processes must conform to the personality and the expectations of subordinates. Employees who do not expect participation and who are dependent upon others for motivation react best to authoritarian patterns of structure and motivation. On the other hand, those who expect participation opportunities are motivated largely from within and react best to organizational processes calculated to give them a voice in what happens.

Congruence of goals means that everybody in the company is heading the same way. Unfortunately, this is not always the case. When goals conflict, leadership is stifled and perhaps counteracted altogether. When the goals of the organization and those of its members are congruent, participation processes can exist and a less formal structure can work well. When organizational goals and members' goals are divergent, greater reliance must be placed upon authoritative processes and formal structure so that adequate control is assured.

Generally, the managers at the top of the organizational hierarchy have a greater opportunity to be in congruence with organizational goals, for they are more likely to have participated in the setting of those goals. Those who are lower on the totem pole receive rulings from on high and may often find themselves balking at commands less because of the content of the command than because of their disassociation from its formulation.

The *level of decision making* can have important consequences for the quality of leadership that is fostered. If decision making (and therefore leadership) is practiced at the level where the decisions will be carried out, it tends to be most effective. That is, if those in the boiler room are making the decisions for and determining the course of the boiler room, chances are that the boiler room will enjoy effective leadership. If those decisions are moved up the organizational ladder and made by someone who hasn't been in the boiler room in twenty years, it stands to reason

[20] "On Leadership," *Antioch Notes*, May 1954, pp. 2–3.

that the boiler crew might be less than enthusiastic. In judging the extent of participative decision making and the degree of participative leadership, management should give the importance and scope of the decisions more weight than the sheer number of decisions.

The *health of the organization* can have a lot to do with the amount and the variety of leadership. In some cases, companies cannot afford the luxury of democratic leadership activities. When an organization is in relatively poor health, more authoritative processes of motivation and structure may have to be brought in to save the day.

An extreme example of an organization's failing to meet its goals is a company showing a loss. Under these circumstances the pattern of leadership of the president or CEO tends to be authoritative. Although the CEO may have long-range plans for improving the company's profit position, an immediate reaction is to reduce variable costs. The greatest potential for a variable cost reduction is achieved by the reduction of payroll costs. To ask subordinates to participate in eliminating their positions is unrealistic. Consequently, these decisions are made without participation, and the means of communicating the decisions are directive in nature.

The Indefinable Ingredient

In this section the chapters have delved into some of the necessary characteristics of the successful manager. We have discussed the abilities to communicate, to motivate, to train, and to innovate. Finally, we have reviewed the evolution of management philosophy regarding the nature of leadership. In each chapter the same type of ultimate conclusion haunts our attempts to quantify and pigeonhole each minute aspect. In the end, we are left with a summary statement something like: "After all has been said and done, after all the theories have been heard, there remains . . . the individual."

The individual is the indefinable ingredient that makes the vital difference. Imagine two identical twins who receive all the same training in management theory and have all the same benefits. Even if such a situation could be created in a test tube, we would not be surprised to witness the management careers of the two heading off in different directions and ending up poles apart.

Why? What makes the difference between the two? There exists somewhere the gist of the manager, the soul, the philosophy of life, a basic approach to life and other human beings. This weightless component cannot be bought, sold, or built into an individual. If it is present, it can be nurtured and cultivated. If it is absent, all the leadership training courses in the world can't make a leader. On the other hand, even the individual who has this mystical component may not succeed as a leader. The relationships of talents to the situation introduce an additional question mark.

Attempts to simplify and quantify the determinants of leadership success have resulted in a library of theories. In many ways, all of the experts can be interpreted as saying the same things in different words. Perhaps Likert's exploitive, authoritative character is the same as McGregor's Theory X man, Maslow's persons stuck at a lower-need fixation, or Argyris' stage of immaturity. At the other end of the continuum, McGregor's easy-going, developmental Theory Y manager does resemble the S-4 of Hershey and Blanchard, the confident, self-actualized person on Maslow's ladder, and the 9.9 balance of Blake and Mouton's emphasis on people and productivity.

Are all the experts saying the same thing? Is any one "righter" than the others? Could all of them be off the mark? Is leadership a commodity that cannot possibly be explained in words and graphs? If so, can leadership be taught, developed, instilled, or only genetically transmitted? The great minds of management thought have struggled with this puzzle for years without conclusive conclusions. Perhaps, for us, there is a message in the pervading similarities of the leading theories. Could it be that our wisest approach is to see all the theories at once (as in the chart in Table 14.3) and, at the same time, draw some consensus theory of our own, which remains most useful to us as long as it remains unwritten.

We must have leaders. We have followed leaders since prehistoric times. Leaders were leading even before we were taking the time to analyze their leadership. Let us be grateful for leadership and study it ever so gently, as we would the goose that continued to amaze us with its golden eggs.

Summary

Leadership is the ability to persuade others to seek certain goals and the technique of taking them there. Leadership is often confused with popularity or with some of its products. Sometimes it is confused with aggressiveness or enthusiasm or success . . . none of which are definite indicators of leadership.

John French and Bertram Raven described five different ways leaders may possess authority. They may be exercising (1) coercive power, (2) reward power, (3) legitimate power, (4) expert power, or (5) referent power.

Various theories have been advanced in an effort to explain the leader. The traitist theories express the idea that leadership can be at-

Table 14.3. Theories of Human Effectiveness

	System 1 (Exploitive-Authoritative)	System 2 (Benevolent Authoritative)	System 3 (Consultative)	System 4 (Participative Group)
Rensis Likert				
Douglas McGregor	Theory X Reductive			Theory Y Developmental
Warren Bennis	Bureaucracy — Authoritarian, Restrictive Management Structure	Traditional	Democracy	Goal-Oriented, Adaptive Management Structure
Robert Blake Jane Mouton	1,1 — Neutrality and Indecision	1,9 9,1 — Unbalanced Concern for People or Production	5,5 — Compromise Middle of the Road	9,9 — Integration of Resources
Chris Argyris	Autocratic Relationships Conflict and Conformity	Manipulative Relationships		Authentic Relationships Interpersonal Competence
Abraham H. Maslow	Lower-Need Fixation — Halted Growth			Self-actualization (Eupsychia) — Realized Potential

	Meaningless Work		Meaningful Work	
Frederick Herzberg	Hygiene Seeking		Motivation Seeking	
Erich Fromm	Escape from Freedom / Conformity, Manipulation, Destructiveness		Freedom / Spontaneous and Responsible Behavior	
Texas Instruments (Myers)	Authority Orientation, Interpersonal Conflict, Meaningless Goals, Restrictive Systems		Goal Orientation, Interpersonal Competence, Meaningful Goals, Helpful Systems	
Keith Davis	Autocratic	Custodial (Maintenance)	Supportive (Motivational)	Collegial
Alvin Zander Dorwin Cartwright	Authoritarian	Democratic		Laissez-faire
Malcolm Shaw	Controlling Communication	Relinquishing	Withdrawn	Developmental
Tom Harris	I'm O.K. and You're Not O.K.	I'm Not O.K. and You're O.K.	I'm Not O.K., and You're Not O.K.	I'm O.K. and You're O.K.

tributed to specific physical, mental, or personality traits possessed by the leader. The behavioral theories suggest that the leader's success lies not in who he is but in the way he acts and reacts. Various approaches to leadership behavior have been suggested (the benevolent autocrat, the democratic leader, the laissez-faire approach, the continuum of approaches, the two-dimensional theory, the managerial grid theory, group dynamics explanations, and situational leadership theory).

Several determinants of leadership effectiveness have been cited. Among them are the size of the organization, the degree of interaction, the personalities of the members, the congruence of goals, the level at which decisions are made, and the health of the organization.

Leadership theories tend to fall into common relationships that are defined with different key words or catch phrases. There remains an elusive, unquantifiable ingredient that can determine leadership aptitude and success. We do not understand leadership perfectly, but we know a lot of things that it is not.

Review Questions

1. Are leaders more intelligent than their followers? Can a leader be too intelligent for his group? Discuss.
2. What is a benevolent autocrat?
3. Describe the laissez-faire leader.
4. What is the optimum style of leadership discussed in the management grid theory?
5. Discuss the change in his leadership philosophy experienced by Douglas M. McGregor after serving as president of Antioch College.
6. In a typical classroom situation, what type of power does a professor possess?
7. If a "Miss America" type of approach were used to select leaders, which type of leadership theory would be emphasized?
8. What famous business leaders would you describe as benevolent autocrats?
9. Describe a situation in which each of the following theories of leadership is appropriate.
   a. Authoritarian.
   b. Benevolent autocrat.
   c. Democratic.
   d. Laissez-faire.
10. Describe how a classroom would be conducted with each of the major managerial grid leadership styles.
11. What are the major dimensions of leadership identified in Fred E. Fiedler's situational theory?
12. What aspect of Fiedler's theory would indicate that a research director might use a different approach to leadership than a supervisor of a chain gang?
13. Can the president of a large organization be "just one of the boys"?

15

Training and Development for Tomorrow

"Excuse me, sir. I think I have some bad news for you."

"Come in! Come in, Parrot. You know you are always welcome in the boss' office. Now, what's this 'bad news' you have for me?"

"Well, sir . . . we . . . uh . . . we're going to have to close down the company . . . liquidate the assets."

"I don't understand, Parrot. As head of our accounting operation, you certainly should know that the company is in better shape than it has ever been . . . with all systems working well and the company assured of the multimillion dollar municipal contract. . . ."

"That's just the point, sir. All the cash reserves have been advanced to move into that municipal contract. And, as I learned in my specialized training, 'Whenever the cash reserves for a company our size fall below $100,000, the company should be closed and the assets liquidated."

"But, Parrot . . . that is rediculous. Within a week, the cash reserves will top twenty million. It would be extremely short-sighted to close the company. The future is not only bright. It is assured."

"Yes, sir. I know that. But if we go by the book . . ."

"This situation is the exception, Parrot. In this case, your book is incorrect."

"But, sir, are you saying that all my specialized training is useless?"

"It's beginning to look that way, Parrot."

Training is almost a sacred word in our society. It has been peddled as the answer to all problems. We have attempted to educate and train people in unheard-of numbers. Education is perhaps the largest legal business in the United States today. Its boundaries extend far beyond the traditional public-school classroom. When the definition is considered broadly enough, most communication activities in most businesses have education as their objective.

In actual fact, a distinction in meaning ought to be made between three words we often toss about as though they were interchangeable. We should distinguish between education, training, and development. Basically, *training* is limited to teaching or developing a specified skill. *Education* tends to emphasize the provision of knowledge or concepts which a person may apply to different kinds of things. *Development* is a similar concept, but places more emphasis on the fact that a person is able to become more than before—practically through a combination of productive education and positive experience.

Leading educators are placing more and more stress on the necessity of turning educational focus to the future rather than the past. They are realizing that the skill and knowledge requirements of educated people are changing rapidly. The same kind of trend may be taking place in business and industry. A steadily reducing segment of our population will be required to produce the goods needed by the society. And those people who are needed will certainly be using a far different set of skills and understandings. The obvious challenge to educators and training personnel is to prepare their students for the future . . . instead of for the past.

The coming age will have different training requirements. The postindustrial era is likely to be more of a learning society than today's. This is being brought about by the *knowledge revolution*, which seeks new business through technological advances rather than volume production. Its chief catalysts are ideas rather than natural resources. The primary institutions in this new society may be universities and education-oriented groups rather than factories.

Few people realize how far the United States has gone in the transition from a production-oriented system to an idea-oriented economy.

Broadly defined, the knowledge industry accounts for over half the entire economy and continues to be one of the most rapidly growing sectors of the economy. To reach this conclusion, we have to consider all activities involved with the creation of knowledge (research), the analysis of information (think tanks, consulting firms, data-processing operations), transmission of the information (including educational institutions, telecommunications, publishing and media), and much of the work of local, state and federal governments.

The American Society of Training and Development estimates that private and public employers in the United Stated spend some $30 billion to $40 billion annually on employee development. The figure does not include allowances for salaries and wages of people being trained. In 1979, the ASTD estimated that the total cost of all higher education, public and private, was approximately $55 billion.[1]

The Impact of Training

As the United States shifts from a society based on natural resources to one based on human resources, the importance of training and education for all organizations will increase tremendously. Even the highly educated professional can quickly become obsolete. Since the graduates of the immediate postwar period left college, the world has more than doubled its body of scientific knowledge. Thomas Stetson, Head of Civil Engineering at Carnegie Institute of Technology, warns that unless a person who has been out of college ten years devotes at least 10 per cent of his or her time to advancing knowledge beyond college training, the individual will not be able to compete with recent college graduates.[2]

When an executive stops learning, he or she is finished. During the next decade, agencies, associations, and businesses must be prepared to shoulder a significant portion of the educational responsibility for their members and employees. Already it is estimated that executives are sent back to school for several weeks each year. No one has accurately estimated the total number of shorter training programs, because thousands of individuals are provided with some educational experiences by their employers. Education and reeducation will be a continuing part of the future executive's career. Progressive companies such as IBM already require every manager to have forty hours of education every year.

It is predicted that the average individual entering the field of management today may return to a university for at least a year of fulltime

---

[1] "The National Report for Training and Development," American Society for Training and Development, September 5, 1979, p. 2.
[2] Robert M. Fulmer, "The Future of Training for the Future," *Training in Business and Industry*, February 1972, p. 41. Much of the material contained in this section is drawn from this article.

study two times during a career.[2] These periods of extended formal study will also be supplemented by an increasing number of short courses and seminars.

Focus on the Future

Managers educated today cannot practice their arts until tomorrow. Consequently, management training and education should be future oriented. In fact, future-oriented training sessions and courses are likely to become the vogue of the 1980's.

While it is possible to predict the skills and techniques that many *workers* will be using for the next few months or even years, it is more difficult to teach managers exactly what they will be doing at any given point in the future. But prophecy is not the key issue. The critical factor may well be whether managers will be able to adapt and cope with tomorrow's "brave new world."

Whenever possible, training activities should alert students to the actual demands they will be meeting after leaving the classroom or conference center. But more than this, an effort must be made to prepare managers so they will be able to deal with tomorrow regardless of what happens. Adaptability, in the future, will be second in importance only to the managerial ability to make the future become what the manager wants it to be.

Three approaches to future orientation are already proving successful.

1. *The crystal ball (trends and projections).* At no other time in history has there been so much concern about forecasting the future. Government agencies, foundations, business firms, and associations are all sponsoring research concerning the long-range future. There is considerable interest in the potential of Delphian forecasting studies about the future of management practices.[3] A few universities are beginning to offer courses in the future of sociology, religion, philosophy, technology, and management.

Several years ago, Kaiser Aluminum developed a game called "The Future" to use for training purposes. At the 1980 Global Conference of the World Future Society, several simulations and exercises were utilized to help people anticipate potential developments throughout the coming years. There is certainly sufficient secondary information to provide a factual basis for future-oriented training activities.

---

[3] See, for example, Robert M. Fulmer, "The Management of the Future," *Business Horizons*, Winter 1973.

2. *Rx for future shock (coping with change).* Change is the only constant that today's manager can expect in tomorrow's world. The rapidity of change has led to the widespread recognition of the phenomenon Alvin Toffler profitably called "future shock."[4] Even where it is impossible to inform managers about specific characteristics of the future, it is possible to prepare them for the phenomenon of change. In addition to the well-established literature concerning the significance and extent of probable change, the reasons people resist change, and ways to overcome this resistance, it is possible to involve training participants in simulated situations that give them a chance to test their adaptability to unusual and unexpected situations.

3. *Inventing the future* (scenario writing). Because management trainees will be asked to practice their skills of supervision in a not yet existent world, it may be appropriate to ask them to plan or even invent the world they expect to manage. Futurists at the Hudson Institute, the Institute for the Future, and other think tanks have long advocated the practice of scenario writing—that is, writing brief descriptive scenes of probable future.

To determine the degree to which students have thought about the future and to help stimulate their thinking along this line, it is often useful to ask them to describe their organization in a year such as 1990 or 2000. It is also useful to ask individuals to describe their own personal situation ten or fifteen years into the future. Often this exercise can dramatize a lack of creative, long-range planning.

Training that points to the past is obviously obsolete. The revolutionary changes and challenges that exist today will not wait for us to make up our minds. As Robert Blakely suggests, "It is not enough to modernize—to catch up with the present—the present doesn't live here anymore!"

Humans—The Multichannel Learners

It will be quite confusing if we approach learning theory with the assumption that all people in all situations learn in the same ways. Quite the opposite is true. The trainer's task is to find the learning channel that is appropriate for the situation under consideration. Channels, or methods, through which humans learn include conditioning, operant conditioning, trial and error imitations, instructions, and problem analysis.[5]

---

[4] *Future Shock* (New York: Random House, Inc., 1970).
[5] Based on Huse and Bowditch, *Behavior in Organizations* (Reading, Mass.: Addison-Wesley Publishing Co., Inc., 1973), pp. 228–229.

Conditioning is the simplest form of learning. Basically it works on the principle of rewards (or reinforcement). Many animals (and humans) learn to perform simple tasks in response to a stimulus, if they have been conditioned to expect a reward after completing the task.

As introduced in Chapter 13, *operant conditioning* is more complicated and tends more to involve learner choice and judgment. Its name comes from the fact that the operation of the subject contributes to the reward-punishment sequence, which in turn leads to the changed behavior sought.

Trial and error is one of the principal methods by which mankind has advanced. Solutions to problems are sought randomly. Trial and error requires a considerable amount of extra time and effort, but can often pay dividends in the depth of the learning impression.

Imitation is the method of learning in which the trainee watches the instructor perform a task and then imitates the observed behavior. Learning to operate machinery is usually done by imitating someone who knows how to do it. Social techniques can also be learned through imitation. Children learn much about grown-up life by copying the behavior of their parents and teachers.

Instruction is a popular method of learning. This method uses written, visual, or oral communications to convey information to the learner. Cookbooks, blueprints, training manuals, vacation guidebooks, do-it-yourself handbooks, films, and spoken instructions are all included in this method.

Problem analysis is the most complex form of learning. With this method, instructors encourage students to seek out problems, take them apart from all angles, and come up with creative and workable solutions. In training, the problems may be actual or invented, so long as they present a challenge in applying knowledge.

These channels of learning often overlap and intertwine. Nonetheless, the manager's awareness of these subtle distinctions can help avoid a lot of wasted effort or reteaching.

It is important for the leader to have a feeling for the components of learning—the kinds of things that cause people to learn, and the indicators that learning has indeed taken place. These components include response to rewards, changes in behavior, motivation, application of learned information or skills, and memory.

Response to rewards. Most people are responsive to rewards and try to avoid punishment. While conditioning techniques are generally used only for very simple behavior changes, the principle can be applied to almost any area of human relations. Training is almost always more effective when the trainer is quick with praise and rewards for those who earn them. Everyone's ego can use a boost now and then, and praise during training serves to reinforce what is being learned.

Change in the individual from learning. An individual changes—whether it is perceptible or not—when something new is learned. Behavior is shaped by a number of things, including genetic inheritance, the physical and social environment, and personality. Behavior is also influenced by knowledge. Individuals are constantly learning about themselves and their surroundings, and every new piece of information serves, no matter how slightly, to alter their approach to the world.

Motivation. Motivation is the pivotal part of the learning process. People rarely learn anything they do not really want to know. Learning involves change, and change is often frightening. Thus, for motivation to provide the impetus for learning and change, the learning situation must be controlled sufficiently to provide reassurance that success is likely. A motivator is anything seen by the individual as promising greater rewards than the threats posed by change.

Application. Application of knowledge is another component of the learning process. In the late 1960's, a cry went up at colleges and universities for relevant coursework. The fact is that all knowledge can be relevant to some aspect of our lives. Problems of relevance arise because it takes a trained mind to see similarities in seemingly diverse material. One of the most basic skills each of us must master is the ability to apply known information to a new situation.

Memory. Without memory, learning would be a pointless exercise. Good trainers know that it is easier to recall what was once learned than to learn something new. Periodic refresher courses are extremely useful in helping people recall the principles and techniques they are expected to apply on the job. Every student knows that it is much easier to spend a few hours reviewing before an exam than to try to read everything for the first time the night before.

Advantages of Training

Because we live in a relatively educated culture, it is almost impossible for us to make accurate comparisons with or even imagine an uneducated society. Familiarity often breeds contempt—we tend to see the failures, inadequacies, and irrelevancies of training efforts. Our critical eyes fall on the failures and overlook the advantages.

An interesting summary of results that can flow from a good training program is contained in the following listing. A properly designed and conducted training course can bring about

1. Increased executive management skills
2. Development in each executive of a broad background and appreciation of the company's overall operations and objectives
3. Greater delegation of authority because executives down the line are better qualified and better able to assume increased responsibilities
4. Creation of a reserve of qualified personnel to replace present incumbents and to staff new positions
5. Improved selection for promotion
6. Minimum delay in staffing new positions and minimum disruption of operations during replacements of incumbents
7. Provision for the best combination of youth, vigor, and experience in top management and increased span of productive life in high-level positions
8. Improved executive morale
9. Attraction to the company of ambitious people who wish to move ahead as rapidly as their abilities permit
10. Increased effectiveness and reduced costs, resulting in greater assurance of continued profitability.[6]

Admittedly there are always improvements to be made in the training process, and book learning is no suitable substitute for common sense and natural skill. Even so, very few of us are willing to have our tonsils removed by a medical school dropout with a natural talent of surgery.

Types of Training

There are many ways to indoctrinate employees regarding new skills, understanding, or attitudes. Some methods come naturally; others require more planning and preparation. Seven methods of employee training are mentioned in this section. They are usable at any level but are generally more appropriate at the lower organizational levels. It should be pointed out in beginning that each of these methods is a substitution for the most natural form of training, in which the internal curiosity of the learner is the motivation to seek out more and more information and assistance. But ideal, self-starting trainees are rare. For the other ninety-nine out of a hundred, one or more of the following methods may be useful.

1. *On-the-job training* is the most common method of employee indoctrination. It requires no special school and no gamble of company money on expensive, time-consuming programs of canned instruction.

[6] E. W. Reilley and B. J. Muller-Thym, "Executive Development," *Personnel*, p. 412.

The trained employee does not have to be reoriented to the actual task after ideological textbook experience. A job is learned by doing it. And, in many cases, a new worker is productively involved long before moving up from a trainee classification. Indeed, some operations exploit the training period to receive the same work at lower cost for a while.

2. *Vestibule training* describes the introductory-course approach. In it, employees are taken through a short course under working conditions resembling actual shop or office conditions. This approach gets its name from the vestibule, or entrance hall, of a house or building where facsimile equipment for training purposes was originally located. These training courses may take a day or a month. They usually are used when the operation involves danger or cost that might prohibit expensive mistakes in on-the-job learning. Thus, training could be simulated for new comptometer operators or aspiring astronauts, assuring their effective performance on the first try.

3. *Apprenticeship training* is traditional in trades, crafts, and technical fields in which proficiency can be acquired only after a relatively long period of instruction by experts. Increasingly, the master craft concept is disappearing from most occupations. Jobs that were once highly skilled and complicated now are merely a matter of pushing buttons. Systems specialists continually endeavor to eliminate craftsmanship from work—replacing it with simplified tasks that are easily taught. The apprenticeship tradition no longer exists in most fields, though it will no doubt remain intact to restrict the entry into certain trades; the apprenticeship time effectively prevents the displacement of experienced workers by learners.

4. *Internship training* refers to a joint program of training in which schools and businesses cooperate. Students take alternate doses of classroom and real-life training. For years, the internship of medical doctors has been a familiar training arrangement. Today more and more internship programs are being planned in connection with highly skilled or professional types of training. Trade and high schools often cooperate with industry in this way to train various workers. Internships have been employed by industry and college for training in management and engineering.

5. *Outside courses* are used by a number of agencies and groups in the solution of their training problems. Apart from the fact that many employees are involved in continuing education for their own purposes, many companies encourage and even arrange outside coursework for their workers and prospective employees. Vocational, correspondence, trade, and evening schools have been a constant source of supply of employees and employee improvement. An ever-present difficulty exists— the classroom instruction must be made applicable to the actual job situation. The school is struggling to make its courses *broad* enough to fit

Rocky (United Artists, 1976). Are there similarities between the developmental activities of managers and boxers?

the many directions a student might take, and the company is struggling to help the student zero in on *specific* job needs and training.

6. *Teaching machines* represent an educational medium that is sure to have a long and ever increasing history of uses. After overcoming the initial objects of instructors who feared for their jobs, mechanical and computerized instructional devices have not become trusted tools of training. The outstanding advantage of the teaching machine is its individualizing of instruction. The data are programmed in such a way that the student may proceed individually and receive immediate reinforcement or correction. Material is always presented in small, orderly segments, requiring extreme care in the programming stage but allowing a more logical progression of thoughts for the learner.

7. *Retraining* is a form of training that may exist because there are too many workers or too few workers. During World War II, it became necessary to retrain industrial workers quickly to (a) make new kinds of products and (b) fill jobs left vacant by those serving in the armed forces. In more recent times, automation has made some jobs obsolete. In almost every case, the same new machine that puts people out of a job creates other new jobs. The task is to retrain displaced workers for the new job slots that have been opened up. Because the problem has been so serious in some areas, the federal government has had to step in with training aid.

Training Techniques

The management of American businesses and associations may soon be spending more to train and educate adult employees than all United States public schools and colleges spend to educate youth. Although exact figures are difficult to come by, it has been estimated that management groups spend in excess of $40 billion annually for educational purposes.[7]

It is not surprising that large business firms such as IBM and General Electric have larger educational budgets than most universities. After all, these industrial giants have far more employees than there are students on any campus. The era when students were educated for their careers in the schools has already ended. Education is and must be a continuing process if an employee, especially a manager, is to keep up with the demands of the job.

Most organizations feel a responsibility to help keep their members abreast of technical developments. Yet the area of management devel-

[7] Projection based on a 1979 estimate of The American Society of Training and Development.

opment is seldom given proper emphasis. Involvement in management education may take several forms, such as developing specialized aids and exercises, developing specific development programs, sponsoring programs that have been developed externally, and screening or publicizing external programs that might be of value to members.

Development of Programs

As will be discussed in greater detail, a well-rounded program should combine instructional materials with group and individual involvement.

Many small firms do not have sufficient personnel to develop and organize a complete training program. In these cases, training or consulting firms may offer expert assistance. Although these organizations are generally familiar with the latest knowledge and techniques in management thought, they may not be fully aware of some of the specialized interests of a given group. It is not usually wise for an organization to buy a "package" training program that has been developed for someone else. Professional trainers are willing to discuss variation and adaptation of sessions to suit a client. An outside agent may also provide assistance in developing special exercises and, in every case, should be willing to discuss his or her capabilities or to prepare a proposal without cost or obligation.

Specific Training Techniques[8]

In training, variety is an essential ingredient if a program is to come to life. Although it may be impossible to combine all of the ingredients mentioned, an appetizing recipe should feature several.

1. *Lecture.* Though tried and true, if used by itself the lecture is almost certain to produce lethal lethargy. This method is useful for disseminating specific information; and if the emphasis is on content, it will, of necessity, be used frequently. But even content should not be served up in a bland formula. The typical lecture has been described as a process by which information passes from the notes of the instructor to the notes of the student without passing through the minds of either. This danger may be partially countered through the use of such visual aids as transparencies, slides, charts, or other demonstrative devices. Additionally, a lecture may be enhanced through any of the other suggested techniques.

2. *Cases.* The Harvard Business School has made famous the case method as a philosophy of business education in which learners are exposed to case histories as the basic content of courses. Supplemented with extra readings, research, and study, this concept is based on the

---

[8] The following section is drawn from Robert M. Fulmer, "Training Techniques for Today and Tomorrow," *Association Management*, July 1969, pp. 55–62.

assumption that detailed, comprehensive descriptions of business situations will provide an opportunity for vicarious experiences. Trainees are confronted with a realistic problem and are asked to deal with a situation that has occurred. Analysis of actual cases may prove particularly interesting because after having reached their own decisions, students may be told what actually took place.

More frequently, the occasional use of cases will be appropriate for management development within organizations. The limited use of cases will not be as successful in developing the analytical skills of trainees as the extended use of the case method; however, there are several important advantages in using them as an occasional exercise. One of the most frequent uses is to illustrate a particular point covered in a lecture. The Intercollegiate Clearing House (Harvard) can provide cases that deal with almost any problem or subject area within the field of management. Cases allow participants to test their ideas and their abilities in selling these recommendations to others. Of course, the use of cases should involve both a preparation period and a discussion session. Problems may be analyzed by individuals or in groups.

3. *Incidents.* The basic distinction between a case and an incident is that the latter is a much shorter description of a situation. A full-blown case is usually longer than ten pages, whereas an incident is generally condensed to less than two. Sometimes condensed-case incident will be used as a springboard for the discussion of a specific topic that has been introduced in lecture or reading material.

Another variation of the same concept is called the incident iceberg (or incident process). This technique begins with a short description of an incident taken from a case that has not been read by the trainees. Participants determine what additional information they need and then "buy" information from the trainer. The facts of the case are parceled out only in response to these questions.

Actual industrial events are not the only source for cases or incidents. Fictional accounts may be written by the trainer or adapted (with permission) from novels, plays, short stories, and other forms of prose. Films for entertainment, as well as those specifically designed for training, may also serve as the basis of a case discussion.

4. *Role playing.* This technique attempts to encourage participants to get inside the skin of the characters in an incident. Dramatic situations are created in which the participants act out different roles that may change their perception of the problem. Role playing seems to work best when each participant is given ample background information and a brief introductory script for the activities. The participant is then expected to carry on the part for some period of time, generally between ten and thirty minutes. Some trainers like to use one set of trainees to present the problem in the form of a short skit. After this presentation, the remainder of the group begins to discuss the behavior of the

"actors." Usually, better results are gained when the training group is divided into several groups of two to four individuals, and each person is asked either to play a role or to serve as an observer. In the latter case, each participant will report reactions to the other participants after the exercise has ended.

5. *Self-development programs.* Too often the sum total of management development takes place within the training room. It is far better for the more formal aspects of training to be supplemented by outside activities on the part of trainees. The two basic ways that this may be achieved are by programmed learning and by reading assignments. In connection with many management development seminars that have been developed for federal agencies and business firms, each registrant must have completed an introductory programmed learning exercise that relates to the seminar content. In other words, they are expected to have read certain background material. In this way, instructors are assured that their audience will have a basic level of familiarity with the materials to be discussed.

Programmed learning may be used in conection with certain key assigned readings. It is extremely wasteful to give trainees nothing more than a blank pad of paper when they begin a program. Even before they arrive at a training session, they should be given access to a reading list and/or reading materials. If this is not possible, reprint copies of articles relating to the subject matter should be placed in the training notebook so that participants may refresh and enhance their knowledge after leaving the session. Some companies with widely dispersed employees have been relatively successful in managing a significant portion of their training through a carefully selected reading program. In these instances, the home office serves as a library/clearing house to recommend, process, and distribute books within several areas of development need or interest.

6. *Group dynamics.* The dynamics of work groups may often be duplicated within the training group. Sparks can fly when individuals are given a chance to express themselves, and expression is a vital part of the learning process. Laboratory or sensitivity training is almost entirely concerned with group activity with little interest or emphasis on subject matter. Without meaning to question the validity of group therapy, it is necessary to mention that the impact of training is maximized when the process of group dynamics is combined with content that is interjected through other techniques. Leadership, techniques of communication, conflict, and almost any other subject that is covered in a management training program may be illustrated and emphasized through group involvement. For example, a lecture on the styles of communication may be followed by a short quiz in which trainees are asked to identify which communication style is illustrated by a series of statements. After reaching individual decisions, participants may be asked

to work together in groups of five to reach a consensus. It is interesting to observe that in most cases, the group score will be significantly better than most individual records. It is simple to see how this concept might be adapted for use with any subject. Not only does it reinforce the lecture, but it exposes the student to many of the challenges of actual management problems. Buzz sessions, brainstorming, discussion groups, and case studies are additional means of generating group involvement.

7. *Simulation exercises.* Simulation is an attempt to construct a situation or demonstration that illustrates a procedure or practice in a realistic manner and teaches or emphasizes a lesson at the same time.

Perhaps one of the most practical and rapidly growing practices of management education is the simulation of reality by reproducing in microcosm a realistic set of problems and challenges (rather than merely talking about the concepts that have been discussed). It has been said that "Experience is a dear or expensive teacher, but fools will learn from no other." Simulation provides the enforcement of experience, but mistakes made in an artificial situation do not have the lasting impact that they would if made in reality.

Simulation is sometimes equated with gaming, and management games are, indeed, one of the most significant management development innovations of the past two decades. There are several computerized games available on a commercial basis that afford players an opportunity to match with competing teams their strategy concerning price, capital improvements, marketing policy, and other variables. Although computerized games are naturally more sophisticated than the noncomputerized variety, it is not necessary to have a substantial investment in hardware or software in order to use this training technique. Management games generally involve an extended period of play to allow trends to develop from several rounds of decisions.

Laboratory or experimental exercises are another means of replicating realistic situations. These are best suited to illustrating specific points and can frequently be conducted in as little time as one hour. For example, leaders in competing groups may be given different sets of instructions as to how they are to go about accomplishing the same task. These instructions can reflect the various styles of leadership, and participants may be shown the impact of leadership styles on group performance. A creative trainer can develop or revise laboratory situations to illustrate most of the major management concepts. Simple children's games (such as construction toys) are useful for this purpose.

An even simpler simulation format involves the use of "in-basket" exercises. These present the trainee with some samples of letters, memos, telegrams, and other communications devices that require judgment as to appropriate action. Within a given time limitation, the participant must deal with a variety of situations. After the participant has dealt with each communiqué, the exercise should be reviewed by the trainer and/or the class to see if each individual has properly allocated time, recognized all of the dimensions in a particular situation, and reached the "best" decision. Generally, each participant will be working on the same material, although interactive exercises can be used. In-baskets are an interesting tool for learners because the students are involved in problems that are realistic to them. These exercises are relatively easy to construct and may be built to fit any available time period and to reflect the problems that a group is studying or experiencing.

It is impossible to construct a complete list of all the techniques that may be used in management training. The methods described in the preceding paragraphs, however, are among the most effective in common use. As has been stressed, no technique may be defined as best. Each may be most appropriate in a particular situation, and generally a top-flight program will incorporate a number of these concepts. A good policy is to incorporate each of the major categories of training techniques in any program that lasts as long as three days.

Management Development

Because the management task requires greater creativity and innovation than most line positions, the various methods of training and developing managers have themselves been more creative and innovative. Several approaches to manager training are mentioned briefly in this section. This review should not, hwoever, be considered final or complete but rather a starting place for the innovative trainers of tomorrow.

1. *Planned progression* is a technique by which the young manager receives a definite idea about the path (or paths) to the top. If a planned promotion route is designed carefully, it can accomplish two valuable objectives. First, the managers can know exactly where they stand and what is expected of them. Second, the path to the top can route them through all the varying kinds of organizational experiences they will need to function knowledgeably at the top.

2. *Job rotation* is a very popular form of management training. Unfortunately, its disadvantages often outweigh its advantages and it *can* breed more dissatisfaction than training. There are several variations on the job rotation plan. Rotations may involve nonsupervisory work slots, supervisors into higher management positions, middle managers into "assistant" positions, rotations for observation only, or for unspecified times and purposes. There is one common problem: the vacant positions are not always available when it is time for somebody's promotion. For this reason, the best job-rotation results are usually secured when young managers are promoted or moved laterally without specified time or sequence.

3. *"Assistant to" positions* permit trainees to broaden viewpoints and background by putting them in close contact with seasoned managers in action. The superior can serve as teacher, tailoring the training period to the assistant's needs and making assignments to test his or her judgment. If the quality of understanding and guidance of the superior could be guaranteed, this would probably be the most effective of all approaches. However, the superior may tend to be biased or authoritarian, a poor communicator. Placed in a position of assistant to a poor manager, a talented trainee will usually go down or out, but rarely up.

4. *Serving on committees* can have its advantages in giving the trainee introductory experience. When young managers are placed on a committee composed mostly of experienced executives, they will become acquainted with the various problems and different points of view. They will witness in comparative safety the interpersonal workings and compromise bargaining that must take place to hammer out a consensus of opinion. This experience, too can be over- or underdone. Committee work should not be *dumped* on unsuspecting newcomers, nor should they be only helpless bystanders in committee proceedings.

5. *Junior boards* have sometimes been created in organizations to supply the young managers with simulated board-of-director experience. Through such an arrangement, junior executives at various levels meet and deliberate over problems they have encountered. They may suggest changes and ideas that they submit to regular managerial boards for consideration. In fulfilling assignments as a board member, the young manager has a chance to develop such important skills as leading a discussion, investigating problems, preparing reports and proposals, and making presentations.

6. *Outside experiences* can often be calculated to enhance the training of the young manager. The company may send trainees to conferences held by trade or management associations. Formal university courses may prove valuable. Group exposure to some leading speaker may be arranged by attendance at conferences. These specialists may be brought in by the company for training purposes.

7. *Psychological approaches* to management training has been developed during recent decades. Young managers have been involved in self-analysis and self-training through the practices of role playing; the participants take the parts of other people and act out a problem situation Wearing the other person's shoes can open many doors to understanding that problems and *our* perceptions of it. In sensitivity training, individuals become involved in a group discussion or experience that results in increased self-knowledge and insights into interpersonal relationships. A wide variance of opinions about the value of sensitivity training can be found. It definitely can be a dangerous activity if not supervised and guided by professional psychological staff.

Organizational Development

In the last few years, the management training boom of the late 60's and early 70's has begun to look at its soft spots. Emphasis on any one thing naturally deemphasizes something else. The mangement training boom tended to emphasize the manager, who was developed into a superstar role, which meant that the organization, its workers, and its interrelationships were neglected.

The term organizational development, usually shortened to "O.D.," refers to the on-going attempts at growth. It gives attention to the big picture—the whole company—and not just the people in the front office.

Organizational development does not take the existing structure for granted, except to note the patterns that exist. Organizational development retains the objective of encouraging individual management development, but is also seeks to change the organizational structure so that flexibility is encouraged. The manager retains the primary responsibility for making sure organizational changes are put into effect and are indeed beneficial for the company, not simply for the sake of change.

The organizational approach realizes that problems are caused as often by structural failings in the organization as by individual failings.

Both management development and organizational development use a variety of techniques for meeting their objectives. Management development techniques, however, tend to focus on educating one or more individuals as individuals. Organizational development programs place the emphasis differently. Instead of focusing on educating the individual to compensate for weaknesses, the organization itself is discussed and analyzed and workshops may still be the medium, but the message is that organizational structure should never be considered as permanently fixed. Problem solving and conflict management are important subjects in organizational development. Actual problems are considered, and group communication techniques are used to solve the problems, even if it means radically altering organizational structure or traditional approach.

The differences between management development programs and programs of organizational development may include the following:

Time frame. Management training is most often a short-term course. Organizational development suggests that the need for growth is permanent, and that businesses cannot survive unless adaptive change is built into the system.

Need for specialists. Most often, well-known professionals are brought in from universities or consulting firms to conduct mangement growth sessions. An optimum program of organizational development requires a permanent specialist, or at least one who is readily available, to record the pulse of organizational processes and suggest areas of improvement.

Continuity. In spite of some outstanding programs of managerial development, it is common for these programs to suffer from faddism. They tend to push the latest and newest terminology. Organizational development needs to be well planned, consistent, and settled in for the duration. Adaptability is important . . . but so is patient whole-organization impact.

Attitude toward change. The management development approach expects to change the leader to solve the problems. Organizational development approaches the problem of change from a systems point of view. If change is to be incorporated into the ongoing processes of the organization, every facet of the organization must be considered and evaluated. The organization can no longer be thought of as a sacred set of isolated departments.

Future of Training

The role of training in the management of tomorrow is destined to become even more significant. Informed authorities predict that by the year 2000, the average executive will spend the equivalent of one day per week in full-time study. They may be trained at home on an electronic console that provides, through programmed courses, videotapes, and other media, the information that needed to stay up-to-date. This same console will probably be used by his children in their own scholastic studies.

It is also estimated that the average individual entering the field of management today may return to a university for periods of extended formal study, supplemented by an increasing number of short courses and seminars. As has been suggested previously, tomorrow's training will probably emphasize neither content (lectures) nor process (group dynamics or sensitivity training) but a combination of the two. Because of the rapidity of change, it will be impossible to teach content that is meaningful in many situations. Rather, basic concepts in content will be taught along with an emphasis on adaptability.

Most of these trends are already evident in progressive organizations.

The number of key executives with advanced degrees continue to climb dramatically. One of the most popular trends in higher execution today is the development of "Executive MBA Programs," where high-potential managers pursue an accelerated graduate program in business while maintaining their regular job responsibilities. This is made possible through special scheduling (typically on weekends) and special classes that recognize and build upon the experiences already gained by seasoned managers. Progressive companies are also requiring regular updating of management skills on a regular basis. IBM insists that every manager should receive 40 hours of management training annually. The phrase that was written to emphasize the importance of physical health also describes the coming emphasis on management education: "The future belongs to the fit."

Summary

Education and training are involved in almost every area of our lives. As a society and as a nation of businesses, we have been committed wholeheartedly to improvement through better understanding through education.

It is becoming increasingly obvious that education and training are going to pick up the pace to keep up with rapid technological change. Not only will preparation have to look to the future rather than the past or present, but education can never stop. When managers are finished learning, they are finished! Adaptability may be by far the most important skill to be given to managers for the 1980's.

Three approaches to future orientation that are proving successful are (1) methods of making projections based on current trends, (2) describing the future in graphic terms to suggest necessary actions, and (3) inventing the likely future of businesses of individuals through scenario writing.

The advantages of training are almost universally agreed upon, though often underestimated. Types of training for lower level employees include (1) on-the-job training, (2) vestibule training, (3) apprenticeship training, (4) internship training, (5) outside courses, (6) teaching machines or programmed learning, and (7) retraining.

Several approaches to the training of mangers are (1) planned progression to the top, (2) job rotation for well-rounded managers, (3) "assistant-to" positions, (4) committee assignments, (5) junior board experiences, (6) outside experiences at universities or conferences, and (7) psychological approaches like role playing or sensitivity training.

Organizations must provide training for their management ranks no matter how small the company. Programs may be developed specifically for and by the company. Or a competent management consultant may be called in. Specific training techniques that are often used are (1) lecture, (2) cases, (3) incidents, (4) role playing, (5) self-development programs, (6) group dynamics, and (7) simulation exercises.

The role of training in the management of tomorrow is destined to become even more significant. As we have seen in every instance, training is usually an expensive undertaking, but it is never as expensive as the lack of it.

Review Questions

1. What is vestibule training?
2. Why should graduation not mark the end of a manager's education?
3. Discuss the junior board as a training technique.
4. What is the case method of instruction?
5. What are the advantages of simulation exercises in education?
6. Will the knowledge industry continue to grow twice as fast as the rest of the United Stated economy?
7. Why is such a small portion of educational activities directed toward the future?
8. Write a brief scenario describing a managment classroom in 1990.
9. What type of training is common in the following activities?
   a. Typing.
   b. Plumbing.
   c. Ditch digging.
   d. Medicine.
10. What ulterior motive might a company have in paying the dues of one of its young management trainees to join the Junior Chamber of Commerce?
11. What training technique is illustrated by the following activities.
    a. You agree to read one business book per week for a year.
    b. You enroll in a sensitivity group.
    c. You participate in a computer game.
12. Discuss some of the ways by which management training can take on a future orientation.
13. What are the major advantages and disadvantages of using trainers from outside the organization?
14. Will tomorrow's education emphasize content or process?

16

Coping with the Challenge of Change

"Oh, Professor! Could I speak with you for a moment!"

"Yes, yes . . . but make it quick, please . . . I really must get back to my office. What did you want to see me about?"

"Well . . . I just wanted to tell you how much I am enjoying your class this semester. And I want you to know that the lecture you just gave on the subject of change was the best I have ever heard!"

"Thank you very much. That lecture ought to be good: I've been giving it exactly like that for seventeen years!"

One of the few things of real permanence in our world is change. Puzzled old-timers remark in every generation, "Things ain't what they used to be . . . and maybe they never was." The phrase "We live in an age of transition" was probably first spoken as Adam escorted Eve from the Garden of Eden. It has never been more appropriate than it is today.

The phenomenal rate of change can be illustrated in a number of ways. It has been observed that if the past fifty thousand years of human existence were divided into lifetimes of approximately sixty-two years each, there have been about 800 such lifetimes. Of these 800, approximately 650 were spent in caves. Only during the past 6 lifetimes have masses of people ever seen a printed word. Only during the past 4 has it been possible to measure time with any degree of precision. Only those who have lived in the past 2 lifetimes have used an electric motor. And the overwhelming majority of all the material goods we use today have been developed in the present, the 800th lifetime.

Another illustration of the rapidity of change is drawn from the world of transportation. Six thousand years B.C., the fastest transportation over long distances that people could use was the camel caravan, which averaged 8 miles per hour. The maximum speed was not significantly changed until three thousand years later, when the chariot was invented, boasting a daredevil speed of 20 mph. Nearly five thousand years later, when the first mail coach began operating in England (1784), it averaged a mere 10 miles per hour. (Of course, some critics of the current postal system can argue that we have regressed since that time.) The first steam locomotive was introduced in 1825 and could muster a top speed of only 13 miles per hour. The great sailing ships of that day labored along at less than half this speed. It was probably not until the 1880's that with the help of a more advanced steam locomotive, we managed to reach the speed of 100 mph. It took the human race millions of years to attain the record. It took only fifty years more, however, to quadruple it. By 1931, airplanes were cracking the 400 mph limit. It took a mere twenty years to double that limit again. And by the 1960's, rocket planes approached speeds of 4,000 miles per hour. Today, we can orbit around the earth and travel to the moon at speeds in excess of 18,000 mph.[1]

And now, curiously enough, we find ourself on the threshold of a new speed challenge, which may be even more difficult to conquer. We must learn to go slower. In the interest of energy supplies, life saving, and emotional stability, we have reduced automobile speed limits to 55 m.p.h. and begun to preach the gospel of "small can be beautiful." In the words of the old farmer, "We have gone about as fer as we kin go." The new frontiers may involve a reversal of direction.

---

[1] The preceding illustrations are drawn from Alvin Toffler, *Future Shock* (New York: Random House, Inc., 1970), pp. 11–26.

Sixty-five percent of all the energy consumed by humans in the history of the world has been consumed within the lifetime of your grandparents. Half of all the people who ever lived have walked the earth while your grandparents were alive. Ninety per cent of all the scientists who ever lived are living now. The amount of technical information available doubles every ten years. Throughout the world, over 100,000 journals are published in more than sixty languages, and that number doubles about every fifteen years.

Few managers would argue with Disraeli's observation that change is inevitable in a progressive culture. Change is perhaps the only constant in today's managerial environment. Yet managers and subordinates seem universally to oppose changes that affect them. Few go as far as an ancient Duke of Cambridge who once emphatically stated, "Any change in whatever direction for whatever reason is strongly to be opposed."

If we stop and look around us at the multitude of trusted devices and practices that at one time were outrageous innovations, we should think that people would learn to welcome change. Yet most experienced managers agree that resistance to change is one of their most perplexing and unchanging problems.

In fact, a manager's ability to be effective might well be measured by the equanimity with which the manager can accept and cope with the inevitability of change. Warren Bennis has said,

> Our social institutions cannot withstand, let alone cope with the devastating rate of change without fundamental alterations in the way they negotiate their environments and the way they conduct the main operations of their enterprise.[2]

Both the theoreticians and the front line fighters can articulate the need to adapt to change, but the specific skills and attitudes by which to make that adaptation remain a topic of continuing popularity. According to J. M. Ewell of Proctor and Gamble, the great challenge is for firms to learn to find methods for anticipating the future and preparing in advance.[3] Chris Argyris emphasizes that creative, change-anticipating *managers* are the only hope of meeting the shifting future successfully.[4] Ewell's summary of the matter is that "the greatest of all managers will be people who can manage change.[5]

[2] Warren G. Bennis, *Organizational Development* (Reading, Mass.: Addison-Wesley Publishing Company, Inc., 1969), p. 18.

[3] J. M. Ewell, *The Effect of Change on Organization*, (Procter and Gamble Co., September, 1971).

[4] Chris Argyris, *Management and Organizational Development* (New York: McGraw-Hill Book Co., 1971).

[5] Ewell, op. cit.

The Nature of Change

The term *change* refers to any alteration that occurs in the organization of the total environment. Professor Keith Davis of Arizona State University illustrates the effect of change with an air-filled balloon.[6] Assume that your finger represents a change and the balloon represents the organization. When your finger is pressed against the exterior of the balloon, the shape of the balloon changes significantly at the point of contact. This obvious pressure, representing change, has produced an obvious deviation at the point of pressure. Though not quite so obvious, it is also true that the entire balloon has been affected and has stretched slightly. This comparison indicates that the entire organization tends to be affected by a change in any part of it. This interrelationship between parts has been one of the significant contributions made by systems theory. Whether we are speaking of the department, a branch office, a government agency, or an entire society, systems operate in an equilibrium in which the parts are directly and harmoniously related to each other. John Donne, the seventeenth-century English poet, suggested the underlying tenets of systems theory and the influence of change in his classic statement:

> No man is an island, entire of itself; every man is a piece of the Continent, a part of the main; if a clod be washed away by the sea, Europe is the less. . . . any man's death diminishes me, because I am involved in mankind; and therefore never send to know for whom the bell tolls; it tolls for thee.[7]

We can carry Davis' analogy of the balloon even farther. The molecules of air could represent a firm's employees. Obviously those at the point of pressure have to make the most drastic adjustment. Though the change has not had direct contact with them, it has affected them. An organizational change may not get anybody fired, but employees are sure to be displaced and have to adjust to new situations. This comparison illustrates an additional principle: technological change is a *human* problem as well as a *technical* problem.

Readers who have extensive empirical experience with balloons may recall the repeated pressure at a certain point tends to weaken the balloon at that point. The same is true with an organization. Pressure and motion create friction and heat. Eventually a rupture may occur, and the organization can collapse or suffer serious damage.

No generalization or analogy is perfect. An organization is much more complex than a balloon, and real people are quite different from the molecules in our illustration. For one thing they are not as free and

[6] *Human Relations at Work* (5th ed.) (New York: McGraw-Hill Book Company, 1977), p. 157.
[7] From *The Complete Poetry and Selected Prose of John Donne and The Complete Poetry of William Blake* (New York: Random House, Inc., 1941), p. 332.

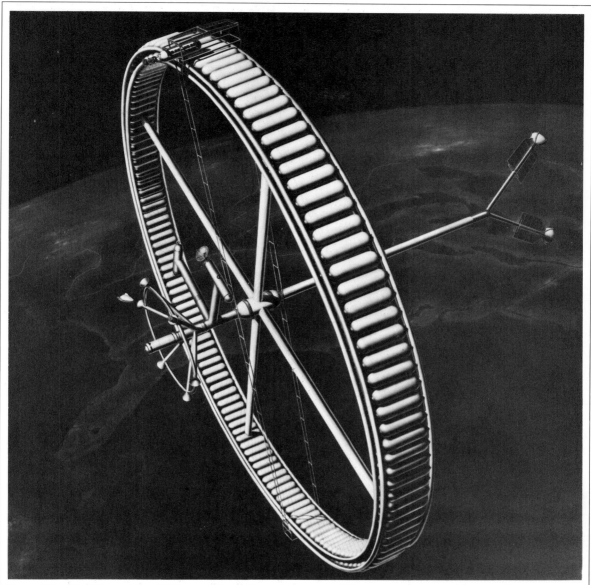

Space city (Lockheed Aircraft Corporation). Can change possibly continue to accelerate at the same pace? How fast will we be moving in 2002?

flexible as air molecules in a balloon. The analogy is merely intended to illustrate what Davis calls molecular equilibrium. Organizations also seek equilibrium. An organization must achieve equilibrium of its social structure. This merely means that people learn what to expect of the various relationships within their surroundings. They learn how to deal with each other, how to perform their jobs, and what to expect

351

next. When equilibrium exists, it is easier for individuals to be adjusted. Change requires new adjustments and a new equilibrium. In general, management's objective in a change is to (1) gain acceptance for that change and (2) restore the group equilibrium and personal adjustment that change upsets. The wise manager is always alert to the complicated human dynamics at work in a changed situation. In fact, it is management's responsibility to create and maintain a kind of "dynamic equilibrium" regarding change. The organization cannot move forward without change, but it must not be vulnerable to the trauma of change. Kast and Rosenzweig suggest that such a dynamic equilibrium includes four important dimensions:

1. Enough stability to facilitate achievement of current goals.
2. Enough continuity to ensure orderly change in either ends or means.
3. Enough adaptability to react appropriately to external opportunities and demands as well as changing internal conditions.
4. Enough innovativeness to allow the organization to be proactive (initiate changes) when conditions warrant.[8]

What Causes Change?

Some managers would rather think about change as little as possible, and then only to "fix" things when a change messes them up. But the wise manager seeks to anticipate changes by attention to the various arenas in which change may be initiated.

Environment, for business, means more than trees and leaves and water and air. The business environment encompasses all the shifting world conditions within which a company must operate. It is futile to say "We would have made a profit if the price of raw materials had not been increased"; or, "We did fine until the weather turned cold." These are the sorts of environmental factors that make life exciting and challenging for business leaders . . . and terrible for those who make no provisions for them. Environmental factors may include governmental regulations, what the competition is doing, technological breakthroughs, political developments, legal complications, the abilities and weaknesses of available workers, and the ever-fickle public opinion which must approve the organization's product or service.

Changes can also come to the organization through gradually changing and adapting morals and taboos of society. Fashion designers know that there may be only a short time lag between what prostitutes are

[8] Fremont E. Kast and James E. Rosenzweig, *Organization and Management* (2nd ed.) (New York: McGraw-Hill Book Company, 1974) pp. 574–575.

wearing today and what the socially chic will be wearing tomorrow. The goals and values that may be the watchwords of the organization today may appear naive and outdated a few years later. These changes in the shifting of human values may result from trends and backlashes of the cumulative social conscience when fortunes or disasters affect society.

Technical developments are continually rewriting the corporate ten-year plan. Early in this chapter we noted some of the accelerating technical developments that have barreled into our presence during this lifetime. Few of them were expected or planned for . . . except by those forward-looking managers who wisely expected the unexpected. Interestingly enough, we almost always limit our expectations of technical development to machines and hardware, even though experience has shown that humans can themselves be continually upgraded and made better able to accomplish assigned tasks. New systematic approaches to problem solving and planning, for instance, have resulted in the kinds of changes that few organizations anticipated.

Organizational changes are many times an unavoidable factor of the environment . . . as when the company is swallowed up by a multinational conglomerate. But other times, organizational changes that produce unsettling alteration can be the result of a board member who fancies a new way of putting the whole puzzle together.

For our purposes in this chapter, managerial change is probably the most important type of change. Managers themselves are the source of many of the changes that managers face. Some managerial change is accidental . . . as when the manager makes one change that has unforeseen repercussions. Other managerial changes are intentional . . . as when the manager's accumulated experience reveals a better way to do things just as the troops are becoming comfortable with the old way. And many times the manager confronts the workers with change when no change was anticipated . . . as when he or she says "we will just keep doing the old thing . . . but twice as fast!"

What Causes Resistance to Change?

Economic Factors.   The most obvious reason for resisting change is economic. Workers resist automation because they fear they will lose their jobs. They are not impressed by arguments that in the long run there will be more jobs in others parts of the country. What concerns them most is the immediate economic welfare of themselves and their families. In a similar way, craftsmen, office workers, and managers may fear that new developments will reduce their economic value. Executives may oppose changes that help the organization as a whole but hurt their individual potential for promotion.

Inconvenience. Equally understandable is the resistance to any change that threatens to make life more difficult. Individuals naturally fight the assignment of extra duties. They know the old job so well that it requires little attention. But any new job requires forgetting old procedures and learning new ones, a most unpopular activity with humans. An executive may be hard to convince of the desirability of being reassigned from one location or responsibility to another one—unless there is a compensating increase in prestige or income. Learning new ways requires the expenditure of energy. Even in the simplest job, there are tricks of the trade that take time to learn. When a person is thrown into a new situation, the old tricks no longer apply and the security of the familiar is lost.

Uncertainty. Just as youngsters fear the dark, adults fear change because of uncertainty. New ways are always strange, threatening, and laden with uncertainties—even when there is obvious improvement over the old. In an old but still important article[9] Robert N. McMurry suggests that the principal cause of hostility toward anything that threatens security or the status quo is *fear* (frequently reinforced and rationalized by accumulated resentments and rivalry).

Often resistance comes from employees who, because of rank, long service, or ability have no real reason to fear. Nevertheless, many feel extremely insecure. This is because deep-seated fears exist within the individual. Everyone knows fear. Even babies are prone to this emotion —it appears to be inborn. Nature is cruel. The law of the fang prevails to a greater extent than many recognize or are willing to admit. As Darwin suggested, the world is a difficult place for the weakling. Business is certainly highly competitive. Rivalry and conflict exist in every organization.

Thus, the real and justifiable fears that beset the average person are numerous. A change may appear relatively insignificant in the total scheme of things, but the person who is directly affected may think it is the most important thing in the world. In looking at the total solar system, an objective astrologer would conclude that the Earth is a minor planet. Yet to all of us it is major indeed. Similarly, everyone evaluates a change in terms of what it means personally.

If a manger is offered a new job with higher pay, several questions must be considered. How hard will it be? How long will it take to learn? Will I be able to meet the challenge? Who will my friends be? The opportunity may be very good, yet there is a natural tendency to let well enough alone. One common reason for fear is the lack of factual infor-

---

[9] "The Problem of Resistance to Change in Industry," *Journal of Applied Psychology*, December 1947, pp. 589–593.

mation. Uncertainty caused by lack of information may be corrected simply by providing answers to questions—assuming that management is aware of what questions are being asked. There is another kind of uncertainty that cannot be answered with information. This is the anxiety that springs from the individual's fears about how to react to the new situation. For this kind of uncertainty there can be no quick remedy.

Threats to Social Relationships.   It is natural for employees to oppose changes that will threaten their status. Every supervisor develops patterns of informal relationships with subordinates. And every new supervisor requires a long period of initiation before being accepted by subordinates. This is partially true because subordinates fear that the new manager will not follow the predecessor's patterns of informal relationships. Some of the early efforts of the scientific management movement failed because adequate attention was not given to the social dimensions of change.

Resentment of Control.   Whenever an organization initiates change, workers are reminded of management's superior authority. This may well lead to resistance, because many people resent having to take orders. Others have become accustomed to a certain level of control and may resist any attempt to strengthen that control. When change occurs, workers become subject to several types of unusual pressures from supervisors and top management. Suddenly they find that someone is checking up on them and giving them far more orders than usual. This increase in control reduces their feeling of autonomy and self-reliance.

Conclusion.   An alert and well-adjusted manager recognizes that change is a way of organizational life. Yet a scholarly observer has concluded that "Managerial behavior (a) is oriented more to the past than to the future, (b) recognizes the obligations of ritual more than the challenges of current problems, and (c) owes allegiance more to department goals (and personal objectives) than to overall company objectives."[10]

Reducing Resistance to Change

Resistance to change is not a new problem. Several hundred years ago Machiavelli wrote in *The Prince*, "it must be said that there is nothing more difficult to carry out, nor more doubtful of success, than to initiate a new thing."

Suggested strategies and solutions are as old as the problem. In 1770, Ben Franklin said,

[10] Larry E. Greiner, "Patterns of Organizational Change," *Harvard Business Review*, May–June 1967, p. 119.

The way to convince another is to state your case moderately and accurately. Then scratch your head and say, at least that's what it seems to you, but of course you may be wrong. This causes your listener to receive what you have to say, and, like as not, come about and try to convince *you* of it, since you are in doubt. But if you go to him in a tone of positiveness or arrogance, you only make an opponent of him.

It is a poor manager indeed whose approach to change is that it is a "necessary evil" with which he or she must cope. Quite the contrary— the better manager expects to *use* change to accomplish desired goals. Better managers see change as an opportunity . . . for organizational improvement and growth.

At the same time, managers must avoid the common misconception that there is no progress unless they keep things stirred up with occasional changes whether needed or not. No change should be undertaken unless it is clearly an improvement: a move that will make the operation (1) more effective, (2) more efficient, or (3) more satisfying to those involved.

Instead of "butting heads" and seeking to effect change through some survival-of-the-fittest approach, the manager proceeds to lessen resistance to change.

1. *Recognize the Social and Psychological Factors in Change.* Management's job would be much easier if there were a simple, direct adjustment to change as suggested in our earlier illustration about the balloon. But reality is far more complicated. Change operates through *each employee's* attitude to produce the response that is conditioned by feelings about the change and the environment. This relationship was illustrated by the famous Hawthorne experiments at Western Electric. In one instance, F. J. Roethlisberger and his colleagues wanted to test the influence of illumination on performance. It was their feeling that better lighting would lead to greater productivity. A test group of the assembly workers was chosen and moved to a special section. When the lighting in the area was increased, productivity rose, as had been expected. Then, because these researchers were good scholars, they decided to decrease illumination to illustrate that the reverse effect would reduce productivity. They were quite surprised when productivity actually increased again! Lighting was again decreased and the result was still greater productivity! Finally, lighting was decreased to 0.06 of a foot candle—approximately equivalent to moonlight. "Not until this point was reached was there any appreciable decline in the output rate."[11]

Doubtless the researchers initally thought that their experiment had failed. Instead, they had discovered an important new truth. They had

[11] *Management and Morale* (Cambridge, Mass.: Harvard University Press, 1941), p. 10.

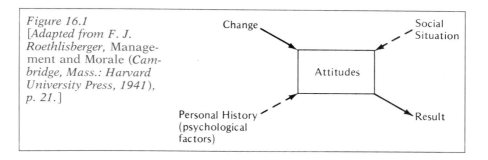

Figure 16.1
[Adapted from F. J. Roethlisberger, Management and Morale *(Cambridge, Mass.: Harvard University Press, 1941), p. 21.]*

mistakenly assumed that there was a direct cause-and-effect relationship in change. If one variable in the situation was changed, they had reasoned that any change in output would be directly attributable to that change. Closer examination of the data, however, suggests that some other influential factor later diagnosed as "employee attitudes" had entered into the situation to upset the expected pattern. Roethlisberger illustrated this new pattern by means of his now-famous X-Chart, shown in Figure 16.1. It identifies other factors that may be operating in the environment.

Roethlisberger's chart illustrates that the psychological or personal factors involved in a change situation, as well as the social dimensions of the situation, contribute to the ultimate result. Each change situation is interpreted by an individual according to personal attitudes about it. The way a person feels about a change will determine the response to it. These attitudes usually depend upon past experiences. Personal history, even from childhood, may have considerable impact. Much of one's attitude toward change may be brought to the work place. Another determinant of the attitude will be the work environment itself and past experiences with it.

Frederick W. Taylor, often known as the "father of scientific management," might have been much more successful if he had recognized Roethlisberger's principle. No one has challenged the accuracy of Taylor's industrial engineering, yet in several instances workers failed to respond because he did not recognize the psychological dimension. Perhaps Frank Gilbreth was more successful in this respect because he had the good fortune to marry the first woman in the United States to receive a Ph.D. in industrial psychology. Lillian Gilbreth's involvement in her husband's work doubtless contributed immeasurably to his success in bringing about increased productivity.

Although each individual interprets change for himself, he often is influenced by his co-workers and by the social relationships that are involved. In the seventeenth century, Samuel Butler wrote, "He that complies against his will, is of the same opinion still." Contemporary research in management and human relations has done little more than confirm this ancient thesis. For change to be accepted, management must convince workers that change is desirable. Being right is not enough.

2. Participation Brings Support. People follow their own decisions best. An experiment with housewives in the Midwest demonstrated this.[12] During World War II, when whole milk was scarce, health authorities wanted more dried milk used. They tried two different ways to increase the consumption. First, they used the logical method. Lectures by experts in nutrition were given to homemakers explaining why they should use dried milk. A month later, only *15 percent* of these women used more dried milk.

The health authorities decided to try the psychological method. Groups of about six women were brought together to talk over among themselves the benefits of using more dried milk. The leader of the discussion did very little taking. The conversation was simply directed to the subject of milk. These small groups of women decided they should use more dried milk. No outsider told them—it was their own decision. A month later, 50 percent of these women were using more dried milk in their homes.

In another experiment—this one conducted in a textile mill—production was too low.[13] The equipment could not be changed, and the only thing to do was to improve the productivity of the workers. The employees were on a piece rate and should have had a selfish interest in seeing how much work they could do. Similar groups of workers in two locations were chosen for the study.

In one group, an industrial engineer was brought in to develop improved methods of production. These methods were explained to the workers; they were told that the new methods would make their job easier and more rewarding and that management expected more production. The workers could have made money for themselves, but practically no one did. In fact, during the next few months, their average output dropped.

In the other situation, the workers were brought together in small groups to talk over what might be wrong with production. The workers did the talking, not the bosses. The discussion leader did not tell them how to turn out more work; the leader left it up to the workers to decide where it might be possible and how. After several discussions, conducted on their own time, these groups decided they could increase the output and they set a goal for themselves. Although their methods were not as "efficient" as those worked out by the professional engineer, their output jumped to a new high. During the next few months it averaged

[12] Related in Donald Laird and Eleanor Laird, *Psychology: Human Relations and Motivation* (New York: McGraw-Hill Book Company, 1967), pp. 410–413.
[13] Ibid., pp. 414–417.

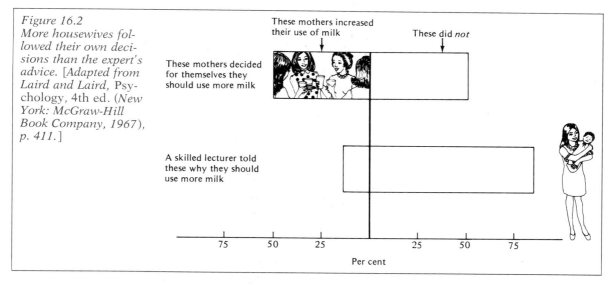

Figure 16.2
More housewives followed their own decisions than the expert's advice. [Adapted from Laird and Laird, Psychology, 4th ed. (New York: McGraw-Hill Book Company, 1967), p. 411.]

These mothers increased their use of milk

These did *not*

These mothers decided for themselves they should use more milk

A skilled lecturer told these why they should use more milk

75 50 25 25 50 75

Per cent

18 per cent higher than it had been before they developed the changes for their procedures.

The final illustration of a work change that led to significant increases in productivity and decrease in absenteeism occurred at Texas Instruments, Inc.[14] A group of women had been assembling radar equipment according to methods suggested by their engineering department. For the study the group was given an opportunity to supervise their own methods and goals. The workers had full access to cost information and could request the assistance of staff specialists. After implementing their own system, the assembly time per unit dropped from 138 hours to 86 hours. At this point, a second goal-setting session was conducted. The workers suggested that they did not need a supervisor. In their opinion, they were ready to practice self-control. They did agree to keep the supervisor informed but requested permission to direct their own activities. The assembly time for the unit was eventually reduced to 36 hours. Although this illustration is unusually dramatic, it does suggest the tremendous potential in allowing people a degree of self-actualization.

3. *Authority of Trust.* It is almost impossible to persuade workers that a change will be beneficial for them when their past experience with change has shown that this is not true. Regardless of what techniques are used, workers will not believe that management has turned over a new leaf until they have definite evidence of sincerity. Consequently, a new supervisor has more trouble in introducing change than one who has established his reputation with the workers. Here again, the importance of leadership emerges. Time after time, the lesson is proven: leadership is not necessarily the same as authority. If one or the other must

[14] Charles L. Hughes, "Applying Behavioral Science In Manufacturing Supervision," *Proceedings of the Ninth Annual Midwest Management Conference* (Carbondale, Ill.: Bureau of Business Research, Southern Illinois University, 1966, pp. 85–89.

be chosen, leadership is far more critical for achieving desired results. Despite Machiavelli's advice that a new leader should "lop heads quickly," aggressive, immediate restructuring of operations by a new manager may lead to disastrous results. A manager can gain a special kind of authority—the authority of trust—only after establishing honesty and interest in the employees. The authority of trust cannot be delegated. It must be earned by each manager.

4. *Force-Field Analysis.* The great social psychologist Kurt Lewin[15] suggested that when a change or an innovation is being resisted, the factors that are operating for and against that change should be analyzed. After the listing of all the factors that would encourage worker cooperation and also those factors that might be causing resistance to the change, Lewin's next step was to analyze the comparative strength of these factors. He identified two ways to gain acceptance. The first was to increase the pressures for the change. No doubt you can think of many incidents in which the pressure far overpowers the resistance. You can imagine the pressure on the positive side increasing to such an extent that the minus qualities are finally pushed down and overcome. The only danger with this is that the resisting factors are not eliminated. Consequently, they eventually build up enough pressure so that they rebound—very much like a coiled spring. In fact, Lewin called this dramatic flareup of resistance after opposition had apparently been subdued, the *"coiled spring effect."*

When there is resistance, we can do one of several things. We can give up . . . which most managers are not allowed to do. We can overpower the resistance . . . which may prove to be a negative act in the end. Or we can reduce the resistance . . . which usually requires less effort and creates far more good will. The process of understanding (and even charting) the force-field situation can be very revealing and inspirational to the manager confronted by resistance.

The more reasonable way of overcoming resistance to change is to eliminate as many of these resisting factors as possible. In one interesting experiment, Lewin was dealing with factory workers during World War II. Workers objected to wearing safety glasses. Dr. Lewin developed the chart of analysis shown in Figure 16.3. The first resistance factor was removed when it was found that lighter, more comfortable hats could be substituted at a cost of about 50 cents more each. The employer was willing to make this additional expenditure in order to gain cooperation. Next, a contest was announced for each worker to decorate the hats in whatever way was appropriate. This not only made the hats more attractive, it gave each individual a chance for self-expression.

---

[15] Based on Kurt Lewin and N. D. Cartwright, eds., *Field Theory in Social Science* (New York: Harper and Row, Publishers, 1951).

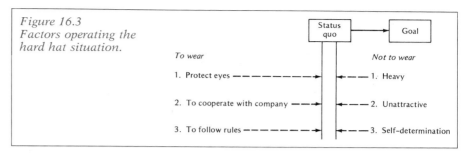

*Figure 16.3
Factors operating the
hard hat situation.*

When the resistance factors were removed, the wearing of hard hats gained positive support and negative pressure was overcome in a lasting and positive way.

5. *Make Only Necessary Changes.* Future shock, or the baffling confusion that comes from an overwhelming stream of changes, is a fact of life in our times. In dealing with a culture that is characterized by future shock, it is important that change not be introduced merely for the sake of variety. There is a price that is paid for each change. Frequently it is the price of confusion, extra effort in learning, and the initital loss of time in developing new procedures. It also builds a climate of distrust. Each person's reaction to change can be analyzed in terms of the chart presented in Table 16.1.

Managers should take care to ensure that their changes are seen as reasonable and necessary. Change is not necessarily improvement, any more than movement is always progress. The change-happy manager should remember that it is possible to saw a board three times and the board may still be too short.

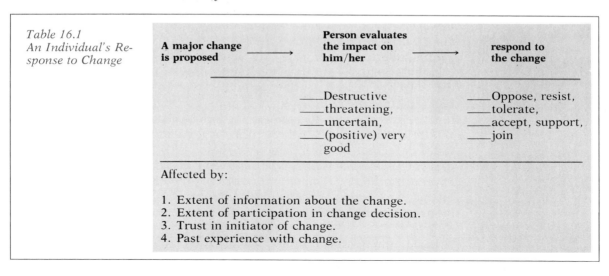

*Table 16.1
An Individual's Response to Change*

A major change is proposed	→	Person evaluates the impact on him/her	→	respond to the change
		____Destructive ____threatening, ____uncertain, ____(positive) very good		____Oppose, resist, ____tolerate, ____accept, support, ____join

Affected by:

1. Extent of information about the change.
2. Extent of participation in change decision.
3. Trust in initiator of change.
4. Past experience with change.

Despite the almost universal longing of middle-aged managers, organizational activities will never retreat to the "good old days." Change is a vital and certain part of each manager's future. Pioneer advertising executive Bruce Barton suggested that "The person who is through changing his mind is through!" The same is equally true today for the manager and the organization. Perhaps the essence of management is to create the correct balance of order and originality. According to Alfred North Whitehead, "The art of progress is to preserve order amid change and to preserve change amid order."

Steps of Change

Edgar H. Schein, a psychologist at Massachusetts Institute of Technology, has developed a model for change that looks at the entire process.[16] According to his model, successful change consists of the following three steps: (1) unfreezing, (2) changing, and (3) refreezing. Schein applied the model he developed to brainwashing in Communist prison camps, the training of a nun, and the development of managers.

Unfreezing. All learning, whether it is the acquisition of skills, knowledge, or changed attitude, depends on the learner's willingness to learn. One must be prepared and motivated for the experience. When attitudes are being changed, it is necessary to eliminate, or unfreeze, the present attitude so that a vacuum can be created for new ones. Coercion may be used as an aid in unfreezing, as in the case of brainwashing. Management development programs often assume that the employees are ready to learn. There is some evidence that this is not the case. If employees can be made to see that the change relates to their own needs, they will obviously be more receptive. In other words, their previous position may begin to thaw.

Changing. According to the scheme model, a changing attitude takes place only when there is *identification* or *internalization*. If a person can identify with another individual who has the desired attitude, it will facilitate the willingness to change. For this reason, it is important for managers to look for opinion leaders as change agents.

Internalization is the process of trying, adopting, and using new attitudes or techniques. If a person's position or belief has begun to thaw, that person may be willing at least to consider the new approach. If this approach proves sufficient and desirable, the change then begins to be internalized and is accepted. It is important that the trials during the internalization period be fair and just. Sometimes tryouts of new ideas

---

[16] "Management Development as a Process of Influence," *Industrial Management Review*, May 1961, pp. 59–76.

resemble the old Indian who heard that feathers were good for sleeping on—he tried one and didn't like it.

Refreezing. Refreezing is the name given to the final acceptance and integration of the desired attitudes so that the innovation becomes a permanent part of a person's personality or procedures. Time and support are needed in this phase of change. As was discussed in a previous section on behavior modification (Chapter 13), behavior that is rewarded immediately and regularly is likely to become part of a person's normal behavior.

Caution. There is a great value in being aware of the unfreezing-changing-freezing theory. However, these steps, particularly the thawing process, happen much faster in a textbook than in the mind of the person being changed. Some mention should be made of the difficulty of

Excalibur (Orion Pictures Co., 1981). Have humans always feared change?

thawing attitudes and practices that were learned in early childhood or have been practiced over a long period of time.

Many are unprepared for change because of childhood imprinting. Early life experiences determine much of adult behavior. Zoologist Konrad Lorenz took half the eggs away from a mother goose and hatched them in an incubator. They followed *him* around, just as the goslings hatched by the goose followed *her* around. From this and other experiments we learn of *imprinting:* childhood learning determines later social behavior.

"As the twig is bent, so is the tree inclined," and so is the forest. Lives are based on a network of beliefs imprinted in us as children. What we have known since childhood is sacred to us, and we teach it to our children. Perhaps the day lies somewhere in the near future when people will become so accustomed to change that unfreezing will become an easy task. But, for now, wise managers and other leaders will continue to be gentle in the replacement of treasured and comfortable beliefs and practices.

Summary

Change seems to happen faster every day. In transportation, communication, and almost every other realm, the rate of change is obviously increasing. One aspect of mankind, however, that has remained more or less constant is the innate resistance to change. It's a fact of life and leadership: people resist change. By its very nature, change is disconcerting. A change is any alteration that occurs in the organization of the total environment. People resist change for many reasons: (1) Many workers fear that a change will cause them to lose their jobs or in some other way affect their economic well-being. (2) A new way of working is always inconvenient and irritatingly unfamiliar. Nobody wants life made more difficult or complicated. (3) Many changes are resisted because of a simple fear—we're afraid of those things we don't understand. (4) Many changes can threaten comfortable social relationships and are therefore resisted, in spite of obvious advantages. Who wants to abolish the superfluous job of his best friend? (5) Workers often resist change because new supervisors or new training processes will impose controls that are resented.

Anyone seeking to bring about a change and meeting resistance can take one of two courses: (1) increase the force with which the resistance is to be overcome; or (2) take steps of an educational and counseling nature to remove the objections that are causing the resisting. Overpowering objections is an unsatisfactory alternative because the objections still exist and, being suppressed, may grow and create greater problems later.

When workers are allowed to participate in the planning and implementation of a change, the job gets done quicker and, often, far more efficiently than with direct instructions alone.

One aspect of resistance to change can be removed even before a specific innovation problem comes to light. Management must foster trust in its workers in day-to-day relationships so that a trust of authority will be present when a problem arises. Trust of the initiator of a change can be a major factor in removing natural resistance to change.

Managers will be wise to make an almost mathematical comparison of the factors *for* and *against* a change. In the process of clarification of the situation, natural next steps are often revealed.

Although change is necessary and prevalent, managers need to be sure that a change is worthwhile. The automatic costs of any change process should be weighed against the advantages to be produced. In some cases, the disruption and dissension will not be worth the dollar gain.

Edgar H. Schein has suggested that any change can be boiled down to three actual steps. *Unfreezing* is the unlearning or breaking-down-resistance stage in the promotion of the innovation. *Changing*, the second stage, has two parts as Schein described the phenomenon: workers must identify with the change agents and internalize the benefits of the change. Once this trust and desire are established, the change process enters a refreezing stage, in which the new process or attitude becomes easy and pleasant by the development of habit.

Management lives with change. Changing things that resist is management's job. Changing things before others change them is creative. The manger must always keep an open mind to new ideas by continuous re-education and exposure to dissident, unfamiliar concepts. In short, he or she must be open and creative if younger employees are not to take over.

There is hope that some day the human race will learn to live gracefully with change. After all, no generation has ever been taught to expect it or to seek it out. Increasingly, an eagerness to deal with change and the ability to live in ambivalence will filter down from the avant-garde and youth to management to the public and be passed along from parent to child. Resistance to change has always been with us. But who knows? Perhaps, this too will change.

Review Questions

1. How can a balloon illustrate the impact of change on an organization?
2. Why do people resist change?
3. Explain F. J. Roethlisberger's X-Chart.
4. What is force-field analysis?
5. Discuss Edgar H. Schein's model of change.
6. Do you believe that transportation will continue to change as rapidly in the remainder of the twentieth century as it did in the first seventy years?
7. Are there any reasons to support the logic of the Duke of Cambridge who suggested, "Any change in whatever direction for whatever reason is strongly to be opposed."
8. How can a change in religious attitudes have any impact on the practice of management?
9. Ken Boulding once suggested that we need social changes to help solve the problems created by our technical changes. Discuss.
10. How would you react if your professor were to suggest that this course would meet one hour earlier each day for the rest of the term? Analyze your reaction.
11. After reviewing the suggestions for reducing resistance to change in this chapter, discuss your reaction to them. Do they appear manipulative?
12. Do the Hawthorne experiments suggest that lighting is unimportant to workers? Discuss.
13. Recently many universities and colleges have begun to add student representatives to faculty committees. Discuss this trend from the perspective of organizational change.
14. Use the Schein model of change to help a young man bring about a favorable change in the attitude of a coed he wishes to date.

part IV

The Management of Operations

17

Managing Production and Operations

IMMEDIATE EMPLOYMENT—Positions are now available for production line workers in the open-heart surgery division at Memorial Hospital. No medical experience is required, since Memorial has pioneered in the reduction of medical costs through the use of unskilled workers on the surgical assembly lines. Openings at present include Position 7B (Sponge Removal), Position 35 (Initial Probe), and Position 86 (Stitch with Decorative Thread). If you are interested in steady work on one of the nation's leading surgery teams, check with our employment office today. Last year, Memorial's gallbladder line led the nation by cranking out an average of 120 patients each day. The supervisor of the open-heart conveyor has committed his teams to award-winning productivity this year, so you can count on lots of excitement as well as steady hours, regular breaks, and all fringe benefits, including our ten percent employee discount on any operation in the hospital. Apply in person and come ready to work.

As consumer, we can appreciate the continuing efforts of the nation's production operations managers. They make it their business to shave each step in each operation in the production of products and services. Their immediate goals are the rewards of personal-achievement bonuses, promotions, and recognition for reducing the costs of creating or shaping a final product. The fringe benefit for the consumer is that each success of these streamliners can potentially save us money or provide us a better product at the same cost.

The American theme—"there is always a better way"—has identified the nation's way of doing things for years. Other nations are, of course, also training personnel in the skills of finding the better way, but it is much more difficult for them to supply the national environment that has made Americans deify the person whose persistence finally results in the breakthrough. What American school child has not thrilled to the story of Henry Ford's institution of the assembly line? And how many hundreds of different filaments did Thomas Edison have to try before he was able to make his incandescent light work? History books and schoolrooms both give praise for those who can find a better way.

As we begin an examination of the production/operations function in organizations, it is interesting to briefly review the development of this area from a historical perspective. In Chapter 2, the important contributions of production managers like Frederick Taylor and Henry Gantt to the early development of management thought and the formation of management as a profession were discussed. As time passed, contributions from technically oriented managers like these continued to be recognized; however, the major emphasis in management seems to have fallen on its behavioral rather than on its technical aspects. The pendulum now appears to be swinging in the opposite direction, and we are experiencing renewed interest in the production/operations area. This change may be attributed to a host of factors, including a decline in productivity and increasing competition from foreign producers. These threats to the superiority of American industry promise a continuing focus over the next decade on finding a better way by increasing efficiency and productivity.

This dedication to refinement by even the smallest amounts might seem strange to anyone who has not learned the lessons of volume that can come only with experience in mass production. Not all people can appreciate the "massness" of mass production. By the same token, it is often difficult to realize how great a savings can be realized by some new discovery which can save a hundredth of a cent of the cost of manufacturing. However, in our modern society we continually have more opportunities to relate to these concepts. Tremendous growth in the service sector of our economy, combined with the application of many traditional production/operations techniques in this environment, allows each of us a chance to observe the "production line" in operation. To appreciate how important even the smallest refinement can become, one has only to stand in a McDonald's as hundereds of "copies" of the same product roll off the "production line" and to realize that this same process is occurring simultaneously in several thousand "factories" throughout the world.

In this chapter, we will scan the world of production and operations management. We will look at some of the formal steps involved in making and monitoring the continuous refinement of any process. But, at the same time, we will seek to give an appropriate place of importance to the human traits that have made us a nation of better-way seekers.

Experience and Expertise

There are skills and formulas which can and must be taught to people who seek careers as managers whose responsibilities will include production/operations. But there are also important aspects of operations management that cannot be reduced to a formula. Practically no working manufacturing process is totally a drawing board product. In order for it to become the best possible approach, it had to wait until the wheels began to turn and the workers had a chance to test and experiment and find the better ways. Indeed, the wise manager of any process soon learns that the real experts—the ones who can provide the vital information for improvement—include the people who work on the machines every day.

This expertise of the experienced is not limited to the world of conveyor belts and machines. Any operation can be understood with peculiar astuteness by those who have worked through it. Whether it be the operation of a military base, an office force, a computer program, or the intricacies of producing a major motion picture, the input of the people who know the ropes is essential.

At the same time, workers and managers can also become so accustomed to the processes and operations as they are, that they become blind to the improvements that could be made. The skills and perceptions of some workers will dictate that they move up through the ranks and into the management of jobs they used to do. Other workers will best be left alone to pursue the work as it has been set up for them. Experience does not always produce expertise or wisdom. It is the task of the operations manager to create and maintain a delicate balance between the knowledge of the textbook and the wisdom that comes only through experience.

Making Things People Want

Our society is set up in such a way that no firm will survive unless it provides something people want at a price they are willing to pay. The charge that heartless businessmen prefer to sell useless junk rather than benefiting the common good is familiar. Yet, one beauty of the profit is self-regulation—to assure that the people get what they want enough to pay for.

It is a different discussion as to whether people are ever going to demand and pay for what they need. An important premise of this chapter is that successful businesses are those that are able to create something that people want . . . more than they want their money. Economists refer to this as *creativity utility*. We can also think of it as adding value by something that is done. The utility of any good or service can be increased in several different ways.

Creating Utility

You may create *time utility* designing and making available a machine that will allow bank customers to secure 24-hour banking services. Your machine will be in demand because it gives people what they want in the time realm. Or, your time utility may result from providing a product that saves time for the buyer.

Place utility is created by putting your product at the place it will be most needed. Suppose you could move the kids' corner lemonade stand to a point in the desert where a millionaire is dying of thirst. The price could easily run to $100,000 for a glass of icy lemonade! All marketing specialists try to create place utility by putting the product where it will most likely be needed. What is the difference in the cost and value of earthworms in your garden and earthworms at the little market on the shore of your favorite fishing lake?

Ownership utility is another important factor in making things the way people want them. Marketing executives know that customers want to *own* their purchases. They want to be able to receive the title to the purchase at the point of sale instead of waiting a long time, going a long way, or enduring a lot of paperwork. It is nearly impossible for us in our marketing society to conceive of bargaining for groceries which will eventually be delivered to us *if* our offer is accepted by the farmer.

Time, place, and ownership utility are usually achieved by the marketing steps of moving a product or service, or packaging it in a more convenient size. These utilities are not usually involved with substantial changes in the nature of the product itself. Purchase a train load of ballpoint pens, and one of them may only cost you two or three cents. But you will gladly pay fifty cents or a dollar to have the same ballpoint pen all by itself at the place where you just ran out of ink. The ballpoint pen is the same—but one has more utilitarian quantities of location and time.

This chapter is more concerned with what is called *form utility*. Form utility is the kind of value-adding factor that is created by changing the nature of the raw materials. In most cases, the other kinds of utility are preceded by form utility to get a product which can be marketed. No matter how convenient your local car dealer's showroom may be, you don't want to buy a car that is delivered in stacks of iron, chrome, rubber, fabric, and glass. You might buy such a pile of raw materials much much cheaper, but you want a car—you are willing to pay somebody to get all those raw materials organized in a drivable arrangement.

Production/operations management as we view it today is the management of the transformation process that provides form utility. A simple depiction of this process is presented in Fig. 17.1 Most people can easily visualize this process in a manufacturing company. However, the transformation process occurs in all organizations whether they produce a tangible product or provide a service. In the service sector, inputs are transformed into a service that is a consumable form. A university builds facilities, employs faculty, determines schedules, and develops curricula so that its "product," education, is in a form that the student can consume. You can easily imagine what the current trend would be if the educational system did not manage this process and each student was solely responsible for his or her own education. Thus the traditional view of production or manufacturing management has broadened to reflect a significant change in our economy, and this has resulted in the adoption of a new label, operations management.

Each of us participates daily in production and operations experiences. We make cookies by mixing dough and "treating" this raw material with a baking process. Or perhaps we pull together paper and ink with an idea to produce a term paper. We go to school or to fast food restaurants which are, in a very real sense, factories mass producing their respective "products." In all these experiences, there are common factors and characteristics that we must understand and use to improve organizations through better management.

Production Processes

There are several processes by which we can add form utility. An *analytic process* breaks down a raw material into one or more usable products, as when the oil refinery divides the black crude oil into many forms with many uses. A *synthetic process* puts several raw materials together, as when a plastics producer takes one of the oil refinery's products and mixes it with other chemicals to make a plastic. *Fabrication* involves the machining, treating, cutting, bending, or weaving of raw materials to create something that did not exist before, as when the pump manufacturer includes an oil-base plastic as liner of the hose of his deluxe pump. *Assembly* is creating value or utility by putting together things that form a product that did not exist before the assembly,

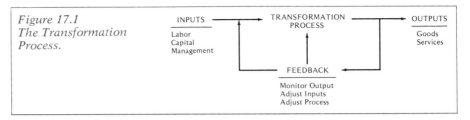

Figure 17.1 The Transformation Process.

as when a builder of drilling rigs puts a deluxe pump together with many other components to create a machine for finding and reclaiming more black crude.

Production/operations management is concerned with creating form utility—making something of value that did not exist before—by analysis, synthesis, fabrication, assembly, or (usually) by some intricate combination of all these processes. In most cases it also involves the production of a combination or bundle of goods and services rather than exclusively one or the other. Obviously, there are innumerable problems to contend with in this area of management. Nevertheless, they usually fall within two major categories, design problems or operating problems. As the name indicates, design problems involve the design of production/operation systems. Where should the plant be located? How should the departments be arranged? How large should capacity be? Operating problems, on the other hand, involve more frequent day-to-day decisions. How much inventory should we hold? What products should be made today? What do we make first? These problems are inherent in all organizations and must be addressed.

Those who are likely to enjoy the work of operations management are those who are as interested in the clock as the time . . . . as fascinated by how a thing is made as what it does . . . . and as intrigued by the components as by the whole. The aptitudes and interests that might lead a person into an enjoyment of work in design or management of operations or production are aptitudes and interests that make life fascinating. This is a dynamic area and one that has implications at almost every level of an organization. Attention to details, components, and the interrelationships of all steps are equally significant in leading an army, running a paint factory, or making a truly great hamburger.

Designing the Productions/Operations System

Successes in production and operations are planned. There are some successes whose planning was not formalized or obvious, but even these were formulated, weighed, and revised in the mind of the founder and initial moving force. As we talk about the formal or informal planning of production facilities and equipment, we will focus on the larger producers, particularly those in the more competitive, lower profit arenas.

Smaller operations are still important in America. They can still make profits and still compete successfully. However, if an engineer in Miami decides to begin a small factory to manufacture his brainchild, the chances are great that the factory is going to be in or near Miami. Unless the savings in transportation or labor can be overwhelming, the budding industrialist is likely to stay close to familiar ground and familiar vendors, and simply let the product carry the burden of the additional costs. The beginning operation is unlikely to be wealthy enough, broadly based enough, or visionary enough to start with a move—even an opportune move.

Most companies start where the founder starts. Geographically speaking, the earliest efforts of most companies have taken place in whatever location the founder lived when the idea came along. In time and with success, the company begins to leave less to chance when it comes to geography. When the time comes to purchase land and build factories, the company—especially the large operation with considerable competition—wants to get its money's worth and even more than that.

Many companies now routinely employ workers whose sole responsibility is to seek out and examine locations and judge how these will fit into clearly specified corporate plans and projections. Retail franchises, for example, have a corps of real estate specialists who are on the lookout for properties entering the market that will fit the population, location, and market specifications created by the parent company.

Large corporations receive a passing parade of mayors and other developers from cities seeking new plants. The competition is heated for a company that lets the word out that it will be building a new plant. Municipalities often bend or even break rules to create industrial parks or other accommodations for promising plants, with their desired payrolls, people, and profits. It is quite common for a city to cut taxes—or even eliminate them entirely—for a few years in order to entice a desirable plant.

These concessions to progress have produced both victories and tragedies for small towns. Some have put themselves on the map and made life better all around by helping dependable industry to get started. Others have found the entire population dependent upon a staggering giant company, or discovered that the town was going to have to pay part of the tab for cleaning up after messy industry. Small towns and rural areas are not as wide-open as they used to be. Industry must now prove that it will be a good clean neighbor.

Principles of Site Selection

Today, we are long past the first generations of factory locating, when both sides seemed bent on exploiting the other. Now, the towns want guaranteed progress for the benefits they can offer. The companies have also learned some bitter lessons about trying to ship its people out to some rural outpost. There is still value in relocation for both the locator and the locatee, but planning is more important than ever. All sides want to look at the long-term implications.

Suppose that you are a land finder for a large company. You are given the assignment of finding the best possible spot for a proposed new factory. What are the questions you must answer before you can be sure that you have pin-pointed the very best location.

What will the product be? A location that is just right for the manufacture of one product could be the worst possible place for another product. Why are there so few steel mills in Houston, Texas and oil refineries in Birmingham, Alabama? As a site locater, you will wisely seek to start with the answer and work backward through the questions, i.e., you will study the proposed product and all that it takes to make it and then follow the path of each raw material and each machine or personnel need.

What raw materials go into it? If your company will be involved in extracting an ounce of something from a ton of rock, you will naturally begin to consider locating the plant and the refining operation as near to the source as possible. It would drive up the final cost unnecessarily to transport that unwanted ton of rock very far. If you are making toothpicks, you will put the new sawmill in the woods rather than in the city.

Does it use more machines or people? If the toothpick factory is totally automated, you will put it as deep in the woods as you can. But if it requires a large number of human workers, you may be wise to put the toothpick works near a small town on the edge of the woods. And if the workers you need have to be highly skilled, the economics of the situation might even force you to consider transporting all the heavy wood to some large city that offers a wider selection of experienced toothpick makers.

Where does the finished product have to go? The distribution to markets can be a deciding factor in the location of your plant. If your product has time limitations to its freshness or its appropriateness, you will have to locate the production facility near the market place. On the other hand, if you have plenty of time, even the heaviest of products can be transported at reasonable rates aboard bulk carriers. The distribution of products is fluctuating more rapidly than it did in the first years of this century. Air freight can put orchids from Hawaii and bread from San Francisco in east coast markets. Unfortunately, the cost of energy for transportation seems to be one of the least predictable factors for the next few years. As a plant location specialist, you would want to give extra attention to your alternatives in taking the finished product to market.

Making the Location Decision

There are really two stages in the selection process. First, you will select a geographic area that has a suitable mix of raw materials, workers, and market proximity. The choices considered should be limited to some reasonable number. Trying to consider 100 alternative locations would be an impossible task. The *limiting factor* concept of decision making is helpful in narrowing the initial alternatives into a workable number. This concept states that there is usually one issue or criterion at the heart of a decision that is critical to its answer. If an alternative does not satisfy this criterion, it can immediately be eliminated from consideration. For example, a brewery requires large quantities of water and must be where this raw material is abundant. This immediately eliminates large sections of our country and substantially reduces the size of the problem. After a suitable geographic area has been selected, the offerings of various choices within the area must be evaluated. This process usually involves both a qualitative and a quantitative evaluation.

How badly does the community want you? One of your first concerns will be the attitudes of communities toward the arrival and long-term stay of your company. The answer to this question will depend on the kind of industry you are offering. Is it clean? Is it a popular public commodity or just a necessary evil? And what are the long-term markets for its product? Some industrial development committees will come to you with promises of tremendous advantages. Others may be more reserved about seeking your new facility. But the experienced manager looks beyond the eagerness of town representatives. Long-term community attitudes are more important than initial ones.

What is the work force? You will want to know the skills that are readily available among the population of the locale. You will want to know what kind of jobs those workers are doing now, and what enticements will be necessary to get them working for you. If your operation can function with unskilled labor, how easily can it be found? How dependable are people? What are the social taboos unique to the area that might conflict with your efforts?

What other companies are already there? At first, it might seem natural to avoid an area where your competitor is already in business. But on second thought, it is easy to see that the reasons for the competitor's presence could be equally important to you. People change jobs, and there may be benefit for both you and the competitor if there are more jobs of the same type in the same area. Furthermore, the competitor may have already done a lot of your work for you by getting rail and truck routes into the area, or by fostering the related companies you also need to supply your raw materials. And eventually, of course, your company may want to buy out the competition when your success begins to demand it.

Is there enough power? Walk through any manufacturing facility and you begin to appreciate the importance of electrical power. Even when adequate power is available, it may be prohibitive in cost or lacking in dependabiity. You will want more than a promise of *enough* power— you need some assurances that the price of the power will remain within the reach of your company's projections for the foreseeable future. You will also want to investigate contingency power sources. What happens in the event of an emergency? What are the alternative methods of keeping your machines turning? What guarantees can be made for the supply of alternative power sources?

Where does the water come from . . . and where does it go? Water is almost the universal solvent. It is used in practically every manufacturing plant. Even when it is not one of the ingredients of the manufacturing process, it is likely to be essential for cooking, heating, or cleaning. You need to know more than that there is *enough* water to meet your specifications. You have to know where the water has been when you get it. If your new facility is to be downstream from some other industrial user, there may be extra costs involved in removing impurities. On the other side of the operation, the water that leaves your plant has to flow on to someone else. The days of dumping your process's waste without treatment are gone. Unless the town is willing to supply these treatment needs, your product's cost will eventually have to bear the additional cost for cleaning up waste water before sending it on to the community where your employees live.

Is it a pleasant place to live? The chances are great that your company will be sending some of its best managerial people to live in the area and operate the plant. In fact, they might send you! If all other factors are perfect and the region is still an unpleasant place for your company's people to live, you'd better pass it up. Many a company has found itself saddled with an outpost that managers dread so much that they will leave the company before moving a family there. In some cases, the plant *has* to be in a certain locale no matter how unpleasant the surroundings may be. In such cases, companies know that they are going to have to bear the extra costs of hazard pay, loneliness pay, or exceptionally high cost-of-living pay to get workers to go there. Unless your investigations impress you with mutual benefits to your company and to the community, you'd better look for another suitable location. No amount of advantages of transportation, power, and water can counteract the negative influence of workers who are unhappy in the work environment.

You will want to know about the schools, community services, and underlying attitudes before you make decisions about the locale. Not only will you want to know how things *are* in the present. You will be even more interested in projections of the way things are likely to be *after* your company's impact begins to be felt in the area. Will there be higher taxes to pay for more police and fire protection or garbage collection? Will your plant cause the school system to be overrun? What happens to the local economy in the event of a cutback in your production needs? What influence do unions have in the area?

Several different quantitative models are employed to assist in finding the best location for facilities. Frequently, models are tailor made for the unique circumstances of a location problem. One well-known example of this type model was used in New York City to determine the best locations for five companies. The objective is to locate firefighting services that will minimize loss of property and life. Different street configurations, varying combinations of commercial and residential property, and other factors contribute to the complexity of the problem and increase the difficulty of its solution. In addition to the tailor-made models, there are some general models that can be adapted to meet the needs of a large variety of location problems.

The simple median model may be the most widely used general model. This technique concentrates on minimizing transportation costs. It considers the movement of standard loads on rectangular paths and ignores diagonal moves. Transportation cost for a load is assumed to be proportional to the distance it is moved, and therefore cost is measured by adding the number of loads times the distance moved.

Figure 17.2 illustrates the formulation of an actual problem. Current facilities exist in Los Angeles, Chicago, and Atlanta. A fourth facility must be built. Table 17.1 provides the necessary data. When the median model is applied to this information, the coordinates selected as the optimal location are $X=900$ and $Y=150$, or a location in the vicinity of Memphis, Tennessee.

A multitude of factors must be considered before making a final recommendation about locations. You must weigh both the individual factors and the inter-relationship of the factors to each other. The lack of one necessity, as we have indicated, may overrule the presence of all the

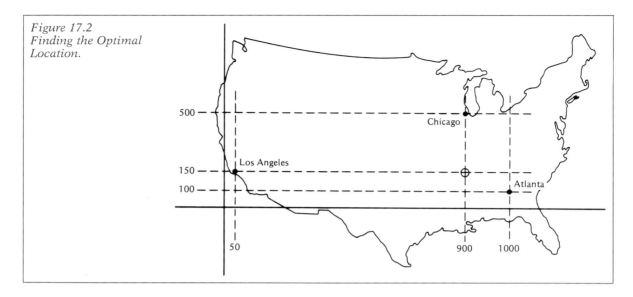

Figure 17.2
Finding the Optimal
Location.

others. A company could gather all the data and feed it into a computer to make the decision without personal evaluative input. However, even though data processing may be used to aid you in your deliberations, the computer cannot read between the lines of the statistics. It cannot "feel" the environment and the community attitudes and willingness. The company assigns a manager to get the facts—but more importantly, to temper those facts with judgment about the place that can offer the best mix of the important factors.

Organizing the Work

Performing the work is far less critical and demanding than designing the best possible layout for the work. The flow of materials and people and work stages must all be simulated to assure that bottlenecks are not going to result in costly losses of time and efficiency.

Time is money, and in one sense the ultimate consumer will be required to pay for every second the product spends in the factory. To keep costs competitive and profit-producing, companies seek to control

Table 17.1
Shipments Between
Current Facilities and
the New Location

Existing Facilities	Annual Number of Standard Loads	Coordinates of Existing Facilities	
		x	*y*
Los Angeles	1000	50	150
Chicago	800	900	500
Atlanta	400	1000	100

every option of time and movement from the beginning of the process until the product is available to the customer. "Time of production" is a term that refers to the time which elapses between the major changes in a product. Production time for one phase of a product's metamorphosis will have to be added to all other production time segments, and all of that added to the standing time to determine the time involved in adding value or new utility to the materials that enter the plant or system.

Layout of Production Processes

As a manager seeks to streamline each rough spot or delay, there are several key terms to remember: continuous process, intermittent process, unidirectional flow, and retractional flow.

Continuous process is the most widely known example of industrial production. This process is used in firms that produce high-volume, standardized products. You have probably seen films of automobile assembly lines with various parts being added as the car moves slowly along. The continuous process line may be set up in a straight line, with raw materials and components and subassemblies coming into the line from all sides and a finished product rolling off the line. Another way of organizing a continuous process is a "U" shape, with raw materials coming in from one loading dock and finished products leaving on the same trucks.

Continuous processes may be laid out in "I" shapes, "S" curves, or even an "O" shape, as when several layers of paint need to be sprayed on and dried and sprayed on and dried before a product has finished its paint cycle. A continuous process does not necessarily run all the time—it should not be confused with a 24-hour operation. Rather, "continuous" applies to the fact that the product moves continuously from one step in its manufacture to the next step in its manufacture. The finished cupcakes go immediately into the icing machine, then to the wrapping machine, and straight through packaging and counting to the loading docks or the warehouse.

Even though the process may be continuous and the product standardized, the products rolling off the end of the line can be different from each other. For example, a car's paint color and accessories may need to be varied. This need to provide variety and choice puts spice into the life of operations and production management. There would be little challenge in cranking out thousands of identical products once the system was set and running. The manager would have nothing to do but run around waking up the workers! The challenge of production management lies in producing many combinations of the product's components without allowing the changes to slow the dynamic operation. An experienced manager of operations feels an instinctive concern when there is lag time or uneven progression toward that exciting moment when it all comes together as a correct, finished product. Though direction of a repetitious operation may appear dull and monotonous to the outside observer, a person with an aptitude for operations management can appreciate many similarities between his job and that of an orchestra conductor. All the components must be present, but unless they are coordinated into exactly the right arrangement, chaos will result. The manager must know every aspect of the production process, just as a conductor must be familiar with each part of a great symphony.

An *intermittent process* is one in which the product moves to a certain state of completion and then hesitates (for a short while or a long time) before moving into the next stage. Hardly any process is *truly* continuous. Even the auto assembly line is in most cases merely assembling parts which have been made at other places and at other times. Usually when we speak of an intermittent process, we are referring to the fact that time lapse is an essential part of the process—as when a bakery mixes the dough and then allows it to rise for a period of time. Another characteristic of the intermittent production process is that all products usually do not follow identical paths through the system. Thus, the bread must be sliced but the rolls are not. In some cases, the immovability of the product dictates that the utility changes must come to the products—as when various subcontractors perform their sequential visits and changes upon a home being built.

Unidirectional flow of the product indicates that everything moves from one end to the other, never retracing any steps. In a *retractional flow*, the product may go around again—as when raw rubber is remixed and recooked in the Banbury mixer several times, adding a different chemical each time, until the finished rubber is ready to be made into tires.

The flow of a product through a factory (or of an idea through an advertising agency) must have logic. It cannot be laid out simply to fill whatever time or space is available, or to involve whatever people might be on hand. Each sequence or activity must have a reason. Designers do not make some factories highrises and spread others over acres from mere architectural preference—the nature of the process must make that determination. If the use of gravity can move bulky or heavy materials along the way at lower cost, then the raw materials ought to start high in the air and drop step-by-step toward the ground. On the other hand, many processes benefit from a single-level plant design.

At every stage, from the time the company sends someone out in search of land through the design and construction of the plant, each thing must be done because it facilitates the optimum production of the final product. Whether the company is winding cables, printing magazines, or canning tuna, the likelihood of success is directly proportionate to the care that is taken in organizing the way to do the work.

However, one final area of concern stands between the well-planned facility and successful production. Unless the actual work is controlled and monitored according to speed and quality, the very best plans can be inefficient and costly. In the next section, we will consider the methods for operating, controlling and maintaining quality and productivity.

Managing the Operations System

The operations manager is responsible for achieving the objectives of the operating system within the constraints set forth by organizational policies. Accomplishing these goals requires a multitude of intermediate and short-range decisions that we normally refer to as operating decisions.

Planning is the first step. This means more than making a few random notations on paper. The front office may request 500 hatchets, but the production manager reads that as "500 handles, 500 ax heads, 500 wedges, 500 labels, 10 gallons of stain, 10 gallons of shellac, and 5 new grinding stones." The production manager also sees a potential problem because he knows the company that usually supplies the ax heads can only turn out about 25 per day. Balancing the needs of the marketing department with the capabilities of the production department over some time period is known as *aggregate production planning*. This procedure is normally for a time horizon of one year. After the aggregate plan is formulated, it must be translated into plans for shorter operating periods.

As soon as the estimates are completed and the order is a firm one, someone must place the orders to the suppliers and request confirmation of the time required to fill those orders. In critical situations, the wise manager also has an alternative plan for securing the necessary quantities of each component if the primary supplier runs into difficulty.

Material requirements planning, a recent innovation in complex manufacturing environments, is an attempt to computerize this task and integrate it with the other functions of the production process. Invoices for components or raw materials are dispatched, and the times of expected delivery are logged into plans for routing the project through the plant.

The routing plan is the road map for the paths the job will take through the operation. In routing the job, the manager establishes the sequence in which events ought to happen and the flow by which all workers can do their part most productively. A home builder might save money by hiring a roofer when work is short in January. These savings will be shortlived unless the walls are up by the end of December. Good routers draw—they try not to ever leave the routing explanation to the spoken word or to a vague understanding in the back of the mind. In explaining a routing plan, nothing beats a diagram because it can show exactly where the orders must go.

Charting Progress

Scheduling is the minute-to-minute charting of the various phases of the project through the required preparations and assemblies. Ideally, the planner would like to see each worker at each station working steadily all the time until the finished job rolls off the line. Of course, there are going to be times when one part of a job takes so long that it will hold up the other phases that must follow it. The planner knows that a worker with nothing to do (even for a few minutes) is adding to the cost of the product and subtracting from the good feelings of the workers who are not getting the same break. Managers can often take advantage of the fact that multiple jobs are moving through the plant at the same time. If the hatchet handles are finished early, the lathe operator can be setting up for the billy club order for the local police department.

A Gantt chart, like the one in Figure 17.3, is a graph that makes a pictorial representation of the work schedules of each worker and discloses overlaps which might not occur to the manager without the chart. Henry L. Gantt introduced the method shortly after the turn of the century. Today, it has been adapted and applied in so many forms that it seems like a commonsense approach to anyone trying to coordinate several inter-related activities. A Gantt chart depicts the sequence in which things need to happen and the time each task is expected to take. More importantly, it allows the timesaving overlapping of activities that do not conflict.

In many situations jobs compete for time on production facilities with limited capacity. Significant differences in the time required to process the jobs can result from the order in which they are done. Table 17.2 reveals the times required to flow chart and program five computer-programming projects. An uninformed manager may decide to complete these tasks in the order that they are listed—A, B, C, D, E. This, in fact, yields an extremely poor schedule. Using Johnson's algorithm, a simple mathematical scheduling technique, the optimal schedule—E, A, D, C, B—is easily found, and substantial improvements in system performance are realized. The make time, the time required to complete all five projects, is reduced from 44 to 32 hours while reductions in both idle time and waiting time are also achieved.

Dispatching orders to the various involved activity centers is one of the chief responsibilities of the operations or production manager. The supply centers need enough warning to make sure that the proper amounts of materials are ready for the start-up moment. The workers who will do the work need a comfortable amount of advance notice but not enough so that they begin to feel swamped. The city editor of a

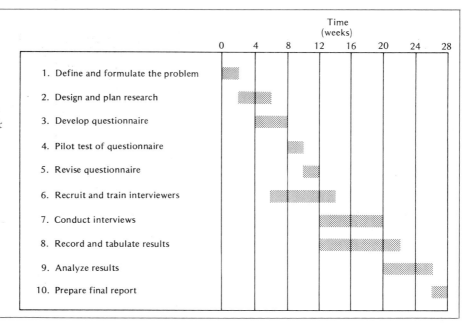

Figure 17.3
Gantt Chart for Research Papers. [Reprinted with permission of the publisher from Robert G. Murdick, Business Research (Scranton, Pa.: International Textbook Company, 1969), p. 118.]

Time (weeks)

0   4   8   12   16   20   24   28

1. Define and formulate the problem
2. Design and plan research
3. Develop questionnaire
4. Pilot test of questionnaire
5. Revise questionnaire
6. Recruit and train interviewers
7. Conduct interviews
8. Record and tabulate results
9. Analyze results
10. Prepare final report

newspaper knows how to help the reporters maintain a productive pace by giving out assignments in a steady flow. Dispatching is far more than posting schedules or giving advance warning. It involves the human relations skills of knowing the workers and their individual motivations.

Once the manager has the entire operation on papaer, has arranged all the materials, and has seen the people going to work, he or she might sit back and relax—and then watch the whole plan fall apart. Follow-up and control are among the final steps in working the plan. They are essential as any of the other steps that precede the beginning of the work.

Production control is never accomplished by snooping and watching the work over the shoulders of the doers. That *will* achieve a result, but it will not be production control! The wise manager establishes, *along with other prior plans*, the milestones that must be reached all the way through the project to make the final goal. No thoughtful manager would be willing to wait until the final days of the project to see how things are moving toward the projected finish. Intermediate goals will

Table 17.2
Task Times in Hours

Project	Flow Chart
A	4
B	4
C	15
D	6
E	2

be set up and clearly communicated to the workers in order that meeting and adjusting all the intermediate goals will add up to the meeting of the overall goal . . . on schedule.

Maintaining Quality

The term *quality control* is a famililar one to all of us, perhaps because of corporate image-building through advertising. It makes an impressive visual to see the company's professional chemist working away in a laboratory to assure that each and every product rolling off the company line is of the highest quality.

The truth may lie in many other degrees of quality control. Few companies, for example, have a product that costs enough so that "each and every one" of them can be inspected thoroughly. Some products could hardly be usable after they are inspected—for instance, firecrackers. And there is some question as to whether the utmost quality level is a realistic aspiration for any company. There is such a thing as goldplating a product unnecessarily and making things better than the market is willing to pay for.

Sampling is the method most often used to provide relative assurance that things are coming off the lines the way they are supposed to. At the distillery, for instance, workers could drink every tenth bottle they produce—or a more dependable laboratory system could be set up to do precise chemical analysis, with less falling into the vats on the afternoon shift. Sampling does not guarantee that the entire production run is perfect. However, if the samples are selected properly, the manager can state with a predetermined level of confidence that the percentage of defective items is above or below an acceptable level.

The type of process often dictates the method of sampling employed in production. Many continuous processes, like the production of wire cable, cannot be stopped while a piece of cable is removed and tested. Non-destructive testing methods that use X-Ray technology are frequently used in these situations. Quality control in the service environment is a difficult task because of the inconsistencies that can result in delivering a service. The quality of health care services may be highly dependent on whether the nurse has had a good day or not. In all phases of quality control, the manager must be aware of operating system characteristics that influence the level of quality. Some companies have discovered that the testing of production can actually be done while the system is functioning by the production workers themselves.

The correct term for this procedure is *process control*. It is an attempt to prevent completion of the entire production process before discovering that a mistake was made in the first step. If the control standards can be clearly and simply explained to workers, the costs and involvements of a large quality control staff can be cut considerably. One way this can be accomplished is through the process control chart. (See Figure 17.4) Measurements of product attributes plotted sequentially over time reveal the underlying behavior of the operation.

However, the system should never be completely turned over to those who can benefit by *not* admitting mistakes. In other words, the machinist who is paid on a piece-work basis is hardly likely to slow down or stop voluntarily as long as his specifications will allow him to keep churning out pieces.

In most cases, companies are not testing products for the benefit of the pieces already made, but for the ones yet to be made. There is a need to continuously monitor the raw materials being received from other suppliers. There is a need to spot the results of shortcutting by some workers in the process. And there is a need to keep top management decision makers informed of defects and weak spots in the product that cannot be corrected in the factory itself.

When an individual craftsman makes something, the product is repeatedly held up to the light for inspection. The craftsman monitors the intermediate results throughout the process, comparing the status with the specifications. But when many semiskilled or even unskilled workers are coordinated to do tiny parts of the craftsman's job, the continuing interest in inspection must be built into the system. Quality control is, in fact, one of the areas where job planners have some options about raising employee interest and participation levels in the midst of what could otherwise be dull, repetitive work.

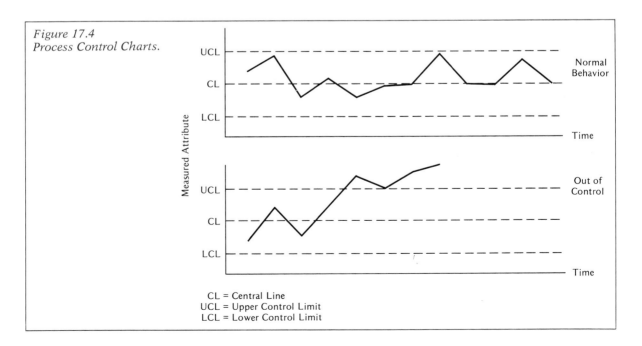

Figure 17.4
Process Control Charts.

CL = Central Line
UCL = Upper Control Limit
LCL = Lower Control Limit

Holding the Line—Organization and Administration

To a child watching the action in any work setting, the lower level employees are really working. Superiors and managers just appear to be standing around watching. But anyone who has ever had to pay the bill for any type of complicated production knows that the comparatively higher salary paid to a firstclass supervisor is an important investment. The annals of military history demonstrate repeatedly that the largest army is not necessarily the winner. The skill with which the soldiers are brought together with a sound strategy and appropriate weapons is very important. A production facility (indeed and type of situation in which many people must work together to accomplish some goal) can never be stronger or more productive than its leadership. The operations manager who may appear to stand and watch is the organizing force. This perspective and overview of the entire operation is the reason there is anything constructive happening.

The operations manager's work often takes place when he is not visible. Before the line workers are even hired, the production planner is conceptualizing . . . analyzing . . . digesting the job and all its parts. He or she may be drawing and redrawing charts and graphs with lots of little arrows that seem meaningless to the uninvolved. The challenge is to be sure that there will not be even one tiny detail to flaw the entire plan. In many cases the worker who enjoys managing production or operations is only incidentally interested in the product itself. The manager's thrill is in a plan that works without any hitches and allows him to reach the objective on time.

There are several basic activities involved in the successful completion of any organized effort. There must be planning, organizing, staffing, directing, and controlling—yes, the five basic functions of management apply to the operations system in the same manner that they apply to the entire organization. Sometimes the steps may happen simultaneously or out of the stated order, but they must all be present if the final product is to be exactly as it was planned. Furthermore, they must fit with some degree of precision within the larger framework of the organization. How can the operations manager obtain new equipment, build new plants, or buy inventory without the assistance of finance? How can he determine what an acceptable level of quality is without consumer preference information obtained by the marketing department? All of the parts must function as a whole. Unfortunately, they exist in a state of tension because their performance is judged by different criteria. The production manager is minimizing cost while the marketing executive attempts to maximize sales. Basic conflicts are inherent in these two goals. This does not preclude cooperation, however, but necessitates coordination through effective strategic and tactical planning and by enlightened management at the senior executive level.

Good management of the operations function does not imply that managers at this level are infallible, or that their planning must be 100 per cent accurate or the entire effort will go down the drain. Just the opposite is true. The manager can hardly have experience in all the things that may be assigned. It stands to reason that the "educated guess" and the strategic rerouting of effort are important skills of the manager. A good production manager knows the skills and weaknesses of workers. He or she knows the limitations of the machinery and the work site. Past experiences have prepared him to scan a proposed task with an eye that is sensitive to trouble spots, hangups, and dangerous assumptions. The reason the company is willing to pay more for a skilled supervisor is his or her ability to mix textbook formulas of production with common sense understanding of the real situation, and to deliver a product of a specified quality on time.

Productivity and the Future of Operations Management

Our society has undergone significant changes over the past quarter century. The unprecedented shift from a society oriented to the production of goods to one that is now predominated by the production of services has had effects that some believe will be more important than any social movement during this time period. This economic revolution has indeed been dramatic. Approximately 75% of the work force is now employed in the service sector. Without a doubt, this shift has changed the course of operation management. Traditional concepts and techniques have found application in new industries, and these industries have served as laboratories for the development of improved techniques and the extension of operational concepts. The digital computer has also opened new horizons to the operations manager. It relieved tremendous clerical burdens in the production planning and control process, and also provided managers with more timely information about the things they were doing. Finally, computerization has facilitated the use of sophisticated mathematical and statistical techniques to assist in providing answers to operations problems.

Today we are faced with new challenges—scarcity of resources, inflation, rising energy costs, declining productivity, and sharp competition from foreign firms. The need to find a better way is more critical than ever before. As a result, operations management is receiving increasing attention from all fronts. Operations can't make an organization grow. That is the role of research and development specialists who develop new products and marketing people who sell them. But the profitability of an organization lies mainly on the shoulders of the operations function.

To achieve the firm's profit goal, the operations manager must concentrate on increasing productivity—that is, output must be increased. Experts agree that this solution is by far the most promising answer to our many economic problems. It's an exciting challenge that will require the skillful use of management principles, scientific techniques, and a basic understanding of human behavior in a rapidly changing environment. The problem will be great—the rewards will be greater.

Summary

Managers of production and operations reap two kinds of benefits: immediate ones for themselves in the form of bonuses and promotions, and more general ones for the consumer by lowering prices, improving products, and generally finding a better way to maintain and improve our standard living. Central to the arena of production/operations management is volume or mass production. This factor multiplies the rewards from even the smallest improvement in production by massive numbers, and it economically justifies the effort expended in developing the most precise method.

The expertise of the manager should not be limited to the realm of conveyor belts and machines. Any operation can benefit by a systematic and determined approach to refining its basic jobs.

Businesses prosper when they are able to produce utility or add value to a product at a price that the customers are willing to pay. A process may add utility of place, of ownership, or of time. The manufacturing world is usually involved in form utility—producing value by changing the form of one thing into a more desired form. This may be accomplished by analysis, synthesis, fabrication, or assembly.

All successes of production and operations are planned. There are some successes whose planning is not formalized or evident, but even these were formulated, weighed, and revised in the mind of the founder and initial moving force in the operation. Each aspect of producing the product—from selection of a plant location to the clean-up operation after the process—can be significant in getting every penny out of the operations dollar.

Production/operations problems can be classified into two major categories: design and operating problems. Design problems involve locating facilities, organizing work, and layout. Planning, scheduling, and quality control are operating problems. Both design and operating problems occur in all production processes. The production processes can be identified by the type of product flow in the system. There are continuous processes, intermittent processes, unidirectional flow, and retractional flow.

The basic activities that must be involved in the successful completion of any organized effort are planning, organizing, staffing, directing, and controlling. The assurance of continuing success must be built into the system itself, both through formal steps of production planning and control, and through leadership in the development of worker attitudes and motivations. The operations manager is more than the person who runs the factory or the office—he is the person who makes the product.

Review Questions

1. Distinguish between the management of production and the management of operations.
2. Identify the major types of "utility" created by managers.
3. Identify the major processes used in the production process to add "form utility."
4. Using the principles of site selection identified in this chapter, evaluate two cities as a possible location for a large petroleum refinery and a medium-sized clothing manufacturer.
5. Identify the difference between "continuous process" manufacturing and "intermittent process."
6. Why is sampling used in the quality control process? What are its limitations?

18

The Modern Manager's Quantitative Tool Kit

"Yes, sir, Mr. Quigley. We're never satisfied until our customer is satisfied. Now what seems to be the problem?"

"It's this saw I bought in your hardware department. It's not half as good as the guy said it was gonna be."

"Not half as good?"

"Right. The salesman told me that with this saw I ought to be able to cut two cords of firewood in half a day. But no matter how hard I work, or how much I sweat, I can't finish more than a half a cord in a day."

"Hmmm, that certainly sounds like a major difference. Let's take a look at the saw."

"Okay. I've got it right here in this case."

"Oh, yes, That's our new Triple-X Deluxe Chain Saw. It's the finest chain saw we have ever had for sale. I can't imagine that you would have any trouble polishing off two cords in a day. Let's start up the motor and see how it runs."

"The motor?"

A person who doesn't know how to use a tool properly might as well not have the tool. Many times the manager may hear others talking about using certain new techniques to make the work move faster or more efficiently. If the manager succumbs to the natural human tendency to want what others have, he may find the new tool to be more of a curse than a blessing.

It seems such a simple thing to say that tools should be chosen to fit the task at hand. And yet over and over business people will saddle their organizations and departments with mandates to use some new and stylish system or technique. The careful manager gives every new tool attention to be sure that its functions are generally understood. When a new task arises, the wise manager studies the problem and proceeds to devise mentally the ideal system or method for its accomplishment. That ideal can then be altered if there is an already existing tool that will do the job as well.

The creative opportunities and excitements that lurk in every management position await the minds that enjoy the chance to find a new way—a labor-saving tool—for getting the job done. It is a thrill that far surpasses the bonus check or higher company profits. Creativity is its own reward.

There are many new tools for the manager to use. There are systems, models, theories, and charts that may assist the manager in accomplishing the assigned task. Just as there is no need for every carpenter to re-invent the hammer, so the manager of a peanut butter factory in Georgia may well be able to benefit from the discovery of an engineer in New Jersey. A tool is a tool, and if it fits the job, it is a discovery of great value.

On the other hand, it would be unthinkable for a carpenter to use his hammer for every task that confronts him. That could make a terrible mess of the concreting and painting! The same principle applies when any tool is applied because it is new, or because it has received high acclaim in the most recent issue of the *Manager's Monthly*.

In this chapter, brief introductions will be given to several tools of management. Some of them have been in use for many years and have gone through revisions and refinements. They have stood the test of time and are widely recognized as valuable assets to managers. Others we will discuss are newer innovations that have been highly acclaimed in more recent years. Regardless of when the tools were developed, there are always two great dangers in their selection: having the wrong tool and trying to make it work anyway, or having the right tool but not knowing how to use it.

As you read this chapter, think of it as a leisurely stroll through the hardware department of your local store. On such a stroll, you can hardly purchase one of each thing that you see. And however much you may admire the craftsmanship of a tool or the way it would obviously save time and effort, you would be foolish to buy tools for jobs that you never do. Rather, you can enjoy browsing through the tool section for the purpose of familiarizing yourself with things that are there, to make mental notes of the functions and costs of the available tools so that you can come back when the need arises.

The management tools described here have one common denominator—they use numbers to represent the situation under study. The process of abstracting real situations by the use of quantitative formulas is called *modeling*. We use this process for several reasons. It is precise and concise. It also allows us to simulate real situations and determine the actions and interactions that result from changes in pertinent variables without suffering the consequences of actual outcomes. The difficult task is to find the best representation, or model, of a real world problem. Models need to be tested and refined, and their assumptions need to be understood. Frequently, selection and refinement of the model is the most time consuming and the most critical step in the use of management tools.

We will not give an in-depth treatment of this subject. The purpose will be to introduce . . . to scan . . . to browse . . . rather than to provide a sales pitch for every tool on the shelf. Make your notes. Be aware of what is available. But remember to keep your approach to each problem open. Let your familiarity with these tools be fuel for your own imaginative approach to any problem, rather than automatic, quick fixes.

Shelves in the Tool Department

Tools are most often placed on the shelves of the hardware store according to the things they do. Things that drill are grouped together. Things that dig are in another place. And things that cut are somewhere else. In this chapter we will group the management tools according to what they accomplish. Tools will be introduced from the shelves of budgeting, scheduling, network analysis, logistics, allocating resources, probability determination and decision making. The categories are arbitrary —merely a way to organize the department.

You will soon become aware that each tool represents a basic principle which can be applied in many other arrangements. A single tool, for example, may be equally important to the tasks of planning or control or decision making—or all these areas at the same time. Likewise, a tool can be used in any functional area of the business. We will discuss linear programming later in the chapter. One of the most widely applied tools among the ones presented here, linear programming, is used in finance for portfolio selection, in marketing for advertising strategy

The Pink Panther Strikes Again (United Artists, 1976). Choosing the right tool is essential for job success.

development, in accounting for manpower planning, and in operating for scheduling. Managers who develop the ability to recognize characteristics in real life situations that make them appropriate places to apply quantitative tools have a distinct advantage over their peers and competitors.

Deterministic Models

One other classification of the tools we will examine is their division into models dealing with certainty and those involving situations of uncertainty. The four models discussed in this section are deterministic models because they represent situations characterized by certainty. For example, if the sales price of a pencil is 10¢ and we know the incremental cost to produce one additional pencil is 5¢, it is certain that a 5¢ contribution will be realized from the sale of that pencil. Hence, the exact number of pencils that need to be sold for $10,000 profit can be calculated. Another deterministic situation occurs when a production manager is trying to decide what products to produce. If two products that use the same limited resources are produced, tables and desks for instance, how many of each are made? The exact amount of each resource required to produce the products is known and the cost of these items is also available. Sales price is also certain. Naturally, one would seek the combination of tables and desks that results in the greatest profit.

It may seem that making decisions under conditions of certainty should be relatively easy. Unfortunately, this is quite rare. Usually, the number of possible solutions is so great that a complete examination of all outcomes is impossible even with a computer. As a result, we must turn to computational procedures that efficiently search for the best solution. The budgeting, scheduling, network analysis, and logistic models are four such procedures.

Budgetary Models

The *variable budget* or *foundation budget* is a tool that may be quite helpful in meeting the problem of inflexibility of budgeting. Few people relish the tasks that must be accomplished when a budget is in preparation. Simply stated, budget preparation asks us to tell the future—to predict accurately the cost of something that has not yet been bought. The reason we have budgets is to eliminate undesirable flexibility from the organization's planning. Whether we are budgeting time, money, people hours, or materials, the ultimate purpose is to avoid surprises. The problem is that, in its rush to absolutism, the budget drives a lot of us crazy because we have to be absolute about things that by their very nature are unpredictable. The variable budget establishes a bottom line of costs which will not change, and that bottom line moves horizontally across the budget picture. If the year is a good one or a bad one, the fixed costs remain the same. But the parts of the budget that change as production increases are more appropriately represented on a line that rises or falls in a constant relationship to the number of units produced —as seen in Figure 18.1.

A good illustration of the variable budgeting application is provided by Muggsy Malone, the enterprising young newspaper boy who peddles his papers on the 5:30 commuter train every workday. Muggsy knows that the more papers he sells, the higher his paper cost, and the higher the profits. He really has no other expenses in selling except the $1.50 he must pay for his ticket on the train. His variable budget might look like Figure 18.1B.

However, if Muggsy could get a price reduction when he bought more papers—and continue to sell the papers at the same price—his variable budget might look like Figure 18.1C.

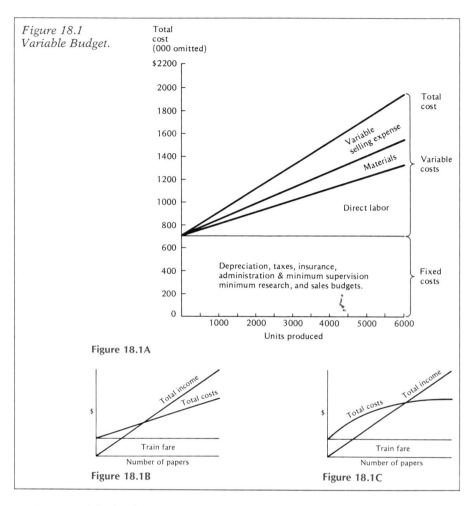

Figure 18.1
Variable Budget.

Figure 18.1A

Figure 18.1B

Figure 18.1C

The variable budget approach facilitates the adjustment of budget amounts on a percentage basis above an established and dependable minimum operational base. Costs that can vary because of changes in environmental conditions, corrective actions, or unforeseen expenses can be absorbed without throwing out the entire budget. The most pleasant aspect of the variable budget is its ability to move without hesitation to provide more materials, more labor, more advertising, as more of the company's product is demanded in the marketplace.

A break-even analysis follows naturally from this type of budgeting model. To the natural-born business person it seems obvious, but it may seem puzzling to others. As the entrepreneur considers a potential project, it is natural for both mind and pencil to be busy, combining all the possible variables that will have a bearing on the eventual profit or loss of the venture. The analysis may be formal or intuitive, but it should be present lest the project produce a lot of hard work and no profits. A break-even search could have greatly benefited the company that foolishly did not know each unit was produced at a small loss and increased sales in an effort to turn the loss into profits through higher volume.

As introduced in Chapter 7, the break-even chart presents all the influential elements of a product's financial life. Any one of the elements may be increased or decreased and its impact on the entire process and on the outcome measured. The five basic elements in a break-even analysis are revenues, costs, contribution margin, profit equation, and break-even point.

Revenues are the monies taken in from the sale of the product to the customers. The more units sold—the higher the revenues. Unless a price break is passed on to the customer who buys in bulk, the revenue line will always move in a linear fashion from the origin across the break-even chart, as in Figure 18.2.

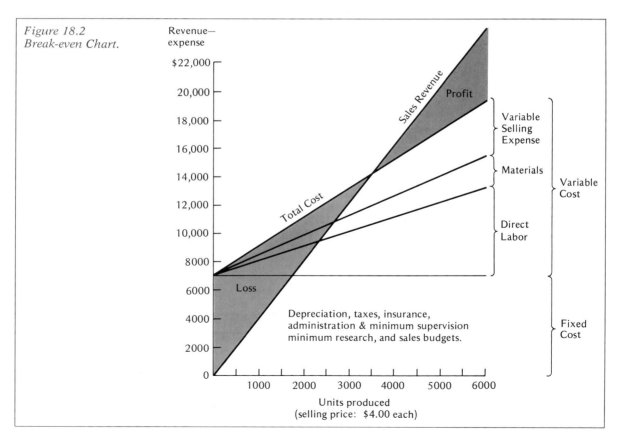

*Figure 18.2
Break-even Chart.*

Revenue—expense

Sales Revenue

Profit

Total Cost

Variable Selling Expense

Materials

Direct Labor

Variable Cost

Loss

Depreciation, taxes, insurance, administration & minimum supervision minimum research, and sales budgets.

Fixed Cost

$22,000
20,000
18,000
16,000
14,000
12,000
10,000
8000
6000
4000
2000
0

1000 2000 3000 4000 5000 6000

Units produced
(selling price: $4.00 each)

Costs are the total amounts the business has to pay out in order to get the product units to a stage the customer considers worth the selling price. As mentioned earlier, every manufacturing system has certain fixed costs, which remain the same up to a given level of activity (as with insurance, interest, and management salaries). There are also variable costs which increase according to the number of units to be produced (as with packaging, delivery, and commissions. Figure 18.2 divides the variable cost into three major components—direct labor, materials, and variable selling expenses.

Because fixed costs are constant, they appear as a horizontal line a given distance from the bottom of the break-even chart, as in Figure 18.2. The variable costs, on the other hand, change every time the production level changes and can be found in a line that rises or falls on the break-even chart with some direct relationship to the number of units produced.

The contribution to margin is the amount of each purchase price that goes toward "retiring" the fixed costs. Or, if the fixed costs have been paid, the contribution margin represents profit. It is the amount left when we subtract the variable cost from the sale price. If an item sells for $10 and the variable cost per unit is $6, then the difference of $4 is a contribution toward the fixed costs. The break-even point is actually determined by calculating how many $4 contributions must be generated to cover the fixed expenses. The appropriate formula is

$$\text{B.E.P.} = \frac{\text{TFC}}{\text{SP/unit} - \text{VC/unit}}$$

where

$$
\begin{aligned}
\text{BEP} &= \text{Break-even point} \\
\text{TFC} &= \text{Total fixed cost} \\
\text{SP/unit} &= \text{Selling price per unit} \\
\text{VC/unit} &= \text{Variable cost per unit} \\
(\text{SP/unit} - \text{VC/unit}) &= \text{Contribution per unit}
\end{aligned}
$$

If the fixed costs are $10,000, then the break-even point is

$$
\begin{aligned}
\text{BEP} &= \frac{\$10,000}{\$10/\text{unit} - \$6/\text{unit}} \\
&= \frac{\$10,000}{\$4/\text{unit}} \\
&= 2500 \text{ units}
\end{aligned}
$$

Thus, 2,500 units, each generating $4 above the direct cost incurred for their production, must be sold to pay the $10,000 fixed cost and break even. Past this level of activity, 2,500 units, the $4 from each unit is added to profit. This is represented on the break-even chart by the ever-widening space between the total revenue line and the total cost line.

To calculate the amount of profit from a forecasted level of sales, we can use the profit equation. It is a formula that reduces to the simplest possible terms the relationship fluctuation between costs, sales and profits. The profit equation may be simplified to, "Your profits are the total amount of money you receive from sales, less what it costs you to make your products and sell them."

$$P = TR - (TVC + TFC)$$

where

$$P = \text{PROFIT}$$
$$TR = \text{TOTAL REVENUE}$$
$$TVC = \text{TOTAL VARIABLE COST}$$
$$TFC = \text{TOTAL FIXED COST}$$
$$(TVC + TFC) = \text{TOTAL COST}$$

The significance of discovering the break-even point, and break-even analysis in general, is not to land on it when the venture is finished. Of course no business person seeks to break even and quit. Break-even analysis functions as a control device through its emphasis on the marginal concept. This analysis provides assistance in the go no-go decision as to whether the risk is too great, the price too high, or the margin too small, and also tends to graphically represent the fact that productivity controls profits. Even those who do not understand all factors of the chart can easily see that in the situation depicted above, the more we are able to make and sell the more we profit.

Another important lesson to be learned from break-even analysis is the relationship between fixed and variable costs. Since fixed costs do not change over large volumes of production, the manager is unable to exercise control over them in the short run. To have any positive effects on profits in the short run, efforts must be directed to reducing variable costs or increasing the selling price. Generally, most managers exercise greater control within the firm and probably would be more successful by concentrating on cost reduction. Chapter 17 discussed the attempts by operations managers to "find a better way." This fundamental relationship between fixed and variable costs reveals the areas in which improvements should be made.

A fundamental principle of supervision also arises from this knowledge. In the short run, managers should be judged on the level of variable cost that falls within their area and not on the level of fixed cost. Why? Because they cannot exercise control over fixed cost. It seems to be a very simple principle, but many firms still evaluate their manager's performance on the basis of both fixed and variable cost. This situation is equivalent to saying, "If it rains next Monday, everyone in the class will make an A. If it does not, everyone fails." Would you like this proposition? Probably not, because you can't control the weather and it has absolutely no relationship to your knowledge of management. Likewise, judging managers on the basis of fixed cost is equally illogical.

Zero-base budgeting is a new technique for controlling discretionary costs more effectively. It was developed in 1970 by Texas Instruments, Inc., and rapidly spread to other companies and many governments. The ZBB advantage is that each expenditure must be rejustified every time the budget is made, rather than simply being carried forward at "last year's" level regardless of productivity or changes in the environment.

ZBB integrates planning with the budgeting process and causes each manager at each level to justify his entire budget request in detail. The heart of the system is the "decision packet," a packet of information about each budgetary alternative. The manager gives a description of the kind of activity that can be expected at a minimum level. In another decision package, the manager describes the same task and shows how much more productivity can be expected if the item receives more than minimum funds. Several levels of funding are given for each item on the budget. These decision packages move up to the next higher manager, who begins the job of picking the ones that will meet his or her own priorities. If he wants to see more emphasis on a certain activity, he will choose the highest proposed funding level for that activity. If he runs out of money before he runs out of decision packets, some tasks have to be eliminated or cut back. Once the manager has arranged the packets as he prefers, they move up the ladder to his own boss, who must compare them with the packets from all other departments below him.

At every level, ZBB forces managers to put expenditures in some priority order, rather than seeking to "build empires" by continuously adding appropriations and never cutting any. It is not an infallible system, but in organizations that tend to be bureaucratic and slow moving, it will force the dropping of useless and nonproductive offices and personnel. Managers are forced to decide (1) which operations are most important in reaching the goals and objectives of their responsibility and (2) how much can be spent for each area without jeopardizing the task as a whole.

Scheduling Tools

It is difficult for us to imagine a society without time charts and schedules and directions. Today, if you visit a hospital, the receptionist directs you to the wing you want by telling you to follow lines and arrows of varying colors that are part of the flooring. When you go to the bank, you notice all customers wait in one line rather than forming a line at each window. The schedules and time tables that are handed out routinely in today's schools and businesses would have baffled the average citizen a hundred years ago. This state of affairs does not mean that our generation is smarter, but that simplified forms of industrial and managerial scheduling tools have become commonplace.

Ideally, the manager would like to see all workers working in steady, consistent paces toward the unified accomplishment of goals. The worker who is idle rings a warning bell in the mind of the manager—time is a-wasting, and time is money. Equally important is the smooth flow of work through the system. If customers trying to pay their bill at a restaurant must wait in a long line, ill will is generated and future business may be lost.

Efficient, gapless planning of the future performance of any task is always based on memory of the past performance of the same task (or of the component tasks). Initially a plan is dependent on someone's estimates of the amount of work to do, the amount of time required to accomplish each phase, as well as transport between the phases. But ultimately the plan must have built into it the ability to adapt, to allow for experience, delays, and windfalls. The schedule is to help in the successful completion of a task—not hinder.

The *Gantt Chart* was one of the first successful attempts at graphically portraying the work flow and the interrelationships of the components of a total job. Henry L. Gantt was a consultant to business in the early 1900's. He came up with a bar-graph approach that made the time relationships of jobs easy to understand and adjust.

There are several types of Gantt charts for different purposes. One of the most familiar Gantt charts is used to clarify the time lines during which each of the workers is involved in a certain project. This type of chart allows both the manager and the workers themselves to communicate with clarity about the amount of time allowed for each phase of the total job, as well as the time savings that may be made in sequencing and transfer from one task to the next.

In a Gantt chart, seen in Figure 18.3, several types of information are depicted on the same chart. The information is related to the same job, but not sequentially. However, the simple process of displaying all pertinent information on the same scale and chart can often be very revealing and helpful in finding points of overlapping and duplication.

The horizontal broken lines in Figure 18.3 depict work that has been scheduled for each department. The short, vertical broken lines stand for work that has not been completed or for work carried over from a previous chart. The wider solid lines are continuous, unbroken representations of the work to be performed. (These solid lines are the same length as the total length of the horizontal broken lines all pushed to-

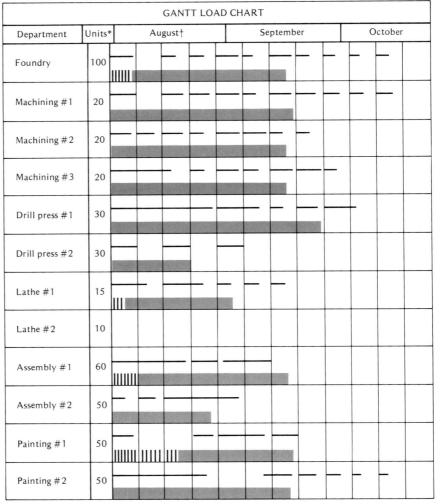

Figure 18.3
Gantt Chart for a
Manufacturing Firm.

Department	Units*	August†		September		October
Foundry	100					
Machining #1	20					
Machining #2	20					
Machining #3	20					
Drill press #1	30					
Drill press #2	30					
Lathe #1	15					
Lathe #2	10					
Assembly #1	60					
Assembly #2	50					
Painting #1	50					
Painting #2	50					

GANTT LOAD CHART

*Weekly capacity in units.
†Each block represents one work week beginning with Monday and ending with Friday.

gether, and are for the purpose of comparing total work time for each department).

The advantages of graphic representation of the work flow on a Gantt chart are numerous:

1. It is possible to schedule accurate completion times for each job.
2. Vacant time periods show up where new work can be scheduled in.
3. Utilization of the facilities can be evaluated at a glance.
4. Total hours of work in the department can be easily calculated.
5. Maintenance and machinery overhaul can be better scheduled.
6. Performance can be compared to this plan for control purposes.
7. Realistic standards of worker output can be established.

8. Bonus compensation systems can be worked out.
9. All activities can be scheduled cooperatively.

Process charts are used in many types of operations. The age-old truth is that one picture is worth a thousand words. If we can see the thing happening in miniature on one sheet of paper, we are able to take a truly productive look at the process from beginning to end, without being distracted by observing the far flung parts of the total operation. A process chart utilizes various simple symbols to represent movement and flow of a product through a process (Figure 18.4).

The decisions about which symbols ought to go in which position are probably the most valuable part of using a process chart. Many a manager has sat down to draw up a process chart of his operation, only to be forced to admit that a step he had been seeing as "activity" was really a "delay." The summary flow chart for a small aspirin manufacturer shown in Figure 18.5 illustrates how these symbols can be used for production planning.

Frank and Lillian Gilbreth were the originators and popularizers of process charting. Of course, charts and picture explanations of processes have been in use since humanity's earliest efforts, but the Gilbreths were able to bring some standardization to the symbols and flow patterns. They also happened to be doing their work at the right time—just after the turn of the century, when American business was eagerly searching for a way to chart the results of the American rush toward total productivity.

When we discuss management tools like process charts, many times we only are able to visualize applications in an industrial setting. This idea is certainly a misconception. Many management tools require a minimum level of mathematical skill; however, others like process charting require none and can be applied in the simplest of environ-

Figure 18.4 Symbols for Process Charts.	SYMBOLS	NAME	DEFINITION
	●	Operations	When something is done to a part of a product in a location in which there may be labor expenditures or other costs.
	➡	Transportation	Change in location from one work place to another.
	◗	Delay or Waiting	A temporary storage situation in the progress of the work.
	▲	Storage	A controlled and planned delay in the overall process of the work in which removal must be authorized.
	■	Inspection	Verification or checking by comparing the product with a quality and/or quantity standard.
	○	Combined Activity	Activities are performed concurrently by the same operator at the same work station.

Operation __Mix asprin materials__

Product __Pronto asprin (325)__

Depts. __Mixing__

Drawing No. __-__ Part No. __42200__

Quantity __1500 pounds of mixed__ __materials for Pronto 325 aspirin__

Present __X__ Proposed _____

Sheet __1__ of __1__ Sheets

Charted By __B. Brown__

Date __3-16__

Approved By __M. Sharp__

Date __3-17__

Summary	
Operation	5
Transport	5
Inspect	1
Delay	1
Store	2
Vertical Distance	–
Horizontal Distance	212
Time (Hours)	1,041

No.	Dist. Moved (Feet)	Worker Time (Hours)	Symbols	Description
1	15	0.200		Unload packages of material from truck to dock and place on pallet.
2	42	0.033		Truck packages of material to storage area.
3				Store materials until needed.
4	25	0.025		Move packages to charge chute.
5		0.330		Unpackage materials and pour into charge chute.
6	20	0.030		Transport charge to mixer.
7		0.100		Charge mixer and begin mixing cycle.
8		0.083		Wait until mixer completes cycle.
9		0.017		Dump mixer charge into receiving vehicle
10		0.020		Inspect materials for proper mixing.
11	50	0.033		Transport vehicle to weighing and packaging station.
12		0.167		Operate machine to weigh and package 1500 pounds of mixed materials.
13	60	0.033		Transport materials to dock.
14				Store materials until truck arrives.

ments by the unsophisticated user with very little expense. For example, you turn in a schedule request form each term when you register for classes. You would like to know as soon as possible if your schedule is approved or if it has been changed. Process charting could be used to study the activities that take place during the registration process. You would examine the process to see if there were any unnecessary delays, if any activities did not serve a useful purpose and could be eliminated, or if some operations could be combined and done by one person. Opportunities for significant improvement may be identified by this analysis.

Network Analysis

Frequently in today's world we find groups of people calling themselves an organization who are anything but organized. It is equally popular to display charts that appear to analyze the totality of everything that happens in the organization. But with only a slightly closer look, we can see that the chart is a representation of an ideal and overlooks many pivotal details.

Network analysis is an approach to planning that recognizes small milestones and potential sidetracks in order to get absolutely specific about reaching a goal. Such attention to each speck of trivia was never possible before the computer. Even when human judgment and productivity are the best that can be hoped for, the manager often has to develop a large and necessary tolerance for sloth and miscellany. The computer has helped us do better. The computer now asks questions we used to overlook and helps us to answer some queries that we would never previously have been asked.

Although the computer has forced this new attention to detail, we do not have to be involved in a computer-assisted operation for the principle of network analysis to benefit us. Actually, the best managers in any century have been those who gave attention to detail and made sure that loose ends and unforeseen delays did not stop their progress.

Yesterday's complicated organization seems like a child's toy next to the complex networks of tasks involved with putting a man on the moon or speeding a brand-new product to a grocery shelf. Any practice can be represented on a network and be done the better for it. Network analysis forces the planner to establish four things that every successful task must be certain about:

1. A clearly recognizable end point or objective.
2. A list of separate, clearly defined, interrelated events.
3. The time required to complete each activity.
4. A starting point.

As you may recognize, network analysis is a refinement of the Gantt chart. It has many of the same characteristics such as the division of a job into separate tasks, estimates of times required, milestones, and a graphical representation of the task schedules. Network analysis goes one step further by showing the relationships between the individual tasks required to complete the job.

PERT/CPM are two of the most commonly used network analysis systems. PERT stands for Program Evaluation and Review Technique. It was developed in 1959 by the Navy in conjunction with a consulting company to coordinate the development and production of the Polaris Fleet Ballistic Missile. It is indirectly involved with cost cutting, but its primary emphasis is finding the most efficient time arrangement for many activities that must work together to accomplish a single result—usually a highly complex result. The Polaris project clearly illustrates how complex. Two hundred fifty prime contractors and over 9,000 subcontractors were involved in this effort. This coordination of so many organizations, not to mention the number of individuals involved, was without question a monumental task.

At about the same time, DuPont was developing the network system called CPM, or Critical Path Method, as a tool to reduce the amount of down time required for plant maintenance. PERT is credited with saving two years on the missile project, and CPM is said to have cut down time for DuPont maintenance from 125 hours to 93 hours. The construction of Atlanta Stadium is another project where this tool was effectively employed. Construction time was less than 12 months, a rarity in this type of project. Successes like these have proven the value of network analysis, and today it is widely accepted in the construction industry for coordinating large-scale projects, in the computer industry for installing hardware and software systems, in government for the control of funded projects, and in many other environments.

A PERT chart is a representation of the activities and events necessary to get all the parts of a project completed. You can see a simple PERT chart in Figure 18.6, and get an idea of the kinds of complex diagrams involved in building a Polaris missile. Some, like the diagram for the Saturn rocket used in the space program, are drawn on huge pieces of paper covering thousands of square feet. These projects literally have hundreds of thousands of activities.

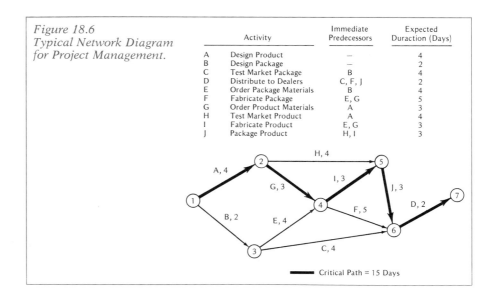

Figure 18.6
Typical Network Diagram
for Project Management.

	Activity	Immediate Predecessors	Expected Duration (Days)
A	Design Product	—	4
B	Design Package	—	2
C	Test Market Package	B	4
D	Distribute to Dealers	C, F, J	2
E	Order Package Materials	B	4
F	Fabricate Package	E, G	5
G	Order Product Materials	A	3
H	Test Market Product	A	4
I	Fabricate Product	E, G	3
J	Package Product	H, I	3

Critical Path = 15 Days

The steps followed in constructing a PERT chart are: (1) the identification of all the activities and jobs necessary to complete the job; (2) the arrangement of these activities in order with respect to the time each requires and the sequence in which it must occur; (3) the charting to determine in days, months, and minutes the time each task will require; (4) the rearrangement or reorganization of any steps which may possibly streamline the job.

For each activity, three possible estimations are made. There is the most optimistic time, based on the assumption that everything goes perfectly. There is the pessimistic time, which takes into account the maximum number of delays anticipated. And there is a most likely time, which assumes the mathematical likelihood that the likely happens more often than the unlikely. By adding all the optimistic times, a manager can see the fastest possible time for completing the entire job. Adding all the pessimistic times will render the slowest time. And by mathematically weighing the computation, the three different times can provide an estimate of the likelihood that the task will be completed on time.

CPM and PERT work well together, since the critical path can and should be designated through any network system. The critical path is the longest path of sequential steps through the network from beginning to end. It sets a lower limit on the time in which the project can be completed. If one activity requires two hours, the project can never be done faster than two hours, even if every other activity takes only 30 seconds. Hence, extra efficiency or savings can only be achieved by directing effort to shorten the critical path, or the longest path between any two points on the chart.

Even though PERT and CPM are similar, there are some differences. The way in which they are graphically represented varies somewhat. CPM also goes beyond PERT in its cost factors. PERT is the most appropriate technique for one-of-a-kind projects like reserch and development work, where CPM is best suited for projects that have been done before.

Neither PERT nor CPM are advisable approaches for mass production systems except in their design and development stages. Once an assembly line is set up and functioning, it would be expensive and wasteful to monitor the repetitious production by network analysis. No doubt, better and better systems of planning and control are yet to be developed. The most recent improvement is GERT, Graphical Evaluation and Review Technique. This variation of network analysis includes uncertain events in the network and incorporates probability theory in the evaluation of possible outcomes. Future improvements will surely continue and will probably utilize PERT, CPM, or GERT to develop better methods.

Logistics

Logistics first came into familiar use as a military word. It originally meant the activities required to keep an army supplied for fighting. It included the very basic concept of always having plenty without having to carry more than was needed. Today, it is applied to the major components of distribution and inventory control systems.

Economic order quantity (EOQ) is most easily understood if we keep in mind the idea of an army on the move. Of course its most common reference today is to the warehousing of things to be used in some manufacturing process, but few of us really appreciate the actual cost of letting things sit in a warehouse. We visit a huge warehouse and have trouble realizing that every inch of space that is used unnecessarily or not used at all is actually draining profits right off the company's balance sheet. Perhaps it is easier to realize that an army on the move has to pay more to carry more with it. There have to be more trucks, more drivers, more fuel, more of everything. So, while any army would love the idea of never having shortages, it must pay dearly for trying to carry more than it needs.

EOQ becomes important in finding the most perfect balance between carrying costs and ordering costs. If there are no carrying costs at all—as when the farmer's barn and labor are all paid for—it makes sense to store up as much of everything as possible—as when the farmer gets ready for the long, cold winter. But more often, industry is faced with increased cost for increased amounts in storage. There is almost always a cheaper price when you make bigger orders, and there is also some cost in the handling and processing of any order. The EOQ allows the modern manager to find the point of balance between storing too much and ordering too often.

EOQ can be brought down to a home example with ease and value. Suppose your pet dog likes Woofers Dog Biscuits. Being a considerate master, you purchase a package of Woofers at your neighborhood store. The trip to the store has some expense, and one bag of Woofers is fairly costly; but it's worth it all to see the smile on your pet's face. Then you discover that you can make a considerable savings on a bag of Woofers if you buy the handy six pack. It costs you more and there is a bit of a storage problem, but the dog is still smiling and you only have to pay for a trip to the store one-sixth as often. Soon, you discover the Woofer truck load deal! This year's supply cuts your trips to the store to only one per year and cost per bag is a fraction of the first bag of Woofers you bought . . . but there is a major storage problem. Because of your experience with the truck load deal, it is not hard to make a decision when you are offered the Woofer Railroad Carload Deal. This lifetime supply is out of the question. There is a point at which the costs of carrying must be balanced against the costs of reordering.

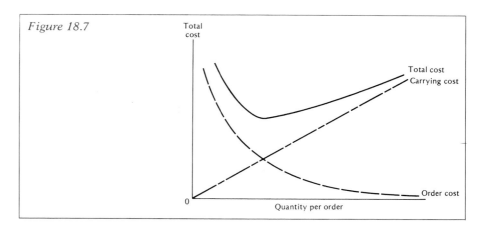

Figure 18.7

Total cost

Total cost

Carrying cost

Order cost

Quantity per order

The relationship between order costs and carrying costs is shown in Figure 18.7. Carrying costs increase forever—the more you store, the more it's going to cost to store it. On the other hand, ordering costs change—the more you order in a single order, the less often you have to pay the ordering costs.

EOQ computations are not always as sure and simple as they may appear in a textbook situation. In order for them to be absolute, several conditions must exist. The rate of demand must be known and continuous—which it is not in most business situations. The planning horizon must be infinite—but more often than not, there are external factors that limit what may be done. The time between placing an order and receiving the goods must be constant—which it rarely is in a world of dock strikes and ice storms. The cost of materials and inventory must be constant and predictable—which it never is in times of inflating costs. If, however, these variables can be pinned down (or even their rate of variation pinned down), mathematical tables like the one in Table 18.1 can enable the manager to know *when* to order, *how much* to order, and *why* that is the ideal time.

EOQ Formula

The basic EOQ formula is a simple mathematical model:

$$EOQ = \sqrt{\frac{2\,RS}{C}}$$

When

R = Annual requirement in units
S = Order (startup) costs per order
C = Inventory carrying cost per unit per year

Values in Table 18.1 have been derived from this formula.

Table 18.1 Analysis of Economic Order Quantity	Number of Orders per year	Size of Order	Average Inventory	Inventory Carrying Cost	Order Cost	Total Cost
	1	6000	3000	600	20	620
	2	3000	1500	300	40	340
	3	2000	1000	200	60	260
	4	1500	750	150	80	330
	5	1200	600	120	100	220 ⎫
	6	1000	500	100	120	220 ⎬
	7	857	428	86	140	226
	8	750	375	75	160	235

Annual Usage = 6000 units
Order Cost = $20 per order
Inventory Cost = 20% or $.20 per unit

As you can see in Table 18.1 the minimum total cost occurs for either 5 or 6 orders a year. If 6 orders are placed, each order will be for 1,000 units. With orders of this size it will cost $100 to carry inventory over the year, and $120 will be expended on ordering activities.

Allocation of Scarce Resources

Linear programming uses the linear equations of algebra to examine the relationship among several variables when the conditions of the situation in which they are found remain the same. Let us consider a simple linear function. For example, if you pay $1.00 for one of something, common sense tells you that two of them will cost you $2.00, three will cost $3.00, and ten will cost $10.00. This is a linear relationship, and it is depicted by the diagonal line in Figure 18.8. If, however, a second dimension is brought into the situation, you will have to find some way to consider the two factors simultaneously. For example, if you have $1.50 coming in every day and need to know how long it will take you to buy seven of those $1.00 items, it becomes necessary to interrelate two linear equations. This problem is shown graphically in Figure 18.8. The point at which the two lines intersect reveals that 4.67 days are required.

By reducing the elements of many product decisions to points on a graph, management science has taken much of the guesswork out of decision making. The hard part no longer is making the decision—the real tasks today are to gather the pertinent information to go into the decision and to make sure that the mathematical approach chosen does indeed deal with the answer it is assumed to deal with.

Linear programming is an operations research tool that is often applied to business-related problems. It is valuable in discovering the

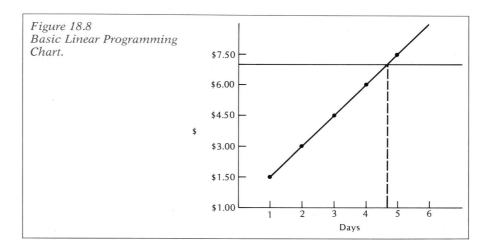

Figure 18.8
Basic Linear Programming
Chart.

exact point of optimum profits from a wide variety of possible product and process mixes. It can also assist in minimizing costs by mathematically isolating the best possible relationships among the organization's limits of equipment, workers, materials, capital, time, and management.

The sample problem given in Table 18.2 shows the resources required to produce two products, A and B. Product A takes longer to manufacture but produces $6 per unit. Product B is quicker to make but has a lower contribution per unit. Another constraint imposed on this problem is the limited number of hours available in each department. Figure 18.9 helps one to visualize the relationship among the variables. Only the points in the area marked "possible solutions" satisfy all the constraints. When the possible solutions are examined, linear programming reveals that making six units of Product A and twelve units of Product B will make optimum use of the time and yield the highest possible return to the company.

Table 18.2.　Hours Required to Produce One Unit of Product

| | Product | | |
	A	B	Total Hours Available
Machinery	18	30	450
Department Painting	29	19	551
Assembly	0	12	480

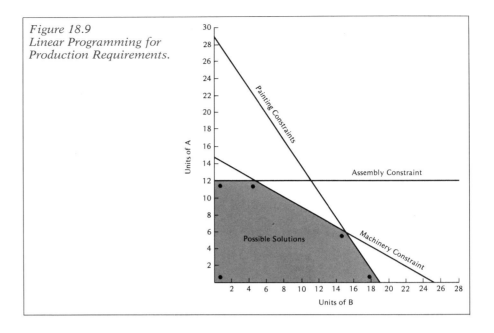

Figure 18.9
Linear Programming for
Production Requirements.

Figure 18.9 graphically portrays the solution to this problem. This simple example involves only two products, represented by the X and Y coordinates, and three constraints, represented by the three linear equations. Larger, more realistic problems often involve 50 or 60 variables and as many constraints. These obviously cannot be solved graphically as a result of their complexity and our physical limitations—we can't draw four-dimensional graphs. Thus, a mathematical technique, the simplex algorithm, is used to work more complex LP problems.

A special application of linear programming is called the transportation method. This technique is used to evaluate the advantages and disadvantages of shipping from various locations. If a company has only one facility, it has little choice but to ship to all outlets from that facility and pay the prevailing price. But suppose a company could open a new factory in another part of the country which could be the supplier for that area. The savings in transportation costs could be sizable. Even if the second factory could save on shipping to market, it would be important to consider the transportation costs of getting raw materials to the second factory. If the product uses raw materials that are available anywhere, the second factory would probably be a helpful investment. But if it required some raw material that was bulky and available only near the first factory, the advantages could soon be offset. This is the reason our country's steel plants tend to remain in the same region.

Using the data presented in Table 18.3 the matrix approach to finding

Figure 18.10A

ORIGINAL PLAN

From Plant:	To Dallas Warehouse	To Chicago Warehouse	Plant Capacity (Units)
A	$ .50 250	$ .70 0	250
B	$1.20 50	$1.50 350	400
Warehouse Requirements (units)	300	350	650

Figure 18.10B

REVISED PLAN

From Plant:	To Dallas Warehouse	To Chicago Warehouse	Plant Capacity (Units)
A	$ .50 0	$ .70 250	250
B	$1.20 300	$1.50 100	400
Warehouse Requirements (units)	300	350	650

Transportation Method

the balance between transportation costs in a company that has two factories and two warehouses is demonstrated (See Fig. 18.10). While simple problems like this can be worked out with ease, imagine the complications in a company with many production facilities and thousands of sales outlets to receive shipments. The analysis would have to evaluate the cost of shipping from any of the plants to any of the outlets. Some would be obviously prohibitive, like shipping from the Seattle plant to the Miami outlet; but others would provide extremely relevant comparisons, like whether to ship to the Nashville store from Memphis or Atlanta. This kind of problem requires sophisticated computer analysis.

Table 18.3. Transportation Problem

Plant/ Warehouses	Transportation Cost per Units	Original Transportation Cost		Revised Transportation Cost	
		Units	Total Transportation Cost	Units	Transportation Cost
A to Dallas	.50	250	$125	0	$ 0
A to Chicago	.70	0	0	250	175
B to Dallas	1.20	50	60	300	360
B to Chicago	1.50	350	525	100	150
			$710		$685

Probability Theory

The second major division of our tools, *statistical models*, involve situations of uncertainty. Many of the situations that we encounter in business occur repeatedly. Customers arrive repeatedly throughout the day at a grocery store. As this situation is observed one is not certain when the next customer will arrive even though there is reason to believe that another will come. If data is collected about the arrival time of customers, a statement can be made about the chance, or probability, of someone arriving within a given time frame. Perhaps the manager would be interested in determining the chance of 100 people arriving at the store in the next hour. After data is collected and probabilities calculated, the store manager can use this valuable information to determine the number of cashier stations that need to be open during the selected hour. Many situations that managers face are similar to this one. Even though uncertainty exists, historical data can be used to determine probabilities and reasonable decisions can be made on the basis of these probabilities.

Particularly in the areas of monitoring activity and decision making, the manager is likely to need to utilize techniques of probability theory. Theoretical approaches to narrowing the guesswork are often helpful but never fool-proof. They provide the manager with an organizational structure for comparing the confusing information that tends to swirl round and round in the human mind when facing a decision or fishing for the most appropriate response to a problem situation.

The normal curve is one statistical tool that can be of use in predicting the count of variation that might normally be expected to occur around the most likely value of a variable. Students are familiar with the results of grades being assigned on the normal distribution or what is known as the bell-shaped curve. The curve is actually the plotting of a frequency distribution in which the number, or frequency, of items is plotted on the vertical axis and the value of the variable on the horizontal axis. Consider the solid line in the center of Figure 18.11 as the class average, or what is known as the mean of the distribution. The standard deviation (SD) is a standard measurement of dispersion (the spread of individual items from the mean). It represents a specific percentage of the items under the normal curve. For example, one standard deviation to the right of the mean represents 34.14 per cent of the data, and one standard deviation to the left of the mean also equals 34.14 per cent of the data. Hence, if the class average is 60 and the standard deviation is 10 points, for the grades to be normally distributed approximately 68% of the students would have scores between 60 and 80. These relationships hold true as long as the curve is bell-shaped, regardless of what values the mean and the standard deviation may assume.

Because experience has shown that things do tend to fall into standard relationships to each other, the normal curve is a helpful tool for

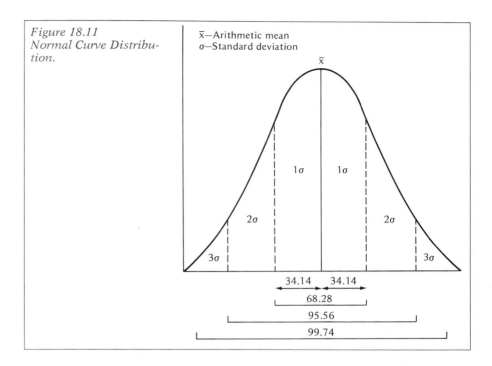

*Figure 18.11
Normal Curve Distribution.*

x̄—Arithmetic mean
σ—Standard deviation

the manager who needs some basis for setting bounds and limitations. Once the mean and the dispersion of the date are known, it becomes a simple matter of mathematics to determine just how far on either side of the mean the various values may be expected to occur.

Statistical quality control (SQC) is application of these formulas for the purpose of (1) computing measurements from a sample; (2) establishing limits of acceptability; (3) determining whether a particular sample falls within acceptable limits; and (4) taking corrective action when quality measurements fall beyond acceptable ranges. For example, historical records show that for every 1,000 light bulbs produced, an average of five are defective with a standard deviation of one. This means that we are almost certain any lot of 1000 bulbs tested will have between two and eight defective bulbs. If a lot of 1000 is tested and we find ten defectives, we are highly suspicious that something is wrong. Having ten defectives is not impossible, but it is highly unlikely. So we test the next lot and discover twelve defectives. This is overwhelming evidence that something in the production process is wrong so we take steps without further delay to isolate and correct the problem.

Decision Theory

Decision models are formularized approaches to representing the multiple alternatives that enter into any decision. Regardless of the arena of a decision, there are always multiple factors that can vary and change the expected outcome. Decision models can allow the manager to plan (at least on paper) for all the things that could possibly come up to affect the outcome.

Variables in any decision usually fall into three areas. Either there can be more than one *strategy*, more than one *state of nature*, or more than one *response from the competition*. Strategies, of course, are the steps taken by the company to try to accomplish its goals—there are almost always several strategies which may be employed in response to any problem situation. When strategy is chosen, it will take place in some environment—some state of nature. The same strategy is sure to bring different results if it is carried out in the desert, in the city, or in the middle of an earthquake! The third variable that can be expected to enter in is the reaction of the competition—in battle, for example, the competition may react to a certain strategy in a certain state of nature by either retreating, counterattacking, or surrendering.

But to complicate the decision maker's job even more, each of the alternatives in each of these three arenas of variation must also be combined with each of the others. The alternatives in a situation are not just the sum of the variables—but the product of all possible conditions.

A *payoff matrix* is a two-dimensional charting of the relationships between the various strategies that might be employed and each of the states of nature or each of the reactions of the competition. In charting the payoff matrix, strategies are listed as S_1, S_2, and so on. States of nature are abbreviated N_1, N_2, and so on, and the reactions of the competition are entered on the chart as C_1, C_2. The payoff in each cell is designated by a capital O followed by two small subscripts indicating the position on the chart, as seen in Figure 18.12.

By assigning probabilities to the various states of nature and/or competitive actions, the manager can find the probable results of one decision as compared with the results of other decisions. Unfortunately, the system is not guaranteed, and its reliability depends totally upon the

Figure 18.12 Payoff matrix

Strategies	States of Nature		
	N_1	N_2	N_3
S_1	O_{1-1}	O_{1-2}	O_{1-3}
S_2	O_{2-1}	O_{2-2}	O_{2-3}
S_3	O_{3-1}	O_{3-2}	O_{3-3}

Figure 18.13

Probability of Occurrence	Possible Sales (States of Nature)	Inventory Positions (Strategies)		
		10	11	12
.2	10	2.50	2.40	2.30
.5	11	2.50	2.75	2.65
.3	12	2.50	2.75	3.00
Expected Value of Daily Profit		2.50	2.68	2.685

accuracy of values and of the probabilities assigned to the variables. Furthermore, the states of nature and competitive actions are almost always outside the control of the manager . . . even if the greatest gain occurs when "strategy 3 is carried out in the rain," there is no way of guaranteeing the weather.

Consider Muggsy Malone once again. Let's say that Muggsy can sell 10, 11, or 12 papers each morning. He would only want to purchase 10, 11, or 12 papers before boarding the train. This creates nine possible outcomes (or profit positions) than can occur. If Muggsy pays 10¢ for each paper and sells them for 35¢, the outcomes are easily calculated. (See Figure 18.13). By collecting data on sales over time, Muggsy has determined the probability of each level of sales occuring. Using this information, Muggsy has calculated the expected value of each inventory position, or strategy, that he can take. The chart shows that Muggsy should buy twelve papers each morning if he wants to maximize the average profit over time.

The decision situations that occur most often are (1) certainty, (2) risk, (3) uncertainty, and (4) conflict. Certainty is rare, because this situation demands that this state of nature be either known or controlled. This is true in laboratory decision making, where every effort is given to controlling the environment so that alternatives can be accurately measured. More often, the manager finds the possible states of nature outside his control. This creates a *risk decision.* Here he must endeavor to determine the likelihood of each state of nature so that it can be multiplied by the assigned mathematical expectation of each strategy as Muggsy did. When there is a history of performance of the states of nature, then some mathematical probability can usually be established. But in many cases, the manager has only wishes, fears, or ignorance as a basis for predicting certain states of nature. In such a case, the manager is involved in decision making under *uncertainty.* Now, the utilization of any probabilities will be influenced by the manager's state of mind. If the manager is optimistic, he will make the *maximax decision* —choosing to go as deeply as possible into the most promising variable in order to maximize the potential maximum positive outcome. If the manager is pessimistic, he will make a *minimax decision* —hedging his bets and placing only a safe number of chips on the most promising variable. If Muggsy were to follow a minimax strategy, he would purchase ten papers each morning, thus insuring that he will make $2.50 each day. The goal of a minimax decision is to minimize the potential negative outcome. If all the alternatives appear dangerous, the manager is likely to seek the safe route—proceeding with the safe, sure, proven steps, and then only at a minimum necessary involvement level.

Decision trees are graphic representations that help managers zero in on the alternatives open in decision situations so that they can choose something, rather than puzzle over everything. Each of us makes a mental decision tree in coming to any decision; but the special values of listing specifics on paper cannot be denied. In many cases, the alternatives tend to swirl around in our heads.

The clearest way to explain the concept is through an example. For purposes of illustration, let us systematically plan the office picnic. Of course, we will not plan the entire function—only the all-important answer to the most universal of all office-picnic questions, "What if it rains?"

The president of the company has assigned us this important task. In his own way, he has reminded us that although everyone should have a good time, the picnic must also be a financial success. We call our committee into session and soon come up with the following potential outcomes:

1. If we plan an *outdoor picnic* there are three potential financial outcomes:
   —If it rains, we lose $350;
   —If we have short showers, we will make $300;
   —If it is sunny all day, we make $500.

2. If we plan an *outdoor picnic* but also provide a temporary shelter and a movie, we must invest an additional $50 but we have the following possible results:
   —If it rains all day, we break even (people will leave early, but our costs are covered);
   —If we have showers, then our emergency plan goes into operation and we still make $450;
   —If it is sunny, we still make $450 (although we have spent money on the safeguards for nothing).

3. If we schedule an *indoor outing* we can predict the following outcomes:
   —If it rains, we lose $100 because of low attendance and the same general and promotion expenses;
   —If we have showers, we still lose $100

Figure 18.14
Payoff Table.

Choices	All–day rain	Showers cloudy	Sunny
1. Commit to outdoors— picnic all day.	−$350	$300	$500
2. Plan outdoors but inside cover for showers	—	$450	$450
3. Plan for an indoor outing and rain	−$100	−$100	−$150

—If it is sunny, we lose $150 because people who planned to come may find personal activities that will enable them to enjoy the out-of-doors.

Based on this set of assumptions, the picnic-planning committee can construct a payoff table (Figure 18.14) that shows, in a concise format, the choices, possible events, and probable results.

If it is possible to estimate the probability of each potential event, we can now construct a decision tree to demonstrate mathematically the best decision to make. In this case, the U.S. Weather Bureau tells us that there is a 70 per cent probability that the day will be sunny, a 20 percent chance that there will be showers, and only 10 percent probability that it will rain all day. (Even without information about probability, the decision tree may be built merely to demonstrate graphically the options and possible outcomes.) The committee constructs the decision tree in Figure 18.15 to discover the relative values of the three approaches.

Figure 18.15
Decision Tree.

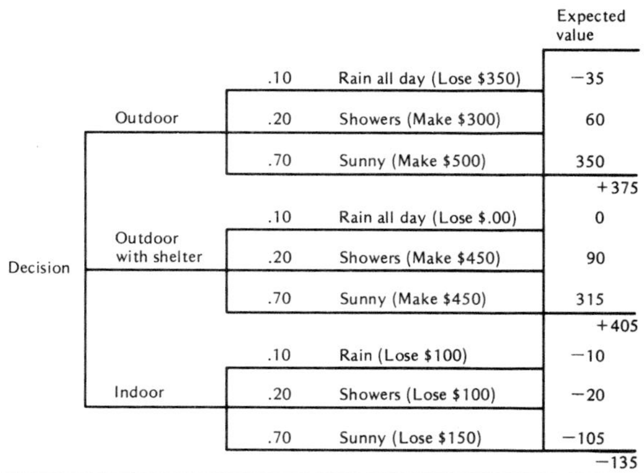

				Expected value
		.10	Rain all day (Lose $350)	−35
	Outdoor	.20	Showers (Make $300)	60
		.70	Sunny (Make $500)	350
				+375
		.10	Rain all day (Lose $.00)	0
Decision	Outdoor with shelter	.20	Showers (Make $450)	90
		.70	Sunny (Make $450)	315
				+405
		.10	Rain (Lose $100)	−10
	Indoor	.20	Showers (Lose $100)	−20
		.70	Sunny (Lose $150)	−105
				−135

According to this analysis, our best decision would be to plan the picnic outdoors with a safety shelter. Because of the low probability of rain, we might even consider gambling on eliminating the emergency shelter altogether. The third alternative is a sure loser. Of course, anybody knows that an indoor picnic is no picnic at all.

Although this illustration is quite simple and the assumptions behind it are open to question, the applications are as numerous as the situations in which an executive can sit down and identify his alternatives and the possible results of these decisions.

Although simple in concept, decision trees can get very complex in application. In the illustration just given, everyone realizes that changes in the weather are among life's most unpredictable probabilities. For purposes of analysis, it is usually desirable to limit the number of alternatives evaluated to a manageable number. In other words, decision trees often need to be pruned. Even in the analysis of a decision tree with three or four branch forks, the trees can get a little out of hand.

Another difficulty in the construction of a decision tree is the making of assumptions and the setting of probabilities from which the "magic" numbers in a decision tree are developed. Many managers are hesitant to assign precise probabilities. Additionally, it must be understood that in most situations a manager does not have totally accurate information concerning probabilities.

Decision trees will not grow in all climates. For instance, if a decision problem is a relatively simple one, the use of decision trees might be unproductive and uneconomical.

Finally, there is some danger that a manager, hypnotized by the logic of the numbers, may take the decision tree as an answer machine rather than carefully investigating the assumptions upon which the outcome figures are based.

These reservations are mentioned not to discredit the use of decision trees but to suggest that they cannot be a utopian solution to decision-making problems. After weighing the risks versus the rewards for using decision trees, we find that the balance tends to be heavily in favor. The fruit produced can be a plum if properly fertilized by careful analysis and sense. On the other hand, it can be a lemon if the dangers and limitations are not well recognized.

The Use and Abuse of Quantitative Tools

There appears to be no imminent danger of managers surrendering their decision-making responsibility to scientific methods. Rex Brown studied twenty large U.S. firms and found that, except at the problem identification stage, the mathematical tools of decision making were not in common use.

Few of us really expect a wideawake manager to blindly follow the advice of some formula, leading the company into disaster and never looking back. Capable managers know that there is little value in being able to blame the chart when the operation goes down the drain.

More often, the reality of the situation is that mathematical models and matrices are called into play to "sell" an idea that someone has generated. This is somewhat short of ideal, but far better than ignoring the formulas altogether. On the other hand, we have all had experience with the ability of statistics to prove those things we strongly want them to prove. Remember the adage, "Figures don't lie, but liars figure."

We have not yet reached the point of developing formulas with intuition and the ability to taste, smell, and sense the real world. A manager knows the tools are important.

In the case of every tool, however, its value lies with the manager. There is no doubt that the decisions can be clarified by the correct use of these mathematical predictors. Like any tool, the formulas are merely an extension of human ability. They increase the power, accuracy, and extent to which we can accomplish necessary activities. Yet the formulas are limited to the input we provide, and the predictors can only accept the prejudices and blind spots of the human user. The skill and sensitivity of the manager cannot be replaced. On the other hand, familiarity with the tools of decision making no more makes one a manager than a well-stocked basement workshop makes one a master builder.

Summary

The mathematical tools of management and decision making must be seen as means to an end—never the end in itself. The wise manager is interested in knowing about new things that may be of help but will never fall ino automatic acceptance of a method just because it is new.

In this chapter, brief introductions have been given to both old and new tools of management that are widely acclaimed. The chapter's objective is not an in-depth explanation of any of the tools but a meaningful and perspective-producing overview for the manager.

Several budgetary models are presented. They include the variable budget or foundation budget, the break-even analysis, and zero-based budgeting.

Tools of scheduling include the Gantt chart and the process or flow chart.

Two tools of network analysis are presented. They are Project Evaluation and Review Technique (PERT) and Critical Path Method (CPM).

Logistics refers to the movement of supplies necessary to do a job and the movement of the products that result from the job. Economic order quantity (EOQ) is explained as a tool for squeezing the last penny out of the organization's activity.

Tools to allocate scarce resources are linear programming and the transportation method.

Probability theory involves the application of mathematical formulas for the purpose of narrowing the guesswork of a decision. The normal curve and statistical quality control are presented. Decision theory is a statistical approach to making logical choices under conditions of uncertainty. The payoff matrix and decision trees are discussed.

Review Questions

1. What are the two major changes in using management tools?
2. Muggsy Malone wants to estimate his break-even point. After paying $1.50 for his train ticket, how many newspapers must he sell if he pays $.10 for the papers and sells them for $.15
3. Where was zero-based budgeting developed? Why?
4. In a decision situation, what three variables must be considered?
5. Develop a Gantt or PERT chart to help you schedule the work for your next term paper.
6. Develop a decision tree to help you choose between majoring in accounting or management.
7. Would PERT or CPM be appropriate for the manufacturing of automobiles? Explain your answer.

19

Systems for Effective Management

"Maybe you should tell it to me one more time. So far, it just doesn't seem to make any sense."

"Sense? Why, it's the most sensible thing in the world, my boy, and, if I do say so myself, it is an idea that is going to make a lot of money for me. As you know, there has been more and more talk about all kinds of systems in the last few years. Scientific systems, business systems, computer systems . . . every part of society is busy finding out how to systematize the parts of its operation".

"Okay . . . so far I understand."

"Since there is such a proliferation of systematic jargon and terminology involving such a multiplicity of disciplines, I believe that people are going to need a helping device to tell which kind of system they are encountering at any given time. Otherwise they will be trying to get one system's results by dealing with some entirely incompatible systematology. Therefore, I have devised a system to help people determine which system is operative, and my invention is naturally called the 'Systematic Sensor of Systems' Symptoms.'"

"I think one more time through it will be enough."

Since World War II, our society has been moving deeper and deeper into a systems frame of mind. Until that turning point in history, we were still busy squeezing the best out of the machine age that had been going since the Industrial Revolution began. For generations the emphasis had been on mechanizing everything . . . finding ways to break things down into the most basic components and then dealing meticulously with the parts. But with the beginning of the systems age, the emphasis shifted to the whole instead of just the parts. The small components were still important, but they received more attention based on their relationship to the whole than on their simple individual importance in isolation.

The mood of our age is one that prefers to see the *gestalt* or total picture. We hear the words *holistic* and *global* commonly used to refer to the wide view, the total perspective, the "big picture." In business and academia we are placing increasing value on the person whose expertise crosses traditional boundaries, because there is an increased confidence that all things tend to be more alike than they are different and that the person who has the grasp of the situation in one arena is likely to be able to quickly take the whole situation into control in a different arena.

The Ecology of Systems

There is also a growing ecological approach to our thinking, even in those realms that have little to do with fish and wildlife. The word *ecology* was little known ten years ago—today it has come into its own and is rightly being applied in many disciplines. The literal meaning of ecology refers to the fact that things are interdependent. To remove one part of nature's cycle is to create new and unforeseen problems in another part of the cycle—if we drain the seaside marshlands to reclaim the land, we soon find that the fish far out to sea are dying from loss of their foodproducing tidelands.

The ecology principle applies to every system and there is a healthy new awareness that making a simple change in one part of an organizational chart is likely to have repercussions on the other side of the chart. Fire one employee and somebody else must do more work. Cut expenses and you can expect to increase profits. There must be balances sought in government-private enterprise, labor-management, quantity-quality. The new attention to the ecological characteristic of systems is opening new doors to true understandings of the businesses we run, the policies we make, and the human interactions that continue to baffle us.

The result is the emergence of a *dynamic* characteristic in place of the traditional but naive assumption that people were like things and could be depended upon to stay where you put them. This new attitude about the things we are trying to organize has brought forth a much more relevant style of systems thinking. At the same time, it has robbed us of some of the quick and simple (and often useless) answers that used to be possible.

To be more specific, we ought to speak less of systems, for the awareness of sequences and steps has been around for a long time. The revolutionary step has been the dynamic quality of the new systems. This concept has filtered down into many aspects of our thinking and has taken concrete form in the techniques and methods we use to solve problems. In the previous chapter, we presented the mathematical tools of project management, PERT and CPM. These serve as an excellent example of system thinking and its dynamic quality.

The systems theorist will look for three things in identifying a system: the common elements that comprise the system, the whole that is formed by these elements, and the existing relationships that tie the parts together. The PERT diagram is a visual representation of all three. Each task or activity is a part of the whole. All the activities taken together make up the project, or the whole. And finally arrows represent the relationships (or interactions) of the tasks to each other. You could go out tomorrow and pour a foundation in your backyard. The following day we can build a roof in your front yard. Completing the tasks required to build a house obviously doesn't make much sense unless they are all done and all placed in the proper "relationship" to each other. PERT helps us to do this.

Once the PERT diagram is drawn the job is not finished—it is just starting. You only have a plan, and plans frequently go awry. The plan allocates four days for painting; however, rain causes delays of six days. The plan must be adjusted to compensate for the delays. This is the dynamic aspect of system thinking. Today, we talk in terms of adaptive systems that can roll with the punches of a fluctuating world. Interactive, adaptive systems are the promise of mankind's ability to survive and progress.

System Characteristics

Systems are usually divided into two major groups, closed systems and open systems. This classification is based on the amount of interchange that a system has with the world that surrounds it. Interchanges with the environment are extremely important to all systems, for this is how systems receive energy and maintain their existence. They take in energy from the outside and use it to create their outputs. These outputs then serve as inputs to other systems.

Closed systems are those systems that have little or no exchange with their environment. A watch is an excellent example of a closed system. We could take the individual parts of a watch and put them in a box, but when we looked into the box, we couldn't tell the time. So we arrange them in such a manner that they work together to reveal time. This system has some exchange with the outside world, but it is not significant. We wind the watch once a day (or, more likely, change the battery once a year). Then the watch functions by itself until it runs out of energy and must be wound again (or the battery replaced).

Open systems are the most common ones in our world. These are systems that have free exchange with their environment. You and I are open systems. We take in air, water, food, and information. From this we receive our energy and are able to create outputs. Work and information are good examples of outputs that we produce, and they serve as inputs to other systems.

The boundary conditions of open systems are frequently discussed. You should be able to see the importance of the boundaries that exist between open systems and their surroundings. They are important because they determine the quantity and quality of inputs. For example, consider the boundaries that exist in the learning process. The teacher talks and information is projected to the student. This information is "absorbed" through the sense of hearing. If the student's hearing is impaired (i.e. the boundary conditions are not ideal), the quantity and quality of the information is distorted, and the effectiveness of the learning process is decreased.

It is a fundamental law of nature that all systems move towards decay. This concept is called entropy. This does not imply that the process is irreversible. Remember our watch? It runs, and if steps are not taken to keep it running, eventually it stops. The human body "runs", and likewise, if steps are not taken to maintain it, eventually it will stop. So we wind the watch to give it energy to run longer. We eat, rest, and exercise to keep our bodies going. This arresting of the entropy process is called negative entropy. In the business world, a more meaningful way to express this concept is to say all organizations move toward a state of disorganization. As in our previous examples, steps are taken to reverse the process. We organize, establish authority, write policies, and develop control devices to reverse and develop healthy, growing corporations.

We mentioned in the previous section that systems have the ability to adapt—that they are dynamic. This characteristic is most common to open systems. Systems theorists have borrowed a biological term, *homeostasis*, to describe the process. It refers to the ability of a system to remain in a state of dynamic equilibrium with its surroundings. Consider the human body. If the room temperature increases significantly, the body responds to this change by perspiring. This occurs in order that the body can maintain a constant temperature, 98.6°F, and function as it should. In a similar manner, businesses respond to changes in their environments. An economic downturn occurs, and the local real estate firm increases its selling effort. This is necessary in order to maintain the current level of sales. Inflationary pressures cause a local wholesaler to raise prices, and the manager of Cunningham's Hardware Store starts looking for another supplier to furnish plumbing hardware.

The adaptive process of systems experience requires that the parts work together. The process of individual parts working together often produces results that could not be achieved unless there was cooperation. We call this *synergy.* In general terms, it means the whole is greater than the sum of its parts. To illustrate, imagine that you and three friends need to move a large desk. You could not move it alone, nor could any one of your friends. Yet, together the four of you can move it quite easily.

Synergy, homeostasis, entropy, and the other characteristics of systems discussed here are found in many types of systems. It is helpful to use these characteristics to identify the way systems function. However, it is also helpful to create ways in which one can distinguish between different type of systems. The next section addresses this topic.

Classification of Systems

Kenneth Boulding has provided us with a system for systematizing the systems of our world. He has listed, in order of ascending complexity, kinds of systems that are alike in principle but different in complexity.

1. The first level is that of static structure. It might be called the level of *frameworks:* for example, the anatomy of the universe.
2. The next level is that of the simple dynamic system with predetermined, necessary motions. This might be called the level of *clockworks.*
3. The control mechanism or cybernetic system, which might be nicknamed the level of the *thermostat.* The system is self-regulating in maintaining equilibrium.
4. The fourth level is that of the "open system," or self-maintaining structure. This is the level at which life begins to differentiate from not-life: it might be called the level of the *cell.*
5. The next level might be called the genetic-societal level; it is typified by the plant, and it dominates the empirical world of the botanist.
6. The *animal* system level is characterized by increased mobility, teleological behavior, and self-awareness.

7. The next level is the *human* level, that is, of the individual human being considered as a system with self-awareness and the abiliy to utilize language and symbolism.

8. The *social system* or systems of human organization constitute the next level, with the consideration of the content and meaning of messages, the nature and dimensions of value systems, the transcription of images into historical record, the subtle symbolizations of art, music, and poetry, and the complex gamut of human emotion.

9. *Transcendental systems* complete the classification of levels. These are the ultimates and absolutes and the inescapable unknowables, and they also exhibit systematic structure and relationship.[1]

Boulding's classification scheme introduces the notion that small systems exist within bigger systems. Depending on what is the *focal system*, the system being observed, we can define suprasystems or subsystems. For example, the operations function in a business is a system. Quality control is a subsystem that exists within the operations system. Broadening our perspective, we see that the operations system is part of a suprasystem, the entire business. If the focal system is changed, the classifications change.

How can you relate to this concept? Consider the school you attend. Following a pattern similar to Boulding's, the system levels could be defined as individual, class, professor, dean, president and community. Of course, this example is greatly simplified. The department or college level administrative structure is implied by the word *dean*, as *president* implies the overall administrative structure. Nevertheless, it ties together in a logical pattern the chain of subsystems, systems, and suprasystems.

When you meet a person today who identifies his occupation as "systems engineer," it is routine to assume that that person works in the computer industry. But, as the pervasiveness of systems expands and as our awareness of the systems of systems becomes more meaningful, you will eventually encounter the systems engineer whose field of endeavor is not limited to the computer world. It *is* likely that the computer will be *used* by this true systems engineer; however, this will not be simply a "computer systems engineer," but a person whose specialty is recognizing and utilizing systems of all types.

The manager may quite naturally be tempted to touch only lightly any discussion about systems, because he may assume that there will always be a specialist around to take care of that kind of thing. However, a valid understanding of the scope of system thinking will reveal that, in one sense, system work *is* the manager's stock in trade. The

[1] Kenneth E. Boulding, "General Systems Theory: The Skeleton of a Science," *Management Science*, April, 1956, pp. 197–208.

manager's ability to recognize, reorganize, and control adapting systems makes that manager worth the salary. Sensitivity to the official and unofficial systems that make up an organization tells a manager *what* there is to be managed and *which* management strategies (i.e., systems techniques) will most appropriately accomplish management goals.

Types of Management Systems

In this chapter, various types of management systems will be introduced briefly. It is important for the reader to understand that, while these system types will be introduced here, they are elaborated upon in almost every other chapter of the book. In one way or another, each chapter of management thought is another expression of systems technique. The kinds of systems to be introduced in this chapter are goal systems, information systems, human systems, authority systems, and operating systems. They are found in all business firms whether large or small. They may be formal or informal, but they exist in some form. They are overlapping and interwoven into a complex maze of relationships that constitute our business organizations. And each one is necessary to support the continued activity of organizations.

Kenneth Boulding gives an interesting illustration to emphasize the importance of these underlying systems. What if a horse were twice as big as normal, say as big as an elephant? Would this work? Probably not, because the legs of the new horse wouldn't support the body. Why? The answer is in the way a horse is made. Its body approximates a rectangular shape. Thus, if we doubled its length, doubled its height, and doubled its width, we would increase the volume of the body ($l \times w \times h$) by a factor of eight. The horse's legs are round. By doubling their size, we would only increase the surface area (r^2) on which the body rests by a factor of four. Hence, the legs would not support the body and the ele-horse (or whatever you want to call it) could not stand. A similar situation is often true in business. We increase sales volume and fail to provide appropriate systems to support the growth. This failure disrupts the interrelationships between various parts of the organization, and disorganization increases. If steps are not taken to adjust, the business is doomed to failure.

The reader will gain most by seeking the similarities of each type of system to the others. There will almost always be new applications of system understanding based on the principles of the ones presented. It is, of course, impossible at any time to provide an exhaustive, complete explanation of all systems knowledge. Rather, it is more useful for the student to distill the basic principles of all systematic phenomena. The information thus gained will always be applicable and up-to-date.

Goal Systems

If we wanted a fresh look at a stale organization, we might wisely rework the organizational chart. Instead of using titles of names in the little boxes, we could write in the goals of each worker. The systematic interrelationships of worker goals would tell us quickly and graphically whether or not that company was moving decisively toward its overall, stated goal.

Every organization, every society has individual goals that are refined versions of each other. The manager's task is to make sure that all goals (both the private, unspoken goals and the overt official goals) are natural extensions of each other.

One of the best uses of goal systems is in the zero-based budget, described in Chapter 18. Zero-based budgeting finds its strength in the fact that each budgetary level of an organization must write down its objectives and relate those objectives to the larger objectives of its superiors. When all parts of the company have stated their goals, the budgetary planners can begin to relate the divisions and offices to each other, and to the overall goals of the organization. The planners can let the money flow down the chart, with special attention to those stated objectives that are in concert with the ones stated above them. The natural conflict between goals in various parts of an organization was discussed in Chapter 17. Operations management tries to minimize cost, while marketing wants to maximize sales. The budgeting process is an attempt to reconcile these differences and respond to conflict in a healthy, logical way. Decisions are made with an overall view of the organization rather than a provincial view. Thus, the goal of all is the ultimate goal.

Chapters about planning, organization, control, motivation, and almost every other area have something to say about the methods of and importance of systematizing the goals of all parts of the organization.

Information Systems

When we hear the term *information systems* we are likely to think first of libraries and other operations, which actually are more involved in information *storage*. As we open our thinking to the multitude of information systems that fill our everyday lives, we can begin to realize that almost every aspect of our relationships with other people involves information systems.

Communications and advertising and training are obvious domains of the systems that transfer information. Sales and marketing and even production cannot facilitate the flow of tangible goods without efficient systems to move intangible information. Even the accounting department is a pivotal information system.

The distinction between the information storage and information exchange systems is well worth making. Even the sometimes nebulous area of managerial decision making is basically an information system. Computers have allowed managers to amass large volumes of information concerning businesses. Unfortunately, many times no thought is given to the usefulness of the information. When this occurs, we often suffer from information overload. The pertinent information is impossible to find because it is hidden in the mass of irrelevant information. Information theorists concentrate on identifying information that is needed to make the decisions with which a manager is faced and eliminating all redundant and irrelevant information. The decision maker's task is then to evaluate the alternatives using the appropriate data and to select the best one. The decision maker must continue seeking and obtaining information until the alternatives begin to eliminate themselves and the decision direction becomes clear.

The manager is a nerve center of corporate communication. The manager is the one through whom all the systems find unity. It is easy enough to order telephones, typewriters, file cabinets, and copy machines. The manager, however, should be able to relate all the tools of communications to each other and to the goals of the organization. This does not mean that any manager must hear and say everything that is said or heard. It certainly would be impossible for any one person to efficiently massage every bit of information that passed through a company; but it is essential for managers to know what information is passing through . . . where it's coming from . . . where it's going . . . and why it is needed. In short, managers should manage the total information system of the organization. Even this grasp will become part of the information that needs communicating.

In every kind of system, the need for the members of the system to understand the total system and their places in it becomes a priority need. Every system needs an information system component.

Human Systems

Human systems have been the pain in the necks of systems enthusiasts for years for one simple reason—people are unpredictable. They tend to do the things that we had not expected or prepared for. Historically, systems people have tried to develop *closed* systems, those which were self-contained, predictable, and under control. People, by their very nature, are members of many systems. Your membership in a family system, an educational system, a corporate system, and a recreational system all interact. None of these systems can *enclose* your part in it without enclosing all the systems of which you are a member.

The *open* system has gradually shown itself to be essential if we seek to accurately explain phenomena. To some degree it is possible to assign quantified values to people and their reactions, but even the most dogmatic chart maker must eventually draw in a box for "miscellaneous responses" and allow for the interaction of the uncontrollable factors.

When we speak of human systems, we are inevitably speaking of systems for motivating and controlling humans. Since the first employee-employer relationship, people have been seeking a foolproof system for motivating and controlling human behavior. Each time another system would come to the forefront and be announced as *the* system, the hopes would soon be dashed and broken because of the fact that a closed system had been proposed, and closed systems will not enclose humans.

Barnard, Simon, and March have proposed several rules of organizational equilibrium. Their theories come close to being a comprehensive theory of human behavior because they endeavor to allow for the open-ended realities of organization members whose lives have many centers outside the organization. The central postulates of this composite theory are listed below:

1. An organization is a system of interrelated social behaviors of a number of persons who are referred to as the *participants* in the organization.

2. Each participant and each group of participants receives *inducements* from the organization, in return for which they make *contributions* to the organization. Such inducements involve not only money or concrete goods and services, but also less tangible factors such as social and psychic satisfaction.

3. Each participant will continue making contributions in an organization only as long as the inducements offered are as great or greater (measured in terms of personal values and the other alternatives that are open).

4. The contributions provided by the various groups of participants are the sources from which the organization "manufactures" the inducements offered to participants.

5. Hence, an organization is solvent—and will continue to exist—only as long as the contributions are sufficient to provide adequate inducements to draw forth these contributions.[2]

Authority Systems

Authority is one of the most ineffectively applied activities of management. There is the common misconception that authority is synonymous with a title or an assignment or even a responsibility. It is not nec-

[2] J. March and H. Simon, *Organizations* (New York: John Wiley and Son's, Inc., 1963) pp. 84–88. See also B. M. Richman and R. N. Farmer, *Management and Organizations* (New York: Random House, Inc., 1975), pp. 63–65.

Flash Gordon (Universal Pictures, 1980). [Copyright © by Universal Pictures, a Division of Universal Studios, Inc. Courtesy of MCA Publishing, a Division of MCA Inc.] Can technical systems create problems for human systems?

essarily so. In Chapter 9, we discussed the problems of formal and informal authority. It is enough to say here that authority has historically been the least systematic and the most emotional field of management endeavor.

We diagram organizational hierarchy and we *think* we have drawn the lines of authority. This is not necessarily so, either. Authority is surrendered by those who are to be directed. They may surrender it because they must . . . as in a dictatorship or prison camp. They may also surrender it by choice . . . as in voluntary support of an admired leader. The differences in the results and the cooperative spirit in either case can easily be seen. Formal authority may be weaker than informal authority . . . but sometimes it is the best that is available.

There are plenty of examples in our daily lives of the fact that sometimes we humans *need* external, imposed, formal authority to push us, kicking and screaming, toward the things that we really ought to do . . . but just don't want to do. How many of us would ever have finished junior high school or taken our cough syrup had it not been for the imposition of formal authority systems? Because we were too immature or too inexperienced to see the long value of unglamorous activities, someone who knew better for us had to coax us to do the things we needed to do.

The necessary balance between formal and informal authority is not easy to attain. It requires a system that can allow both extremes to exist in the presence of one another. Mankind can give up the dream of eventually attaining and maintaining a perfect system, for the most successful human structures of authority have always been in transition. It becomes not so much a matter of what we are like, as it is of what stage we are in as we pass along a never-ending journey.

As introduced in Chapter 9, responsibility and accountability are two words that figure significantly in an understanding of authority systems. Responsibility refers to the fact that managers (or other leaders) have obligations for the behaviors, successes, and failures of those who work for them. We often assume responsibility when it ought not to exist. The job of the open system is to counteract this failure. For example, the young sales rep is responsible for making thirty calls this week. If the rep does not make the calls, it may not be his or her fault; illness or disaster may be responsible. An open system recognizes the existence and influence of external factors and provides for such contingencies appropriately. The closed system simply (and ignorantly) fires the salesman for not making the calls!

Accountability describes the built-in results—success or failure—of those assigned responsibility. Accountability is a valuable motivational tool . . . as long as it is applied through an open system and not blindly through a closed system of authority. Skillful managers search for ways to tie worker reward directly to worker performance. Motivation grows whenever the worker sees that laziness costs and industry pays more. On the other hand, there is nothing that can create bitterness and discouragement quite so fast as a worker's discovery that the reward system is based on some criteria that are totally outside the worker's control or influence.

In devising a workable authority system, the manager must give attention to the existence and influence of many subsystems the inputs of which affect results. The system must be open to the real variables if it is to merit authority.

Operating Systems

One part of managerial plan making has always been a favorite: physical facilities and tools involve the kind of simple decision that any manager can love. Of course, as our organizations become larger these decisions become more complicated. Nevertheless, they still represent problems that are relatively easy to handle. The catalogues describe exactly what is available. The manager makes a selection and orders it, and what gets delivered is either right or wrong.

Because the operating systems are tangible and easily dealt with, it has been common for managers to give these greater attention. In many cases, this has resulted in a loss of flexibility. The operations function in effect was overmanaged. Schedules were set, inventories ordered, people assigned to tasks, and other detailed plans made. When changes to these plans were necessary, great resistance was encountered. Furthermore, many operations managers lost sight of the individuals' role in the operations process. Emphasis was placed on machines and plans rather than on people.

While it is true that a new machine or a new process or a new tool can streamline production in any operation, it should not be assumed that the tangible facet of the job deserves more attention. In most cases, the lag in productivity is a result of poorly motivated workers rather than poorly equipped work stations.

Attention to the operating systems is a potential problem in any kind of managerial situation. It is definitely not limited to factory or conveyor belts. The office manager, the physician, the rancher, or the minister can yield to the temptation to buy a new tangible thing rather than work on an old, nagging problem with some intangible facet of the operation. Motivated soldiers with inferior equipment can often defeat well-equipped mercenaries who have little to fight for. A great artist can do more with a piece of charcoal than an unskilled artist with all the most expensive equipment.

The operating systems are of undeniable importance. Wickham Skinner, Harvard professor of business administration, has clearly outlined the important role of operations in developing corporate strategy.[3] He has discussed the detrimental effects of failing to consider operations in the long range plans and has clearly illustrated the rewards to be gained from including it. The slightest changes and improvements can result in dollars-and-cents progress, as well as savings in time, talent, and effort. However, the relative importance of the tangible systems (and even of the knowledge and expertise of the process) can be overshadowed by the importance of the motivational and authority systems. A balance among these systems must be maintained to achieve the overall goals in the most efficient and effective way.

---

[3] Wickham Skinner, "Manufacturing—A Missing Link in Corporate Strategy." *Harvard Business Review*, vol 47, No. 3. (May-June, 1969), p. 143.

Summary

This chapter is a brief one, but an important one. It is brief because it introduces the systems approach to viewing the manager's world. It is important because of its emphasis on the extent to which many subsystems interact to influence the results of any managerial decision.

Since World War II, our society has been moving deeper and deeper into a systems frame of mind. The new emphasis has been on the ecological nature of the manager's system-making world. Each decision is likely to have unforeseen consequences and implications. The wise manager becomes aware of the many interlocking factors and designs an open system instead of an impossibly closed one.

Various types of management systems are mentioned in the chapter. These types of systems are only the tips of icebergs covered in many other chapters throughout the book, but they are brought together in this chapter to assure that the manager will recognize their interlocking nature. The types of systems described are goal systems, information systems, human systems, authority systems, and operating systems.

Review Questions

1. How does ecology relate to management?
2. Provide one example of a "goal system."
3. "The manager is a nerve center of corporate communication." Explain this statement.
4. Which is more complex, a human system or an information center system? Explain.
5. Distinguish between an authority and an information system.
6. Distinguish between an open and closed system. Give an example of each.
7. Identify and provide an example for each of the major types of systems introduced in this chapter.

part V

The World Outside

20

The Challenging Environment of the Manager

We were all impressed when Johnson first stood up and started talking. It was the first PTA meeting of the year, and he was certainly a man with a cause. We listened intently as he graphically described the rampant lawlessness of our neighborhood schools. We nodded in agreement as he told of petty thievery that made our children's possessions disappear daily.

Johnson rambled on with evangelistic fervor. He had us all ready to march with him to lynch the young thieves. But, unfortunately, he had to add that one final illustration of the school's moral depravity . . . he had to tell about the pencils.

"My boy has anywhere from five to ten pencils stolen from him every week in this school," exclaimed Johnson. "I think something ought to be done!"

Then, glancing around and fearing that his concern over pencils might sound petty, Johnson continued: "Now, don't get me wrong. It's not the pencils—it's the principle of the thing. Why, I can get all the pencils I need for free because I work for the government."

After an embarrassed silence the PTA meeting moved on to the next item of business. Johnson had lost his position as the group's conscience.

In an earlier era, the environment of the manager was much less demanding and challenging. The businesses were operated with single minded purpose. Cornelius Vanderbilt responded to a charge that his actions might have been illegal by exploding, "Law? What do I care about the law? Ain't I got the power?"[1]

In this chapter, we will examine the ethics of business (generally called social responsibility), the ethics of managers, and the international environment in which today's managers must operate.

The Ethics of Business: Social Responsibility

George Bernard Shaw once remarked that every profession is a conspiracy against the public. He was implying that members of every profession are so deeply involved in the getting that they lose sight of the giving. Shaw's idea tends to support the suspicions of many citizens, even those who are in the world of management and quite conscious of their job's social service aspects. Perhaps it is the very nature of management that it is unable to maintain consistent devotion to service. Perhaps service to society is a goal secondary to the majority of managerial pursuits . . . a nice thing if you can afford it but not to come before profits or income.

Models of Social Responsibility

The conflict over the extent to which corporations are socially responsible lies in two mutually exclusive theories—the theory of the traditional corporation and the theory of what Richard Eells and Clarence Walton have called the metrocorporation.[2] In the *traditional corporation* the shareholders are the kings, and maximum profits are the objectives. The job of managers is nothing more or less than steering the company toward profits. There is nothing to give away. The corporation recognizes no public responsibilities except legal ones. The unions will take care of the working man—the corporation must take care of itself. Although this traditional, hard-nosed approach has been often attacked as shortsighted and counterproductive, there are still some experts who support a return to this simplistic arrangement.

---

[1] N. Eberstadt, "What History Tells Us About Corporate Responsibilities," in *Managing Corporate Social Responsibility* (ed. Archie Carol) (Boston: Little, Brown and Co., 1977), p. 21.
[2] *Conceptual Foundations of Business* (Homewood, Ill.: Richard D. Irwin, Inc., 1961), pp. 468–472.

Theodore Levitt,[3] a Harvard professor, declares that what began as a pious intonation of social service and Christian brotherhood and modifier of the big-business profit mania eventually caused more trouble than it cured. Levitt feels that this social responsibility syndrome clashes with sound business philosophy, which he would describe as "The business of business is profits." He foresees the day when the whole society may stand around the corporations' doors demanding care, nurture, and support.

Nobel Laureate, Milton Friedman[4] has declared that "if anything is certain to destroy our free society, to undermine its very foundations, it would be a widespread acceptance by management of some social responsibilities in some sense other than to make as much money as possible."

The *metrocorporation*, by contrast, is as extreme in its social responsibility as the traditional corporation is irresponsible. It is a major social institution and, as such, recognizes its obligation to serve its society. It does not confine itself to pure activities of a business nature. It emphasizes its rights and duties as a "citizen" and endeavors to get involved in many types of benevolent, social, and cultural betterment projects. Some companies, driven by a relentless public relations person and a warm feeling deep down, have in fact overextended themselves in public service. Even those supporters of the involved metrocorporation recognize the danger that the company may become an overly paternalistic and meddling intruder in the affairs of those it is trying to help.

Thus, two extreme positions exist with regard to the ethical relationship between business profits and business service: (1) that business does not and should not do anything but maximize profits; and (2) that business should forget all about profit motives and the profit measure and simply settle down to do social good. Two extremes—it is easy enough to see that the answer must lie somewhere in the middle. The profits are necessary to pay for the service, but the profits will not last long if the social situation goes to pieces. It is another chicken-egg problem. Both aspects are necessary. Some balance must be sought. Managers must decide exactly what it is they are aiming to do with their business. Managers are in the position of leadership. They must bring about the recognition that this deliberation is needed. This is not an intellectual calisthenic. It is not just a topic to fill the agenda of some convention. The obvious fact is that unless a manager (or anybody) knows why

---

[3] The Dangers of Social Responsibility," *Harvard Business Review*, September–October 1958, pp. 41–60.

[4] "Three Major Factors in Business Management: Leadership, Decision-Making, and Social Responsibility," *Social Science Reporter's Eighth Social Science Seminar* (San Francisco, March 19, 1958), pp. 4–5.

they are doing their job, then they are probably doing it poorly and are not likely to be doing it long. Nothing is quite so critical to a journey as a clear understanding of the destination.

The Levels of Social Responsibility

Certain levels of social responsibility are required for business to function in our society. Employees must be paid a minimum wage. Certain types of pollution controls are mandated. Discrimination is forbidden by law. It can be argued that when a firm goes beyond the requirements imposed by law and regulation, it is exercising social responsibility. A model developed by the Chamber of Commerce of the United States has identified the lowest level of acceptable responsibility as when a firm operates in such a way as to satisfy the legal demands that are required for it to engage in business. (Figure 20.1) The traditional corporate manager or the profit-maximizing manager would probably remain at this level.

A manager who was somewhat more responsible would be willing to go beyond the law to meet the recognized expectations of the public. An even greater level of social responsibility would be to anticipate new social demands before the ground swell of public opinion develops. Contemporary firms that have developed programs to recognize the particular demands of working women or dual-career families would fall into this category. The final level of responsibility is where a firm or its executive team exercises leadership in setting new standards of business performance. In our time, Reg Murphy of General Electric and Irvin Shapiro of DuPont are sometimes cited as chief executive officers demonstrating this unusual quality of leadership.

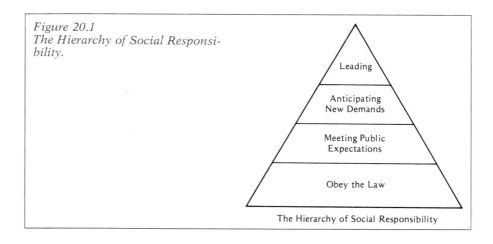

Figure 20.1
The Hierarchy of Social Responsibility.

Leading

Anticipating New Demands

Meeting Public Expectations

Obey the Law

The Hierarchy of Social Responsibility

Evolution of Emphasis

As America grew and changed, its business community's attitudes towards social responsibility changed with it. In fact, Robert Hay and Ed Gray[5] have argued that these attitudes have gone through three distinct phases.

Initially, business managers were believed to have but one objective —to *maximize profits*. The view originated with Adam Smith, who believed that an individual's drive for maximum profits and the regulation of the competitive marketplace could interact to produce the greatest amount of national wealth and therefore the maximum public good. This position was accepted in the United States through the early part of the twentieth century because it helped the country realize its national goals of economic growth and the accumulation of aggregate wealth. This would be level number one of the Chamber of Commerce model of social responsibility—meeting the law.

But in the 1920's and 1930's the diffuse ownership of American corporations and the development of a pluralistic society resulted in the emergence of the *trusteeship* concept. According to this idea, corporate managers were responsible for maintaining an equitable balance among the competing claims of customers, employees, suppliers, creditors, and the community, as well as the stockholders. The trusteeship concept would include meeting the recognized public expectations and some modest participation of social goals.

More recently, the *quality of life* concept has come into prominence among business managers. Its emergence is directly tied to some great changes in America's societal goals. As the United States became increasingly affluent, the scarcity of basic goods and services was no longer the fundamental problem. Instead, attention shifted to issues like the deterioration of the cities, air and water pollution, and the defacement of the landscape. This shift of emphasis has been accompanied by society's demand that business employ its technological and managerial skills to help solve these major problems and thus provide a better quality of life for all this country's citizens. The quality of life concept would be more aggressive in anticipating new social demands and move to genuine leadership in the area of ethical and social concern.

Recent evidence suggests that business is becoming increasingly aware of its social responsibilities. As early as 1956, Ralph Cordiner of General Electric argued that a new type of capitalism was coming into existence in America.[6] He called it "mass capitalism" and claimed that

---

[5] Robert Hay and Ed Gray, "Social Responsibility of Business Mangers," *Academy of Management Journal*, March 1974, pp. 135–138.
[6] Ralph J. Cordiner, *New Frontiers for Professional Managers* (New York: McGraw-Hill, 1964), p. 1.

it valued the spiritual and cultural life as well as the material. David Rockefeller put forward this idea even more clearly when he stated,

> Corporations have developed a sensitive awareness of their responsibility for maintaining an equitable balance among the claims of stockholders, employees, customers and the public at large.[7]

Nor is this position limited to only a few isolated individuals. In a *Harvard Business Review* study of the ethical attitudes of business persons, Brenner and Molander[8] discovered that a large majority of their respondents believed that social responsibility was an ethical issue for both the individual and the corporation. Only 28 per cent of those replying endorsed the traditional dictum that "the social responsibility of business is to stick to business." In fact, when asked to rank the areas to which they felt the greatest responsibility, these executives ranked profit maximization below the efficient use of energy and the assessment of their company's technology upon the environment. They also felt it was to their customer that they owed the greatest responsibility. Stockholders and employees were ranked second and third.

But if managers don't view themselves as conspirators, neither do they see themselves as naive idealists. Fifty-eight per cent of the respondents in the *Harvard Business Review* study felt that the "socially aware executive must show a net short-term profit or long-term economic advantage to the coporation in order to gain acceptance for any socially responsible measure."

The Social Audit

One way that firms have of showing their social responsibility as well as monitoring the degree to which they are meeting their own statements of intent is the use of a social audit. In Chapter 7, we discussed how some of the concepts associated with financial auditing had led progressive firms to develop management audits in order to assess the overall performance of the organization. The third generation[9] of this same concept is the development of a social audit which attempts to evaluate an organization's performance in achieving specific goals in the various areas of social responsibility.

There are two basic approaches to a social audit. In the first, a firm will evaluate the environment in which it operates and establish specific objectives that it intends to accomplish. Subsequently, the firm's

---

[7] David Rockefeller, *Creative Management and Banking*, (New York: McGraw-Hill Book Co., 1964), p. 23.

[8] Steven N. Brenner and Earl A. Molander, "Is the Ethics of Business Changing?" *Harvard Business Review*, January, 1977, pp. 57–71. Subsequent references to the 1977 study of business ethics are to this source.

[9] Council on Trends Perspectives, The Corporation In Transition (Washington, D.C., Chamber of Commerce of The U.S., 1971)

public or board can evaluate how well they have done in meeting those objectives.

A second approach is an attempt to develop a comprehensive checklist of social responsibility concerns and to compare the performance of various companies in recognizing the spectrum of socially responsible actions. A similar approach has been the measurement of references in annual reports to social goals and achievement.[10]

Jim Higgins also asserts that social auditing is becoming more quantitative today. Indeed, it is appropriate because of the tremendous investment required today for social overhead. A study of 185 firms from the largest 1,000 U.S. corporations indicated that only about half had established specific objectives in the area of external affairs.[11]

Still there is little agreement about what should be involved in a social audit or who should be responsible for this activity. There are, however, advances being made. The American Accounting Association has established a committee on measurement of social costs. The National Association of Accountants has set up a group to establish goals for the accounting profession in dealing with social responsibility and improving social performance of the business community. The American Institute of CPA's has organized a committee on social accounting. In 1975, the Securities and Exchange Commission created guidelines on how organizations should report their environmental performance to investors. The area of measuring and monitoring social responsibility is as likely to be a key growth area during the next few years.

Ethics and the Manager

Occasionally, it will be said of an individual that he or she is a person of high ethics. Almost without doubt the purpose of the statement is to pass on a compliment regarding the person. We understand easily that this is a compliment. Yet most of us would be hard pressed to explain exactly what is meant by "high ethics" (or even "ethics" for that matter). We talk about ethical problems and codes of ethics and perhaps never stop to think about the import of our terms.

Like many intangibles, ethics are often most easily perceived when they are weak or absent. In our day there is a disproportionate number of prophets of doom who preach the sad news that the world has abandoned its ethics. The moral crises of our times are attributed by these folks to a rather catchall phrase: "moral and ethical breakdown." Our language is filled with new terms for old human philosophies. *Situation ethics* and the *new morality* could be identified in most other centuries under slightly different names.

---

[10] James M. Higgins, *Organizational Policy and Strategic Management* (Hinsdale, Ill.: The Dryden Press, 1979), p. 147–148.

[11] W. Hegarty, J. Aplin, and R. Cosier, "Achieving Corporate Success in External Affairs: A Management Challenge," *Business Horizons*, Winter, 1978.

Is the world losing its ethics? The question has perhaps never had greater significance. Charges of corporate irresponsibility with regard to the critical issues of the 1960's and 1970's (minority relations, consumerism, and the environment) combined with continuing disclosures of corporate wrongdoing at home and abroad call into doubt business's ethical standards.

Watergate and Abscam have raised even more serious questions, not only about our nation's leaders, but also about the moral fabric of the society as a whole.

Whether the world, despite its current rash of problems, is any worse than ever is open to debate. Certainly no one can doubt that societal ills are definitely present. And yet, there is a lingering question about the nature of ethics. Are ethics culture-wide factors, or are our ethical considerations made on a more personal, one-to-one basis? Are people really any different today than in ancient Rome or medieval Europe? Are humans inherently good—or inherently bad?

The deeper we delve into the discussion of ethics and the nature and morals of humanity, the more confused we can become. As our thoughts begin to spiral in confusion and indecision, we want to drop the whole discussion. What good, after all, is it to discuss such things? Why trouble ourselves? Ethics have nothing to do with production and quotas and markets . . . do they? Ethics are fit topics only for those who are not worried about competition and profits . . . aren't they? There is no reason for association managers to get overly involved with consideration of ethical questions . . . is there?

Obviously, the answer is yes. Managers not only should but must give thought to ethics. If they are to be any more than spineless automatons they must evaluate and refine the ideals and principles upon which their actions will be based. They must question the motivations and methods and consciously establish those beliefs to which they will hold. A person without a clear-cut, conscious ethical position is a ship with neither sail nor anchor.

Definition

Sometimes called moral philosophy, the word *ethics* is derived from the Greek word *ethos*, which refers to character. Webster defines an *ethic* as "the discipline dealing with that which is good and bad and with moral duty and obligation." In general, ethics deal more with good than with evil. Our code of ethics provides a small voice that tells us what other people should do. Actually, our ethics describe our aspirations rather than our behavior. We are not as concerned about people *doing right* as we are about their knowing what is right to do. (Some apologists for our new morality might well argue that we live in a more honest society that despises the old practice of saying one thing and doing another and so has chosen to do and then explain why.)

In simplest terms, we can define *ethics* as "a system of moral principles." More broadly, our definition might expand to "that branch of philosophy dealing with values relating to human conduct, with respect to rightness or wrongness of certain actions and to the goodness or badness of the motives and ends of such actions."[12]

From the standpoint of the organizational manager, *ethics* may be seen as "the rules or standards governing the moral conduct of the members of the organization or management profession." Ethical discussions, for individuals or for organizations, are real-life concerns. They are no ivory-tower affair. They are an attempt to consolidate, understand, and give intellectual coherence to the motives and impulses that characterize our actions.

We want to know what to expect from organizations, other individuals, and ourselves. For this reason, we demand organization policies and consistent individual behavior. Ethics allow us the luxury of standardizing our expectations.

> Ethics is an attempt to make a science of what is in reality an art, the art of right living. Every art has had its traditional precepts and techniques, not so much reasoned out as felt out and handed on to beginners dogmatically, often as sacred mysteries. This is eminently true of the art of right living: its codes have been transmitted rather than explained; and anyone who undertakes to replace authority by a reasoned system takes a long risk.[13]

Ethics are not simple. They do not fit into neat textbook situations. They are not a matter of choosing the obvious, clear-cut good over the obvious, clear-cut evil. Anyone can do that. The difficulty of ethical consideration is that the alternatives are most often almost equally worthy objectives or else the lesser of two evils. Some forms of warfare are commonly agreed to be unethical. Poison gas and hydrogen bombs are mutually excluded because there would be no way to control such devices once they were unleashed. We may agree to disagree with bullets, but nuclear weapons are somewhere on the other side of the international ethics line. By the same token, some management practices (like lying, cheating, and fraud) might give us initial advantages. Yet we realize that if everybody played that way chaos would reign. Therefore, we establish ethics . . . policies . . . no lying, no stealing.

The entire phenomenon of ethical action is beautifully capsuled in the prizefighting ring: two men are locked in vicious battle, straining every

[12] *Ethical Problems of the Association Executive* (Washington, D.C.: U.S. Chamber of Commerce, 1972), p. 2.
[13] William Ernest Hocking, quoted by Clifford Clarke, *Ethical Problems of the Organization Executive* (Atlanta, Ga.: Georgia Business and Industry Association, 1971), p. 5.

muscle to gain advantage. Through all their efforts, they consistently refrain from hitting below the belt. Why? Ethics. There have to be standards. Without predictable performance, there would eventually be no prizefighting at all. The same is true of business and personal relationships. Without ethics, there could be no working together.

Today, business managers operate in a pluralistic society—they must respond to the interest of many institutions in society. Stockholders, employees, suppliers, customers, the government and the general public all have a claim on the attention and interest of today's manager. Moreover, these constituencies are becoming widely diverse. The interest of many companies extends beyond the national boundaries. As a result, managers must be concerned with ethics, morality, economics and culture in a variety of settings.

The American Ethic

We often hear jokes about the sacred things of American society—the flag, motherhood, apple pie, and so on. Yet for all our sophisticated snobbishness, there really have been certain basic principles—certain ethics—that have pushed our nation toward success and accomplishment. One great advantage that the United States has enjoyed is the benefit of history. The best of many ethical systems have been blended together. America is not only a melting pot of *ethnic* groups but of many and varied *ethic* groups. The moral tradition of this country is a network of three broad interrelated intellectual and spiritual strands: (1) the humanistic doctrines of the great philosophers of all ages; (2) the teachings of the great religions; and (3) the egalitarian ideals of the founding patriots.

The great philosophers and legalists of the ancient civilizations conducted considerable trial-and-error experimentation that has been invaluable in framing the constitutional ethics of our country. Not only is our legal system based on the Graeco-Roman traditions of democracy and jurisprudence, but many of our institutions have grown out of the great reawakening of the Renaissance. The welding of the best of both worlds has yielded an American ethic . . . an American feeling . . . for rights, justice, loyalty, and accomplishment.

The great religions came to America with the immigrants from every land. Though the Judeo-Christian faiths gained early majority and influence, many other religious systems have added their strength to the composite American ethic. The Christian and Jewish traditions have systematized the broadest understandings of personal duty and moral responsibility. There is great emphasis in biblical teaching upon a person's relations to fellow citizens. Religion has probably influenced

American society more than any other factor. The future of American ethics is uncertain, for the changing nature of American religious practice is sure to affect the way we live.

The founders of America came to these shores in search of things. Some were looking for religious freedom; some sought philosophical freedom; others wanted to find new and exciting commercial potentials and the freedom to capitalize upon their potentials. They came seeking these great freedoms. They found a country where these goals could be achieved. The government we enjoy today is the benefactor of those people's hunger and thirst for specific opportunities.

Hurley summarizes the centuries-old struggle to find a system of ethical explanation. He says, "Down through the centuries, people suffered and wrote at great length, describing how he practiced virtue and longed for vice, or practiced vice and longed for virtue."[14]

When we try to isolate qualities that can motivate ethical action, there are several human traits that come to mind: (1) *Wisdom.* Intelligence is a basic need of the moral life. The great thinker tests the validity of ideas and evaluates their significance. (2) *Courage.* We may admire the person who knows what to believe and is determined to stick by it. (3) *Temperance.* The extremes on almost every issue leave something to be desired. It's true in politics, envy, ambition, egotism, or eating and drinking. (4) *Justice.* We all appreciate and admire fairness, respect for other's rights, and the honoring of obligations. Nothing infuriates us like injustice; the shout of "That's not fair!" is enough to stop all proceedings. (5) *Conscience.* Some describe conscience as intuition about what should or should not be done. Others consider conscience to be the voice of God within us. Still others feel that it is a sensitivity developed within each individual on the basis of accumulated experience. Conscience must be obeyed, but it can hardly be trusted as a sole dictator of ethics. The consciences of individuals and the consciences of organizations can be trained. A mature person will be working to keep the conscience educated and objective. A false conscience is a dangerous influence on life. Table 20.1 identifies the basic value perceptions that people have and places them under three major headings—religion, philosophy, and culture.

The Case for Business Bluffing

This need to make a profit is at the root of Albert Z. Carr's controversial argument that there should be and always has been a double standard applied to the morality of business.[15] Carr believes that business and poker should be played by different rules than those which apply to

---

[14] Hurley, op. cit., p. 21.
[15] Albert Z. Carr, "Is Business Bluffing Ethical?" *Harvard Business Review*, January–February 1968, pp. 143–153.

	Category	Source	Instrument	Major Value	Term
	1. Religious	Deity	Faith	Charity Love of God Neighbor	Moral theology
	2. Philosophic	People	Reason	Justice Exchange Equity	Ethics Descriptive Normative Critical
	3. Cultural	Society Nation Ethnic group Corporations	Experience	Progress Pluralism Competition Individualism	

Table 20.1 Basic Value Perceptions*

* Adapted from material contained in Richard Fells and Clarence Walton, *Conceptual Foundations of Business* (Homewood, Ill.: Richard D. Irwin, Inc., 1961).

polite society. He argues that we should not expect to approach a used car salesperson with an open, straightforward statement of what we will pay, anymore than we expect a poker player to tell us what cards were just dealt. When companies begin negotiations with union representatives, what would happen if all cards were laid face up on the table? Do managers have to be allowed a special set of standards of morality? Is there always going to be an accepted organizational bluffing allowance? As management attempts to refine its motivations into a more noble future, is it a foregone conclusion that "poker game ethics" must apply to businessmen?

In defense of the management community, it should be said that if business is a conspiracy, as Shaw claimed, then society is conspiring against itself, for any organization exists only by the will and participation of the people. No matter how high its social consciousness, an organization is destined for extinction if it is not ultimately able to pay its bills. The finest record of public service will not keep the doors open if the ability to continue is not there. Therefore, the manager is faced by an initial dilemma that assaults the very nature of our business system. Traditionally, business has had the job of making a profit and doing it fairly and honestly and in the process rendering service to the community. But in the last few years such a role has been classed as crass, money-grubbing social insensitivity. Public opinion is demanding that because business appears to be about the richest thing around, it ought to take action outside of its primary roles, either directly or by influencing government, to heal the wounds of society. Some businessmen would like to answer, "Sure. . . . It's a nice idea, but who is going to mind the store while I am out serving the poor?"

The manager is continually over some ethical barrel involved in trying to make the decision that will keep the company moving forward

Cheyenne Autumn (Warner Brothers, 1964). Do businessmen play by poker rules?

and at the same time serve the interests of employees, customers, and family. Ecological problems are an excellent example: managers' production necessarily interrupts the operation of nature's cycles in order to make life better for consumers; the interruption of ecological balance may eventually make life worse for the consumers or for their grandchildren; on the other hand, the pollution may not affect the consumers as much as loss of the company's product. The manager has to be able to look with respect at the person in the mirror every morning. If managers take an exclusively ecological position, they may be out of work and have no mirror to look into each morning.

Once again, it is the manager who will have to serve as the conscience prod to draw attention to these significant problems and then serve as a counselor and sounding board in their resolution. He or she occupies a unique position of responsibility and opportunity with respect to the ethics of the corporation.

Shapiro has suggested four general ethical problems that typically concern executives:[16]

1. *What is the limit of our job responsibility?* To what extent must we be bound to producing only those products that we know to be of the highest quality? In most cases, the consumer is not sophisticated enough to tell first class from good enough. Is it unethical for the profession to produce less than perfect goods? If so, how much less than perfect?

2. *Do we make the decisions, or must we involve our clients or customers?* Obviously, the managerial team are the ones with the knowledge of their situation. Would their decisions be more wise and farsighted than decisions in which the competitors and customers participated? Should business be encouraged to allow the consumers a voting voice in business decisions? Do people know what is really best for them?

3. *Shall we manipulate the people for their own good?* "The consequences of benevolent autocracy and popular apathy may be very grave. In some trade unions, the individual member possesses fewer rights with respect to his own organization than is possessed as a citizen with respect to the government."[17]

4. *Which is more important—the system or the individual?* Does business provide needed structures or liberating opportunity for workers? For all its faults, does the world of giant organizations provide more effective opportunity for individual freedom and expression than would ever have been possible under the microorganization system that preceded it? Is it futile for the individual to struggle against the omnipotent organization, or is the resistance of the individual the provider of a dynamic tension required for progress? How can the organization be in conflict with its members if it is founded and operated upon a system of representative participation?

Obviously, ethical problems and discussions are going to be among the most difficult and time-consuming activities of the manager. People see things differently. There are many sides to every question. It is the task of the leadership to bring consensus and unity out of the natural diversity of members. This task is not easy, but it is imperative.

The questionnaire in the following section was designed to discover the varying attitudes of business groups regarding several familiar statements of ethical principles. If you have trouble believing that agreement on ethical questions is difficult, try getting a unified opinion about one of these statements from any five of your associates.

---

[16] Op. cit., pp. 4–8.
[17] Sidney Hook, *Bureaucrats Are Human,* quoted in Shapiro, op. cit., p. 6.

Ethical Opinions and Attitudes

The classic study of business ethics was conducted in 1961 by Raymond C. Baumhart S. J., who surveyed over fifteen hundred executives from a variety of firms and management levels. This work was updated by Stephen Brenner and Earl Molander in 1977. The changes which occurred during the sixteen years between the two studies are interesting, if not particularly encourging.

In the aftermath of Watergate we might have expected a greater sensitivity to ethical issues and somewhat higher standards. But this was not the case. In 1961, three out of four executives claimed to have experienced ethical dilemmas; but in 1977 only four out of seven claimed to have encountered them. We could assume that there are fewer conflicts in the 1970's, but no evidence indicates this. The more probable explanation, according to the authors, is that ethical standards have declined so that situations which once caused ethical discomfort have now become accepted practice.

Not only were the 1970's characterized by fewer ethical conflicts, but the areas in which they occur have also changed. No longer are problems associated with firings and layoffs especially important. Rather, respondents complain most frequently of a superior's pressure to support incorrect views, sign false documents, overlook the superior's wrong doing, and do business with the superior's friends. Employees do not seem as willing as they once were to accept instructions without question. This situation, whatever its explanation, does suggest a weakening of the corporate authority structure, and an attendant impact upon business conduct in the future.

Perhaps the most encouraging aspect of Baumhart's survey was the discovery that years of business experience do not tend to dull a person's ethical sensibilities. Indeed, according to his analysis, older executives and those with longer experience in business reported higher ethical standards and opinions than those who are younger and less experienced.

Two possible explanations were cited for this phenomenon. First, there was the possibility that the older respondents had already achieved their career plateau and no longer had to engage in the shady, aggressive activities that had helped them reach their various positions. The second and more positive interpretation was that older and experienced managers had learned that it is not only morally but also economically advisable to practice good ethics.[18] Future business leaders have agreed with this corollary of the Protestant ethic. In a 1967 survey

---

[18] "How Ethical are Businessmen?" *Harvard Business Review*, July 1961, pp. 6–8; and *An Exploratory Study of Businessmen's Views of the Ethics of Businessmen.* An unpublished Ph.D. dissertation (Boston: Harvard Business School, 1963), p. 145.

of MBA graduates, 90 per cent responded affirmatively to the statement, "Sound ethics are good business in the long run."[19]

Purpose, Pragmatism, and Profits

At least since Plato, the question as to whether individuals and groups behave in an ethical fashion because of moral conviction or because of the attendant advantages of ethical behavior has been debated. Moral responsibility stimulates trust, and trust is frequently attended by material rewards.

The contemporary business community seems to disagree with Theodore Levitt, who stated,

> The businessman exists for only one purpose: to create and deliver value satisfactions at a profit to himself. If what is offered can be sold at a profit, then it is legitimate. The spiritual and oral consequences of the businessman's actions are none of his concern.[20]

When asked to comment on this statement, 89 per cent of the M.B.A. respondents in the study disagreed and almost three fourths identified their reaction as "strong disagreement." An even more impressive 94 per cent of executive respondents expressed disapproval of this position.

Of course, the Carthaginian Creed (At Carthage, nothing that results in profit is regarded as disgraceful") receives some support in practically every economic text used to introduce the business student to the underlying discipline of the curriculum. Robert Anthony asserts that all five of the leading economics texts identify profit maximization as the supreme, if not the only, objective of modern business. Despite this indoctrination, 76 per cent of the respondents reported that in their opinion profit maximization is immoral. An even larger number of business executives (83 per cent) had reacted affirmatively to Anthony's assertion, "For corporation executives to act in the interest of shareholders alone, and not also in the interest of employees and consumers, is unethical."[21]

Although the ethical opinions expressed by graduating M.B.A.'s correspond very closely to those expressed by businessmen in almost every instance, Table 20.2 shows that a higher percentage of managers reported opinions that would generally be viewed as more ethical.

---

[19] This section is drawn largely from Fulmer's "Business Ethics: Present and Future," *Personnel Administration*, September–October 1971, pp. 48–56.

[20] "Are Advertising and Marketing Corrupting Society?" *Advertising Age*, October 6, 1958, p. 89.

[21] "The Trouble with Profit Maximization," *Harvard Business Review*, November–December 1960, p. 126.

		M.B.A.	Executive

Table 20.2
The Business Scene

Respondents were asked how they felt about the statements listed below. Except for item two (2), all percentages indicate the number *agreeing* with the statement.

	M.B.A.	Executive
1. "Sound ethics is good business in the long run."	98%	99%
2. "The businessman exists for only one purpose: to create and deliver satisfactions at a profit to himself. If what is offered can be sold at a profit, then it is legitimate. The spiritual and moral consequences of the businessman's actions are none of his concern."	(89%)	(94%)
3. "For corporation executives to act in the interest of shareholders alone, and not also in the interest of employees and consumers, is unethical."	76%	83%
4. "Whatever is good business is good ethics."	15%	15%
5. "Let the buyer beware."	24%	20%
6. "Competition is stiffer than ever. As a result, many businessmen find themselves forced to resort to practices which are considered shady, but which appear necessary to survive."	42%	—
7. "The American business executive tends to ignore the great ethical laws as they apply immediately to his work. He is preoccupied chiefly with gain."	42%	50%

Creating an Ethical Code

One of the most far-reaching company activities designed to improve business ethics is the adoption of a code of ethics and/or standards of practice. Although it is true that codes range from arbitrary, legalistic documents to vague generalities written in such misty, grandiose terms that they become meaningless, the potential contributions from codes make them worthy of consideration by any progressive organization. Seventy-five per cent of the managers studied in 1977 favored some sort of code because they believed it would help executives to raise the ethical level of their industry, define the limits of acceptable conduct, and refuse unethical requests.

More than anything else, the code of ethics is evidence of concern on the part of the adopter. Interest in ethical behavior intense enough to develop and adopt a code brings subsidiary contributions to all parties who have contact with the code or its creator. Some of these advantages are discussed in the following paragraphs.[22]

Internal Benefits. One can reap significant rewards by merely stopping to ask the searching question, "Why are we in business?" and then to identify what the firm or group recognizes as desirable practices or acceptable standards. The American Management Association has con-

[22] This section is based on Robert M. Fulmer, "Creating an Ethical Code," *Manage*, August 1968, pp. 28–33.

cluded, "The process of formulating the creed is often more valuable than the finished product." Hopefully, every internal and external relationship is explored with penetrating thoroughness, and cynics are given the opportunity to test their attitudes against sincere beliefs. The result of clarification and careful consideration is as significant as any benefit that comes from the concern demonstrated in the creation of an ethical code.

From a selfish standpoint, there is considerable status associated with subscribing to a code of ethics. Codes are sometimes criticized because they appear framed and hung in public places, apparently for display. Although the display should not be the only reason for adopting a code, it should be pointed out that among its other contributions, this can be a valid and practical sales device or public relations gimmick. While critics frequently attack such labels, no one has gone to the trouble to spell out exactly what is wrong with a firm's informing others of its intentions to conduct business in an honorable and ethical fashion.

It is generally recognized that effective self-regulation can often prevent external controls. It is difficult to explain the logic that leads an employer to provide better working conditions than competing union shops in order to discourage the organization of his workers, or the willingness of business firms to police themselves more carefully than government even considers. Yet almost every individual who respects freedom is able to understand the basis of these actions. Government, as well as management, tends to operate on the exception principle. Consequently, firms, industries and professions are less likely to attract the attention of legislators or regulatory agencies if their reputations and practices remain above suspicion.

Advantages for Employees. Of course a firm interested in attracting high-caliber employees must develop a reputation for ethical practices. At the same time, employees can expect consistent dealings from a firm with high standards and are more likely to enjoy association with an employer of this type. Codes can provide evidence of a firm's ethical concern, strengthen the resolve of employees to be ethical, and also provide a source of coercion against ethical apathy.

From the standpoint of the new employee, written codes eliminate a great deal of the uncertainty often associated with learning a job. The creation of a code helps an employee avoid the confusion of attempting to determine just what is ethical. The code becomes particularly significant if older and wiser individuals have already wrestled with and reached a solution to a particular problem. There seems little reason for each subsequent employee to spend the time and energy to reach the same or a similar conclusion.

Another major advantage in having a code of ethics is that it helps an individual refuse an unethical request without seeming sanctimonious.

Advantages for Customers. Although firms benefit from having a sales document that is designed to give their customers a sense of confidence, it should be recognized that these customers also benefit if they have reason for being assured that they will be treated in an ethical fashion.

Advantages for the Industry. Machiavelli once warned that the good or ethical man was often an easy prey for the unscrupulous. Frequently, the "weak" or ethical members of an industry may decide to band together and through their united strength insist that all members of the industry behave in a predictable, ethical fashion. The net effect of such a decision is often enough to raise the level of competition within the entire industry or profession involved. If sanctions are sufficiently strong, unethical practices may be eliminated.

But although this may be the ideal result, codes have seemed to have a limited impact. The majority of managers studied believe that people would violate a code whenever they thought they could avoid detection. This evidence suggests that a code's real value lies not in its capacity to eliminate unethical actions, but in its capacity to retard the commission of such acts. Even if this is not accomplished, the creation of standards may at least retard the degree of unethical action. For example, a speedster traveling in a forty-five-mile-per-hour zone will generally drive somewhat more slowly than he will in a fifty-five-mile-per-hour zone. The establishment of definite standards may also be compared to posted speed-limit warning signs. These standards make it much easier to identify and to punish those who behave in an undesirable fashion.

Codes can be valuable apart from their role in professionalization. Still, practically every treatment of professionalization recognizes that a well-defined code of ethics is essential for a vocational specialization to become a full-fledged and legitimate profession. Advocates of professionalization for management must, of course, unite their constituency behind a code before their goal can be achieved.

Even the most talented managers will find it difficult for those lightning fingers to emulate successfully the code of a higher but less bureaucratic Being. Obviously, each code should be tailor-made for the adopting group. Nevertheless, there are some general principles that should simplify the process for a group attempting to develop its own standards of practice.

1. *Study what others have done.* Borrowing ideas, however, is valid only if the activities, employees, and problems are similar.

2. *Don't do it all yourself.* A manager usually has too many operating pressures to find time to acquire extensive knowledge concerning the usual format and composition of codes. Consequently, outside assistance is often a very desirable investment.

3. *Participation brings support.* Those who are to be governed by a code are much more likely to support the provisions that it contains if they have had a voice in its formulation. Although final decisions about

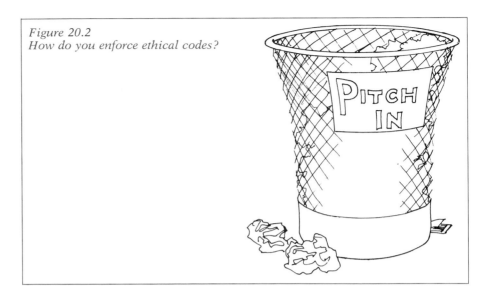

Figure 20.2
How do you enforce ethical codes?

company policy will be made by top management, representatives of all segments within an organization should be asked to approve both the procedure and the content of a code at each stage of its development.

4. *Provide for enforcement.* Former Secretary of Commerce Luther Hodges has asserted that "A code that doesn't provide for enforcement isn't worth the paper it's written on." The process of "enforcement" should be explained in a set of written provisions either in the code itself or in a policy manual. These enforcement activities should be designed to deprive unethical managers of privileges, benefits, and prestige while at the same time protecting the public and other members of the work group from injury. Companies generally charge each employee's superior with the responsibility of seeing that he conducts himself in an ethical fashion. Sanctions generally are applied in terms of compensation, promotability, or job maintenance.

5. *Keep the code up to date.* Ethical codes cannot be adopted and then forgotten. Periodic revision not only keeps the code up to date but will also maintain a sense of involvement on the part of employees or members, provided, of course, they have a voice in the revisions.

Although these suggestions will not make the job of writing a new decalogue painless, they should eliminate some of the most common pitfalls.

Codes of ethics have already made significant contributions in areas in which they have been given a chance. Greater good can and will result when serious attempts are made to eliminate some of the empirical weaknesses that have damaged the reputation of these instruments and when uniform attention is directed to the development of a consistent pattern of ethical codes.

International Environment

The late Marshall McLuhan once compared the world to a shrinking "global village." It is no longer possible for a nation or a tribe that doesn't like its neighbors to ignore them or to move somewhere else. A popular song of a few years back asked, "Where do you go when there's no place to go . . . and you don't want to be where you are?" The answer for us is that there is no place to go. We must face our problems. Our shrinking world has left no more space to be alone, at least in business matters.

Economist Kenneth Boulding has used the phrase *cowboy capitalism* to describe the American economy of yesterday. He compares yesterday's capitalism to the early American West. The land was so rich and resources so vast that people could abuse their environment with impunity. They could cut down trees, kill buffalo, and plow the grassland. And if erosion began to take the land, or the animals got sparse, the answer was easy. Move on to virgin territory and leave the wornout land behind. There was always more over the horizon.

Another analogy used is to describe our "spaceship earth." All of humankind is part of one survival system, hurtling through space together. Each one's actions affect everyone else on the spaceship. We can no longer afford to use up resources. We must recycle and use them again.

Managers in the international global village must recognize that the time of cowboy capitalism is over. The abuse of any part of the world's environment must be seen as hazardous to the progress of all one's fellow travelers on spaceship earth.

Currently, there are over 4 million workers in American industry and business whose jobs are directly dependent upon the health of the U.S. world trade. Yet current trends are disconcerting. The future of U.S. world trade is far from secure. The political shifts and slips are sources of continuing danger. Devaluation of the dollar, foreign attitudes toward U.S. business, and U.S. public opinion are likely to bring continued problems for managers with international responsibilities.

Organization for Activities

There are several routes by which domestic companies become international. The most common is when a successful domestic company begins to have sizable foreign requests for its product. Or strategic planners may find some overseas market ripe for the harvest. Initially, the company becomes an exporter. It opens the minimal required offices to distribute, advertise, sell, and service its product.

A similar basic stage exists when a company is an importer only.

Such a company develops a flow of foreign products which it markets or a flow of foreign raw materials which are incorporated into its own domestic products.

Frequently a domestic company sells a *license* or franchise to some foreign company. The major management challenge created by this arrangement is legal. Licence agreements depend greatly on careful contract wording. Many American firms have learned bitter lessons in the licensing arena. In some cases, the franchise was granted without sufficient stipulations about quality control of the product. Some foreign holders of the franchise have merely learned the ropes through the license period. Then they introduce a similar—and often better adapted —product. Indeed, many licensing companies have found themselves training their own competitors.

The joint venture is similar to the licensing approach. But it stipulates the percentage control of the participating companies. Some countries (such as Japan, England, and Mexico) will not allow an outside firm to own controlling interest in certain domestic joint ventures. The joint venture is, of course, more stable than the licensing situation. It is cheaper than holding the entire ownership. But it is difficult to control, because it involves cooperation, communication, and organization across national boundaries.

A wholly-owned operation may be of two types. It may be a branch of the domestic corporation. It may also be a wholly-owned subsidiary, frequently a company with its own management and objectives. But it is owned completely by a parent corporation outside the country.

Some American manufacturers have developed substantial overseas operations. They have done this through either joint ventures or wholly-owned operations. In companies such as Ford, IBM IT&T, 3M, Exxon, National Cash Register, Singer, Colgate-Palmolive, and Gillette, over 30 percent of their total sales are done abroad. Budgets, laws and regulations, meetings, personnel procedures and, in fact, every aspect of management becomes more complex when a firm is truly multi-national.

The day of the multinational company is no longer in the future. Corporations occasionally suffer abuse or even loss at the hands of political changes, as happened in recent years in Chile. But it is becoming far more likely for the powerful foreign business interests to wield considerable power over deliberations and decisions of national governments.

Multinational Management—Why?

The multinational company is an often-used term today but was not included in most dictionaries even a decade ago. Typically, a multinational company is one that has plant operations and managerial personnel and ownership of a mix of foreign countries.

In the late 1800's, there had been a few border crossings. Du Pont purchased a few Canadian powder mills. Edison started the Canadian General Electric Company. It was not until the mid-1900s that advantages of multinational status swung open the doors on an era of global cooperation that has not yet reached its zenith.

Today, the strength of multinational corporations is such that many companies have more financial resources than the countries in which they do business. In fact, if a corporation's sales were equated with a nation's output of goods and services, over half the world's 100 biggest powers would be international corporations. Large international companies currently do business outside their home country equal to about one sixth of the world's gross product.

Managerial Advantages for International Operations

There are three major reasons for the swing to international operations. The first and most commonly assumed reason is *cheaper labor.* Once production processes are streamlined as much as possible, the cost of labor is the remaining adjustable variable. In many cases, the extra costs of transportation, construction, and tariffs can be regained many times over by reductions in costs. Wages in other countries are generally much lower than in the United States. But wages in certain countries like Germany and Japan have been rising fast. Of course, low wages must be accompanied by reasonable productivity for this advantage to be important.

A second reason for companies to establish foreign operations is the *location of raw materials.* Why should a company buy raw materials in one country (which has cheaper labor or labor of equal cost) and ship them to home factories where labor is more expensive? If the production facility can be set up where the resources are, there will be savings on transportation, tariffs, and talent.

A third type of expansion motivation is the *availability of new markets.* With competition getting stiffer at home, the corporation often realizes that there are untapped markets waiting across the border. Singer has created demand for sewing machines in places where no modern sewing equipment had ever been seen. In 1973 Pepsi-Cola was given permission to sell its products in Russia. Here was a market where no American soft drink had ever been sold. Most recently Coca Cola was allowed to enter the People's Republic of China.

Besides these three positive motivators for making a company multinational, there have been negative pressures. These have pushed successful firms across borders whether they wanted to go or not. As certain companies grow larger and more powerful, they come under the scrutiny of governmental agencies looking for monopolies. Seeing impending difficulty connected with domestic expansion, management moved its emphasis to world markets. In many cases, this has proved a happy move—though initially it was prompted by expansion limitations.

Unique Challenges of Multinational Management

Domestic companies may make rash assumptions as they rush into multinational expansion. Otherwise intelligent managers will make major decisions on the basis of a movie stereotype about a country or after making a single visit. The general need for careful planning is even greater in a foreign country. The manager has no experience to fill in the information gaps.

Problems sneak up on executives of multinational firms in the most unexpected ways, including the following:

Americans often take *reading skills* for granted, as they do a common language. India has over 500 million potential buyers, but only 15 percent are literate, and 51 languages are spoken.

Local attitudes and tastes may be important. If a product is thought to be mainly for men or children, or even crooks, its sales would be affected. International attitudes toward milk are a case in point. They range from the Norwegians, who drink 516 pounds per capita each year, to the French and Italians, who think milk is only for children.

Stereotypes about foreign countries are often incorrect and misleading. Would it make marketing different to discover that the average Frenchman uses twice as many cosmetics as his wife; or that Italians eat only half as much spaghetti as the Germans.

Climatic differences and currency problems are two areas in which difficulty is anticipated but still encountered.

Local laws, trade barriers, and quotas can make the free practice of business very difficult. Special laws about taxation, shipping, and employment must be considered. Any U.S. manager who assumes all foreign ports will meet American standards in unloading ships or delivering goods deserves every delay encountered. Business customs and ethics are rarely part of written law. Still, they are certain to affect marketing strategy. Sometimes the differences in custom are merely irritating. Americans are not accustomed to extended price negotiations common in other countries. In other cases, differences may create key moral and legal questions. For example, bribery of public officials in certain countries is a common business practice. This is unethical and illegal in the United States. Should managers adopt these international market practices? There may be strong resentment about the power of both the USA and the company. During the past decade, IT&T was accused of contributing money to political parties in Chile to bring down the Allende Marxist government. Gulf Oil was accused of making massive contributions to influence elections in South Korea. As a result of actual and perceived corporate abuses of power and because of rising nationalism, multinational firms are often viewed with suspicion by host countries. In the event this suspicion turns to hostility, every multinational firm faces the potential risk of government takeover (expropriation).

The number one problem of the multinational corporation is not a function of the country at all. There is a *critical shortage of qualified management personnel* for multinational operations. Schools are now training for international management. Some corporations are beginning to try to make overseas experience attractive. It is now a requisite for advancement within the corporation. But training U.S. managers for foreign operations is only a half-step toward maturity for the multinational company. Full maturity cannot be realized until managerial ranks of overseas subsidiaries include able personnel from the local scene. Headquarters of American-controlled multinationals must include foreign nations in managerial posts.

A final organizational problem often occurs in the upper echelons of the multinational company at the critical *interface of divisions*. Relationships between divisions can become strained. Competitiveness among division executives is increased by nationalistic pride. Great care for detail and fairness must be tied into the agreements. Plans for marketing areas and responsibilities of each corporate arm must be made. There is danger of aggression among national divisions of the multinational company. Boundaries and interrelationships must be spelled out and carefully supervised.

Summary

In today's pluralisic society, managers must respond to the demands of stockholders, employees, suppliers, customers, government, and the general public. All of these demands create a tremendous challenge for managers in coping with their complex environment.

This chapter has examined the social responsibility of the business, the ethics of managers, and the international environment in which today's managers must operate.

Most corporations have moved beyond the *traditional* emphasis on profit maximization, or doing what the law requires, to a well-tempered approach of trusteeship which meets and sometimes anticipates the expectations of the public. A few progressive firms can be described by the "metro-corporation" concept that stresses "quality of life" and provides genuine leadership in the area of organizational ethics and social responsibility.

Public sentiment, along with the efforts of several professional organizations has increased the popularity of the "social audit." Social audits will typically be used by firms to identify the degree to which they are meeting specific social objectives or the extent to which they compare favorably with other organizations in meeting their social expectations.

Three major studies about ethical attitudes and opinions of business managers have been conducted since 1961. Major conclusions are as follows:

There is substantial disagreement as to whether ethical standards in business today have changed from what they were.

Managers are somewhat more cynical about the ethical conduct of their peers than they were.

Most managers favor ethical codes, although they strongly prefer general precept codes to specific practice codes.

The ethical code was pointed out as one of the most useful tools in upgrading ethical awareness and practice. The extra consideration involved in establishing a code is likely to be as valuable as the code itself. Some of the advantages of developing a statement of ethical policy are internal benefits of morale and public relations, employee advantages, customer advantages, and advantages for the industry or profession.

Steps for the establishment of a code of ethics should include (1) studying what others have done, (2) having more than one code-maker, (3) involving those who will be affected, (4) providing for enforcement, and (5) keeping the code up-to-date.

Management may decide to become international or multinational in order to obtain cheaper labor. They may want to secure cheaper raw materials or to reach new markets. These motives are often logical and provide genuine benefits for the firm. But in considering a potential multinational move, managers must consider language, local attitudes, and differences in tastes, culture, climate, laws, and other variables which exist between nations. Perhaps the greatest problem facing the multinational firm is the critical shortage of qualified management personnel.

Students now in school will influence and be influenced by the future level of ethical practice in business. There are always plenty of prophets of doom ready to predict the downfall of our present environment. Of course, the downfall of the present situation will be no problem at all . . . if something better replaces it.

Review Questions

1. Is business bluffing ethical?
2. What is Theodore Levitt's theory of social responsibility? Do you agree with him?
3. Are graduate business students more ethical than practicing businessmen?
4. What is the metrocorporation?

5. Identify some real-life parallels to the story contained in the opening vignette.
6. Is there any relationship between ethics and ethnics?
7. What are the major philosophical and religious contributions to the American ethic?
8. Is the metrocorporation more acceptable today than it was in the 1950's?
9. Identify and discuss the Carthaginian Creed.
10. Are young managers more ethical than experienced executives?
11. Compare the ethics of business to the ethics of a poker game.
12. Distinguish between ethics and social responsibility.

21

The Changing Environment of Management

"Professor, we understand that you are the outstanding authority on the future. So we have come to you for advice about management practice in the next era."

"Yes, ladies and gentlemen. I am without doubt the leading leader and most expert in charting the uncharted, seeing the unseen, and doubletalking the unspeakable."

"Our first problem is one of terminology, Professor. We do not know what to call the emerging era. There was a time when agriculture was the dominant activity of our society."

"Yes, I like to refer to that time as the Agricultural Society."

"Agricultural Society—that's very good. And what wise designation do you give to the great industrial period that followed?"

"I call that one the Industrial Society."

"Brilliant! And what age do you predict we will enter next? The space age? The computer culture? The leisure society? The robot years?"

"I think we can say without fear of contradiction that we are approaching the Postindustrial Society."

"Amazing!"

The Postindustrial Society

One of the dominant social trends predicted for the next decade and a half is the emergence of the "postindustrial" society. For some 250 years, from the founding of Jamestown until around 1870, the United States existed as an agricultural society. For the next 90 or so years, it became an industralized society.

Our changing needs and capabilities now indicate that a new lifestyle is on the horizon. We are on the brink of something different—a form of society that the world has not seen before. Some of the features of this society can be discerned, but lack of precedent dictates caution in making our predictions too specific. The commonly accepted term among futurists, *postindustrial society*, is scarcely descriptive of its characteristics and merely fixes its position on the development time-scale.

In one sense, however, the term *postindustrial* does indicate a characteristic of the new form—the relative decline of industry as a prime force in our society. To a generation that has grown up with the notion that industrialization is the hallmark of the United States, such a prospect may seem farfetched and even alarming. However, a comparison with the agricultural society may serve to put the future in historical perspective.

Agriculture is still a vital force in the United States today. It supplies most of our food and fibers. It accounts for nearly a quarter of our exports. Its productivity is exceptional, even by our own standards. Even so, no one would describe this country as an agricultural society. Agriculture employs less than 5 per cent of our work force. It is not the source of major innovations in our society. And, perhaps most significantly, it no longer determines our values and way of life.

Today, industry is faced with the same sort of decline—in a modified form and over a long period. In a sense, it will be a victim of its own success. Secondary industries (those that process primary products) have not yet dominated the employment picture the way primary activities (farming, forestry, fishing, mining) did prior to 1870. And, just as fewer farmers now raise more food than in the agricultural society, the manpower requirement for industrial production is also steadily declining.

The secondary industries' share of both employment and the GNP will continue to be a steadily declining one. In their place will rise the *tertiary* sector (which supplies goods and services to primary and secondary organizations and the *quaternary* sector (which supplies services to organizations, individuals, and to society as a whole). The quaternary sector is primarily concentrated in education, the professions, government, and nonprofit institutions. More and more of our market activity will take place outside the traditional market economy. As affluence in-

		Jobs in Goods-Producing Industries	Jobs in Service Industries
Figure 21.1 *Where the Opportunities Will Be.* [*Source estimates by USN & WR Economic Unit based on data from U.S. Dept. of Labor.*]	1990	30,700,000	74,570,000
	2000	32,200,000	82,260,000
	Change 1976–2000	UP 20.1%	UP 35.5%
	Note: Goods-producing industries include agriculture, mining, construction and manufacturing. Service industries include transportation, public utilities, trade, finance, insurance, real estate, services, government and others.		

creases, profit-making institutions will decrease in their proportion of the national effort and power structure.

As shown by Figure 21.1, jobs in the service sector of our economy will continue to grow at a faster rate and with larger absolute numbers than the goods-producing sector of the economy.

The Twentieth Century; Retrospect and Prospect

Historians often suggest that the past is prologue to the future. Herman Kahn, Director of the prestigious Hudson Institute (one of the leading futuristic think tanks in the world), describes the twentieth century as suggested by Figure 21.2.[1] In the period ending in 1913 (*La Belle Epoque* —The Good Era), the advanced capitalist nations (the countries sometimes referred to as the Atlantic Protestant Community) experienced economic growth that was twice as high as had been common before this period. It was a good era, in which the United States and a few other countries began to move ahead of most of the world.

The period from 1914 to 1946 was a bad era, for it was an era of instability. A worldwide depression helped cause the economic growth rate to drop to about half what it had been in the preceding period. Two World Wars and two communist revolutions added a pervasive feeling of political uncertainty to the economic discomfort that already existed.

Immediately after the end of World War II, entered a second prosperous period. The economy began to boom, and progress was apparent in almost every area. A recent television program labeled this"Happy Days." One observer has remarked, "Americans felt that they could

[1] Herman Kahn, World Economic Development: 1979 and Beyond (New York: Morrow Quill Paperbacks, 1979). pp 184–185.

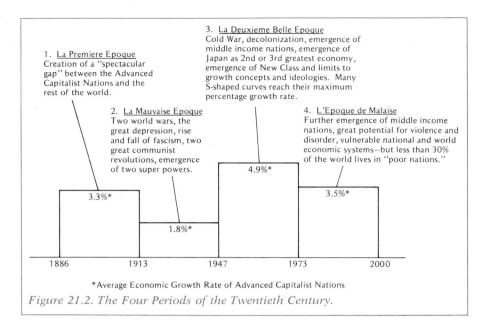

Figure 21.2. The Four Periods of the Twentieth Century.

eliminate poverty, make the world safe for democracy, explore outer space, and enjoy a drip dry, permanent press existence with instant cake mix, coffee and dollars."[2] Despite the apparent prosperity, a few people began to question whether we could continue to grow so rapidly. The Club of Rome sponsored a study using massive computer simulations at MIT to probe this question. Published in 1972, D. H. Meadows[3] and her associates describe the problems that will be encountered unless we immediately adopt a policy of zero economic growth. Although subsequent studies have challenged this conclusion, growth will certainly be less dramatic in the future than it has in the past.

In 1974 the OPEC nations helped usher in the final era of the twentieth century. (*L'Epoque de Malaise*—The era of disquiet) According to the Hudson Institute, our ability to cope with the challenges of this epoch depend on "good luck and good management." We are already recognizing the tremendous potential for disorder that results when there is dependence on very venerable national and world economic systems. Hopefully, some of the concepts presented in this book will be helpful to students who will be faced with some of the challenges of management in the world of 1990, which will be even more complex than the one we know today.

[2] G. F. Abert, *After the Crash* (Atlanta, GA: Bradford Press, 1979).
[3] *The Limits to Growth* (New York: Universe Books, 1972)

Demographic Trends

The immediate post-World War II period was a boom period for the United States. Dramatic increases in population, income and expectations reshaped the American character.[4] The baby boom, with increasing birth rates, lasted until 1958. The extremely large group of people born in this period will continue to shape our nation's character and personality. Social Scientists (demographers) who study population trends report that their charts over the past few decades resemble a python swallowing a pig. In other words, the baby boom became the group of children who created record-high enrollments in elementary schools during the 1950's and early 1960's. They accounted for the explosion of college enrollment during the late 60's and 70's. Now most of them have families of their own and as is suggested by Table 21.1, most of them will be in their late thirties and forties by the end of this decade. The extremely low percentage of the population between the ages of

[4] Lewis Mumford, *Great Expectations* (New York: Coward, McCann & Geoghegan, 1980).

Table 21.1. How Age Mix Will Change			
	Under Age 20		
1980		70,525,000	Up
1990		71,972,000	2.1%
	Age 20–29		
1980		39,848,000	Down
1990		38,122,000	4.3%
	Age 30–39		
1980		31,275,000	Up
1990		40,178,000	28.5%
	Age 40–49		
1980		22,718,000	Up
1990		31,220,000	37.4%
	Age 50–64		
1980		32,866,000	Down
1990		32,198,000	2.0%
	Age 65 and Over		
1980		24,927,000	Up
1990		29,824,000	19.6%

USN & WR chart—Basic data: U.S. Dept. of Commerce.

fifty and 64 represent the people born during the Great Depression and World War II.

At the beginning of this decade, the U.S. population was about 222 million. In 1990, we can anticipate a population of approximately 242 million. Although the birth rate will probably not increase, we can expect another, but smaller, baby boom. This will be caused by the fact that many of the women born during the baby boom have deferred having children. Sociologists anticipate that many of these women will decide to have children before they become too old and that this will fuel a more modest baby boom in the 1980's.

Although the total number of people under the age of twenty will increase 2.1 per cent by the end of this decade, most of this growth will be among the very young. During the decade of the 1980's, the average age in the United States will rise from thirty to 32.5. About eighty per cent of the total population growth will come among people in their thirties and forties. From a business standpoint this is good news, because these people usually are in high earnings stages of their lives.

Another dramatic area of growth will be among older people. By 1990, 12 per cent of the U.S. population will be over 65. This represents a twenty per cent increase since 1980. By the year 2020, Americans over 55 will account for more than 28 per cent of the population. (Up from about 19 per cent in 1970). Seven out of ten people over 65 own their own homes. Of these, nearly 85 per cent have paid off their mortgages. While median family income for the elderly is only 57.5% of the national average, older people also tend to have fewer expenses than young families. Almost half the men over 55 worked in 1950; now only one fifth do. Dr. Robert M. Butler, Director of the National Institute on Aging, says that most people today remain vigorous until 75 or older. Only five per cent of the elderly population lives in nursing homes and other institutions, and the average age of admission is eighty.[5]

Education and the Individual

Education is viewed as a revolutionary force for changing the all important self-image. The better-educated person has more self-respect, wants to be treated more as an individual, is far less tolerant of authoritarianism and organizational restraints, and has different and higher expectations of what to put into a job and what to get out of it. Such attitudinal changes will clearly be most marked among the college-edu-

---

[5] The preceding statistics are based on *U.S. News & World Report*, September 1, 1980, pp. 50–52

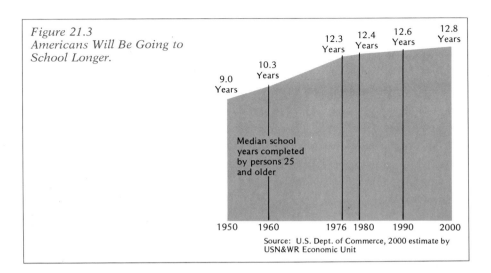

Figure 21.3
Americans Will Be Going to
School Longer.

Median school
years completed
by persons 25
and older

Source: U.S. Dept. of Commerce, 2000 estimate by
USN&WR Economic Unit

cated, who will form the managerial, professional, and technical ranks
of tomorrow. Attitude changes will also increase, though more slowly,
to influence the thinking of the high school graduate who becomes a
production or service worker.

In past years a college education was considered a basic investment
in a person's future. Until recently, there was good evidence to support
a claim that college education pays off financially as well as helping the
student become a better-informed citizen. Today, the financial value of
a college degree, especially in the arts or humanities, is open to question.[6] The estimated rate of return on a college investment fell from
11–12 per cent in 1969 to 7–8 per cent at the present time. This unprecedented decrease is computed from projected lifetime earnings for the
college graduate, minus tuition and other costs such as lost income
while in college.

College graduates with good training in practical disciplines such as
business usually tend to do much better than their classmates in the job
market, regardless of general economic conditions. And even though
there is a growing tendency to question the desirability of college for all
young people, it appears that the length of time spent in formal education will continue to grow. As indicated by Figure 21.3, the rate of increase will not be as fast as it was during the 1960s.

More money, more facilities, more courses, new methods—these
physical manifestations were merely reflections of a new public attitude
toward education and learning. Americans have always placed value on

[6] This section is based on Andrew Spekke, "Is Going to College Worth the Investment?"
The Futurist, December 1976, pp. 297 ff.

education for economic reasons. The new attitude values education for the ways it can help solve problems and make people happier. We are beginning to realize that change demands versatility and flexibility and that these, in turn, demand even better education and a continuing flow of new knowledge.

The Trouble with Cities

Yet another social problem facing tomorrow is the urban crisis. It is predicted that by the year 2000 nearly 74 per cent of the U.S. population will be living in three hundred major metropolitan areas. The air will be dirtier, the slums more unlivable, the traffic more immovable, and the psychological tolls of overcrowding even greater—and the budgets of these cities will be even more strained than they are today.

America today is clearly an urbanized nation. For the past century, economic growth has been associated with the growth of large cities which have grown considerably faster than other locations. The Conference Board[7] estimates that major metropolitan areas with populations of 500,000 will account for only 55 per cent of the total population in 1990. In 1970, these same areas counted for 57 per cent of the total population. Although certain major cities will grow, they will be drawing migrants from other cities. The sixteen largest metropolitan areas in the United States (those with population above two million) are likely to decline in relation to the other 45 major metropolitan areas, defined as places where the population is between 100,000 and 2 million. As Table 21.2 indicates, these cities will experience the most rapid growth during the next few years. Smaller cities and nonmetropolitan areas can also expect significant growth.

Somehow things have to change, and somehow even the most cynical person realizes that we can solve our problems . . . whenever we get ready to. It is hoped that improvement in the quality of city life will come from the practical application of present technological knowledge. Many research efforts are now underway to discover methods for combating such chronic problems as air pollution, inadequate transportation, water shortage, and overcrowding.

To indicate some of the problems faced by cities, consider the facts. The Environmental Protection Agency estimates that municipalities would have to spend $96 billion to build the facilities necessary to meet requirements of the 1972 Water Pollution Control Act. To prevent pollution from industrial waste waters would cost another billion. The Fed-

[7] Juan de Torres, "The New Pattern of Urban Migration," *The Conference Board Record,* May 1976, pp. 29–30.

Table 21.2 *Past and Projected Residence of U.S. Population, 1950–1990*		1950	1970	1990	Implicit Growth Rate	
					1950–70	1970–90
		(millions)			(percent per year)	
Major Metropolitan		55.6	115.0	130.0	3.7	0.6
Over 2,000,000		36.3	75.2	79.6	3.7	0.3
500,000 to 1,999,999		19.3	39.8	50.4	3.7	1.3
Minor Metropolitan (50,000 to 499,000)		23.0	34.8	42.0	2.1	0.8
Nonmetropolitan (under 50,000)		56.9	53.5	62.6	−0.3	0.7
Total U.S.		135.6	203.3	234.6	2.0	0.7

Source: Conference Board Record

eral Highway Administration estimates it would cost $23 billion to replace the more than one hundred thousand bridges that were officially classified as dangerous.[8]

Changing Nature of the Work Force

During the 1980's, the American labor force will not grow as rapidly as it did during the past two decades. The average amount of experience will increase as fewer workers seek jobs. This should mean higher productivity since older, more experienced workers usually produce more.

Unemployment of young men between the ages of 16 and 24 has always been a major problem. This should not be as significant in the 1980's, because there will be fewer people in this category.

Although the number of people involved in blue collar jobs may rise, the portion of total employment will probably drop to about 33 per cent. A substantial increase in women working is projected. In 1980, there were about 42 million women in the U.S. work force, which represents a forty per cent increase since the previous decade. In 1980, almost 46 per cent of the work force were women as compared with 36 per cent in 1966.

About half the labor force in 1980 was between 25 and 44. This means there will be heated competition for promotions. Many people will not be able to move up in organizations as quickly as they would like. The pressure for top jobs may be increased by the reluctance of older workers to step aside. As a result of increased life expectancy, continuing inflation, and legislation to forbid discrimination against older workers, fewer people will choose to retire at 65.

Of the 31 million people to enter the work force during this decade, about 23 million will be women and blacks. Despite the increased num-

[8] Quoted by Abert, op. cit. pg. 8.

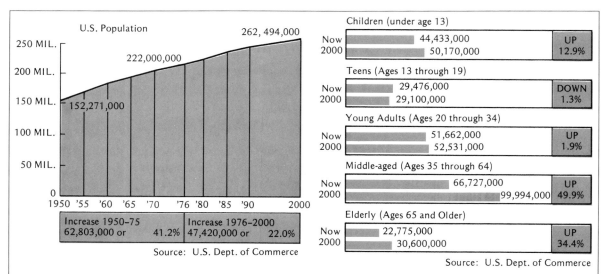

U.S. Population

250 MIL.
200 MIL.
150 MIL.
100 MIL.
50 MIL.
0

152,271,000

222,000,000

262,494,000

1950 '55 '60 '65 '70 '76 '80 '85 '90 2000

Increase 1950–75		Increase 1976–2000	
62,803,000 or	41.2%	47,420,000 or	22.0%

Source: U.S. Dept. of Commerce

Children (under age 13)
Now 44,433,000
2000 50,170,000
UP 12.9%

Teens (Ages 13 through 19)
Now 29,476,000
2000 29,100,000
DOWN 1.3%

Young Adults (Ages 20 through 34)
Now 51,662,000
2000 52,531,000
UP 1.9%

Middle-aged (Ages 35 through 64)
Now 66,727,000
2000 99,994,000
UP 49.9%

Elderly (Ages 65 and Older)
Now 22,775,000
2000 30,600,000
UP 34.4%

Source: U.S. Dept. of Commerce

Figure 21.4. By the Year 2000 Population's Climb Will Slow and Age Mix Will Change. [Source: U.S. Department of Commerce.]

ber of job holders in these categories, they will still probably not have achieved an equal share of top jobs. Many young workers may be disappointed if they believe in what has been called the psychology of entitlement. It is a belief that they deserve good jobs, a rising standard of living, plus a satisfying work experience.

Increased competition for promotions will encourage even more young workers to improve skills and knowledge. Graduate business programs have grown about three hundred per cent in the past ten years. If disappointment increases in the work force, unions will attempt to capitalize on these dissatisfactions. Less than one fourth of all the nation's workers are now union members. This is the lowest figure in recent history and will probably decline slightly in the 1980's.

Changing Attitudes Toward Business and Work

Increasingly, businesses will have to develop an instinct for survival in a political world. Managers will have to become more involved in the problem-solving process of governmental and community affairs. The public will expect business to place greater emphasis on the quality of life, particularly concerning the continuing education and personal development of employees, expectations about the quality of products, and business' contribution to the social cost of urban problems—which business has helped create.

478

Significant increases are expected in governmental regulation and pressure on business to meet higher standards in the public interest. Groups representing consumer interests and the increasing public concern with environmental hazards and quality will force the politicians to tighten the screws.

Increasing affluence, increasing education, continuing automation, and a vastly changed future environment are likely to change people's attitudes toward the value of work. The concept of hard work as a consuming necessity has already been called into question by the younger generation. To complicate the question, we are using fewer hard workers every year. Currently less than thirty per cent of the work force is directly involved in manufacturing products, mining, growing crops, and constructing buildings.

In the late 1960's, about half of working Americans looked to their jobs as a source of personal fulfillment. Today, only about one worker in four feels this way. In fact, only thirteen per cent of all working Americans find their jobs more important to them than leisure-time pursuits. Research by the Yankelovich organization reveals that traditional incentives still work for only about 58 per cent of the work force, but mean nothing to the other 44 per cent.[9] These traditional "tools" include the use of money as an incentive, economic fear, productivity measures that don't depend on worker motivation, and the assumption that people who aren't interfered with will naturally want to do a good job. While all of these four tools have lost power in recent years, they are especially insignificant to the 17 per cent of workers who are young, highly educated middle-managers and professionals who feel that challenge and responsibility are most essential to them. The least motivated of all workers are the 27 per cent who can be described as poorly educated, low income blue-collar workers who are not influenced by the traditional protestant work ethic.

Paychecks and Fringe Benefits

Part of an organization's bid for talent will be through higher compensation and improved benefits programs. The emphasis will shift to providing work that is satisfying and motivating in itself. As changing conditions make obsolete the old theory of compensation, work challenges will become key elements in the compensation package. The employment opportunities ad of the future may include, along with salary, a description of the opportunities for education, self-development, and self-fulfillment. In fact, many ads already evidence this trend.

[9] Based on Daniel Yankelovich, "Today's Workers," *Best of Business*, Spring, 1980, pp. 67–72.

Phyllis Diller on Andy Williams Show (NBC). How will the role of women in business change?

Among the trends that are expected in compensation and benefits is the disappearance of the wage-salary difference. The growth of benefit programs (especially income security programs and short work week provisions) over the past twenty years has laid some groundwork for a shift to salary status for the workers who are paid by the hour. Also likely is a gradual transition to annual earnings guarantees for regular workers in some industries. Labor market conditions may make guarantees of salaried status virtually a necessity to attract and hold skilled workers. Actually, the cost of substituting salaries for hourly wages—in a full-employment economy with few layoffs—may be negligible.

Because of the relatively small number of entry-age workers, companies will be more creative in scheduling work time. Such concepts as job sharing, flex-time and part-time work will increase in popularity. Alvin Toffler describes the future potential of the "cottage office."[10] This is a concept where individuals contract to perform certain types of work in their own homes. This may involve creating illustrations for advertisements, software programs for computer operations or training materials to be used by the personnel department.

Since more than half the workers in the economy will be between the ages of 25 and 44, there will be increased competition for promotions. The creative approaches to work scheduling mentioned in the preceeding paragraph will not be as common for individuals who seek to move up in the organization.

Women as well as blacks, the handicapped, aliens, and other minority groups will demand more promotions. Despite the rhetoric, these groups are still under-represented in average earnings and management positions.

A general trend is also expected to move away from compensation plans that stress individual output and toward those that focus the attention of the whole organization on all aspects of economic achievement. New technology often removes control of output from the individual worker. It doesn't matter if Jo works harder—she's only one member of a team. It will be almost impossible to tie Jo's bonus to her individual extra effort.

Managerial philosophy is changing in the direction of eliminating inequities within the organization, as witnessed in the trend toward an all-salaried work force. Management is becoming aware that the elimination of "disincentives" is as important as the construction of new incentives.

In designing compensation plans that take advantage of these developments, profit sharing may take on added attraction.

There are numerous other trends relative to compensation and benefits that are expected to develop. Double time for overtime could be-

[10] Alvin Toffler, *The Third Wave* (New York: Random House, 1980).

come more popular than sharing the work. As higher income taxes start to affect the take-home pay of even production workers, they may become more interested in deferred compensation plans. Vacations may get longer, and be paid for at premium rates, to take care of employees' extra expenses.

There is not expected to be a trend to substantially earlier retirement, though the norm may go down. New legislation now gives older workers more of a choice of staying on the job after 65. Also, in some fields such as trucking, airlines, and police work, job requirements may dictate a retirement age in the mid fifties. Pensions may be increased to a point at which, together with OASI benefits, they will approach 80–90 per cent of latest career earnings. Other recent moves have legislated funding requirements for pension funds, and increased portability of pension credits through earlier vesting rights.

Challenges of Next Decade

As the United States moves into an era of continued turbulence and uncertainty, business will be faced with several key environmental challenges that will demand knowledge, skill, and ingenuity from managers. Six challenges suggested in the previous edition of this text are still present today, except for a possible easing of government regulation and a lessening of the challenge to the private enterprise system. The major challenges for management in the 1980s will focus on the following concerns:

1. *High Political Turbulence and Uncertainty.* The first major challenge to business will be how to operate at a profit in a very dynamic political environment. The United States, as well as other industrial democracies, will face difficult problems involving inflation, unemployment, energy supplies, environmental improvement, consumerism, and minority rights. The nation will be attempting to reconcile competing claims from organized labor, farmers, minorities, stockholders, public employees, and other interest groups. Increased unionization of professionals and public employees will result in more confrontations between labor and the public, with some resulting work stoppages. Financial crisis in major cities will add to the uncertainty of the business environment.

2. *Slow Economic Growth.* After the exciting "go-go" years of the 1960's, managers will have to adjust to a growth rate substantially below their wishes and expectations. As suggested earlier in this chapter, both population growth and productivity gains will be relatively small during this period. Huge capital investments will be needed to

clean up the environment and to develop domestic sources of energy; however, there will be less capital available to invest in either technology development or improved production equipment. Expenditures for research and development have dropped about six per cent during the past decade. This means that new technologies, industries, and products are less likely to be launched in the immediate future. Traditional growth industries, such as oil, automobile, and metals will play a relatively diminished role.

All in all, some industries and many companies will experience economic growth. Still, managers cannot expect growth to be a way of life during the next decade. Growth will be something earned, rather than an unexpected dividend. In many instances, managers will move from the challenge of managing growth to the challenge of managing stability or decline.

3. *Expensive Capital and Credit.* In order for business to prosper, sufficient capital and credit must be available to finance new ventures and expansion of successful activity. There is considerable evidence that there will be a strong demand for capital, but a relatively weak supply to meet this need. As a result, interest rates will probably continue to be quite high. Extremely large sums of money will be needed to finance energy developments, mass transportation systems, urban renewal, plant modernization, and energy developments. Because of increased inflation and higher deductions for Social Security and other public benefits, the amount of personal savings will probably decline. This will further reduce the amount of capital available for business borrowing and investment.

4. *Weakening Industrial Discipline and Support for the Work Ethic.* Industrial psychologists report that the attitudes of many Americans toward authority in general and their own job in particular have gone through significant changes. Working conditions in business have been receiving increased criticism on the basis that jobs in plants and offices are monotonous and dehumanizing. These criticisms are likely to undermine the authority of business managers and to create increased pressures for employees to participate in decisions that affect their well-being. Another possible result will be that new structures for operations and management will be required to convince workers that their aspirations can be more closely identified with those of their employer.

5. *Public Demands and Governmental Regulation.* Demands from consumers, environmentalists, and civil rights proponents, along with increasing governmental regulation, will continue to make the job of management more complex and confusing. Many formerly passive, unorganized interest groups have become very outspoken in their demands for detailed government regulation of business. Legislation and regulation of business activities have permeated almost every aspect of

business, including product design, production methods, employment practices, warranties, marketing, and finance. Compliance with governmental regulation is generating mountains of costly paper work.

The cost of useless and wasteful regulation by federal agencies is estimated to be over $130 billion per year—the equivalent of $2,000 annually for every U.S. family. It has been estimated that U.S. businesses spend over $20 billion per year just to prepare government reports, and that another $15 billion is spent by the government in processing the data. Many more taxpayers' dollars are spent by the thousands of government employees who develop and enforce the regulations.

A farm family may spend four hours a week on government paperwork. Standard Oil company of Indiana annually sends about 250 final reports totaling 24,000 pages (backed by 20,000 subsidiary reports totaling many times that number of pages) to 41 different government agencies. Goodyear Tire and Rubber Company says that it is spending over $30 million per year to handle the load of federal regulations.

Many observers feel, however, that the pendulum has begun to swing away from increasing government regulation. While the total cost of government in 1950 averaged about $2,000 per family, by 1979 the cost had reached a figure in excess of $9,000 per family. The election of 1980 seemed to indicate that a large number of Americans were ready to reconsider Thomas Jefferson's notion that "the government that governs best, governs less." Business and public sentiment against increasing regulation will probably somewhat ease the burden of paperwork for managers in this decade—especially for managers of smaller companies.

6. *A Challenge To the Private Enterprise System.* Recent public opinion polls indicate that Americans in general, and young people in particular, seem to have a limited understanding of the private enterprise system. This is often accompanied by suspicion and hostility toward business managers and corporations. Few people in our society seem to be impressed with what socialism and communism have achieved in other countries. Yet, the market economy is threatened by ignorance and neglect. Many fear that the spirit of enterprise will be stifled by overregulation and overtaxation.

In the past few years, businesses have begun to do a better job of presenting their case to the public. Enrollments in business schools are increasing dramatically while the student-count in other disciplines is declining. Many people are beginning to feel that since a pervasive federal government cannot solve the problems of our economy, the private enterprise system with its dramatic history of achievement may offer a better hope.

Summary

The Postindustrial Society will bring the declining influence of agriculture and industry and the increase of the service (tertiary and quaternary) sectors of society. Because of growing emphasis on innovation and problem-solving skills, a new educational emphasis will emerge. Education will be more available to a higher percentage of workers, both prior to and during employment.

The urban crisis will demand the marshaling of business and government effort. There will be greater leisure in the future, but nothing approaching the fantasizing of science-fiction writers of the past. The American labor force will grow to 135 million civilians by the year 2000.

Businesses will have to develop an instinct for survival in a political world. The nature of work will alter—with occupational challenge becoming as important to many as salary considerations. There will be higher percentages of women, nonwhites, and college graduates in the work force.

Managers will have to move faster, know more, and accept payments in many forms besides money. Vacations will be longer, retirement earlier. Things will cost more, but workers will earn more, and buying power will be greater.

Review Questions

1. Which of the following organizations are primary, secondary, tertiary, or quarternary?
   a. General Motors.
   b. The Southwest Research Institute.
   c. IBM Corporation.
   d. The King Ranch.
2. What major categories of workers will experience greatest growth by 1980?
3. Discuss probable trends in the average work week and retirement age. Do these trends have implications for the travel industry?
4. Is it possible for people in the twenty-first century to have less money and a higher standard of living than today? Discuss.
5. How can education realistically be considered an investment?
6. Some authorities believe that cars will be banned by most cities before 1990. Evaluate the probability and impact of this decision.
7. If you were offered $15,000 a year to remain as a full-time student (at least ten hours per term) for the rest of your life, would you agree? Explain.
8. List in the order of popularity (current number of employees) the following employment categories:
   a. Government.
   b. Farming.
   c. Manufacturing.

9. Discuss the pros and cons of scheduling all college classes on Monday and Thursday. Identify some other alternatives to scheduling.
10. Discuss differences in the work ethic possessed by your classmates and by your parents.
11. Identify some of the major structural changes that may take place in the U.S. economy during the next decade.

22

The Changing Practice of Management

The scientist certainly learned a valuable lesson, even if it had to be a result of a freak accident. She had finally completed her time machine and was prepared for the first voyage into the future. She rechecked all the mathematical computations, set the destination dial for fifty years in the future, and climbed into the capsule. She pushed the button and closed her eyes.

After a few minutes, she climbed out and, with great eagerness, walked about observing the strange new world. She marveled at new styles and methods. She could hardly believe the progress that had been made. And the attitudes of the people— how infinitely more mature! The future was everything it had been predicted to be.

The scientist returned to the time machine only to find her assistant with puzzling news. There had been a power failure. The machine had not worked. The scientist had never left the present. Her expectations of a better world had opened her eyes to the beauty and wonder of the present.

The cynic might well laugh at our attempts to delve into the future that holds us all so spellbound. For as the scientist learned with her time machine, few of us have studied the present well enough to understand our surroundings. Today is yesterday's tomorrow, and we're hardly up to date on today—let alone a mystical future that never really comes.

Is there good sense in the great emphasis upon planning for the future? What's the value of those fifteen- and forty-year plans that gather dust on so many office shelves? Why should we sink many hours and great sums into guesses and wishes about a future that cannot be known for sure until it is the present?

Obviously, we must plan. Otherwise, we lay all our future prospects in the hands of happenstance. Individuals and nations, junior achievers and giant conglomerates must prepare for the future. And, in preparing, the degree to which we can second-guess the unpredictable is exactly the measure of our probable good fortune.

Still, for all our interest in the future, we are hopelessly bound to the present. We study the trends and try to shake loose from preconceptions long enough to predict open-mindedly. Yet, we are greatly limited—we never think big enough or anticipate freely. Many of the "facts" we refer to today are destined to be the exploded myths of tomorrow. "Incurable diseases" are not incurable—we just don't know the cure *yet*. The great challenge facing any student of the future is the development of an anything-is-possible attitude.

In 1870, Bishop Milton Wright declared from his pulpit, "Flight is reserved for the angels. To think anything else is blasphemey." Almost at the time he spoke these words, his two sons were attempting to put wings on a bicycle. In the years before the Wright brothers flew at Kitty Hawk, it was a fore-gone conclusion that a heavier-than-air machine could not possibly fly. Stop for a minute and think of factual absolutes in our time—how able are we to accept the possibility that these truths may be changed in the future? Can man breathe in water? Is the law of gravity indisputable? Can humans learn the languages of animals? Is it necessary for everyone to die?

An old Chinese proverb says that it is very difficult to make predictions—especially about the future. Even so, astute executives can never give up their enthusiasm for knowing the future. After all, they plan to spend the remainder of their careers—and lives—there.

From Buck Rogers to Business as Usual

It is interesting to note the extent to which the futurists think the future will differ from the present. The excitement of the predictions ranges from a conservative attitude that things will probably go along pretty

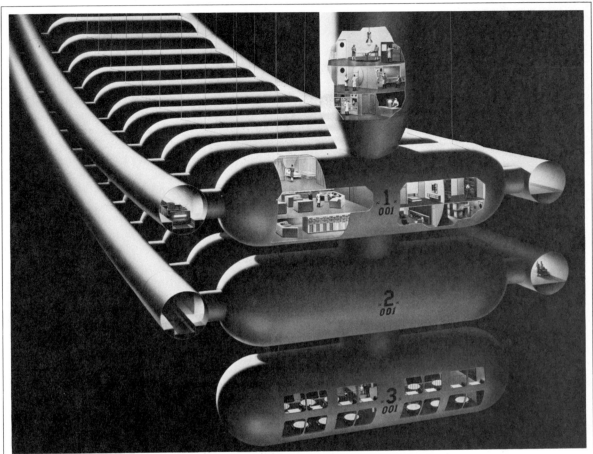

Home away from home. This cutaway shows how people might live and work in the space city of the 1990's as pictured by Lockheed Missiles and Space Company engineers. The modules containing work areas, living spaces, and a restaurant are part of a giant wheel silently circling Earth (see Figure 19.2). People might live in the space city for six months at a time, and vacationers from Earth could treat themselves to the city's resort hotel. Will management in space differ from management on Earth?

much the same, all the way to the fantasies of a Buck Rogers world. The truth, no doubt, lies somewhere in between. We have all been exposed to enough surprises and fascinating new things that we can hardly believe that things are going to change imperceptibly. In fact, people seem to be getting more and more expectant about change. No longer are the citizens threatened by falling traditions. On the contrary, the public is beginning to forsake products and leaders who are not continuously flaunting their newness and pointing to their more-modern-than-tomorrow qualifications. We might well wonder if the day is upon us when there will be as much resistance to tradition as there used to be in change. None of us can accept the unimaginative no-change theories about what is to be.

The Buck Rogers theories are sometimes equally far from the mark. The world now has a sufficient backlog of science-fiction literature to make some evaluation of the accuracy of these predictions. From Jules Verne to George Orwell's *1984*, the reading public has been enthralled by the seeming fantasies of writers. In many cases, the innovations predicted have remained impossible and occasionally become humorously undesirable. In almost every case, writers have dealt with mechanical predictions and ignored the great potential renovations that now seem quite feasible. Even so, we must tip our hats to the foresight of writers like Aldous Huxley, who was able in 1932 to describe life conditions in a *Brave New World* that at that time were laughable but now seem just over the horizon.

So . . . what stance are we to take in our evaluation of the contradictory assurances of the futurists? We may agree with the story of the investor who had himself cryogenically returned to life one hundred years after his "death." He hurried to the phone to call his stockbroker. To his great pleasure, he discovered that his IBM stock had gone up to $3 million per share. His AT&T was up to $4 million. He was about to ask about his other holdings when the telephone operator interrupted to ask him to deposit another $150,000 for the next three minutes. He was discovering (as many have guessed) that the names and amounts will be changed, but life will remain essentially the same.

When all our guessing is done and we have given up our arguments about what is to come, one simple fact remains: the future hasn't happened yet. There is no way to *know* the future—we can only guess. We must take up the challenge to be, at the same time, sufficiently open-minded and realistically conservative about what is to come. Regardless of the difficulty, we must try to see what lies ahead. After all, the future is where we are all going . . . we want to be properly dressed when we arrive.

The Manager Faces the Future

Most managers share a general interest in the future. The manager knows that survival is largely dependent upon predictions and forecasts. Because of the increased pace of change and technological development, managers are progressively becoming more concerned with the future.

Traditionally, references to the future cause most managers to think about sales predictions, staffing forecasts, and other statistics that measure the performance of their particular company. Furthermore, executives tend to think of these statistics as they relate to the present organizational structure. As sales and staffing forecasts increase, managers interpret this as growth and expansion of the present organizational pyramid, with continued application of current concepts of authority, leadership, and administration. Such naive faith in the stability of the status quo is a dangerous pitfall for all extrapolists who assume that the future will be like the past and fail to consider the impact of opposing trends or potential discontinuities. If plans are made on the assumption that the current role of authority and the organizational structure will continue indefinitely, planners may well be building their houses on the sand.

We all give lip service to the ever-presence of change and the necessity to honor contingencies when we plan. Yet merely observing that changes do occur does not provide sudden clarity to our crystal ball. If we are determined to make predictions, we must first attempt to understand *why* certain changes have occurred and *why* certain trends emerge. The ability to be a skilled and accurate prophet does not lie so much in knowing *what* has happened . . . but *why*. It is the *why's* of behavior that are most likely to tell us the events that will take place.

There have been many individual expressions about the future of management. Most of the professional periodicals like to sprinkle in an occasional article on the future for interest's sake. The predictions of those writers who fall somewhere between the Buck Rogers ideas and the more-of-the same concept have been drawn together in this section. Their opinions on specific events affecting the future practice of management are homogenized into a sort of majority opinion. The specific areas emphasized are organizational changes, automation and information technology, labor relations, working conditions, and professional development. Obviously the opinions of experts have value only as they are able to stimulate the thinking of each reader. How foolish we would look protesting some new development on the basis that professor so-and-so predicted it would never happen. The opinions of experts provide an excellent launch pad, but each of us must make a solo flight into the future.

The Tried and True Pyramid

For many the pyramid is almost an automatic approach to organizational planning. For five thousand years activities that involved large numbers of people have been charted in the pyramid form—with the person or small group of primary power-wielders sitting on the pinnacle. Below these kings of the mountain, there are arrayed in ever increasing numbers the layers of workers. The farther down the pyramid we go, the less responsibility the individuals have and the farther they are removed from original motivations for the actions they are performing. The foot soldier in the Roman army would be unlikely ever to see the emperor, but the events of his life (and death) were controlled by decisions of that single individual at the top of the Roman pyramid. And in this characteristic are demonstrated both the chief advantage and the greatest disadvantage of the pyramid system. The chief advantage of the pyramid is that each worker need be concerned only with his own job and his own supervisor. The greatest disadvantage of the pyramid system is that each worker is concerned only with one job and one supervisor.

Communication of group goals (i.e., what the guy at the top has decided the whole pyramid ought to do) is next to impossible. The pyramid mentality has no doubt coined and overused the familiar "Ours is not to reason why, ours is but to do and die."

Numerous alternative organizational patterns have been suggested to overcome the communications deficiencies of the traditional pyramid. One familiar pattern is the wheel arrangement, which endeavors to move all parts of the organization into a closer (or at least equidisant) proximity to the policy makers. Although many management thinkers favor the wheel as the most logical successor to the pyramid, some use a more complicated approach in describing the organizational chart of the future. Harold J. Leavitt and Thomas L. Whisler, suggest that the organizational chart may look more like a football balanced upon the point of a church bell. Their idea is that

> within the football (the top staff organization), problems of coordination, individual autonomy, group decision making, and so on should arise more intensely than ever. We expect that they will be dealt with quite independently of the bell portion of the company, with distinctly different methods of remuneration, control and communication.[1]

The future of bureaucracy as we now know it is far from agreed. Some feel that it will be forced to give way to more adaptive, problem-solving, temporary systems of diverse specialists who function on a project-completion basis. These short-term specialists will have their projects coordinated and evaluated by a much smaller division that operates continuously. If such a project orientation can short-circuit the bureaucracy's unfortunate tendency to perpetuate and feed on itself, then there may indeed be a bright future for the traditional forms of organization. Still, there remain those more realistic prophets who say "The inherent forces that have made the pyramidal form dominant for 5,000 years

---

[1] "Management in the 1980's," in *Management Systems*, ed. by Peter Schoderbek (New York: John Wiley & Sons, Inc., 1967), p. 233.

haven't disappeared."[2] When a panel of leading management experts was asked to make a probability estimate regarding the pyramid's place by the year 2000, the median of the response was that 75 per cent of the organizational structures will remain in the form of a pyramid.[3]

Some predictions have been advanced that indicate that the changes in general management will be of major proportions. To accommodate these changes, there will have to be corresponding changes in organizational structure. The most significant single change is likely to be a shift from *activities*-oriented systems to *results*-oriented systems. Managers will be likely to devise means for directing their organizations towad foreseeable needed objectives and toward unsolved problems. This could prove to be a gigantic leap forward for management, shifting the emphasis from the *process* (which may or may not be productive) to the *product* (about which there is no doubt).

Greater emphasis is already being planned upon the total systems concept. There will continue to be a shift from a role of autocratic, centralized decision making to one of support and linkage with decentralized decisions. Organizational plans will be drawn to achieve specific, measurable, and realistic results. Many organizations that are beginning the use of the project approach have indicated that it may allow a greater opportunity for an individual feeling of satisfaction and accomplishment than the more impersonal pyramid.

In summary, there are many factors, such as the attitude of people toward authority, the impact of the computer, and the changing challenges of business environment, which may cause a gradual erosion in the use of the organizational pyramid. This change will probably take place with all the speed associated with the erosion of the original Egyptian pyramids. In other words, the modern pyramid is likely to be made of a more modern, pliable substance than was found in the past. Perhaps the dominant organizational structure of the future will be a "plastic pyramid," where change can take place but where there is also a continuing sense of structure and unity.

Farewell to the Chief?

One of the predicted changes that experts have debated is the idea that a single chief executive will not be able to cope with the future demands of this job. The sheer volume of work and the demand for a broad range

[2] James E. Morrow, *A Delphi Approach to the Future of Management*, unpublished Ph.D. dissertation, Georgia State University, Atlanta, 1971. Subsequent references to predictive statements made by management scholars, without footnotes, are taken from Delphi questionnaires received in this study.
[3] Ibid.

of critical skills and talent will make the tradition of the big boss impractical. Accordingly, some authorities have suggested that top-level decision making will have to be performed by an executive team or plural executive in the future. For example,

> the tasks of the organization will be more technical, complicated and unprogrammed. They will rely on intellect instead of muscle. They will be too complicated for one person to comprehend, to say nothing of control. Essentially, this will call for the collaboration of specialists in project or team form of organization.[4]

Similarly, Pfiffner and Sherwood, writing over a decade ago, suggested that many factors will operate "to make the image of a top executive a decision maker and coordinator increasingly untenable. The executive in fact will be a group and will encompass many forces within the organization."[5]

However exciting the plural executive may be to us, many of the experts seem to be skeptical that this prediction will ever be a reality. The late Cyril O'Donnell felt that the prediction had little strength, especially in smaller firms: "Small and medium firms will shy away from plural executives. . . . A few large firms have tried this form and received all the publicity. Most of these have abandoned the idea. The idea is largely propagated in universities—not in business."

Others suggested that regardless of the organization, one individual will make the final decision in most cases. There is likely to be considerable experimentation along the way, but ultimately (by 2000) we will certainly return to the primacy of the individual. The strongest statement of objection to the fulfillment of the stated prediction comes from Columbia's Harold Smiddy, who emphasizes that "a decision is only made between two ears on the opposite sides of the head. Committee palaverings bring no information of use that a responsible decision maker cannot get from individuals. . . . With human nature as it is, team decision making will emphasize compromise and trimming versus decisiveness and risk."

On the other side of the coin, some experts suggest that complexity *will* increase rapidly—especially the need to weigh diverse noneconomic forces in the environment. The plural executive would be better able to deal with this complexity. Group decision making is already being done in associations (civic or voluntary organizations, trade associations, and so on) in which business executives participate. This is another influence toward acceptance of group decision making by executives in their companies.

Since the earliest predictions have been made about the plural execu-

[4] *Management Review*, August 1969, p. 8.

[5] John Pfiffner and Frank P. Sherwood, *Administrative Organization* (Englewood Cliffs, N.J.: Prentice-Hall, Inc., 1960), p. 444.

tive, we have seen a move toward a division of responsibility at the top of large organizations shared by several individuals. For example, it is quite common today for the Chief Executive Officer (CEO) to be responsible for strategic management and the external relationships of the firm. At the same time, the Chief Operating Officer (COO) will typically assume responsibility for day-to-day decisions affecting people and activities within the organization. In some instances, a Chief Financial Officer (CFO) will work with the other two executives to handle the financial questions that arise. These three individuals may function as a triumvirate. While their responsibilities are well defined, all of them together are making the kinds of decisions that a single executive would be making at the top of a much smaller firm. Even so, it is difficult for us to conceive of voting for a group instead of an individual for the nation's presidency.

Centralization or Decentralization

For years management scholars and computer specialists have discussed, debated, and argued about the potential impact of computers on information systems and decision making. In one of the earliest discussions of the subject, George P. Shultz and Thomas L. Whisler suggested that the use of high-speed computers and associated techniques (information technology) "will be enforced with centralization of decision making."[6] John F. Burlingame took an opposite position, "The anticipated advancement in information technology can strengthen decentralization in those businesses that have adopted it. This will encourage more management to experiment and operate in accordance with decentralization policy. There is no denying that corporations will be deeply affected by the computer revolution. We are sure to see some shifts from centralized operation to decentralized management and control and increases in the number of people in a corporation who participate in the management decision-making process."[7]

Top scholars are still divided in their opinions. It is interesting to see that although some are certain that computers will lead to greater decentralization of decision making, others credit computers with aiding a move toward centralization. One of the strongest positions has been articulated by George Steiner of UCLA: "I insist that there is a 100% probability that computers will continue to lead to centralization of decision making. There is a 100% probability now . . . (on the other hand there are, and will continue to be, other powerful forces toward decen-

[6] *Management Organization and the Computer* (New York: The Free Press, 1960), p. 28.
[7] "Information Technology and Centralization," *Harvard Business Review*, November–December 1961, p. 121.

tralization)." Billy Goetz, a specialist in the area of planning and control, agrees and adds his expectation that multiple-access on-line real-time use of computers will increase until it becomes the dominant mode. The decision about how decisions are to be made is likely to become more centralized in top-level decision-making teams.

Harold Koontz adds, "Computers do not make decisions, except where algorithms are simple or decision rules definite. They do, or should, help managers make better decisions. As managers become more sophisticated and do more of their job at all levels, I would expect greater decentralization."

Computers certainly have the ability to permit more participation in decision making by people at all levels, but it seems likely that final decisions will continue to be made at the top. Decentralization may become the dominant trend at some point in the future, but not for the next few years. There will be many field decisions, but basic long-range planning and resource allocation will be centralized, particularly in the United States. Innovation and other creative functions will be assumed to a greater degree by top management, which will have an expanded staff and make maximum use of information technology.

On the other hand, those who anticipate more decentralization are equally confident that the ability of computers to provide additional amounts of data will not promote centralization of decision making. Decisions must be made promptly and at the actual work points where the knowledge and experience that cannot be computerized is located. Computer access is easily available to managers at lower levels and will assist them in making decisions and also encourage a greater input of data into the system. An added benefit may be a greater flow of communication within the organization in general. The social demand for more participation in decision making will encourage decentralization, making use of the young intellectuals who can use computer access equipment at the lower levels. The growth of the inexpensive "mini" computer will permit sophisticated decisions at lower levels and be a source of better data for the central system.

Willis Harmon of SRI International suggests that one of the major trends affecting the future of our culture is an almost universal desire for greater decentralization.[8] In other words, we have greater capability for centralization, but the mood of the times seems to favor more decentralization.

The computer is basically neutral as far as the focus of authority is concerned. It will work in whatever way management decides to employ it. The computer does, however, help give top and middle managers greater competence to perform their respective tasks better.

---

[8] Presentation at the Global Conference of the World Future Society, Toronto, Canada, July 22, 1980.

The Manager in the Middle

One of the major areas of speculation about coming organizational change has been concerned with the effect that computerization will have on middle management. One possibility is that the organizational chart of the future may be shaped like an hourglass. The larger portion of jobs on the bottom half of the chart would require little skill, training, or sophistication. The upper half of the chart would remain the area of creativity, innovations, and decisions that computers could not make. The traditional role of middle management would be assumed by computers. Levitt and Whisler predict that the roles of all management levels will change substantially, particularly the role of middle management.

> A radical reorganization of middle management levels should occur with certain classes of middle management moving downward in status and compensation (because they will require less autonomy and skills), while other classes move upward into the top management groups.[9]

These and other writers feel that machines will increasingly take over more and more of the routine work of middle management. By the end of the century, this could mean that there would be few middle managers, and that most of those who did remain would be routine technicians rather than thinkers. Although there has not yet been sufficient time to assess all the impact of computers on middle-level management jobs, today there seems to be general agreement that middle management job content has already changed, with some jobs becoming more routine and some becoming much more demanding.

The major disagreement in this area comes about in deciding what to call middle management. The real organizational result of computers in business has been a redefinition of middle management, and a greater expectation of managers at all levels. The role of middle management has not been eliminated or significantly reduced. Rather, increasingly competent middle managers have assumed more responsibility, and will ultimately have greater responsibility for planning decentralized operations. Today's top managers already spend large amounts of time dealing with the demands of diverse societal institutions. The increased role of middle managers will free top executives to do an even better job of handling these external expectations. Managers who are between the supervisory and top executive levels in firms of the future will still be in the middle, even though the nature of their work is significantly altered.

[9] Levitt and Whisler, op. cit., p. 41.

The Oriental Connection

After a period of thinking that they had all the answers, American managers have begun to realize that there is much to learn from managers in other cultures. The dramatic productivity increases achieved by the Japanese have made this fact particularly significant. After a brief summary of the traditional American management model as compared to the traditional Japanese model, we will attempt to identify a mode that draws from both experiences in a way that will probably reflect the practice of management in the next decade.[10]

The American experience has emphasized the following concept:

• *Short-term Employment* - The average college graduate stays in the first post-graduate job an average of only three years. Throughout the past, the "mobi-centric" manager has been characterized as an individual who moves frequently from company to company in the search of greater challenges and opportunities for advancement.

• *Individual Decision Making* - We are accustomed to believing that if you give one individual the right information, he or she should be able to come to a decision about what should be done.

• *Individual Responsibility* - Just as we expect an individual to make speedy decisions, we expect to be able to identify the person who is responsible when something goes right—or wrong.

• *Rapid Evaluation and Promotion* - Consulting companies, universities and accounting firms have typically employed an "up or out" philosophy. Individuals are expected to advance rapidly. If they fail to do so, they are encouraged to seek employment elsewhere. After short periods of employment, many companies make decisions about the ultimate potential of an individual.

• *Explicit, Formal Control* - The American need for exactness has lead us to develop control systems so that employees can know at all times how well they were doing in meeting standards. This need for specific information is generated through grading systems in schools and continues through formalized control systems in most companies.

• *Specialized Career Paths* - Individuals who enter an organization through the accounting function will probably spend most of their career in that function. It is relatively unusual for an accountant or marketing specialist to be moved into production or finance. Americans seem to believe that specialized training and certain kinds of personalities fit in various types of functional areas.

• *Segmented Concern* - For many reasons, U.S. companies have been concerned only about the time an individual spends on the job. People reacted negatively to the paternalism that some companies demon-

---

[10] This is based on William G. Ouchi, "A Corporate Alternative to Village Life," *Outlook*, Spring, 1980, pp. 12–17.

strated during the 1950's. As a result, business corporations have concluded that whatever an individual does on his or her own time is not their concern. They do, however, expect that problems associated with childcare, health and other domestic matters will not interfere with job expectations.

Conversely to the ideas expressed in the preceding section, Japanese companies view an employment decision as a lifetime contract. One of the reasons that Walt Disney Productions chose a joint venture approach to their Tokyo venture was the fact that they did not want to make long-term employment commitments to people in an amusement park. The oriental emphasis on "saving face" has lead to more consensus in decision making and a great degree of collective responsibility. The group shares in the decision-making process and the responsibility for that decision.

Because of the lifetime commitment for employment, the Japanese take a longer time in evaluating employees and are more patient in expecting advancement through the organization. Control measures are more implicit and informal. Japanese workers feel more comfortable without what they view as rigidly defined standards that may not recognize the uniqueness of a situation or provide opportunities for flexibility. Because of the slower career paths, specialization is not as acute as it is in the United States. Finally, Japanese employers take a more holistic view. They are more interested in the employee's physical fitness (coffee breaks are sometimes replaced with calisthenics breaks); they are also interested in the individual's family and try to make accommodations for the special needs of working parents.

As we face an era where American management is more open to influences from abroad, we will probably develop a consensus model of management which recognizes the characteristics identified in Figure 22.1. This will include long-term employment. It simply is too expensive for individuals to change jobs and move from city to city as frequently as was done ten years ago.

Much of the research discussed in this and any other management text has stressed the importance of participation and involvement in the decision-making process. At the same time, our culture is not likely to give up its emphasis on individual responsibility. We like to know

---

Figure 22.1.   TYPE Z/MODIFIED AMERICAN

- Long-Term Employment
- Consensual Decision Making
- Individual Responsibility
- Slow Evaluation and Promotion
- Implicit, Informal Control with Explicit, Formalized Measures
- Moderately Specialized Career Paths
- Holistic Concern, Including Family

where the blame rests when something goes wrong. Similarly, we like to receive the credit when we have achieved heroic results.

Because of slower economic growth in our culture and a large number of workers in the 25–45 age category during the next decade, we will become accustomed to slower evaluation and promotion. While control systems will become more informal, there will still be explicit formalized measures to let American managers know when things are not going as they should.

With increasing complexity in all areas of business, a certain degree of specialization will be required. Nevertheless, it is becoming increasingly necessary that managers understand how the various aspects of an organization work together to achieve objectives. In a similar way, corporations are beginning to realize that it is impossible to separate an employee from the problems he or she faces away from work. Companies are developing programs that relate to physical fitness, stress management, and financial planning. They are developing day-care centers and revising nepotism rules to allow a husband and wife to work together for the same organization.

This modified American management model offers more of a humanistic concern for individuals involved and at the same time will probably provide more opportunities for profitability, changing the nature of our economy and workforce.

The Last Word?

We can only guess at the possible developments in and implications of organization, automation, working conditions, and professional development. The wide divergence of opinion, even among experts, points up the limitations and uncertainties that surround all planning. It will be interesting to compare the real thing with our predictions about it. No doubt, we will be too conservative on some points and too much like Buck Rogers on others. However, our failures are not likely to bother us greatly, for we will be at that time preoccupied with predictions about the next era.

In a presidential address to the Academy of Management, George Steiner[11] listed some predictions about the changing emphases and approaches of business in the future. (See Table 22.1.) Steiner's management characteristics are all in line with a "death of the entrepreneur— rise of the social manager" concept. Each area of endeavor seems to have purified its motivations in Steiner's future and emphasized the

[11] George Steiner, Presidential Address, Academy of Management, Minneapolis, Minn., August 11, 1972.

Table 22.1
Steiner's Predictions
of Future Managerial
Practices

Recent Past	TOWARD	Future
Assumption that a business manager's sole responsibility is to optimize stockholder wealth		Profit still dominant but modified by the assumption that a business manager has other social responsibilities
Business performance measured only by economic standards		Application of both an economic and social measure of performance
Emphasis on quantity of production		Emphasis on quantity *and* quality
Authoritarian management		Permissive/democratic management
Short-term intuitive planning		Long-range comprehensive structured planning
Entrepreneur		Renaissance manager
Control		Creativity
People subordinate		People dominant
Financial accounting		Human resources accounting
Caveat emptor		Ombudsman
Centralized decision making		Decentralized and small group decision making
Concentration on internal functioning		Concentration on external ingredients to company success
Dominance of economic forecasts in decision making		Major use of social, technical, and political forecasts as well as economic forecasts
Business viewed as a single system		Business viewed as a system of systems within a larger social system
Business ideology calls for aloofness from government		Business-government cooperation and convergence of planning
Business has little concern for social costs of production		Increasing concern for internalizing social costs of production

Source: George Steiner, Presidential Address, Academy of Management, Minneapolis, Minn., August 11, 1972.

more noble reasons for enterprise. It is certainly to be wished that this predicted world of cooperation and consideration will come to pass.

As Harvard philosopher Alfred North Whitehead once suggested, "It is the business of the future to be dangerous." In management, a part of the danger lies in the uncertainty about what is to be expected. Although the analysis provided in this chapter cannot provide a crystal clear vision of the future, it should suggest important considerations for the student and the decision maker. The modern oracle Marshall McLuhan asserts, "There is absolutely no inevitability as long as there is a willingness to consider the alternatives." The alternatives are presented and described throughout the book. Executives must decide if they will accept what appears to be an undesirable inevitability or if they will use their insight and ability to create the kind of future they desire. The future belongs to those who prepare for it. As a familiar Chinese proverb points out, "All the flowers of all the tomorrows are in the seeds of today." The future of the future is certainly in the present.

Summary

For all our need to plan for the future and our fascination with the nature of things that are yet to be, we are hopelessly bound to the present. The foundation task of any person who needs to project the future is simultaneously to be free enough of the present to consider any alternative and yet to be cognizant of the present to keep predictions realistic and relevant. Our enjoyment of the Buck Rogers type of predictions must be brought into productive coexistence with our natural tendency to assume that things will remain pretty much the same as we know them. There is no way to *know* the future, but it is imperative that we guide the present by sighting on the future.

This chapter has presented some of the divergent views and possibilities of the management climate that might be anticipated for the 1980's and for the year 2000. The specific areas emphasized are organizational structure, automation and information technology, labor relations, and fringe benefits.

One of the areas of organizational structure that is almost certain to be affected by the streamlining of the passing years is the location, distribution, and exercise of power through new approaches to structure. It is hard to see how the pyramid chart could ever be replaced . . . yet it has so many obvious deficiencies. Also in question is the position of the chief—can a single individual possibly cope with the snowballing complexities of management? Yet on the other hand, can any group act as one person?

There is considerable disagreement among the experts as to the degree to which decision making processes will be centralized in the future. Interestingly enough, both the centralizers and the decentralizers point to the computer as the key that will make their predictions come true. The computer is certain to change the nature of all jobs, but that of the middle management positions remains most in question.

Progress is anticipated in the field of labor relations, with forced arbitration, representation of the consumers, and a strike tax being factors that could change the whole labor-management relationship.

Executives must decide if they will accept what appears to be an undesirable inevitability or if they will use their insight and ability to create the kind of future they desire. The future belongs to those who prepare for it.

Review Questions

1. Will the organizational pyramid survive? Discuss.
2. Discuss the future of the strike as a tool of labor relations.
3. What major lessons will management practice learn from the Japanese during the 1980's?
4. Discuss the future of the profit motive and entrepreneurship.
5. Discuss the impact of computers on tomorrow's manager.
6. Explain the statement, "A trend is not a destiny."
7. Explain why the organization of the future might look like an hourglass.
8. Many futurists believe that most highly trained individuals will change careers during their work life. What other careers appeal to you? Do these relate to your current study of management?

23

So Manage!

The coach was a real stickler for obedience. He wanted obedience from his boys more than he wanted anything else . . . even more than he wanted touchdowns. To him, football was secondary: those boys had to learn to do as they were told with no questions asked.

And that is just the reason that he took his first-string quarterback out of the game right at the toughest point. The coach had a standing rule that his teams were to punt on the fourth down. It was a simple rule. There was no room for discussion in the huddle. No matter how sure the boys were that they could make the yardage for the first down, the rule stood: punt on the fourth down.

The first-string quarterback tried for the yardage—the coach put him on the bench for the rest of the game. The second-string quarterback was doing fine until he came up with fourth down and a yard to go for a first down. The temptation was too great and the youngster called a quarterback sneak. He made a beautiful run and picked up eight yards and a first down, and the coach slapped him on the bench.

The third-string quarterback had his big opportunity. He proved to be a man after the coach's own heart. He marched the team eighty-five yards down the field and then, with fourth down and one yard to go for a touchdown, he punted the football out of the stadium right over the end-zone bleachers.

One of the tragic misemphases of our educational processes is the tendency to teach information rather than students. In almost every field there are students who are trained to recite rather than react. Especially at the most advanced educational levels, students are told to absorb the opinions of the experts and espouse one leader or another. There is certain to be value in drawing upon the accumulated wisdom and experiences of our predecessors. However, it is only in our most thoughtless moments that we would allow (much less encourage) our students to give blind allegiance to professional tradition.

Throughout the chapters of this book we have tried to insert a continuing reminder to the reader to value his or her own management capability. We have described the heritage and developmental stages of the science of management. We have talked about various leaders who have pioneered the subfields that today compose the field of management. We have tried to show a humanistic and social-science approach to management. The worst possible result of all this discussion and description would be for the reader to attempt to pick a favorite set of managerial ideas and try to conform to fit those ideas.

It does not matter that the ideas were popular or appropriate for others. As students of management you should be trying to find out about the manager who exists inside your own skin. It matters not, after all, how many respected management writers you can quote but how well *you* can accomplish *your* objective. Managers are people who are trying to get things done through other people. It is quite common to meet a manager who has fallen far short of the stated goal but who has done everything right . . . according to the book. Even with convincing excuses to readily show that the failure was not his or her fault, excuses are useless. If the project did not successfully arrive at its objective, the manager is held responsible.

The message of this final chapter is not one of anti-intellectualism. It is not suggesting that we burn all the books or cast off the valuable accumulation of experiences that are available to aspiring professional managers. Rather, this chapter seeks to make one final underscoring of a concept that has been woven throughout every chapter: *Absorb ideas but don't waste time memorizing them.* Read. Discuss. Observe. Take in all the information you possibly can. But do not become a librarian of names, dates, and theories. Become a manager. Don't be a parrot—be yourself.

Every day, you are in a management position regardless of your age or status in life. You are managing as much time as the most successful entrepreneur in the world—twenty-four hours each day. You are managing people—the hard way, without benefit of wages or other levers. You are encountering problems to be solved, decisions to be made, and priorities to be set. If you miss the daily opportunities to perfect your

Machiavellian Manipulator

Without question, conditions improved in the postwar period. Although appearances and conditions did change, it is questionable that motivation was significantly different. Psychology and sociology were discovered as tools that could be used to encourage greater output from the most undependable of the factors of production. These were the days of what Robert Blake would describe as "country club management." The "happiness disciples" in schools of business began to preach their "cow psychology." Based on the premise that contented cows gave more milk, it was assumed that contented workers would show their appreciation in a similar way. Many a manager reacted as likable Linus in the "Peanuts" comic strip. When told that people were placed on earth to make others happy, he decided, "I guess I'd better start doing a better job . . . I'd hate to be shipped back."

Managers did not want to run the risk of being shipped back. Consequently, they developed training courses by the dozen and studied the behavioral and social sciences in the apparent hope that these disciplines would reveal the secret of how to use people effectively. Much useful and valuable knowledge was developed, and some of it was put to highly productive and proper uses. Still, there was a tendency for supervisors to manipulate rather than truly manage.

The Profits Persuader of the 1950's

As the second half of the twentieth century dawned, a profit was never without honor in its company. Dale McConskey wrote with great persuasion about management by results, and Peter Drucker suggested that management should be by objectives. Achieving objectives should not be objectionable. Some companies, however, learned that the pressure for profits today could easily be bought with future profits and sometimes at the risk of the future itself.

One tendency during the 1950's was to decentralize into "profit centers." No longer were managers frequently evaluated on how they spent their time but rather on the results that they achieved. Profits (or the more precise consideration of return on invested capital) was and still is an invaluable tool for management evaluation. Yet many firms learned that unless profit maximization is tempered with some long-run considerations, it can be an inequitable and undesirable yardstick. General Electric, for example, introduced its "key area results" analysis, and Genesco has adopted a complex evaluation system, considering both quantitative and qualitative aspects of management.

Management can never be a simple, single-minded pursuit. Undue emphasis on even such an important consideration as profit can lead to the kind of tunnel vision illustrated by Schroeder, the budding piano virtuoso of "Peanuts." When Lucy says, "I'm looking for the answer to life, Schroeder. . . . What do you think is the answer?" she is told "BEETHOVEN IS IT!! CLEAR AND SIMPLE!! DON'T YOU UNDER-STAND?" Music (and certainly life) is more than Beethoven, and management is more than profits.

The Situational Specialists of the 1960's

George Odiorne predicted that the manager of the 1960's would be "more of a manager of situations than any prior counterparts." In identifying this new-style manager, Odiorne suggested that this manager would be judged by what his followers did rather than by personal actions. This manager was seen as a generalist and the kind of person who made things happen. The situational specialist was results- and responsibility-oriented and able to work through the organization rather than through personal effort.

The 1960's can be accurately described as an era of rapid change. It was necessary for managers to adapt and to deal with complex and diverse situations. This was the decade of the new morality or situational ethics. Both managers and moralists were asked to deal with complex challenges without all of the traditional guidelines that had previously been applied. Ministers and managers cannot be chamelions who change with every shift of the environment. A certain amount of flexibility is fine, but there must be moorings to help provide a sense of continuity and consistency.

The Systems Synchronizer of the 1970's

Model managers of the 1970's were able to find a type of fixed flexibility. Although highly adaptive, they were more than firefighters. They had the ability to relate many activities to the overall objectives. They had a broader view of the big picture. Even if responsible for a specific division or department, they saw this area as merely a subsystem of the corporate totality. When Charlie Brown was asked if he knew the mystery of life, he promptly responded, "Be kind, don't smoke, be prompt, smile a lot, eat sensibly, avoid cavities and mark your ballot carefully . . . avoid too much sun, send overseas packages early, insure your belongings, and try to keep the ball low. . . ." Although managers of the 1970's did not always have the answer so well in hand, they did recognize the diversity of their responsibilities. They were both decision makers and delegators.

The Contingency Coordinator of the 1980's

One of the earliest attributes associated with successful management was *coordination*. One of the most recent advances in management theory is the recognition of the importance of the uniqueness in each situation and the *contigencies* which apply. The model manager of this decade will combine these two important characteristics. This approach also recognizes and builds upon the situational emphasis of the 1960's and the systems orientation of the 1970's.

Contingency coordinators recognize that every situation is somewhat unique. Thus, they will not attempt to apply hard and fast rules. They will anticipate developments and be able to draw from past education and experience to keep things moving toward predetermined objectives. The watch-words of this manager are *anticipatory*, *adaptive*, and *assertive*. The contingency coordinator anticipates the uncertain and unpredictable nature of the future. Yet, he or she works to keep surprises small. While vision into the future is seldom crystal-clear, this manager has a healthy concern for what is about to happen.

Although the model managers of the 1980's will try to avoid surprises, they recognize that uncertainty is the only sure prediction about the future. Consequently, there is a major emphasis on being able to adapt approaches, plans, and practices to situations as they evolve.

Despite tremendous uncertainly in a period of continued rapid change, this manager must be prepared to move assertively in order to cope with the internal demands of the organization and the external challenges of the organization. While management has never been a comfortable career for the timid recluse, the future demands both courage and commitment.

Perhaps the primary characteristics of the model manager of the next decade can be summed up as follows:

1. *No manager can be an island in the 1980's.* To borrow an idea of John Donne, the manager of tomorrow will recognize a dependence upon an interrelationship with people throughout the world. As Marshall McLuhan suggests, the world is becoming a global village, and to carry this analogy a bit farther, the manager will operate a corporate tribe with extensions that may reach beyond the Earth itself. Although a generalist, he or she will have to be a communications specialist, using techniques for communicating with colleagues, subordinates, and superiors that would confound people in the past. Facsimile reproduction and home communication centers are but two of the more predictable tools they will employ.

2. *They will be concerned with productivity, profitability, and people.* Many managers may remember when they were evaluated on how much they produced. Then evolution took them through periods when morale or profitability was viewed as the most significant factor in their

performance. The managers of tomorrow will recognize that achieving their ultimate objective will depend upon a successful integration of these three subsystems. They will be interested in productivity because this will help employees achieve the satisfaction of doing a job well and will serve as a sound base for continued profits. Managers will continue to be interested in profits because they are the fuel that keeps our system of private enterprise in operation and because profits ensure the continued existence of the firm. They will be interested in people because they are essential to achieve the production management seeks and because they can, if they work together, make that production even more profitable. People will also be respected because they are human beings and possess a spark of divinity.

3. *Managers and supervisors of the 1980's will not have completed their education.* This does not imply that uneducated people will be able to rise to positions of importance. Conversely, more knowledge, training, and education will be required than ever before. A successful manager will simply never find that it is possible to stop learning or, for that matter, to end formal education. Without continual renewal, managers will become obsolete more quickly than the machinery that they control.

In the 1980's managers must be coordinators because they must make many things work together and because they must draw upon many areas of knowledge and many previous experiences. The manager of tomorrow will use the best of the past to make the future even better.

Review Questions

1. Why do "A" students in management not always make the best managers?
2. What was so good about the "good old days" of management?
3. Is there anything better for a manager than to maximize profits? Discuss.
4. What role will be most appropriate for the managers of the 1980's? Discuss.
5. Considering the models of management developed in this chapter, identify the model of previous individuals or concepts that we have studied in the text:
   a. A Robber Baron
   b. Country club management.
   c. The operational manager.
6. Does the opening vignette encourage managers to violate rules?
7. What resource do you have in the same quantity as the world's richest person?
8. How long will it be before you will be able to practice the concepts of management taught in this text?

Name Index

Subject Index